Criticizing Photographs

An Introduction to Understanding Images

FIFTH EDITION

Terry Barrett

University of North Texas

Professor Emeritus

The Ohio State University

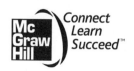 Connect
Learn
Succeed™

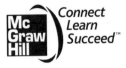

Connect
Learn
Succeed™

CRITICIZING PHOTOGRAPHS: AN INTRODUCTION TO UNDERSTANDING IMAGES,
FIFTH EDITION

Published by McGraw-Hill, a business unit of The McGraw-Hill Companies, Inc., 1221 Avenue of the
Americas, New York, NY 10020.

This book is printed on acid-free paper.

1 2 3 4 5 6 7 8 9 0 DOC/DOC 1 0 9 8 7 6 5 4 3 2 1

ISBN 978-0-07-352653-9
MHID 0-07-352653-3

Vice President & Editor-in-Chief: *Michael Ryan*
Vice President EDP/Central Publishing Services: *Kimberly Meriwether David*
Publisher: *Christopher Freitag*
Associate Sponsoring Editor: *Betty Chen*
Executive Marketing Manager: *Pamela S. Cooper*
Senior Managing Editor: *Meghan Campbell*
Project Manager: *Robin A. Reed*
Design Coordinator: *Margarite Reynolds*
Cover Designer: *Mary-Presley Adams*
Photo Research: *Sonia Brown*
Cover Image: *© William Wegman (ca. 1945–present), "Intruder," 2006 (Pigment print photograph,
24 X 30 inches)*
Buyer: *Laura Fuller*
Compositor: *Laserwords Private Limited*
Typeface: *10/13 Berkeley Old Style Medium*
Printer: *R. R. Donnelley*

Library of Congress Cataloging-in-Publication Data

Barrett, Terry, 1945-
    Criticizing photographs : an introduction to understanding images/
Terry Barrett. —5th ed.
        p. cm.
    Includes bibliographical references and index.
    ISBN-13: 978-0-07-352653-9 (alk. paper)
    ISBN-10: 0-07-352653-3 (alk. paper)
  1. Photography, Artistic. 2. Photographic criticism. I. Title.
    TR642.B365 2012
    770.1—dc22
                                    2011003518

www.mhhe.com

Contents

Preface

YEARS OF TEACHING ART CRITICISM HAVE CONVINCED ME THAT ONE OF THE BEST ways to appreciate an image is to observe, think, and talk about it. This is what art criticism entails, and it's what this book is about. My goal is to help both beginning and advanced students of photography use the activities of criticism in order to better appreciate and understand photographs.

This book is organized according to the major activities of criticism identified by aesthetician Morris Weitz, the author of the "open definition of art," in his study of *Hamlet* criticism—namely, describing, interpreting, evaluating, and theorizing. These activities are presented in this book as overlapping and interdependent. I believe that Weitz's breakdown is sufficiently broad so as not to exclude any considerations about criticism and sufficiently narrow to provide a directed and clear consideration of the complex activities of criticizing photographs. Although Weitz distinguished these activities in 1964, I think they readily accommodate post modernism concerns and are amenable to a diverse range of theoretical persuasions and political stances. The spirit of the book is pluralist, inclusive of many different voices, and resistant to dogmatic thinking.

The following chapters consider describing photographs, interpreting and evaluating them, and theorizing about photography, in that order. I've placed major emphasis on the interpretation of photographs because I believe that discussion of meaning is more important than pronouncements of judgment and that interpretation is the most important and rewarding aspect of criticism. Interpretive discussion increases understanding and thus deepens appreciation whether that appreciation is ultimately negative or positive. A judgment rendered without an understanding is irresponsive and irresponsible. Unfortunately, *criticism* is too frequently confused with negative value judgments because of its everyday connotations. The term *criticism* in the language of aesthetics encompasses much more.

For the present, at the risk of oversimplification, the four activities of criticism—describing, interpreting, evaluating, and theorizing—can be thought of as seeking answers to four basic questions: What is here? What is it about? How good is it? Is it art? This book explores the criticism of photographs by means of these major questions.

The book also provides a variety of answers to these questions by critics, including student critics in Chapter 8, who sometimes agree and sometimes disagree about the same photographs. I've cited dozens of critics and many more photographers. In my selections I've tried to present a diversity of critical voices to responsibly provide readers a range of critical stances and approaches from which to choose. I chose these particular critics and photographers as being especially appropriate to the points being discussed; no hierarchy of critics or photographers is implied by my choices.

NEW TO THIS EDITION

The changes in this edition are mostly to keep the book current. Thus, minor changes have been made throughout. I've streamlined examples of photographs in each of the categories in Chapter 6 based on a reviewer's recommendation; I've eliminated many references to works that students do not know. Most of the exemplary photographs mentioned in a category are now reproduced in the book. This should help make the categories more understandable and thus more useful. Student writing examples have been changed, and there are more of them. Reader responses are most welcome from students and instructors (terry.barrett@unt.edu).

ACKNOWLEDGMENTS

This book may never have happened without my serendipitous meeting of Jan Beatty, then an editor at Mayfield Publishing Company, the first publisher of this book, and her continued gentle and joyful handling of the entire editorial process from the initial conception of the book through its third edition. This latest edition was most ably guided by the people at McGraw-Hill, including editors Betty Chen and Meghan Campbell, and the production team of Robin Reed, Margarite Reynolds, Sonia Brown, and Laura Fuller.

Thanks to Robert Milnes, my dean, and my colleagues at university of North Texas, for their generous support of time and a pleasant and supportive research atmosphere in which to work. Thanks especially to my wife, Susan Michael, who kept love, joy, and enthusiasm in the revision project.

Past editions of the book have benefited from manuscript reviews by Thomas Barrow, University of New Mexico; Ron Carraher, University of Washington; Daryl Curran; Doug Dubois; Carol Flax; Gretchen Garner, University of Connecticut; Victoria Hirt, University of South Florida; Sybil Miller; Bea Nettles, University of Illinois; Dan Powell, University of Oregon; David Read; Susan Ressler, Purdue University; Adrienne Salinger, University of New Mexico; Ernest Scott, University of Illinois; Robert Smith, Milwaukee Institute of Art and Design; Richard Stevens; Stan Strembicki; Christopher Tsouras, Community College of Southern Nevada; John Upton, Orange Coast College; and Jon M. Yamashiro, Miami University.

This fifth edition has been reviewed by Carol Flax, University of Arizona; Mary Frey, Hartford Art School; Marita Gootee, Mississippi State University; Jessica Hines, Georgia Southern University; Dean Kessmann, The George Washington University; Leesa Rittelmann, Hartwick College; Prince V. Thomas, Lamar University; Anthony Thompson, Grand Valley State University; Margaret Doell, Adams State College; Corinne Diop, James Madison University; Mariah Doren, Central Michigan University; Marcella Hackbardt, Kenyon College; Karen Norton, Purdue University; Carol Scolllans, University of Massachusetts, Boston; David Taylor, New Mexico State University, Las Cruces; Gwen Walstrand, Missouri State University; Samuel Winch, Pennsylvania State University, Harrisburg; and Sue Wrbican, George Mason University.

About Art Criticism

THIS BOOK IS ABOUT READING AND DOING PHOTOGRAPHY CRITICISM SO THAT YOU CAN better appreciate photographs by using critical processes. Unfortunately, we usually don't equate criticism with appreciation because in everyday language the term *criticism* has negative connotations: It is used to refer to the act of making judgments, usually negative judgments, and the act of expressing disapproval.

In mass media, critics are portrayed as judges of art: Reviewers in newspapers rate restaurants with stars, and critics on television rate movies with thumbs up or thumbs down or from 1 to 10, constantly reinforcing judgmental aspects of criticism. Of all the words critics write, those most often quoted are judgments: "The best play of the season!" "Dazzling!" "Brilliant!" These words are highlighted in bold type in movie and theater ads because these words sell tickets. But they constitute only a few of the critic's total output of words, and they have been quoted out of context. These snippets have minimal value in helping us reach an understanding of a play or a movie.

Critics are writers who like art and choose to spend their lives thinking and writing about it. bell hooks, a critic and scholar of African American cultural studies, writes this about writing: "Seduced by the magic of words in childhood, I am still transported, carried away, writing and reading. Writing longhand the first drafts of all my works, I read aloud to myself, performing the words to hear and feel them. I want to be certain I am grappling with language in such a way that my words live and breathe, that they surface from a passionate place inside me."[1] Peter

Schjeldahl, a poet who now writes art criticism as a career, writes that "I get from art a regular chance to experience something—or perhaps everything, the whole world—as someone else, to replace my eyes and mind with the eyes and mind of another for a charged moment."[2] Christopher Knight, who has written art criticism for the *Los Angeles Times* since 1989, left a successful career as a museum curator to write criticism precisely because he wanted to be closer to art: "The reason I got interested in a career in art in the first place is to be around art and artists. I found that in museums you spend most of your time around trustees and paperwork."[3]

Some critics don't want to be called critics because of the negative connotations of the term. Art critic and poet Rene Ricard, writing in *Artforum,* says: "In point of fact I'm not an art critic. I am an enthusiast. I like to drum up interest in artists who have somehow inspired me to be able to say something about their work."[4] Michael Feingold, who writes theater criticism for the *Village Voice,* says that "criticism should celebrate the good in art, not revel in its anger at the bad."[5] Similarly, Lucy Lippard is usually supportive of the art she writes about, but she says she is sometimes accused of not being critical, of not being a critic at all. She responds, "That's okay with me, since I never liked the term anyway. Its negative connotations place the writer in fundamental antagonism to the artists."[6] She and other critics do not want to be thought of as being opposed to artists.

DEFINITION OF CRITICISM

The term *criticism* is complex, with several different meanings. In the language of aestheticians who philosophize about art and art criticism, and in the language of art critics, *criticism* usually refers to a much broader range of activities than just the act of judging. Morris Weitz, an aesthetician interested in art criticism, sought to discover more about it by studying what critics do when they criticize art.[7] He took as his test case all the criticism ever written about Shakespeare's *Hamlet.* After reading the volumes of *Hamlet* criticism written through the ages, Weitz concluded that when critics criticize they do one or more of four things: They *describe* the work of art, they *interpret* it, they *evaluate* it, and they *theorize* about it. Some critics engage primarily in descriptive criticism; others describe, but primarily to further their interpretations; still others describe, interpret, evaluate, *and* theorize. Weitz drew several conclusions about criticism, most notably that any one of these four activities constitutes criticism and that evaluation is not a necessary part of criticism. He found that several critics criticized *Hamlet* without ever judging it.

When critics criticize, they do much more than express their likes and dislikes—and much more than approve and disapprove of works of art. Critics do judge artworks, and sometimes negatively, but their judgments more often are positive: As Rene Ricard says, "Why give publicity to something you hate?"

When Schjeldahl is confronted by a work he does not like, he asks himself several questions: "'Why would I have done that if I did it?' is one of my working questions about an artwork. (Not that I *could*. This is make-believe.) My formula of fairness to work that displeases me is to ask, 'What would I like about this if I liked it?' When I cannot deem myself an intended or even a possible member of a work's audience, I ask myself what such an audience member must be like."[8] Michael Feingold thinks it unfortunate that theater criticism in New York City often prevents theatergoing rather than encourages it, and he adds that "as every critic knows, a favorable review with some substance is much harder to write than a pan."[9] Abigail Solomon-Godeau, who writes frequently about photography, says there are instances when it is clear that something is nonsense and should be called nonsense, but she finds it more beneficial to ask questions about meaning than about aesthetic worth.[10]

"What do I do as a critic in a gallery?" Schjeldahl asks. He answers: "I learn. I walk up to, around, touch if I dare, the objects, meanwhile asking questions in my mind and casting about for answers—all until mind and senses are in some rough agreement, or until fatigue sets in." Edmund Feldman, an art historian and art educator, has written much about art criticism and defines it as "informed talk about art."[11] He also minimizes the act of evaluating, or judging, art, saying that it is the least important of the critical procedures. A. D. Coleman, a pioneering and prolific critic of recent photography, defines what he does as "the intersecting of photographic images with words."[12] He adds: "I merely look closely at and into all sorts of photographic images and attempt to pinpoint in words what they provoke me to feel and think and understand." Morris Weitz defines criticism as "a form of studied discourse about works of art. It is a use of language designed to facilitate and enrich the understanding of art."[13]

Throughout this book the term *criticism* will not refer to the act of negative judgment; it will refer to a much wider range of activities and will adhere to this broad definition: *Criticism is informed discourse about art to increase understanding and appreciation of art.* This definition includes criticism of all artforms, including dance, music, poetry, painting, and photography. *Discourse* includes talking and writing. *Informed* is an important qualifier that distinguishes criticism from mere talk and uninformed opinion about art. Not all writing about art is criticism. Some art writing, for example, is journalism rather than criticism: It is news reporting on artists and artworld events rather than critical analysis.

A way of becoming informed about art is by critically thinking about it. Criticism is a means toward the end of understanding and appreciating photographs. In some cases, a carefully thought-out response to a photograph may result in negative appreciation or informed dislike. More often than not, however, especially when considering the work of prominent photographers and that of artists using photographs, careful critical attention to a photograph or group of photographs will result in fuller understanding and positive appreciation. Criticism should result in what Harry Broudy, a philosopher promoting aesthetic education, calls "enlightened cherishing."[14] Broudy's "enlightened cherishing" is a compound concept that combines *thought* (by the term *enlightened*) with *feeling* (by the term *cherishing*). He reminds us that both thought and feeling are necessary components that need to be combined to achieve understanding and appreciation. Criticism is not a coldly intellectual endeavor.

SOURCES OF CRITICISM

Photography criticism can be found in many places—in photography classrooms, lecture halls, and publications. Published criticism appears in books, exhibition catalogues, art magazines, photography magazines, and the popular press. Exhibition catalogues list the exhibited works; reproduce several, if not all, of the pictures; and usually have an introductory essay explaining why the curator selected this group of works for an exhibition. Such essays often offer insightful interpretive commentary on photographs and photographers. After the exhibitions, the catalogues are marketed as books and take on a life of their own.

Barbara Kruger has combined her critical essays, which previously appeared in several publications, into a single volume titled *Remote Control: Power, Cultures, and the World of Appearances*. Rosalind Krauss's critical essay on Cindy Sherman's photographs accompanies the artist's work reproduced in *Cindy Sherman 1975–1993*. Arthur Danto has published critical essays on Cindy Sherman's *Film Stills* and the photographs by Robert Mapplethorpe in comprehensive books by those artists. Susan Sontag's criticism of photography began as a series of articles and became the book *On Photography* in 1978, which she followed with more articles and then another book on photography, *Regarding the Pain of Others*, in 2003. Much critical writing about photography appears in exhibition catalogues such as *In Response to Place* and *Only Skin Deep*. *In Response to Place* is both a book and a traveling exhibition of landscape photographs by a variety of current photographers sponsored by the Nature Conservatory, with essays by Terry Tempest Williams and Andy Grundberg. *Only Skin Deep* is an exhibition and book that explores the themes of race and identity as expressed in photographs accompanied by lengthy essays, some historical and others written especially for the volume, by different authors. Jonathan Green's book *American Photography* is a critical treatment of recent American photography. Much critical writing about photography has appeared in exhibition catalogues such as *The New Color Photography*, by Sally Eauclaire, and *Mirrors and Windows*, by John Szarkowski. These two catalogues are based on exhibitions these curators have organized. As past curator of photography at the Museum of Modern Art in New York, Szarkowski organized many exhibitions and often prepared accompanying exhibition catalogues. Sally Eauclaire is a freelance curator who designs shows for museums and prepares catalogues.

The majority of photography criticism, however, is found in the art press—the large art magazines such as *Artforum* and *Art in America,* and regional art journals such as *Dialogue* from Columbus, Ohio, *New Art Examiner* from Chicago, and *Artweek* and *Photo Metro* from California. Much photography criticism is also published in journals specifically devoted to photographic media, such as *Afterimage,* or in photography publications including *Aperture* and *Exposure.* Reviews of photography exhibitions appear in daily newspapers of national import, such as the *New York Times,* and in local newspapers. Some critics choose to write for very large audiences and publish in mass media circulations: Abigail Solomon-Godeau has published her criticism in *Vogue,* and Robert Hughes and Peter Plagens write art criticism for *Time* and *Newsweek.*

Each of these publications has its own editorial tone and political ideology, and critics sometimes choose their publications according to their style of writing, their critical interests, and their personal politics. They also adapt their styles to fit certain publications.

Editors often provide direction, sometimes quite specifically. The *New Art Examiner,* for instance, instructs its reviewers that "the writer's opinion of the work is the backbone of a review. Set up your thesis by the third paragraph and use the rest of the space to substantiate it."[15] The editors add: "Keep descriptions brief and within the context of the ideas you are developing." *Dialogue* similarly defines reviews as the "personal assessments of individual shows or of more than one related show or event."[16] *Dialogue*'s editors also ask that writers include only sufficient description for intelligibility but add: "Use descriptions to help the reader see the work in a new way and/or to illuminate connections between the exhibited work and the larger art world." Both publications distinguish short reviews from feature articles and have different editorial guidelines for each.

Policies about what they cover vary from publication to publication, too. Grace Glueck, who writes art criticism for the *New York Times,* explains that her paper covers important museum and gallery shows because that is what the readers expect. Similarly, because his magazine is national and devotes comparatively little space to art, Peter Plagens of *Newsweek* covers museum shows, almost exclusively, but tries to write about as many museum shows of contemporary art as possible.

Many critics have editorial independence about what they cover. Kay Larson, who writes for the weekly *New York Magazine,* says, "I write about what interests me."[17] She explains that she tries to see everything in town that she can manage to see, looks for things that she likes, and then makes her choices about what to write: "Ultimately I base my decisions not only on whom I like but whom I feel I can say something about. There are many artists every week whom I do like and whom

I feel I can't say anything about." Robert Hughes, who writes around twenty-four pieces a year for *Time*, is subject to no editorial restrictions or instructions, and he covers what he chooses. However, because *Time* is a newsmagazine and needs to be timely, the exhibitions must still be showing when his article runs, and because the magazine is distributed internationally, he writes many of his reviews of shows outside New York City.

When critics write for different publications, they are writing for different audiences. Their choices of what to write about and their approaches to their chosen or assigned topics vary according to which publication they are writing for and whom they imagine their readers to be. A review of an exhibition written for the daily newspaper of a small midwestern city will likely differ in tone and content from a review written for the Sunday *New York Times* because the readers are different. The *Times* has national as well as regional distribution, and its readers are better informed about the arts than are average newspaper readers; a critic writing for the *Times* can assume knowledge that a critic writing for a regional newspaper cannot.

KINDS OF CRITICISM

In an editorial in the *Journal of Aesthetic Education,* Ralph Smith distinguishes two types of art criticism, both of which are useful but serve different purposes: exploratory aesthetic criticism and argumentative aesthetic criticism. In doing *exploratory aesthetic criticism,* a critic delays judgments of value and attempts rather to ascertain an object's aesthetic aspects as completely as possible, to ensure that readers will experience all that can be seen in a work of art. This kind of criticism relies heavily on descriptive and interpretive thought. Its aim is to sustain aesthetic experience. In doing *argumentative aesthetic criticism,* after sufficient interpretive analysis has been done, critics estimate the work's positive aspects or lack of them and give a full account of their judgments based on explicitly stated criteria and standards. The critics argue in favor of their judgments and attempt to persuade others that the object is best considered in the way they have interpreted and judged it, and they are prepared to defend their conclusions.

Ingrid Sischy, editor and writer, has written criticism that exemplifies both the exploratory and argumentative types. In a catalogue essay accompanying the nude photographs made by Lee Friedlander,[18] Sischy pleasantly meanders in and through the photographs and the photographer's thoughts, carefully exploring both and her reactions to them. We know, in the reading, that she approves of Friedlander and his nudes and why, but more centrally, we experience the photographs through the descriptive and interpretive thoughts of a careful and committed observer. In an essay she wrote for the *New Yorker* about the popular journalistic photographs made by Sebastião Salgado, however, Sischy carefully and logically and cumulatively builds an argument against their worth, despite their great popularity in the art world.[19] She clearly demonstrates argumentative criticism that is centrally evaluative, replete with the reasons for and the criteria upon which she based her negative appraisal.

Andy Grundberg, a former photography critic for the *New York Times,* perceives two basic approaches to photography criticism: the applied and the theoretical. *Applied criticism* is practical, immediate, and directed at the work; *theoretical criticism* is more philosophical, attempts to define photography, and uses photographs only as examples to clarify its arguments. Applied criticism tends toward journalism; theoretical criticism tends toward aesthetics.[20]

Examples of applied criticism are reviews of shows, such as those written by Edward Leffingwell for *Art in America.*[21] Critics also write theoretical essays that may appear as feature essays in magazines and scholarly journals. For example, Louis Kaplan applied the theoretical insights on the topic of community by contemporary French philosopher Jean-Luc Nancy to the photographs of a community of lovers by American photographer Nan Goldin: "A photographer and a philosopher share with us the fundamental acknowledgement that sharing constitutes each of us, that our being-in-the-world is always already a being-with."[22]

Theoretical explorations of photography are also of book length: Roland Barthes's book *Camera Lucida: Reflections on Photography* is a theoretical treatment of photography that attempts to distinguish photography from other kinds of picture making. In *Burning with Desire,* Geoffrey Batchen uses the methodology of Michel Foucault to explore the ideological and ideational origins of photography and why early photographs look the way they do.

In her writing about photography, Abigail Solomon-Godeau draws from cultural theory, feminism, and the history of art and photography to examine ideologies surrounding making, exhibiting, and writing about photographs. Her writing is often criticism about criticism. Chapter 7 of this book explores in detail theories of art and photography, theoretical criticism, and how theory influences both criticism and photography.

Grundberg also identifies another type of criticism as "connoisseurship," which he rejects as severely limited. The connoisseur, of wine or photographs, asks "Is this good or bad?" and makes a proclamation based on his or her particular taste. This kind of criticism, which is often used in casual speech and sometimes found in professional writing, is extremely limited in scope because the judgments it yields are usually proclaimed without supporting reasons or the benefit of explicit criteria, and thus they are neither very informative nor useful. Statements based on taste are simply too idiosyncratic to be worth disputing. As Grundberg adds, "Criticism's task is to make arguments, not pronouncements." This book is in agreement with Grundberg on these points.

THE BACKGROUNDS OF CRITICS

Critics come to criticism from varied backgrounds. Many art critics have advanced degrees in art history and support themselves by teaching art history as they write criticism. Several come from studio art backgrounds. Some critics are also exhibiting artists, such as Peter Plagens, who is a painter and a critic for *Newsweek,* and Barbara Kruger, who exhibits photographic art and writes criticism. Rene Ricard is a poet and art critic; Carrie Rickey writes film criticism for the popular press and art criticism for the art press.

Michael Kimmelman, chief art critic for the *New York Times,* studied art history as a graduate student but wrote music criticism for a daily newspaper in Atlanta, then for the *Philadelphia Inquirer, U.S. News & World Report,* and the *New York Times.* At the *Times* he started writing about art as well as music and became chief art critic in 1990. Robert Hughes, art critic for *Time* magazine since 1970, is Australian and a Jesuit-trained, ex-architecture student, ex-painter, ex-political cartoonist. He also writes essays for the *New York Review of Books* and the *New Republic,* has produced an eight-part television series on modernism, *The Shock of the New,* and is the author of several books on art.

A. D. Coleman can be an inspirational figure for those interested in photography but who are not photographers themselves. Coleman's academic background is one of English literature, creative writing, and communications theory. He thinks of himself as a voice from the audience of photography and wrote more than four hundred articles from that vantage point between 1968 and 1978, some of which are contained in his book *Light Readings.* In 1994 he published another collection of his essays, *Critical Focus,* about issues of contemporary international photography. Coleman became a full-time, freelance critic of photography in 1968. Before that, he wrote theater criticism for the *Village Voice.* He began writing about photography because he was "excited by photographs, curious about the medium, and fascinated—even frightened—by its impact on our culture." As a photography critic he has published widely and frequently, both nationally (for example, in *Afterimage, Artforum, Art in America, Camera 35, Popular Photography,* and the *New York Times*), and abroad. He continues to write, lecture, curate, and teach, and maintains The Nearby Cafe Web site (http://www.nearbycafe.com/). Although he publishes in a wide range of publications, Coleman prefers a regular forum in a large-circulation publication because he wishes to reach the broadest possible audience, and he regrets that he has been "reluctantly ghettoized in art and photography publications."[23]

Before writing photography criticism, Abigail Solomon-Godeau was a photo editor with an undergraduate degree in art history, and she had her own business of providing pictures for magazines, textbook publishers, educational film strips, and advertisers. She eventually became bored with her work and also became aware that she was part of what culture critics were deriding as the "consciousness indus-try." About that she says: "Here was an enterprise that was literally producing a certain reality that people, or students, or whoever, wouldn't question because it was perceived as real [because it was photographed]. That's when I started think-ing that I would really like to write about photography."[24] After trying for two years to make a living as a critic in New York, she realized that the only way she could survive economically as a critic was to teach. She earned her PhD in art his-tory to gain access to jobs in higher education. While teaching, she has written for publications as diverse as *Vogue, Afterimage,* and *October* and has published a col-lection of her essays in *Photography at the Dock.*[25]

Grace Glueck believes that to become educated, the critic needs to look at as much art as possible and at "anything that deals with form including architecture, movies, dance, theater, even street furniture." Mark Stevens agrees and stresses the importance of spending time in museums: "Immersion in excellent examples of different kinds of past art is the best training for the eye."[26]

STANCES TOWARD CRITICISM

Critics take various stances on what criticism should be and how it should be con-ducted. Abigail Solomon-Godeau views her chosen critical agenda as one of asking questions: "Primarily, all critical practices—literary or artistic—should probably be about asking questions. That's what I do in my teaching and it's what I attempt to do in my writing. Of course, there are certain instances in which you can say with certainty, 'this is what's going on here,' or 'this is nonsense, mystification or falsification.' But in the most profound sense, this is still asking—what does it mean, how does it work, can we think something differently about it."[27]

Kay Larson, who is also concerned with explanation of artworks, says that she starts writing criticism "by confronting the work at the most direct level possible—suspending language and removing barriers. It's hard and it's scary—you keep wanting to rush back in with judgments and opinions, but you've got to push your-self back and be *with* the work. Once you've had the encounter, you can try to fig-ure out how to explain it, and there are many ways to take off—through sociology, history, theory, standard criticism, or description."[28]

Grace Glueck sees her role as a critic as being one of informing members of the public about works of art: She aspires to "inform, elucidate, explain, and enlighten."[29] She wants "to help a reader place art in a context, establish where it's coming from, what feeds it, how it stacks up in relation to other art." Glueck is quick to add, how-ever, that she needs to take stands "against slipshod standards, sloppy work, impre-cision, mistaken notions, and *for* good work of whatever stripe."

Coleman specified, in 1975, his premises and parameters for critical writing:

> A critic should be independent of the artists and institutions about which he/she writes. His/her writing should appear regularly in a magazine, newspaper, or other forum of opinion. The work considered within that writing should be publicly accessible, and at least in part should represent the output of the critic's contemporaries and/or younger, less established artists in all their diversity. And he/she should be willing to adopt openly that skeptic's posture which is necessary to serious criticism.[30]

These are clear statements of what Coleman believes criticism should be and how it should be conducted. He is arguing for an independent, skeptical criticism and for critics who are independent of artists and the museums and galleries that sponsor those artists. He is acutely aware of possible conflicts of interest between critic and artist or critic and institutional sponsor: He does not want the critic to be anyone's mouthpiece but rather to be an independent voice. Coleman argues that because criticism is a public activity, the critic's writing should be available to interested readers, and that the artwork which is criticized should also be open to public scrutiny. This would presumably preclude a critic's visiting an artist's studio and writing about that work, because that work is only privately available.

Coleman distinguishes between curators and historians who write about art, and critics. He argues that curators, who gather work and show it in galleries and museums, and historians, who place older work in context, write from privileged positions: The historian's is the privilege of hindsight; the curator's is the power of patronage. Coleman cautions that the writer, historian, curator, or critic who befriends the artist by sponsoring his or her work will have a difficult time being skeptical. He is quick to point out, however, that skepticism is not enmity or hostility. Coleman's goal is one of constructive, affirmative criticism, and he adds: "The greatest abuses of a critic's role stem from the hunger for power and the need to be liked."[31]

Mark Stevens agrees that distinctions should be maintained between writing criticism and writing history: "The trouble with acting like an art historian is that it detracts from the job critics can do better than anybody else, and that is to be lively, spontaneous, impressionistic, quick to the present—shapers, in short, of the mind of the moment."[32]

Lucy Lippard is a widely published independent art critic who assumes a posture different from Coleman's, and her personal policies for criticism are in disagreement with those of his just cited. She terms her art writing "advocacy criticism."[33] As an "advocate critic" Lippard is openly leftist and feminist and rejects the notion that good criticism is objective criticism. Instead, she wants a criticism that takes a political stand. She seeks out and promotes "the unheard voices, the unseen images, or the unconsidered people." She chooses to write about art that is critical of mainstream society and which is therefore not often exhibited. Lippard chooses to work in partnership with socially oppositional artists to get their work seen and their voices heard.

Lippard also rejects as a false dichotomy the notion that there should be distance between critics and artists. She says that her ideas about art have consistently emerged from contact with artists and their studios rather than from galleries and magazines. She acknowledges that the lines between advocacy, promotion, and propaganda are thin, but she rejects critical objectivity and neutrality as false myths and thinks her approach is more honest than that of critics who claim to be removed from special interests.

RELATIONS BETWEEN CRITICS AND ARTISTS

Lippard and Coleman raise a key question in criticism about the critic's relation to the artist. And they each have different answers: Coleman advocates a skeptical distance between critic and artist, and Lippard a partnership between them. Critics take various positions between these two polar positions. Peter Schjeldahl says that "intimate friendships between artists and critics, as such, are tragicomic. The critic may seek revelation from the artist, who may seek authentication from the critic. Neither has any such prize to give, if each is any good." He adds: "A critic who feels no anguish in relating to artists is a prostitute. A critic who never relates to artists, fearing contamination, is a virgin. Neither knows a thing about love."[34]

Kay Larson feels that to be informed she is required to study history and also to "talk to artists."[35] She struggles with the issue of responsibility and states, "Your responsibility to the artist is to be as fair as possible," and in a second thought adds, "You have a responsibility to your taste and values."

Mark Stevens sees his primary responsibility being "to his own opinion." He also tries "to be fair, and not to be nasty," and he regrets the few times he's been sarcastic.[36] He thinks that knowing artists is difficult because he doesn't want to hurt their feelings or champion work that he doesn't think is good. He thinks "it's probably a bad idea to know artists too well, to accept works of art or to know dealers too well."

Jerry Saltz states, "There ought to be an uneasy alliance between artists and critics. You should not want to 'love' your critic. For the critic this means not being 'loved' by everyone. But a critic shouldn't want love. He or she wants *respect*." He acknowledges consequences of his stance: "If you write negative things you may not get asked to all those sexy dinner parties or you may not be the one to write the juicy catalog essays but at least you'll be doing your job."[37]

Christopher Knight likes to associate with artists but does not talk to them about their work until after he has written about it: "I never talk to an artist about the work until I've written something because it only confuses me. I don't see myself as being a translator of the artist's intentions to the public."[38] Michael Feingold believes that criticism "is not a part of the artistic process. That is a matter between artists and their materials, artists and their colleagues, artists and their audiences. Criticism comes later. When it tries to impose itself on the process, it usually ends by corrupting art while making itself look insipid or foolish."[39]

Editors of periodicals that publish criticism are also sensitive to issues of integrity and possible conflicts of interest between a critic and an artist or institution. The *New Art Examiner,* for example, declares in bold type in its reviewer's guidelines: "Under no circumstances are manuscripts to be shared with outsiders (the artist, dealer, sponsor, etc.)." *Dialogue* disallows reviews from writers who have a business interest in a gallery where the show is located, a close personal relationship with the exhibiting artist, any position within the sponsoring institution, or previous experiences with the artist or sponsoring institution. These policies are instituted to avoid damage to a publication's and a writer's credibility.

There aren't easy answers to questions of the ethics of criticism or to deciding personal or editorial policy. The question is less difficult, however, if we realize that critics write for readers other than the artist whose work they are considering. Critics do not write criticism for the one painter or photographer who is exhibiting; they write for a public. Grace Glueck thinks that, at best, the critic gives the artist an idea of how his or her work is being perceived or misperceived by the public.

The relation between the critic and the artist also becomes less clear when we realize that criticism is much more than the judging of art. This point is easily forgotten because in art studios, in schools, and in classrooms of photography, criticism is often, unfortunately, understood solely as judgment. The primary purpose of school criticism is usually seen very narrowly as the improvement of art making; little time is spent in describing student work, interpreting it, or in examining assumptions about what art is or is not.[40] Thus we tend to think that published professional criticism is judgment and, more specifically, judgment for the artist and the improvement of art making. This conception of professional criticism is far from accurate.

THE ART OF CRITICIZING CRITICISM

Although the critics quoted in this chapter have seriously considered their positions regarding criticism, their positions differ; and their theories and approaches do not combine into a cohesive and comprehensive single theory of criticism. Quite the contrary. Critics frequently take issue with one another's ideas. Art critic Hilton Kramer has dismissed Lucy Lippard's writing as "straightout political propaganda."[41] John Szarkowski is frequently accused by social-minded critics of "aestheticizing" photographs—turning too many of them into "art," particularly socially oppositional photographs. Allan Sekula's writing is so suspicious of photography that it has been called "almost paranoid" and has been likened to a history of women written by a misogynist.[42] These conflicting views contribute to an ongoing, interesting, and informative dialogue about criticism and photographs that enlivens the reading of criticism as well as the viewing of photographs.

Jerry Saltz thinks too much published criticism is positive: "A critic's job is simply to look and then record his or her responses as honestly and clearly as possible. That means positive *and* negative response. Look at art magazines. The reviews are either descriptive or they're positive. Seldom is heard a discouraging word. Is that because of the tacit connection between galleries taking out ads and favorable opinion? I'm not saying they're all in cahoots. The question is raised because of the lack of negative response. Perhaps it's that our critics are not up to it. They—we—are too locked in, too much a part of the art 'community.'"[43]

Art critic Donald Kuspit is the editor of a series of books that anthologize the major writings of such contemporary art critics as Lawrence Alloway, Dennis Adrian, Dore Ashton, Nicolas Calas, Joseph Masheck, Robert Pincus-Witten, Peter Plagens, and Peter Seltz. In his foreword to their writings, he calls them "master art critics" and provides some reasons for his positive appraisal of their criticism. He thinks they provide sophisticated treatment of complex art. They have all thought deeply about the nature of art criticism and have seriously considered how they should go about doing it. He praises the independence of their points of view and their self-consciousness about it. Kuspit knows they have all expanded their criticism well beyond journalistic reporting and have avoided promotional reporting of the artist stars of their day. He admires these critics for being passionate about art and their criticism and for depending on reason to prove their point. In their passion and reason they have avoided becoming dogmatic—they "sting us into consciousness."

In these statements Kuspit provides criteria for good criticism by which he can measure and weigh the writings of others about art. Mark Stevens offers these criteria for good criticism: Critics should be "honest in their judgment, clear in their writing, straightforward in their argument, and unpretentious in their manner."[44] He adds that good criticism is like good conversation—"direct, fresh, personal, incomplete." Not all criticism is good criticism, and even if all criticism were good criticism, critics would have differing points of view and would want to argue them. Those in the business of criticizing art and criticizing criticism understand that what they do is tentative, or "incomplete" in Stevens's terms, open to revision, and vulnerable to counterargument. The best of critics realize that they cannot afford to be dogmatic about their views because they can always be corrected. They can be passionate and often are, but the best of them rely on reason rather than emotion to convince another of their way of seeing a work of art. Critics believe in how they see and in what they write, and they try to persuade their readers that their way is the best way, or at least a very good way, to see and understand. Writing about Robert Hughes's criticism, Nicholas Jenkins says that Hughes's "strong opinions seem shaped almost as much by his love of the surge of powerful rhetoric as by his sense of intellectual conviction." Hughes concurs: "*Of course* there's an element of performance in criticism."[45] Critics are also open to another's point of view, but that other will likewise have to persuade them, on the basis of reason, before they change their views.

Several readers and critics themselves have complained that criticism is too often obscure, too difficult to read, and at times incomprehensible. Saltz puts it this way:

> Why is it that so much art criticism is indecipherable—even to "us"? If art has lost its audience then surely this type of smarter-than-thou "criticism" played its part. Criticism isn't the right word for it anyway. Much of this writing feels cut off from its objects. When a critic reports back about what he or she has seen it should be in accessible, clear language and not a lot of brainy gobble-dygook that no one understands. A critic should want to be understood. But the price you pay for this accessibility can be dear. You can lose your "pass" into certain academic circles, or it might mean that you don't get asked to be on all those panels that discuss art and its relationship to biogenetic whatever, and it may mean you won't get asked to too many CAA [College Art Association] conventions—but that's okay.[46]

Peter Schjeldahl, with some self-deprecating humor, writes that "I have written obscurely when I could get away with it. It is very enjoyable, attended by a powerful feeling of invulnerability." Then, with less sarcasm, he adds: "Writing clearly is immensely hard work that feels faintly insane, like painting the brightest possible target on my chest. To write clearly is to give oneself away."[47] This book tries to give ideas away by making them clear and thus accessible—especially when they are difficult ideas—to anyone interested in knowing them.

THE VALUE OF CRITICISM

The value of *reading* good criticism is increased knowledge and appreciation of art. Reading about art with which we are unfamiliar increases our knowledge. If we already know and appreciate an artwork, reading someone else's view of it may expand our own if we agree, or it may intensify our own if we choose to disagree and formulate counterarguments.

There are also considerable advantages for *doing* criticism. Marcia Siegel, dance critic for the *Hudson Review* and author of several books of dance criticism, talks about the value for her of the process of writing criticism: "Very often it turns out that as I write about something, it gets better. It's not that I'm so enthusiastic that

I make it better, but that in writing, because the words are an instrument of thinking, I can often get deeper into a choreographer's thoughts or processes and see
more logic, more reason."[48]

Similarly, A. D. Coleman began studying photography and writing photography
criticism in the late 1960s because he realized that photography was shaping him
and his culture; he wanted to know more about it and "came to feel that there
might be some value to threshing out, in public and in print, some understandings
of the medium's role in our lives."[49] For him the process of criticizing was valuable
in understanding photographs, and he hoped that his thinking in public and in
print would help him and others to better understand photographs and their effects
on viewers.

If the process of criticism is personally valuable even for frequently published,
professional critics, then it is likely that there are considerable advantages for others
who are less experienced with criticizing art. An immediate advantage of thoughtful engagement with an artwork is that the observer's viewing time is slowed down
and measurably prolonged. This point is obvious but important: Most people visiting museums consider an artwork in less than five seconds. Five seconds of viewing compared to hours and hours of crafting by the artist seems woefully out of
balance. Considering descriptive, interpretive, and evaluative questions about an
artwork ought to significantly expand one's awareness of an artwork and considerably alter one's perception of the work.

In criticizing an art object for a reader or viewer, critics must struggle to trans-
late their complex jumble of thoughts and feelings about art into words that can
be understood first by themselves and then by others. Everyday viewers of art can
walk away from a picture or an exhibit with minimal responses, unarticulated feelings, and incomplete thoughts. Critics who view artworks as professionals, however, have a responsibility to struggle with meaning and address questions that the
artwork poses or to raise questions that the artwork does not.

Critics usually consider artworks from a broader perspective than the single picture or the single show. They put the work in a much larger context of other works
by the artist, works by other artists of the day, and art of the past. They are able to
do this because they see much more art than does the average viewer—they consider art for a living. Their audiences will not be satisfied with one-word responses,
quick dismissals, or empty praises. Critics have to argue for their positions and
base their arguments on the artwork and how they understand it. Viewers who
consider art in the way that a critic would consider it will likely increase their own
understanding and appreciation of art—that is the goal and the reward.

Describing Photographs

What Do I See?

MARY ELLEN MARK, A RENOWNED PHOTOJOURNALIST USUALLY ASSOCIATED WITH DOCUMENTARY photographs, offers an elegant description of a photograph from *The Bathers* by Jennette Williams (Plate 1):

> It doesn't matter that these bodies are not conventionally ideal—when these women are in front of Jennette's camera, they are proud to reveal their full femininity. Jennette's photographs could only have been taken by a woman— a woman with passion, a strong personality, and great talent—a woman who is gentle, kind, and engaging. . . . I asked Jennette about her process in taking these pictures—how she convinced these women to let her photograph them nude, how they came to trust her. First of all, of course, she was willing to be nude herself . . . Jennette told me that she would shoot in the baths and then go back to her hotel room each night to process the film so that she could read the negatives. She would make prints back home and return to the baths with boxes of photographs to show and give to the women. When the women saw the photographs, they allowed her to continue to photograph them. I'm sure it was the beauty and dignity of her images as well as her approach that put them completely at ease in front of her camera. . . . Jennette's lounging women not only revel in intimate feminine moments but in the camaraderie of women as well. They relax together, soaking in the steamy atmosphere. . . . Jennette's frames are always perfectly resolved, both technically and graphically, and made dynamic by her unique sense of composition. Another powerful quality of these surprising images is how Jennette utilizes scale in them. Some pictures become

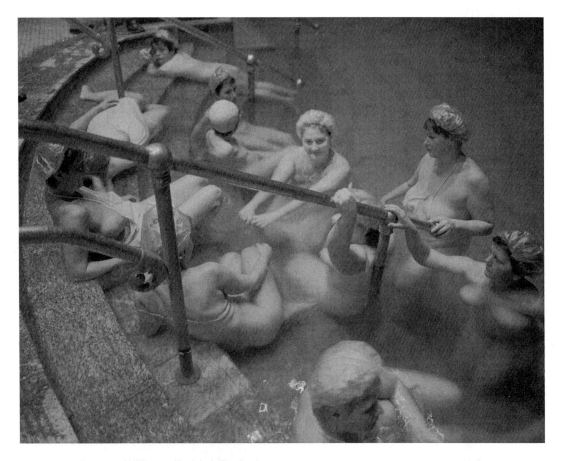

PLATE 1. Jennette Williams, *Untitled, The Bathers*, c. 2006.
© Jennette Williams.

landscapes . . . while others are taken from middle distance, as (Plate 1) the women lounging on the steps of a pool (the frame brilliantly cut into different shapes by the banister). At times Jennette moves her camera in even closer, and female forms become abstract shapes that merge into the steam of the baths. Jennette treats her subjects with the greatest of respect; she has brought back dignity, beauty, and romance to the female nude in a way that inspires me.[1]

DEFINING DESCRIPTION

To describe a photograph or an exhibition is to notice things about it and to tell another, out loud or in print, what one notices. Description is a data-gathering process, a listing of facts. Descriptions are answers to the questions: "What is here? What am I looking at? What do I know with certainty about this image?" The answers are identifications of both the obvious and the not so obvious. Even when certain things seem obvious to critics, they point them out because they know that what is obvious to one viewer might be invisible to another. Descriptive information includes statements about the photograph's subject matter, medium, and form, and then more generally, about the photograph's causal environment, including information about the photographer who made it, the times during which it was made, and the social milieu from which it emerged. Descriptive information is true (or false), accurate (or inaccurate), factual (or contrary to fact): Either Richard Avedon used an 8- by 10-inch Deardorff view camera or he didn't; either he exposed more than 17,000 sheets of film or he didn't. Descriptive statements are verifiable by observation and an appeal to factual evidence. Although in principle, descriptive claims can be shown to be true or false, in practice, critics sometimes find it difficult to do so.

Critics obtain descriptive information from two sources—internal and external. They derive much descriptive information by closely attending to what can be seen within the photograph. They also seek descriptive information from external sources including libraries, the artists who made the pictures, and press releases.

Describing is a logical place to start when viewing an exhibition or a particular photograph because it is a means of gathering basic information on which understanding is built. Psychologically, however, we often want to judge first, and our first statements often express approval or disapproval. There is nothing inherently wrong with judging first, as long as judgments are informed and relevant information is descriptively accurate. Whether we judge first and then revise a judgment based on description, or describe and interpret first and then judge, is a matter of choice. The starting point is not crucial, but accurate description is an essential part of holding defensible critical positions. Interpretations and judgments that omit facts or are contrary to fact are seriously flawed.

Critics inevitably and frequently describe, but in print they don't necessarily first describe, next interpret, and then judge. They might first describe to themselves privately before they write, but in print they might start with a judgment, or an interpretive thesis, or a question, or a quotation, or any number of literary devices, in order to get and hold the attention of their readers. They would probably be dreadfully boring if they first described and then interpreted and then judged. In the same sentence critics often mix descriptive information with an interpretive claim or with a judgment of value. For our immediate aim of learning the descriptive process of criticism, however, we are sorting and highlighting descriptive data in the writing of critics.

DESCRIBING AN EXHIBITION:
AVEDON'S "IN THE AMERICAN WEST"

When Richard Avedon's photographs "In the American West" (Plate 2) were first shown, in 1985, Douglas Davis was in the difficult position in which art critics often find themselves—he had to write some of the first words about some new and

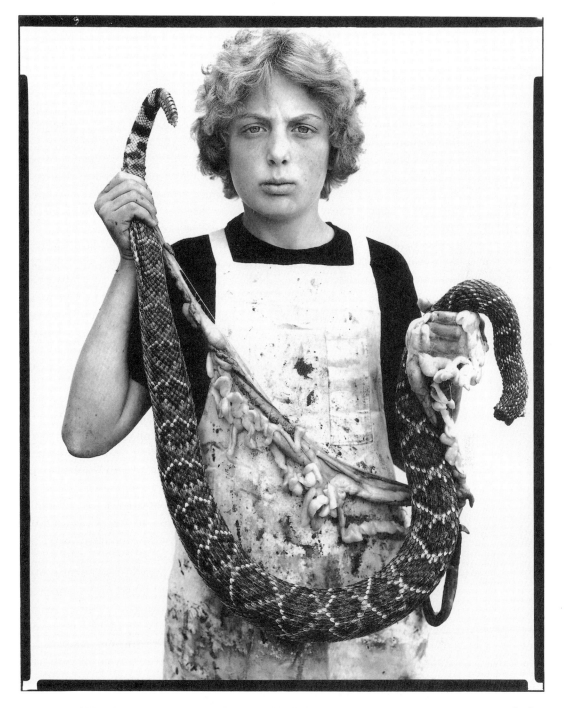

PLATE 2.   Richard Avedon, *Boyd Fortin, Thirteen Year Old Rattlesnake Skinner, Sweetwater, Texas, 3/10/83.*
© Richard Avedon.

challenging work. He also had to write for an audience of readers who had not seen the work. Avedon's American West work is now relatively well known because it has been exhibited and has been available in book form since 1985,[2] and it has been considered by several critics. But the work wasn't known when Davis wrote about it for *Newsweek,* shortly after its inaugural exhibition opened. Davis's review is one magazine page plus a column in length, about 1,000 words, and is accompanied by four of Avedon's photographs from the exhibition. It is full of descriptive information—facts and verifiable observations about the work in question.

Davis opens his article with this sentence: "In the thick of the crowd of portraits on display in Ft. Worth by famed fashion photographer Richard Avedon to document the American West, there is one immensely ambitious—and revealing—triptych."[3] Thus, because his readers may or may not know of Richard Avedon, Davis quickly and without condescension informs them that Avedon is a famed fashion photographer. He also explains that the show is of portraits, that there are a lot of them—"in the thick of the crowd of portraits"—and that they are on display in Ft. Worth. That they are on display in Ft. Worth, although basic, is interesting to note because major shows by a famed fashion photographer, and by Avedon, are more likely to open in New York City than in a city in Texas. That they were made "to document" the American West becomes important for Davis's ultimate judgment of the show.

Davis begins his review of the show by discussing one piece, which he calls "immensely ambitious" and "revealing." It is a complicated piece and not reprinted with the article. Our mental image of it depends on Davis's description: "More than 10 feet long, almost 5 feet high, it is the largest image in an exhibition dominated by life-size faces and torsos." The work is very large by photographic standards; Davis emphasizes the dimensions of it and also reveals that most of the show is life-size: "Here we stand face to face with four grimy coal miners lined up across three separate photographs." Readers who may not know the term *triptych* can now decipher that this piece is composed of three separate photographs. Davis identifies the subject matter of this piece as four coal miners whom he describes as "grimy" and as "lined up." He also describes the experience of viewing this large image: "we stand face to face" with them.

Davis's description of the image's size is important to note because if his readers see these photographs, they will likely see them as pages in Avedon's book, small reproductions in magazines or newspapers, or perhaps as slides on a screen in a classroom, but not as they were presented life-size in the Ft. Worth exhibition. One purpose of descriptive accounts is for understanding in the present; another is to accurately record for posterity. Some of today's criticism of new work will eventually become part of art history for future generations long after exhibitions have closed.

Davis then explains that one of the four miners in the triptych appears twice, with his face split by the separation between two of the three pictures. Davis finds this split "hypnotic and arresting." In one picture the miner has a beard and in the other he does not. Davis explains that Avedon photographed the miner twice, at three-month intervals: The first time the miner had a beard, the second time he did not.

All of this description of the one triptych appears in Davis's first paragraph of the article. And this information sets up his ensuing interpretation of what the work is about and then his evaluative conclusion about how good it is: "In many ways, Avedon's long awaited new body of work . . . is as two faced as this miner."

For Davis, this new work is two-faced because, first, it has been promoted as a forthright, direct, and "documentary" treatment of the West and as a departure from Avedon's high-fashion style for which he is famous. But according to Davis, although the photographs may seem candid and spontaneous, they are highly contrived: "As always he pursued style, manner and effect." The show, Davis concludes in the last sentence of the article, does not document the West, but rather documents Avedon himself and his style. Thus, Davis's judgment is mixed: The show fails because it is not an accurate documentation of the West as it was promoted and as it pretends; but it succeeds as the continuation of a photographer's "exhilarating pursuit of the perfect photographic style."

Between the opening paragraph about the triptych and the concluding paragraph containing Davis's judgment of the work are three paragraphs of descriptive information. Not only are descriptions interesting and enlightening in themselves, but they are also used to support a critic's interpretation and judgment. Davis's interpretation of the work is that it is very stylized, and his judgment is that the work both fails and succeeds because of its stylization. We and other critics may agree or disagree with Davis's decisions about Avedon's work, and in Chapters 3–6 we will fully consider interpreting and judging photographs, but our primary concern here is description. Although description, interpretation, and evaluation overlap in a critic's writing, often in the same phrase or sentence, we will continue sorting out Davis's descriptive language and consider all the descriptive information he provides in his brief article.

In the next paragraph we learn that the work was long awaited and that it has been highly advertised as different from the work that made Avedon famous in the 1960s. Davis typifies the style of earlier work as "mannered high-fashion." In the first paragraph he said there were many photographs; now he specifies that 124 pictures are on display and that they are reproduced in a book published by Abrams. In a judgment and not a description, Davis calls the book "handsome." He also adds that the photographs have "seeming candor and spontaneity."

In the third paragraph Davis informs readers that this work was commissioned in 1980 by the Amon Carter Museum of Ft. Worth, where the show opened. Davis tells us that Avedon traveled extensively and went to the Rattlesnake Roundup in Sweetwater, Texas, to a rodeo in Augusta, Montana, and to coal mines in Paonia,

Colorado. He held 752 photo sessions and shot 17,000 pictures. Davis states that Avedon's project was as immense as the documentary efforts of William Henry Jackson and Edward Curtis, who surveyed regions of the American West in the late nineteenth and early twentieth centuries.

In the fourth paragraph Davis discusses Avedon's method of shooting. He tells us that Avedon has "a bare chested beekeeper stand before the lens with scores of bees crawling across his skin." Davis claims that Avedon's subjects seem relaxed and real; he attributes this to Avedon's method of photographing, which he also describes. He relates that in making these photographs Avedon used an 8- by 10-inch Deardorff view camera, permitting him to stand close to the subjects, talk with them, and snap the shutter while standing away from the camera. Davis observes that the backgrounds are all uniformly white, made with a sheet of seamless paper hung behind the subjects; that the exposures were by natural daylight; and that all the prints are enlarged from uncropped and unretouched negatives.

In the final paragraph Davis quotes Avedon as saying that when looking at one of these photographs he wants us to believe that the subject "was not even in the presence of a photographer." He offers more descriptive language about Avedon's stylistic treatment of the subjects—"the deadpan stare into the camera, the slouch of the body, the cropped arm or head at the edge of the frame." He describes the subject matter of another picture as a "burly lumber salesman holding his impassive baby upside down" and mentions a coal miner who has a face "painted with rock dust" before he draws his conclusion in his final sentence, quoted earlier, that Avedon exhilaratingly pursues the perfect photographic style.

Davis's article is written for a mass circulation magazine with readers of diverse interests. It is relatively short, of "review" length rather than "feature" length. Another review of about the same length was published in *Artforum* in the same month that Davis's appeared in *Newsweek*.[4] It was written by William Wilson, identified in a byline as a writer and editor. A feature article called "Avedon Goes West" was written by Susan Weiley and published in *Artnews* six months later.[5] Both *Artforum* and *Artnews* are national in scope and devoted exclusively to visual art. Whereas the Davis and Wilson reviews are about one magazine page in length and about 1,000 words, Weiley's is six pages and about 3,500 words. One photograph accompanies Wilson's review, and four are printed with Weiley's article.

Davis and Wilson generally agree in their appraisals of the show. Although they both approve of the work, they have reservations. Like Davis, Wilson does not accept the work as an accurate documentation of the West. He sees it as Avedon's fiction, but he doesn't mind that; rather, he enjoys the photographs as he would a good story. Although he faults some of the photographs as "self-important" and "patronizing" and mere "fashion,"[6] he is positive about the exhibition. Susan Weiley, however, clearly disapproves of the work. Although she admires Avedon's "flawless craftsmanship," for her the American West project is "cold and mechanical" and "without that power to deeply disturb."[7] For her it is "fashion, not art." With these brief overviews of the positions taken by Wilson and Weiley, we have two more critical positions on Avedon to consider as we continue to explore description in criticism. In addition to analyzing descriptive statements about Avedon's work by these three critics, we will also consider descriptions of other types of photographs.

DESCRIBING SUBJECT MATTER

Descriptive statements about subject matter identify and typify persons, objects, places, or events in a photograph. When describing subject matter, critics name what they see and also characterize it.

Subject matter is different from *subject. Subject,* however, is synonymous with theme or meaning and is more of an interpretive than descriptive endeavor. The following example helps to distinguish between subject matter and subject. Spencer Tunick is famous for his "Nude Adrift" series of large group photographs of nude people in public spaces. While visiting Santiago in 2002, he organized a photo shoot of 4,500 enthusiastic participants who disrobed in a park adjacent to the presidential palace:

> Riding a wave of free speech and expression that has swept the country since the end of the Pinochet dictatorship, many Chileans saw Tunick's work as symbolizing a new beginning for Chile. The phenomenal success of the event, however, shocked many others. Even before the shoot took place, a team of lawyers had tried to prevent it and a crowd of 400 protesters gathered outside the artist's hotel room to chant "Tunick is immoral!" TV and newspaper images of the event sparked outrage throughout the country. In the end, however, Tunick provoked a broad debate about personal freedoms and emerged as something of a hero in the process.[8]

He continues this project all over the world (Plate 3). Although the *subject matter* of Tunick's photograph is 4,500 nude people in a park, its *subject* is interpreted as a call for personal freedom.

Because there are 124 portraits in the Avedon exhibition, many of which are group portraits, there are too many to list individually. Davis chooses to summarily describe the subjects of the show as "ranchers, housekeepers, rodeo riders and oil drillers, pig men, meatpackers and an army of unemployed drifters."[9] Some of these nouns were supplied by Avedon as part of his titles—for example, *David Beason, shipping clerk, Denver, Colorado, 7/25/81*—and Davis has included several of them in his review. But he invents the phrase "an army of unemployed drifters." He adds that one of the coal miners is "tall and enigmatic," and he writes of a boy "with a snake wrapped coyly around his arms." These descriptions of subject

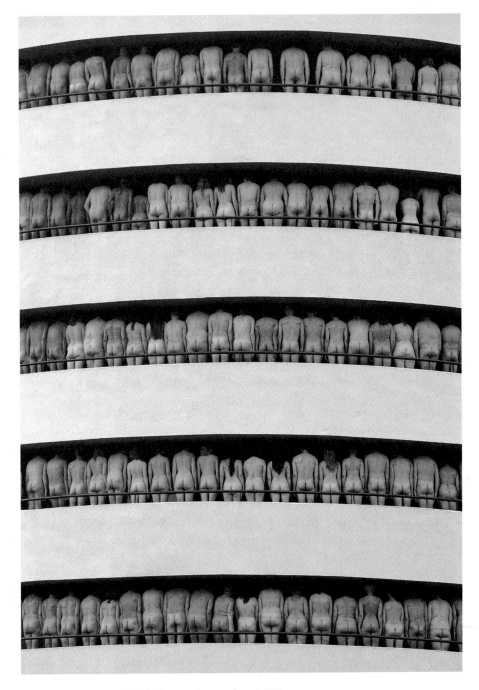

PLATE 3.   Spencer Tunick, *Dream Amsterdam*, 2007.
© STR/Reuters/Corbis.

matter seem simple, straightforward, and obvious when we read them, but Davis had to fashion these subjects with carefully selected words. The photographer gives us images; the critic gives us words for the images.

In his *Artforum* review, William Wilson describes the same subject matter that Davis saw but summarizes it differently. He calls the subject of the show "a human cyclorama" and says that the show includes not only the expected "cowboys and Indians" but also "a couple of mental-hospital patients; a physical therapist; three sisters from Wildhorse, Colorado."[10] About the three sisters, Wilson adds that they have served as co-presidents of the Loretta Lynn Fan Club for the past twenty-five years. In colorful descriptive language utilizing alliteration, Wilson mentions "soot and grime and rips and rashes and blood" and states that the heads of slaughtered sheep and steers are important inclusions in these portraits.

In her feature article in *Artnews,* Susan Weiley had considerably more space than the one page allotted to the reviews by Davis and Wilson, and she chose to describe a lot of Avedon's work, starting with his older fashion work which, she tells us, began in 1946. She discusses how his work differed from that of his peers who photographed fashion, and she explains that he freed the fashion photograph from the still studio pose. She uses lively descriptive language to discuss the subject matter of his fashion work and how he presented it: In real and recognizable places he photographed models as they "leaped off curbs or bounced down a beach or swirled their New Look skirts through Parisian streets or gamed at a roulette table."[11] Weiley also relates that in addition to his commercial fashion work in the sixties and seventies Avedon made portraits of celebrities. Beyond merely identifying the subjects as portraits of artists, writers, and politicians, she characterizes them in carefully chosen descriptive language: "Avedon presented the frailties of the body: the sags and bags, lines and pouches that flesh is heir to, the double chins, enlarged pores, glazed eyes and sullen expressions of the rich, the powerful, the famous." She also describes a "devastating series" of portraits Avedon made of his father as he was dying of cancer.

When she discusses his American West work, Weiley not only describes the subjects he photographs but also those he does *not* photograph: "fearless gunslingers or stalwart lawmen or fierce cattlemen or Houston oil barons, or any of the stock characters that live in our imagination of the West." As do Davis and Wilson, she lists the persons in the photographs by their jobs but further describes the lot as "a catalogue of the odd, the bizarre, the defective, the deformed, the demented and the maimed." And like Wilson, but unlike Davis, she mentions the bloodiness of some of the subjects: "Slaughterhouse workers and their implements are drenched in blood, and severed, bloodied calf, steer and sheep heads all have their likenesses immortalized."

Weiley concludes that Avedon's choice of subject matter is more interpretive than descriptive: "After a short time one realizes the westerners were selected solely for their strange physical characteristics." She is not alone in her conclusion. Richard Bolton, writing in *Afterimage,* considers Avedon's work exploitative and asks of the subjects of the photographs: "Were they told that, had they been less dirty, less debilitated, or had better taste, or better posture, they might not have been chosen to be photographed?"[12]

These critics have seen the same work and write about the same exhibition, but in describing the subjects of the photographs, they have us notice different aspects and characteristics. There is much overlap in their observations about the subject matter, because they are writing about observable facts, but there is also room for different selections of what to include and what to exclude as well as considerable variance in the language they use to describe the subject matter once they have named it.

Avedon's subject matter is mostly people and is relatively uncomplicated—usually one person to a photograph. But as we have just seen, describing that subject matter is not an easy task. The subject matter of many other photographs is also simple, but when criticizing it, we characterize what is there. Edward Weston's subject matter for an entire series of photographs is green peppers. The subject matter of a Minor White photograph is bird droppings on a boulder. Irving Penn's subject matter for a series of photographs is cigarette butts.

Some photographers utilize *a lot* of simple objects as their subject matter. In a series of still lifes, Jan Groover "took her camera to the kitchen sink" and photographed complicated arrangements of kitchen utensils such as knives, forks, spoons, plates, cups, plastic glasses and glass glasses, pastry and aspic molds, metal funnels, whisks, plants, and vegetables.[13] Most of the objects are recognizable, but some are abstracted in the composition so that they are "surfaces and textures" and not recognizable on the basis of what is shown. Although in real life Groover's subject matter is a pie pan, on the basis of what is seen in the photograph it can be identified only as "a brushed aluminum surface" or "a glistening metallic plane." The subject matter of many abstract works can be described only with abstract terms, but critics still can and should describe it.

The subject matter of some photographs is seemingly simple but actually very elusive. Cindy Sherman's work provides examples (Plate 4; see Color Plate 1). Most of these photographs are self-portraits, so in one sense her subject matter is herself. But she titles black and white self-portraits made between 1977 and 1980 "Untitled Film Stills." In them she pictures herself, but as a woman in a wide variety of guises from hitchhiker to housewife. Moreover, these pictures look like stills from old movies. She also made a series of "centerfolds" for which she posed clothed and in the manner of soft-porn magazine photographs. So what is the subject matter of these pictures? In a *New York Times* review, Michael Brenson names the subject matter of the film still photographs "stock characters in old melodramas and suspense films."[14] Eleanor Heartney, writing in *Afterimage,* says that both the self-portraits and the film still photographs directly refer to "the cultural construction

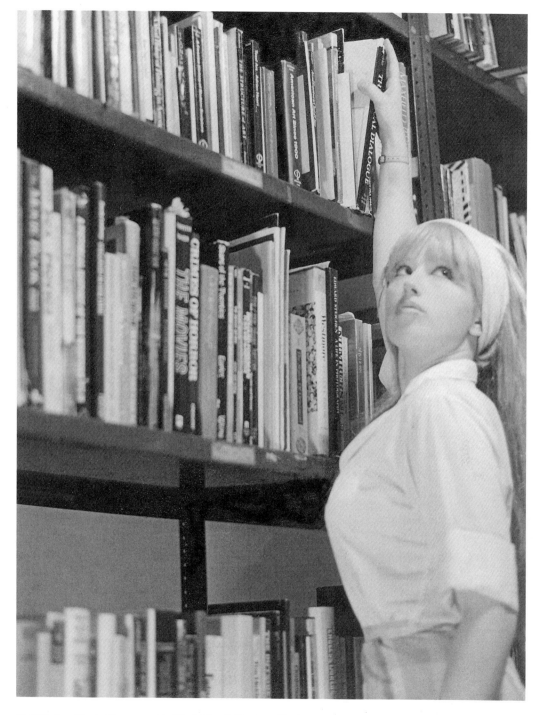

PLATE 4.   Cindy Sherman, *Untitled Film Still*, 1978. Black and white photograph, 10 × 8 inches.
© Cindy Sherman. Courtesy of the artist and Metro Pictures, New York City.

of femininity."[15] They are pictures of Cindy Sherman and pictures of Cindy Sherman disguised as others; they are also pictures of women as women represented in cultural artifacts such as movies, magazines, and paintings, especially as pictured by male producers, directors, editors, painters, and photographers. Arthur Danto identifies these iconic characters he sees in the Film Stills:

> The invariant subject is The Girl in Trouble, even if The Girl herself does not always know it. In Barbie-doll garments, in the suburbs or at the beach or in the city, The Girl is always alone, waiting, worried, watchful, but she is wary of, waiting for, worried about, and her very posture and expression phenomenologically imply The Other: the Stalker, the Saver, the Evil and Good who struggle for her possession. She is the Girl Detective; she is America's Sweetheart; she is the Girl We Left Behind, soft and fluttering in a world of hard menace: the Young Housewife, pretty in her apron, threatened in her kitchen; Cindy Starlet, Daddy's Brave Girl, The Whore with the Golden Heart, Somebody's Stenog, Girl Friday, with obstacles to meet, enemies to overcome, eyes to lift the scales from, hard hearts to soften, the Kid in the Chorus, love light burning in her big, big eyes, with a smile for everyone, a kind word for all, not a mean bone in her body, The Girl Next Door, Everyman's Dream of Happiness.[16]

In 1968 Roland Barthes, a French semiotician, author of the book *Camera Lucida* on photography and novelist of *The Name of the Rose,* announced "the death of the author." By that phrase he meant to destabilize the sole authority of the author as the meaning-maker for passive readers and to encourage readers to be active makers of meaning. Barthes conjoined the death of the author with the "birth of the reader."[17]

Sherman jettisons her self-hood as author and individual and suggests "that the very condition of selfhood is built on representation: on the stories children are told or the books adolescents read; on the pictures the media provide which social types are generated and internalized; on the resonance between filmic narratives and fantasy projections." They are also permeated with Sherman's own enjoyment of the time-honored adolescent girl's game of dress up. They are powerful reminders that there is a feminine form of pleasure that cannot be theorized out of existence.

Sherman says: "I like making images that from a distance seem kind of seductive, colorful, luscious and engaging, and then you realize what you're looking at is something totally opposite. It seems boring to me to pursue the typical idea of beauty because that is the easiest and the most obvious way to see the world. It's more challenging to look at the other side." Sherman invites interpretations of her work: "I try to get something going with the characters so that they give more information than what you see in terms of wigs and clothes. I'd like people to fantasize about this person's life or what they're thinking or what's inside their head, so I guess that's like telling a story."[18]

A writer for Sherman's gallery offers this careful and detailed description of some new work, pointing out things we well may not notice without it (see Color Plate 1).

Sherman's latest photographs depict wealthy middle-aged American women, past their prime physically but at the height of their social powers, protected by their sartorial armor yet utterly exposed by the camera—and our scrutiny. These savage portrayals suggest a disconcerting liminal space between fiction and reality where pathos rules. Expensively attired, expertly coiffed and made-up, and framed by the elaborate architectural or landscape settings of their privileged lives, these carefully constructed women begin to crumble under the camera's impassive gaze. At first glance, each of them is projected from a vantage of comfort and success, rendered on a scale that recalls the impressive portraits commissioned by wealthy patrons during the Renaissance. But the enlarged scale has a cruelly adverse effect, drawing attention to their every imperfection—the age-spots, the wrinkles, the sagging skin, and ill-fitting, sometimes garish clothes. Moreover, on closer scrutiny, the backgrounds reveal themselves to be separate from the characters that they frame, shot elsewhere and after the fact, and then added digitally to complete—and at the same time, undermine—the composition.[19]

To simply identify her photographs as "portraits" or "portraits of women" or "self-portraits" or "self-portraits of Cindy Sherman" would be inaccurate and in a sense would be to misidentify them.

Some photographs, such as those of Joel-Peter Witkin, have obviously complex subject matter. His subject matter is sometimes difficult to decipher and always demands attention because it is usually shocking. In a feature article in *Exposure,* Cynthia Chris characterizes Witkin's subject matter as sexual, violent, and perverse and itemizes it in this litany: "fetus, child, male, female, hermaphrodite, corpse, skeleton, the beautiful, the deformed, the obese, live animal and taxidermic specimen."[20] Hal Fischer, in *Artweek,* describes Witkin's subject matter in the following way: "tortured figures, obese women, carrot dildos, fetuses and anything else which may enter this photographer's imagination are fabricated into enigmatic, often grotesque tableaux."[21] Witkin uses models whom Fischer describes as "earth-mother goddesses, transsexuals, masked and bound men and other inhabitants of the demimonde." In her article Chris states: "Usually nude, they are less dressed than entangled in hats, hoods, masks, wings, rubber hoses, flora, fauna, food, and sex toys."[22] The subjects are sometimes further altered by scratching and other manual manipulations done to the negatives before they are printed, and many of the photographs are collages of different negatives.

Witkin also includes other art objects or segments of them in his tableaux, and he frequently refers to artworks by artists of earlier times. Van Deren Coke details some of these art objects and art references in his introductory essay to an exhibition catalogue of Witkin's work.[23] A 1981 photograph by Witkin titled *The Prince Imperial* refers to a portrait of the son of Napoleon III made in the 1860s. Witkin's *Mandan* is based on a painting done in the 1830s by George Catlin, and *Courbet in Rejlander's Pool* refers to both the painter Courbet and the photographer Rejlander.

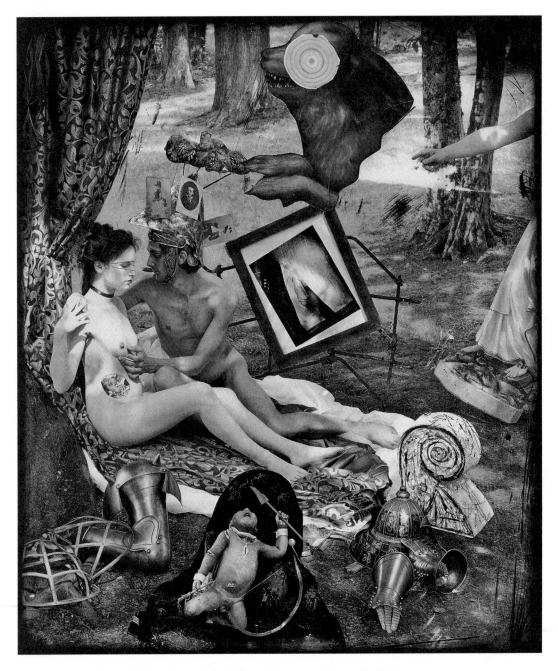

PLATE 5.   Joel-Peter Witkin, *Thoraxic Park, Paris,* left panel of triptych, 2002.

Courtesy of Joel-Peter Witkin and Ricco/Maresca Gallery.

Some of Witkin's photographs refer so closely to other artworks that Coke includes the historic paintings in the catalogue of Witkin's contemporary work: *The Little Fur,* painted around 1638 by Peter Paul Rubens, is printed opposite Witkin's *Helena Fourment.* In a footnote, Coke relates that Witkin's photograph parodies a portrait of Rubens's wife, Helena Fourment. Witkin also parodies portraits by Goya and Grant Wood (*Portrait of Nan*) and a sculpture of Venus by Canova. In another of Witkin's photographs, *Pygmalion,* segments of reproductions of Picasso's paintings are part of the photograph. Thus the subject matter of this photograph is other art, which is observable only if the viewer knows the other art or is told of the references by someone else, such as a critic. The parodies in particular are problematic because a parody is not effective unless the reader or viewer knows that it is a parody and how it ridicules what it refers to. In these examples of Witkin's work, the subject matter is not obvious, so the critic must describe it accurately and completely.

DESCRIBING FORM

Form refers to how the subject matter is presented. Ben Shahn, the painter and photographer who made photographs for the Farm Security Administration in the 1930s, said that form is the shape of content. Descriptive statements about a photograph's form concern how it is composed, arranged, and constructed visually. We can attend to a photograph's form by considering how it uses what are called "formal elements." From the older artforms of painting and drawing, photography has inherited these formal elements: dot, line, shape, light and value, color, texture, mass, space, and volume. Other formal elements identified for photographs include black and white tonal range; subject contrast; film contrast; negative contrast; paper contrast; film format; point of view, which includes the distance from which the photograph was made and the lens that was used; angle and lens; frame and edge; depth of field; sharpness of grain; and degree of focus. Critics refer to the ways photographers use these formal elements as "principles of design," which include scale, proportion, unity within variety, repetition and rhythm, balance, directional forces, emphasis, and subordination.

Edward Weston identified some of the choices of formal elements the photographer has when exposing a piece of film: "By varying the position of his camera, his camera angle, or the focal length of his lens, the photographer can achieve an infinite number of varied compositions with a single stationary subject."[24] John Szarkowski reiterated what Weston observed over fifty years ago and added an important insight: "The simplicity of photography lies in the fact that it is very easy to make a picture. The staggering complexity of it lies in the fact that a thousand other pictures of the same subject would have been equally easy."[25]

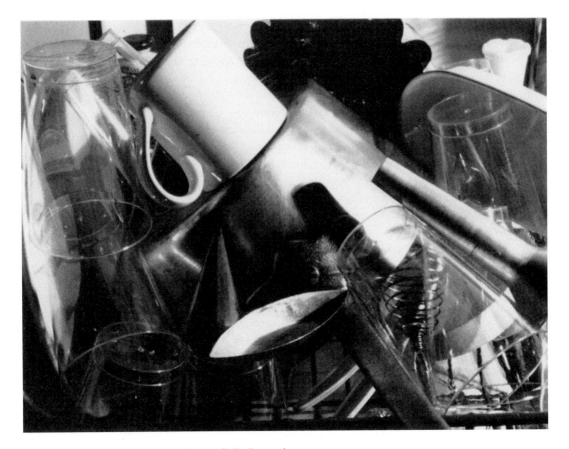

PLATE 6.   Jan Groover, *Untitled*, 1977. Palladium print.
© Jan Groover. Courtesy of Janet Borden Gallery, Inc.

In an essay for an exhibition catalogue of Jan Groover's work (Plate 6), Susan Kismaric provides a paragraph that is a wonderful example of how a critic can describe form and its effects on subject matter:

> The formal element put to most startling use in these pictures is the scale of the objects in them. Houseplants, knives, forks, and spoons appear larger than life. Our common understanding of the meaning of these pedestrian objects is transformed to a perception of them as exotic and mysterious. Arrangements of plates, knives, and houseplants engage and delight our sight through their glamorous new incarnation while they simultaneously undermine our sense of their purpose in the natural world. Meticulously controlled artificial light contributes to this effect. Reflections of color and shapes on glass, metal, and water, perceived only for an instant or not at all in real life, are stilled here, creating a new subject for our contemplation. The natural colors of the things

photographed are intensified and heightened. Organic objects are juxtaposed with manmade ones. Soft textures balance against, and touch, hard ones. The sensuous is pitted against the elemental.[26]

The formal elements to which Kismaric refers are light, color, and texture; the principles of design are scale, arrangements of objects, and juxtapositions. She cites scale as the most dominant design principle and then describes the effects of Groover's use of scale on the photographs and our perception of them. She identifies the light as artificial and tells us that it is meticulously controlled. The colors are natural; some of the shapes are manufactured and others are organic, and they are juxtaposed. She identifies the textures as soft and hard, sensuous and elemental. Kismaric's description of these elements, and her explanation of their effects, contributes to our knowledge and enhances our appreciation of Groover's work.

Kismaric's paragraph shows how a critic simultaneously describes subject matter and form and also how in a single paragraph a critic describes, interprets, and evaluates. To name the objects is to be descriptive, but to say how the objects become exotic and mysterious is to interpret the photographs. The tone of the whole paragraph is very positive. After reading the paragraph we know that Kismaric thinks Groover's photographs are very good and we are provided reasons for this judgment based on her descriptions of the photographs.

DESCRIBING MEDIUM

The term *medium* refers to what an art object is made of. Identifying or describing medium is important because medium significantly inflects meaning or expresses meaning itself. For example, Rashid Johnson made a Van Dyke photograph in 2001.[27] (It is a very abstract monochromatic photograph with no recognizable subject matter.) The medium could simply be said to be "photograph," or "Van Dyke photograph." It is also a photogram, a further identification of its medium. Most significantly, however, to make the photogram, Johnson used chicken bones, watermelon seeds, red beans, rice, and other materials. These materials themselves carry connotations. The cultural connotations that they carry are reinforced by the title of the image: *Jiggabooboo Holy Field Negros*. Without this information about the medium of this image, it would be difficult to arrive at meaning consistent with what is actually there, although it is not visible in the image itself. The medium of Sandy Skoglund's *Walking on Eggshells,* 1997, can simply and accurately be said to be "Cibachrome," or "color photograph," but in the installation she constructed for the photograph, Skoglund uses the media of whole, empty eggshells (some filled with plaster), cast paper bathroom fixtures (sink, bathtub, toilet, mirror), cast paper wall tiles with relief-printed images, cold-cast (bonded-bronze) sculptures of snakes and rabbits, over a variable floor space of thirty square feet. To make *Spirituality of the Flesh,* she bought eighty pounds of raw hamburger with which to cover the walls in the final photograph, and she used orange marmalade and strawberry preserves to color the walls and floor of *The Wedding.* Descriptive statements about a picture's medium usually identify it as a photograph, an oil painting, or an etching. They may also include information about the kind and size of film that was used, the size of the print, whether it is black and white or in color, characteristics of the camera that was used, and other technical information about how the picture was made, including how the photographer photographs. Each of the critics of "In the American West" writes about how Avedon made the pictures.

Davis tells us that Avedon's prints are uncropped and not retouched, that the subjects were illuminated with natural light in front of white paper, and that Avedon held 752 photo sessions with the subjects of the portraits and shot 17,000 sheets of film. He also relates that Avedon used an 8- by 10-inch Deardorff view camera, which allowed him to stand close to the subjects and talk to them as he shot.

Wilson mentions the camera and tripod, the rolls of white paper for background, and Avedon's ability to stand by his subjects rather than behind the camera when shooting. He also tells us that Avedon held 752 shooting sessions and adds that he did this work over five consecutive summers, traveling through seventeen western states, from Kansas to California.

Weiley does not detail much technical information, but she describes Avedon's positioning of the subjects in front of white paper on location and tells us that two assistants loaded his camera. She describes his method of photographing and interprets the psychological effects of his method: "He is in total control, has complete authority over his subjects. He selects, arranges, directs, just as he would a fashion shot."[28]

In her essay on Groover's work, Kismaric specifies that some of the still lifes are done in the platinum-palladium process. She explains that this method of working was invented in 1873 for its permanence, but she also details its aesthetic qualities—"delicacy, soft grays, and warm tones."[29] Kismaric considers further Groover's choice of photography rather than painting, even though Groover was trained as a painter: "By using photography instead of painting, Groover complicates the notion of representation, and emphasizes the capacity of photography to make works of the imagination."

Critics of Witkin's work usually discuss how he uses the medium of photography. Gary Indiana, in a review in *Art in America,* says that "many of the prints have been made to look like daguerreotypes salvaged from partial decomposition" and adds that "the edges are scored with black lines and smudges suggestive of Action Painting."[30] In a review in *Artweek,* Hal Fischer also describes how Witkin treats the medium of photography and posits some of the effects of his treatments: "By etching into his negatives and selectively bleaching and toning the prints, this artist imbues his imagery with a nineteenth century aura without compromising the sense of photographic reality."[31] In the same publication a year later, Jim Jordan agrees that Witkin's formal treatments of his photographs make them look old, from the eighteenth century and the court of Louis XVI. Jordan further relates that Witkin uses a Rolleiflex camera, prints on Portriga paper, sometimes through a tissue paper overlay that he sprinkles with water and toning chemicals.[32]

Uta Barth makes photographs in the spirit of conceptual art that examine and pointedly utilize distinctive characteristics of the medium of photography, such as camera movement, position, nonstationary subject, scale, or focus. According to critic Andrew Perchuk, Barth's photographs are "boiled down to an almost topological study of how the photographic apparatus orients and disorients the viewer."[33]

To make the images for the exhibition and book *Attracted to Light,* Mike and Doug Starn photographed moths on the porches of their homes in upstate New York. They used custom-made macro lenses and invented a specialized printing method during which the silver emulsion softened and tiny flakes of the image washed away, thus mimicking the moths' delicate and tattered wings. They printed the images on soft paper that echoes the velvety texture of the moths. Knowing this bit of technical information about the Starns's manipulations of a traditional medium and method can increase our understanding of the meaning of the images and our appreciation of them.

Annette Grant, writing about Gregory Crewdson's photographs for the *New York Times,* describes the elaborate postproduction Photoshop manipulations made to Crewdson's *Untitled (Woman at the Vanity)* by Geraldine Lucid at Laumont Digital in Manhattan, aided by the printer Kylie Wright:

> The man and woman in the bedroom scene on Page 1 of this section, for example, come from two different shots. One central scan was used for the room and the man on the bed and another for the woman, who was dropped in. The shadows she casts had to be adjusted; a transferred figure never fits perfectly. The ceiling was altered slightly to join the wall seamlessly. Birds that once perched on the grass outside the bedroom door were deemed distracting and excised. The brand name was erased from the lotion bottle on the vanity table to make the image feel more outside of time. The curtain on the left was extended slightly for compositional reasons. The telephone, on a table at right, looked too prominent and was toned down. The stem of the lamp behind the phone had nearly disappeared and was highlighted. The floor had too many shadows, a result of using multiple lighting sources, so lighter carpet was morphed into some areas. The effect? To Mr. Crewdson, the difference between good and beautiful.[34]

Thus the description of medium involves more than just using museum labels, as in labeling Jan Groover's images as "three chromogenic color prints," or "platinum-palladium print," or "Gelatin-silver print." To fully describe the medium a photographer is using is not only to iterate facts about the process he or she uses, the type of camera, and kind of print, but also to discuss these things in light of the effects their use has on their expression and overall impact. Critics might more fully explore these effects as part of their interpretation or judgment of the work, but they ought to explicitly mention the properties of the medium in the descriptive phase of criticism.

DESCRIBING STYLE

Style indicates a resemblance among diverse art objects from an artist, movement, time period, or geographic location and is recognized by a characteristic handling of subject matter and formal elements. Neoexpressionism is a commonly recognized, recent style of painting, and pictorialism, "directorial" photography,[35] and the "snapshot aesthetic"[36] are styles of photography.

To consider a photographer's style is to attend to what subjects he or she chooses to photograph, how the medium of photography is used, and how the picture is formally arranged. Attending to style can be much more interpretive than descriptive. Labeling photographs "contemporary American" or "turn of the century" is less controversial than is labeling them "realistic," or "straight," or "manipulated," or "documentary." The critics of Avedon's work being considered here are particularly interested in determining whether his style is "documentary," or "fictional," or "fashion." Determining Avedon's style involves considerably more than describing, but it does include descriptions of whom he photographs, how he photographs them, and what his pictures look like.

Of all the treatments of Avedon's style considered here, Weiley's is the most complete. She begins with his earlier portraits, claiming that he "Avedonizes" his subjects.[37] She generalizes his early portrait work as "confrontational" and typifies it as "frontal, direct, with a single subject centered, staring directly out at the viewer." She explains that he undermined the glamour of the famous people he photographed—that he stripped them of their masks and "brought the mighty down to human scale, assassinating all possibility of grace or vanity." Weiley is much less sympathetic to Avedon's treatment of his subjects in the American West work; she finds his manner of working "disagreeable," "condescending to his subjects," and "frankly arrogant" in its exploitation. Whereas the famous people he photographs are media smart and accustomed to being photographed and publicized, the westerners are not, and she thinks that in the hands of Avedon they are "like innocents led to slaughter." Thus, on the basis of descriptive facts about Avedon's style, namely, whom he photographs and how he photographs them, Weiley goes beyond describing and interpreting his style and forms a negative judgment about it.

COMPARING AND CONTRASTING

A common method of critically analyzing a photographer's work is to compare and contrast it to other work by the same photographer, to other photographers' works, or to works by other artists. To compare and contrast is to see what the work in question has in common with another body of work and how it differs. Each of the critics under consideration here descriptively compares Avedon's work to that of other photographers.

Davis compares the size of Avedon's American West project to the late nineteenth- and early twentieth-century documentary projects of William Henry Jackson and Edward Curtis.[38] Jackson was an explorer, writer, and photographer who, over a period of twenty-five years, produced tens of thousands of negatives of Indians and the western landscape. Curtis published twenty volumes of *The North American Indian* between 1907 and 1934. Although Davis compares the three photographers, he does not equate Avedon with the other two in terms of merit. In a judgment, not a description, Davis states that "Avedon is no Jackson or Curtis."

Critics need not limit their comparisons of a photographer to another photographer. Wilson makes comparative references between Avedon and several others of various professions, most of whom are not photographers but rather literary sources he knows and figures in fashion and popular culture: Sam Shepard, Edward Curtis, Mathew Brady, August Sander, Joan Didion, Norman Mailer, Truman Capote, Evil Knievel, Salvador Dali, Elsa Schiaparelli, Charles James, Andy Warhol, Tom Wolfe, Calvin Klein, Georgia O'Keeffe, Ansel Adams, and Irving Penn. Wilson compares Avedon to other storytellers and to others who bridged the gap between fashion and art because he interpretively understands Avedon to be telling stories and attempting to transcend fashion with his photographs.

Of all the critics considered here, Weiley makes the most use of in-depth comparisons, paying particular attention to the similarities and mostly the differences between Avedon's work and that of Robert Frank, August Sander, and Diane Arbus. She cites Robert Frank's book, *The Americans* (1959) because like Avedon's it is "a harsh vision of America"[39] and because both men are outsiders to the cultures they photographed: Frank is Swiss, and Avedon is not a cowboy. To compare Avedon with Frank, Sander, and Arbus, Weiley has to describe each one's photographs and manner of working and then specify how each photographer's work is different from and similar to that of the others.

IDENTIFYING INTERNAL AND EXTERNAL SOURCES OF INFORMATION

We have seen that a critic can find much to mention about the photograph by attending to subject, form, medium, and style. And, as mentioned earlier, critics often go to external sources to gather descriptive information that increases understanding of that photograph. In their writings the critics of Avedon's work each used much information not decipherable in the photographs. By looking only at his American West photographs, a viewer cannot tell that Avedon's exhibited photographs were selected from 17,000 negatives, that he held 752 shooting sessions, that the work was commissioned by the Amon Carter Museum, or that they were made by a famous fashion photographer who had a large body of images made previously. This information comes from a variety of sources, including press releases, interviews with the artist, the exhibition catalogue, and knowledge of photography history. To compare and contrast Avedon's work with his own earlier work and with the work of others, including nonvisual work, each of the critics went to external sources.

In an example different from the critical treatments of Avedon's work, Van Deren Coke relies primarily on external information to provide an introduction to Witkin's work in an exhibition catalogue.[40] Coke gathered the information from Witkin's master's thesis, written at the University of New Mexico in 1976, and from statements that Witkin has made about his work. Much of the information Coke provides is biographical, about the facts of Witkin's life and about his psychological motivations for making specific images. Coke believes that information about Witkin's life illuminates his photographs, and he includes as psychological motivation Witkin's shocking story of how at the age of six he witnessed a car accident and stood close to the decapitated head of a little girl. Coke also relates that Witkin's father was an orthodox Jew and his mother a Catholic and that they divorced over religious differences, that Witkin's first sexual experience was with a hermaphrodite, that he studied sculpture in the evenings at Cooper Union School of Art in New York, that he was an army photographer during the Vietnam War, and that one of his assignments was to photograph accident and suicide victims.

In her article on Witkin, Cynthia Chris relies on external information that includes Coke's catalogue essay and a lecture Witkin delivered at the Art Institute of Chicago. She particularly notes how Witkin obtains the unusual subjects for his photographs—by searching the streets, by following people, through want ads, and through an afterword in his book "that reads like a shopping list"—because she finds his methods objectionable.[41]

Critics and theoreticians of criticism differ on the importance and desirability of external information, on certain types of information, and on the means of gathering it. As we saw in Chapter 1, A. D. Coleman, for example, advocates distance between the critic and the artist, and distinctions between curating and criticizing and between writing history and criticism. Lucy Lippard, however, assumes a partnership with the artists she writes about and feels comfortable interviewing them and seeking their views of their work. In the past, critics rejected biographical and psychological information about artists as irrelevant and advocated instead that the artwork be the source of criticism, that the rest is distracting. Most contemporary critics, however, embrace a more contextual view of criticism and art and carefully consider the photograph's causal environment, including the context in which it was made. The importance of considering context will be explored in Chapter 5.

The test of including or excluding external descriptive information is one of relevancy. The critic's task in deciding what to describe and what to ignore is one of sorting the relevant information from the irrelevant, the insightful from the trivial and distracting. When engaging in criticism, however, one would not want to substitute biography for criticism or to lose sight of the work amid interesting facts about the artist.

Michael Fried, historian and critic newly interested in photography, offers this excellent description of a photograph by Mitch Epstein, *Amos Coal Power Plant, Raymond City, West Virginia 2004* (see Color Plate 2). Fried is known to be very concerned with the form of a piece and a careful describer of what he sees. Here he presents a thorough description of Epstein's photograph based on internal information, that is, what he sees in the picture:

> The camera has been set up in a somewhat elevated position at the side of
> a grassy yard; a white frame (aluminum siding?) house is to the left, next to a
> modest concrete patio with chairs, a table, and plants; to the right is part of a
> garden, and almost in the middle of the picture rises a tree with bare branches
> (though trees elsewhere in the photo are full of foliage—our first clue that
> something untoward may be going on). Alongside the tree is a white garden
> shed and beyond it, following a small rise, are another yard and a house with
> yellow siding, and more trees. The neighborhood, in other words, is typical
> American suburban, not wealthy but not depressed either. And beyond the
> yellow house and the trees, dimmed as if by distance—but not very far away—
> we see two broad cooling towers and two tall narrow smokestacks, with
> Mitch Epstein steam issuing from the tower on the left." "One also senses the
> care Epstein must have taken to select exactly the right point of view, from
> which the scene would appear at once to open itself unguardedly and to hang
> together—to compose itself—as an aesthetic whole, his ideal throughout the
> book. It matters, too, that a small bush just off the patio and a few others in
> the garden bear bright red blossoms, and that a red car is visible in the narrow
> space between the house at left and the one in the middle distance: Eliminate
> any of those and the scene would lose crucial éclat.[42]

DESCRIBING AND INTERPRETING

It is probably as impossible to describe without interpreting as it is to interpret without describing. A critic can begin to mentally list descriptive elements in a photograph, but at the same time he or she has to constantly see those elements in terms of the whole photograph if those elements are to make any sense. But the whole makes sense only in terms of its parts. The relationship between describing and interpreting is circular, moving from whole to part and from part to whole.

Though a critic might want to mentally list as many descriptive elements as possible, in writing criticism he or she has to limit all that can be said about a photograph to what is relevant to providing an understanding and appreciation of the picture. Critics determine relevancy by their interpretation of what the photograph expresses. In a finished piece of criticism, it would be tedious to read descriptive item after descriptive item, or fact after fact, without having some understanding on which to hang the facts. That understanding is based on how the critic interprets and evaluates the picture. At the same time, however, it would be a mistake to interpret without having considered fully what there is in the picture, and interpretations that do not (or worse, cannot) account for all the descriptive elements in a work are flawed interpretations. Similarly, it would be irresponsible to judge without the benefit of a thorough accounting of what we are judging.

DESCRIBING AND EVALUATING

Joel-Peter Witkin (see Plate 5) is a controversial photographer who makes controversial photographs. Critics judge him differently; and their judgments, positive or negative or ambivalent, influence their descriptions of his work. Cynthia Chris clearly disapproves of the work: "Witkin's altered photographs are representations of some of the most repressed and oppressed images of human behavior and appearance,"[43] whereas Hal Fischer writes that "Joel-Peter Witkin, maker of bizarre, sometimes extraordinary imagery, is one of the most provocative artists to have emerged in the past decade."[44] And Gene Thornton of the *New York Times* calls Witkin "one of the great originals of contemporary photography."[45] Their evaluations, positive or negative, are often mixed into their descriptions. For example, Gary Indiana uses the phrases "smeared with burnt-in blotches" and "the usual fuzz around the edges" to describe some formal characteristics of Witkin's prints,[46] and Bill Berkson describes the same edges as "syrupy."[47] These are not value-neutral descriptors but rather descriptors that suggest disapproval. Another critic, Jim Jordan, talks about "Witkin's incredible range of form definition within the prints" and claims that Witkin's surface treatments "inform the viewer that these are works of art."[48] Jordan's phrase "incredible range of form definition" is also a mix of description and judgment, with positive connotations.

In published criticism, descriptions are rarely value-free. Critics color their descriptions according to whether they are positive or negative about the work, and they use descriptors that are simultaneously descriptive and evaluative to influence the reader's view of the artwork. Critics attempt to be persuasive in their writing. Readers, however, ought to be able to sort the critic's descriptions from judgments, and value-neutral descriptions from value-laden descriptions, however subtly they are written, so that they can more intelligently assent or dissent.

Novice critics can find it beneficial to attempt to describe a photograph without connoting positive or negative value judgments about it. They may then be more sensitive to and aware of when descriptions are accurate and neutral and when they are positively or negatively judgmental.

THE IMPORTANCE OF DESCRIPTION TO READERS

As we have seen throughout the chapter, description is a vital activity for critics, established or novice, because it is a time for "getting to know" a piece of art, especially if that art is previously unknown and by an unfamiliar artist. Descriptions are also important to readers because they contain crucial and interesting information that leads them to understand and appreciate images. Descriptions provide information about photographs and exhibitions that readers may never get to see and otherwise would not experience at all. Descriptions are also the basis on which they can agree or disagree with the critic's interpretation and judgment.

Describing photographs and reading descriptions of photographs are particularly valuable activities because people tend to look through photographs as if they were windows rather than pictures. Because of the stylistic realism of many photographs, and because people know that photographs are made with a machine, people tend to consider photographs as if they were real events or living people rather than *pictures* of events or people. Pictures are not nature and they are not natural; they are human constructs. Photographs, no matter how objective or scientific, are the constructions of individuals with beliefs and biases, and we need to consider them as such. To describe subject, form, medium, and style is to consider photographs as pictures made by individuals and not to mistake them for anything more or less.

Description is not a prelude to criticism; description *is* criticism. Careful descriptive accounts by insightful critics using carefully constructed language offer the kind of informed discourse about photographs that increases our understanding and appreciation of photographs.

PRINCIPLES FOR DESCRIBING PHOTOGRAPHS

The following principles for describing photographs summarize the points in this chapter and may be used to guide future descriptions.

- Description is criticism.
- Descriptions are factual.
- Description can be a data-gathering process or a data-reporting process.
- When gathering descriptive data, everything matters.

- Facts about artist, title, medium, size, date, and place or type of presentation are meaningful descriptive data.
- Formal analysis is a combination of description and interpretation.
- Description, interpretation, and evaluation are interdependent activities.
- Reported descriptions should be based on relevancy to interpretive, evaluative, and theoretical ideas.
- Description is especially dependent on interpretation.
- Interpretations and descriptions are meaningfully circular.
- Descriptions should offer information drawn from within and outside of a photograph.
- Descriptions can be (productively or nonproductively) infinite: Relevancy is the determining factor.

CHAPTER 3

Interpreting Photographs
What Does It Mean?

TWO EXEMPLARY INTERPRETATIONS

Following is a fully quoted interpretation written by Susan Sontag about a photograph by Jeff Wall (Plate 7). The essay and reproduction of Wall's photograph appeared in the *New Yorker* magazine as a stand-alone piece for a generally sophisticated audience, but not one necessarily knowledgeable about the medium of photography or the work of Wall. Sontag's piece is offered here as an excellent example of an interpretation. An analysis of it follows the essay.

LOOKING AT WAR: Photography's View of Devastation and Death[1] SUSAN SONTAG

Among single antiwar images, the huge photograph that Jeff Wall made in 1992 entitled *Dead Troops Talk (A vision after an ambush of a Red Army Patrol, near Moqor, Afghanistan, winter 1986)* seems to me exemplary in its thoughtfulness, coherence, and passion. The antithesis of a document, the picture, a Cibachrome transparency seven and a half feet high and more than thirteen feet wide and mounted on a light box, shows figures posed in a landscape, a blasted hillside, that was constructed in the artist's studio. Wall, who is Canadian, was never in Afghanistan. The ambush is a made-up event in a conflict he had read about. His imagination of war (he cites Goya as an inspiration) is in the tradition of nineteenth-century history painting and other forms of history-as-spectacle that emerged in the late eighteenth and early nineteenth centuries just before the invention of the camera—such as

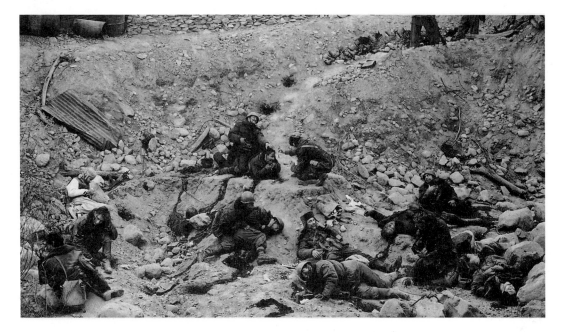

PLATE 7.   Jeff Wall, *Dead Troops Talk (A vision after an ambush of a Red Army patrol, near Moqor, Afghanistan, winter*, 1986. Photograph (original in color), 1992.

Courtesy of Jeff Wall.

tableaux vivants, wax displays, dioramas, and panoramas, which made the past, especially the immediate past, seem astonishingly, disturbingly real.

The figures in Wall's visionary photowork are "realistic," but, of course, the image is not. Dead soldiers don't talk. Here they do.

Thirteen Russian soldiers in bulky winter uniforms and high boots are scattered about a pocked, blood-splashed pit lined with loose rocks and the litter of war: shell casings, crumpled metal, a boot that holds the lower part of a leg. The soldiers, slaughtered in the Soviet Union's own late folly of a colonial war, were never buried. A few still have their helmets on. The head of one kneeling figure, talking animatedly, foams with his red brain matter. The atmosphere is warm, convivial, fraternal. Some slouch, leaning on an elbow, or sit, chatting, their opened skulls and destroyed hands on view. One man bends over another, who lies on his side in a posture of heavy sleep, perhaps encouraging him to sit up. Three men are horsing around: one with a huge wound in his belly straddles another, who is lying prone, while the third, kneeling, dangles what might be a watch before the laughing man on his stomach. One soldier, helmeted, legless, has turned to a comrade some distance away, an alert smile on his face. Below him are two who don't seem quite up to the resurrection and lie supine, their bloodied heads hanging down the stony incline.

Engulfed by the image, which is so accusatory, one could fantasize that the soldiers might turn and talk to us. But no, no one is looking out of the picture at the viewer. There's no threat of protest. They're not about to yell at us to bring a halt to that abomination which is war. They are not represented as terrifying to others, for among them (far left) sits a white-garbed Afghan scavenger, entirely absorbed in going through somebody's kit bag, of whom they take no note, and entering the picture above them (top right), on the path winding down the slope, are two Afghans, perhaps soldiers themselves, who, it would seem from the Kalashnikovs collected near their feet, have already stripped the dead soldiers of their weapons. These dead are supremely uninterested in the living: in those who took their lives; in witnesses—or in us. Why should they seek our gaze? What would they have to say to us? "We"—this "we" is everyone who has never experienced anything like what they went through—don't understand. We don't get it. We truly can't imagine what it was like. We can't imagine how dreadful, how terrifying war is—and how normal it becomes. Can't understand, can't imagine. That's what every soldier, and every journalist and aid worker and independent observer who has put in time under fire and had the luck to elude the death that struck down others nearby, stubbornly feels. And they are right.

What does Sontag do when she interprets the image? She first praises it as "exemplary in its thoughtfulness, coherence, and passion." Critics frequently combine interpretation and judgment, and one's judgment and interpretation are mutually influential on one's thinking about an image.

She also offers selective descriptive information about the object itself. It is huge, was made in 1992, has a title that she provides within her essay even though it is also given with the reproduction, and she identifies the image as a Cibachrome transparency mounted on a light box.

Sontag also describes the making of the photograph. It is "the antithesis of a document," constructed in the artist's studio. She writes that the photograph shows figures posed in a blasted hillside, a scene set in Afghanistan in 1986, although Wall, a Canadian, has never been to Afghanistan.

She cites the sources of the artist: Goya, nineteenth-century history painting, and dramatic spectacles such as wax displays and dioramas that were made before the invention of photography.

Sontag draws our attention to the narrative detail of the image: thirteen Russian soldiers in winter uniforms scattered about "a pocked, blood-splashed pit." She points out a leg in a boot that has been removed from its body, soldiers with opened skulls and destroyed hands, one with "red brain matter" foaming from his mouth. A white-garbed Afghan scavenger rummages through a dead man's belongings, and two Afghans seem to have already taken the dead soldiers' rifles because Kalashnikovs are stacked near their feet. The Russian soldiers are dead and unburied, although they talk to one another.

Amidst this information that describes the photograph and explains its historical context, Sontag offers interpretive claims both about the photograph and about history: Wall's photograph is "the antithesis of a document," the war is "colonial" and a "folly." The image is "accusatory." Most significantly, Sontag interprets the image to be the dead soldiers saying to us that the dreadful horrors of war are unimaginable and unthinkable to us who "don't get it" because we have not experienced it. She forcefully concludes that the soldiers "are right."

Sontag's essay is exemplary of good interpretive criticism in many aspects. She tells us only what she thinks we need to know and no more, providing some information about the photographer, the medium, relevant art historical influences, and historical information about what the scene represents.

She does not bother telling us things that she has decided we don't need to know to understand the image and her interpretation of it. For example, she assumes that readers of the *New Yorker* will know Goya and his images of war. Although many critics of work made by Wall emphasize his elaborate use of film technology and digital media, she deems it sufficient to let her readers know that this image is fictional, based on Wall's imagination of a place to which he has never been.

The descriptive, contextual information that she presents allows her interpretive conclusion that this image is a powerful condemnation of the dreadful, incomprehensible normality of war. The photograph is a story told in images, and Sontag retells the story in her words. Her interpretation builds as a story would build. She tells her story passionately, paralleling the passion of the photograph.

Graham Nash, the musician who was a member of Crosby, Stills, and Nash, and writer of the popular song "Teach Your Children" (1968), offers a personally relevant interpretation of an iconic photograph.

> One day, in a San Francisco gallery, I came upon an image that would stay with me forever. It was *Child with a Toy Hand Grenade in Central Park, N.Y.C.* and it was taken by Diane Arbus in the early '60s. While standing before this masterpiece, I realized that the sensibilities I was reacting to perfectly matched my new song. I understood that if we didn't teach our children a better way of dealing with our fellow human beings then the very future of humanity was in dire straights. She pictured a child of about ten or eleven years old, clenching a toy hand grenade and threatening the very world upon which he stood. In Central Park, at his back, stands an elderly lady . . . was she his mother, grandmother, nanny or stranger? Whoever she was, she couldn't possibly protect anyone from the child's maniacal expression. Diane's image makes me realize that we have to do better, as parents, to raise our kids in a more affectionate way. We must help them deal with their lives, their friends, and their fellow human beings in a much more compassionate manner because violence is not the way to deal with our differences. I praise Diane for her great courage in making images that disturb one's realities and cause one to reflect on why the world is as it is and the need to accept it as it is. This image by Diane Arbus haunts me to this day.[2]

ABOUT INTERPRETATION

To interpret an image is to make sense of it. To interpret is to see something as "*representing* something, or *expressing* something, or *being about* something, or *being a response to* something, or *belonging in a certain tradition,* or *exhibiting certain formal features,* etc."[3] To interpret a photograph is to ask and answer questions such as these:

What is this object that I see?
What is it about?
What does it represent or express?
How does culture influence its construction?
What did it mean to its maker?
What is it a part of?
What are its references?
What is it responding to?
Why did it come to be?
How was it made?
Within what tradition does it belong?
What ends did it possibly serve its maker?
What purpose does it serve its owner or distributor?
What pleasures or satisfactions did it afford the person responsible for it?
    The persons for whom it was made?
Whom does it address? Whom does it ignore?
What problems does it solve, allay, or cause?
What prejudices and preconceptions does it reinforce or disrupt?
What needs does it activate or relieve?
What does it mean to me?
Does it affect my life?
Does it change my view of the world?

As a culture we are perhaps more accustomed to thinking of interpreting poems and paintings than photographs. But all photographs—even simple ones—demand interpretation in order to be fully understood and appreciated. They need to be recognized as pictures about something and for some communicative and expressive purpose. Joel-Peter Witkin's bizarre photographs attract interpretive questions and thoughts because they are different from our common experiences, but many photographs look natural and are sometimes no more cause for notice than tables and trees. We accept photographs in newspapers and on newscasts as facts about the world and as facts that, once seen, require no scrutiny.

Photographs made in a straightforward, stylistically realistic manner are in special need of interpretation. They look so natural that they seem to have been made by themselves, as if there had been no photographer. If we consider how these photographs were made, we may accept them as if they were made by an objective, impartial recording machine. Andy Grundberg, reviewing an exhibition of *National Geographic* photographs, makes this point about these kinds of photographs: "As a result of their naturalism and apparent effortlessness, they have the capacity to lull us into believing that they are evidence of an impartial, uninflected sort. Nothing could be further from the truth."[4]

Nothing could be further from the truth because photographs *are* partial and *are* inflected. People's knowledge, beliefs, values, and attitudes—heavily influenced by their culture—are reflected in the photographs they take. Each photograph embodies a particular way of seeing and showing the world. Photographers make choices not only about what to photograph but also about how to capture an image on film, and often these choices are very sophisticated. We need to interpret photographs in order to make it clear just what these *inflections* are.

When looking at photographs, we tend to think of them as "innocent"—that is, as bare facts, as direct surrogates of reality, as substitutes for real things, as direct reflections. But there is no such thing as an innocent eye.[5] We cannot see the world and at the same time ignore our prior experience in and knowledge of the world. Philosopher Nelson Goodman puts it like this:

> As Ernst Gombrich insists, there is no innocent eye. The eye comes always ancient to its work, obsessed by its past and by old and new insinuations of the ear, nose, tongue, fingers, heart, and brain. It functions not as an instrument self-powered and alone, but as a dutiful member of a complex and capricious organism. Not only how but what it sees is regulated by need and prejudice.[6]

If there is no such thing as the innocent eye, there certainly isn't an innocent camera.

What Goodman says of the eye is true of the camera, the photograph, and the "photographer's eye" as well:

> It selects, rejects, organizes, discriminates, associates, classifies, analyzes, constructs. It does not so much mirror as take and make; and what it takes and makes it sees not bare, as items without attributes, but as things, as food, as people, as enemies, as stars, as weapons.

Thus, all photographs, even straightforward, direct, and realistic-looking ones, need to be interpreted. They are not innocent, free of insinuations and devoid of prejudices, nor are they simple mirror images. They are made, taken, and constructed by skillful artists and deserve to be read, explained, analyzed, and deconstructed.

DEFINITION OF INTERPRETATION

While describing, a critic names and characterizes all that he or she can see in the photograph. *Interpretation* occurs whenever attention and discussion move beyond offering information to matters of meaning. Hans-Georg Gadamer, the European philosopher known for his extensive work on the topic of interpretation, says that to interpret is "to give voice to signs that don't speak on their own."[7] To interpret is to account for all the described aspects of a photograph and to posit meaningful relationships between the aspects.

When one is acting as a critic, to interpret a photograph is to tell someone else, in speech or in writing, what one understands about a photograph, especially what one thinks a photograph is about. Interpreting is telling about the point, the meaning, the sense, the tone, or the mood of the photograph. When critics interpret a work of art, they seek to find out and tell others what they think is most important in an image, how its parts fit together, and how its form affects its subject. Critics base interpretations on what is shown in the work and on relevant information outside of the work, or what in Chapter 2 we called the *photograph's causal environment*. Interpretations go beyond description to build meaning. Interpretations are articulations of what the interpreter understands an image to be about. Interpreters do more than uncover or discover meaning; they offer new language about an image to generate new meaning.

Another way of understanding interpretation is to think of all photographs as metaphors in need of being deciphered. A *metaphor* is an implied comparison between unlike things. Qualities of one thing are implicitly transferred to another. Verbal metaphors have two levels of meaning: the literal and the implied. Visual metaphors also have levels of meaning: what is shown and what is implied. A photograph always shows us something as something. In the simple sense, a portrait of a man shows us the man as a picture—that is, as a flat piece of paper with clusters of tones from a light-sensitive emulsion. In another simple sense, a photograph always shows us a certain aspect of something. A portrait of Igor Stravinsky by Arnold Newman shows us Stravinsky *somehow, as* something. In Goodman's words, "*the* object before me is a man, a swarm of atoms, a complex of cells, a fiddler, a friend, a fool, and much more."[8] The photograph represents the thing or person as something or as some kind of person. Newman's portrait of Stravinsky shows the man sitting at a piano. In a more complex way, however, the portrait of Stravinsky shows him not only as a man sitting at a piano but also as a brilliant man, or a profound man, or a troubled man. The more complex "as" requires interpretation. To miss the metaphoric and to see only the literal is to misunderstand the expressive aspects of photographs.

Roland Barthes, the late French scholar, was a semiotician who investigated how culture signifies or expresses meaning, and he paid particular attention to how photographs signify. He identified two signifying practices: denotations and connotations.[9] A photographed still-life arrangement may *denote* (show) flowers in a vase on a wooden table; it may *connote* (suggest, imply) peace, tranquility, and the delightfulness of the simple. These connotations may be conveyed by the lighting, colors, and the absence of superfluous objects. A fashion photograph may denote a model wearing a coat and a hat but may connote flair, sophistication, and daring by the look and pose of the model and the setting. To look at the photographs and to see only flowers in a vase on a table, or a hat and a coat on a woman, and not to recognize what they express is to miss the point of the pictures.

The distinction between denotations and connotations is made clearer by an interpretation of a magazine advertisement that Barthes provides.[10] The advertisement is a photographic ad for Panzani spaghetti products that appears in a French magazine. The ad shows cellophane packages of uncooked spaghetti, a can of tomato sauce, a cellophane package of Parmesan cheese, and tomatoes, onions, peppers, and mushrooms emerging from an open string shopping bag. The color scheme is formed by yellows and greens against a red background. The Panzani label is on the can and cellophane packages. Barthes identifies three parts of the ad: the linguistic message, the denoted image, and the connoted image. The linguistic message is the word *Panzani,* which is both denotational and connotational. Barthes explains that the word denotes a brand name of the packaged products but that it connotes, just by the way it sounds, "Italianicity." The word would not have that connotation in Italy for Italian readers because they would not perceive that the word sounded Italian.

The photographic image itself denotes what it shows: a can, spaghetti packages, mushrooms, peppers, and so forth. But Barthes explains that the image connotes several other messages. The ad represents a return from the market, and it implies two values: freshness of the products and the goodness of home cooking. The variety of the objects connotes the idea of total culinary service as if Panzani provided everything needed for a carefully prepared dish. The vegetables imply that the concentrate in the can is equivalent to the vegetables surrounding it. The predominance of red, yellow, and green reinforces Italianicity. The composition, focus, lighting, and color transmit a further value: the aesthetic goodness of a still life.

Barthes's schema can be applied to all photographs, not only photographic advertisements. It is another way of emphasizing that photographs need to be interpreted. All photographs connote; and without some understanding that photographs connote or imply or suggest, viewers will not get beyond the obvious and will see photographs as reality rather than pictures of reality.

THE OBJECTS OF INTERPRETATIONS

Sometimes critics interpret single photographs, but they often interpret whole bodies of work by a photographer and even the photography of a country or a period in history. In this section we will look at a series of interpretive statements by several critics, each considering the work of a different photographer. These interpretive statements show a range from the particular to the general: from consideration of a single photograph to a set of photographs to a photographer's career and to a historical decade of photography.

John Szarkowski interprets 100 individual photographs, one at a time, and one page to each, in his book *Looking at Photographs*. In discussing a Josef Koudelka photograph (*Untitled*. No date. 7¼″ × 11½″) he explains that Koudelka is dedicated to photographing the Gypsies of eastern Europe, who are in danger of vanishing. Szarkowski relates that the photographs contain specific information about Gypsies' everyday life, but adds that "such anthropological data does not seem their real point." So Szarkowski is providing general descriptive information about the photographer—that he is committed to the subject of Gypsies—and general descriptive information about the photographs—that they give us much detailed anthropological data about the Gypsies' way of life. But then he states that even though this information is apparent on the surface, it is not what the photographs are *really* about. He adds: "They seem instead to aim at a visual distillation of a pattern of human values: a pattern that involves theater, large gesture, brave style, precious camaraderie, and bitter loneliness. The pattern and texture of his pictures form the silent equivalent of an epic drama."[11] Szarkowski then discusses the specific untitled photograph and tells how it is an epic drama about human values.

This statement by Sally Eauclaire offers interpretive insights into a set of photographs: "As a black American, he vowed to record this part of his heritage and to revive interest in this custom, which has been dying out since World War II."[12] She refers here to Daniel Williams's photographs of Emancipation Day celebrations. She explains that these events are held sporadically around the country, depending on the initiative of local people. The photographs themselves depict African Americans in family gatherings at picnics; and without some explanation beyond the photographs themselves, a viewer would not know that these pictures had anything to do with slavery, emancipation from it, or Emancipation Day celebrations.

Shelley Rice writes about the photographer Mary Ellen Mark (see Color Plate 4): "In other words, Mark's career—and photographic production—have been characterized by an almost dizzying diversity, a catch-as-catch-can quality that is as dependent on chance in the assignments offered to her as it is upon her own personal choices of subjects and themes."[13] Rice writes the statement after describing the diversity of subjects Mark has photographed for *Life, Look, Esquire, Paris-Match, Ms.*, and other publications and lists some of her subjects: celebrities, women in a psychiatric ward in Oregon, prostitutes in Bombay, battered wives, abused children, famine victims in Ethiopia, and neo-Nazis in the United States. Rice's statement about Mark is interpretive in her generalization about the whole of the photographer's life work, her typifying it as having "dizzying diversity." Rice also explains that Mark's work is the result of a combination of accepting assignments from others and choosing topics for herself.

About photography made over a period of more than ten years, Jonathan Green states: "In the seventies straight photography moved away from documentation of the outcast, the bizarre, and the freak and turned back to the most basic source of

American myth and symbol: the American land."[14] Green is writing about American photography and, particularly, a style, straight photography. He summarizes the straight photography of the 1960s as documentation of unusual people and then generalizes that in the 1970s photographers who were working in the straight mode began making landscapes. He also states that their choice of the land as subject matter was a return to the past. In the same sentence, Green then says that the American land is the most basic source of American myth and symbols. Thus in this one sentence he offers several general interpretive statements about large time periods, huge amounts of work, and grand ideas about the land. This sentence by Green is the first sentence of the eleventh chapter of his book *American Photography*.

In an introductory essay to a book of John Pfahl's color photographs utilizing picture windows, Edward Bryant writes: "Since the 1950s the picture window has been commonplace in the American visual vernacular. Its ubiquity has coincided with that of the wide-screen movie, the undivided windshield, the big painting, and that ultimate picture window, the television set."[15] This too is an interpretive statement, although it is not directly about the photographs of Pfahl. It is about the importance of the picture window in American society, and it helps us think about aspects of our cultural environment and prepares us to consider the pictures of picture windows by Pfahl. Just as Green writes about the land as a source of symbols for photographers, Bryant considers the picture window. Interpretive statements about photographs are not limited to photographs: As Ronald Dworkin states, they "may be of more general importance, helping us to an improved understanding of important parts of our cultural environment."[16]

INTERPRETIVE CLAIMS AND ARGUMENTS

These quotations of Szarkowski, Eauclaire, Rice, Green, and Bryant not only provide descriptive information about photographs and photographers but also provide interpretations of the photographs. Although they are declarative sentences, usually stated with unflinching authority, these statements should all be considered to be interpretive *claims*. Even though the authors do not express any doubts about their ideas and assert them as if they were self-evident and undeniable truths, they realize, and informed readers of criticism realize, that their interpretive statements are claims to truth and that if readers of criticism are to accept them as true or reasonable, they will want evidence for the claims before they accept the interpretations.

Each of these quoted sentences is from a larger piece of writing. The sentence by Szarkowski is part of a one-page essay, and the sentence from Green is from a whole book. In the complete pieces, the critics do provide reasons for their understandings of the photographs they are writing about.

Interpretations are more than the single or few sentence statements quoted earlier. Such statements are claims in need of arguments, or hypotheses in need of a convincing body of evidence. A fully developed interpretation is an argument that has premises leading logically and forcefully to a conclusion. But a fully developed interpretation is rarely written as a logical argument, with premises one, two, three, and four clearly stated and a conclusion clearly drawn. Instead, interpretations are often mixed with descriptions and sometimes with evaluations. Nonetheless, a reader can analyze a fully developed interpretation by identifying its premises and conclusion and then by seeing if and how the premises lead to and support the conclusion.

Interpretations are answers to questions people have about photographs. The main interpretive questions that critics ask of photographs are "What do these photographs mean? What are they about?" All interpretations share a fundamental principle—that photographs have meanings deeper than what appears on their surfaces. The surface meaning is obvious and evident about what is pictured, and the deeper meanings are implied by what is pictured and how it is pictured. If one looks at the surface of Cindy Sherman's self-portrait photographs (see Plate 4 and Color Plate 1), for example, which were discussed in Chapter 2, they seem to be about a woman in a library or a circus clown. Less obviously, however, they are pictures of the artist herself, in various guises, and they are self-portraits. Because of how the subject is photographed, the film stills can also be understood to refer to media representations and to how popular and fine art media represent women. And, in an interpretive statement by Eleanor Heartney, they are, less obviously still, about "the cultural construction of femininity."[17] Heartney and other critics who consider Sherman's work are not content to understand the film stills simply as pictures of women doing various things, self-portraits of Cindy Sherman, or self-portraits of an artist in artful disguises. They look beyond the surface for deeper meanings about femininity, the representation of femininity, and culture.

INTERPRETIVE PERSPECTIVES

Critics interpret photographs from a wide range of perspectives. Following are brief interpretations by several photography scholars, each written from a different vantage point to show the variety of strategies critics use to decipher images. The first three interpretations are by different writers on the same images, Harry Callahan's photographs of his wife, Eleanor, which are titled *Eleanor, Port Huron, 1954* (Plate 8). These examples show how critics can vary in their interpretations and how their various interpretations of the same images can alter our perceptions and understandings. Then interpretations of other photographers' works are used as examples of a variety of interpretive strategies.

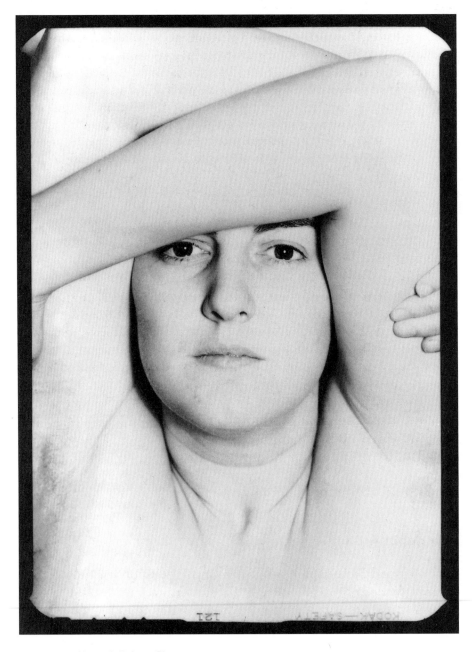

PLATE 8.   Harry Callahan, *Eleanor*, ca. 1947.

Collection of the Akron Art Museum. Purchased with funds donated by Eleanor W. Aggarval. Photo by Richard Haire.

Three Interpretations of *Eleanor*

A COMPARATIVE INTERPRETATION   John Szarkowski claims that most people who have produced lasting images in the history of photography have dealt with aspects of their everyday lives and that Callahan is one of them. For many decades he has photographed his wife, his child, his neighborhoods, and the landscapes to which he escapes. Szarkowski notes that Callahan is different from most photographers who work from their personal experiences. Whereas they try to make universal statements from their specifics, Callahan, according to Szarkowski, "draws us ever more insistently inward toward the center of [his] private sensibility. . . . Photography has been his method of focusing the meaning of that life. . . . Photography has been a way of living."[18]

AN ARCHETYPAL INTERPRETATION   In *American Photography,* Jonathan Green devotes several pages to Callahan and reproduces five of the *Eleanor* photographs.[19] In contradistinction to Szarkowski, Green sees them as elevating Eleanor the woman to an impersonal, universal, mythical, and archetypal status. About a photograph of Eleanor emerging from water, he writes: "We experience the *fons et origo* of all the possibilities of existence. Eleanor becomes the Heliopolitan goddess rising from the primordial ocean and the *Terra Mater* emerging from the sea: the embodiment and vehicle of all births and creations." Green continues:

> Over and over again, Callahan sees Eleanor in the context of creation: she has
> become for him the elemental condition of existence, she is essential woman-
> hood, a force rather than an embodiment, an energy rather than a substance.
> As such she appears cold and inaccessible, beyond the human passions of lust
> or grief. She is the word made flesh.

A FEMINIST INTERPRETATION   In a personally revealing critique, and one quite different from the two preceding interpretations, Diane Neumaier traces the development of her thinking regarding women, particularly photographers' wives, including Eleanor, as the subject matter of photographs. She recounts when as an undergraduate she discovered photography and excitedly changed her concentration from printmaking to photography. She became acquainted with the work of such prominent photographers as Alfred Stieglitz and Emmet Gowin and their photographs of their wives, Georgia O'Keeffe and Edith Gowin. Neumaier was thrilled with the romanticism of these three famous couples, and she hoped to be like them and do similar work. However, as years passed, and as her consciousness grew through the experiences of being simultaneously a wife, mother, and artist, her conflicts also increased:

> I simultaneously wanted to be Harry, Alfred, or Emmet, *and* I wanted to be
> their adored captive subjects. I wanted to be Eleanor, or Edith and have my
> man focus on me and our child, *and* I wanted to be Georgia, passive beauty
> and active artist. Together these couples embodied all my most romantic, con-
> tradictory, and impossible dreams.[20]

Neumaier unsuccessfully attempted to photograph her husband as these men had photographed their wives: "To possess one's wife is to honor and revere her. To possess one's husband is impossible or castrating." In years following her divorce, she attempted to immortalize her son in her photographs, as Gowin has his children. But these efforts also failed because she could no longer manipulate her son into the photographs and because her time for art was limited by her role as a mother. She had to reevaluate those early pictures of the photographers' wives, and for her, feminist conclusions strongly emerged; she could now see them as pictures of domination:

> These awe-inspiring, beautiful photographs of women are extremely oppressive. They fit the old traditions of woman as possession and woman as giver and sacrificer. . . . In this aesthetically veiled form of misogyny, the artist expects his wife to take off her clothing, then he photographs her naked (politely known as nude), and after showing everybody the resulting pictures he gets famous. . . . The subtle practice of capturing, exposing, and exhibiting one's wife is praised as sensitive.

Other Interpretive Strategies

PSYCHOANALYTIC INTERPRETATION   Laurie Simmons has made a series of photographs using dolls and figurines in different dollhouse settings. In writing about Simmons's work, Anne Hoy states that these female dolls are trapped in environments in which they are dwarfed by TV sets and out-of-scale grocery items. In contrast to the trapped dolls, Simmons later suggested freedom by photographing cowboy dolls outside, but their liberation was illusory because even the grass in the pictures outsized them. In the early 1980s, Simmons made a series of swimmers using figurines and live nude models underwater. About these, Hoy writes: "In a Freudian interpretation, they suggest the equivalence of drowning and sexual surrender and the sensations of weightlessness associated with those twin abandonments."[21]

Donald Kuspit applies psychoanalytic criticism to Sally Mann's series "Proud Flesh" (2004–2009), which shows many bodies with missing limbs. According to the critic, Mann focuses on "what psychoanalysts call part objects; there is no whole object, only fragments of a distinguishing object, and a peculiar kind of insubstantiality to all the flesh on display." Mann's "photograph process confers upon the photographs themselves a diseased, wasted look, as if the disease has also infected their surface making them to seem tragically sick unto death." Poignantly, the model for the images is her husband of forty years who is suffering from muscular dystrophy. *Hephaestus,* (see Plate 9), "suggests that the skin has been burned away by death, even as half the body remains irradiated by light, which lends it a certain ghostly presence." "Proud Flesh" are photographic interpretations that offer "no solace, but relentlessly focus on the trauma of decay we must all face, the death that slowly but surely wastes our bodies."[22]

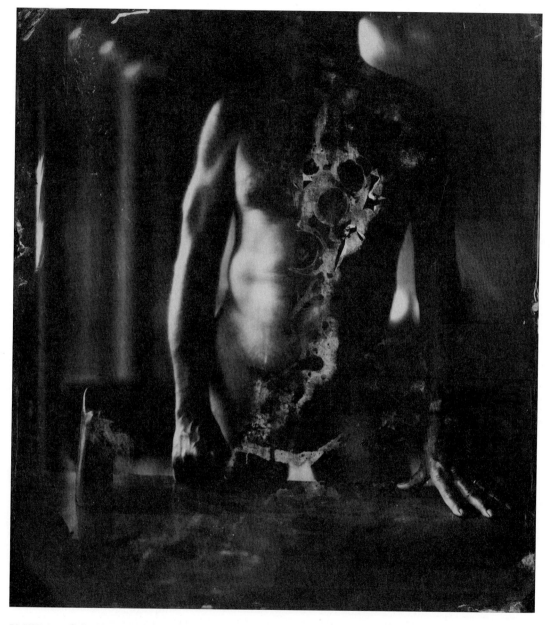

PLATE 9. Sally Mann, *Hephaestus,* 2008. Photograph, 15 × 13 ½ inches.

© Sally Mann. Courtesy of Edwynn Houk Gallery, New York City.

FORMALIST INTERPRETATION   Some interpreters base their interpretations of images solely or primarily on considerations of the image's formal properties. Richard Misrach has been photographing the desert for a number of years, first at night with flash in black and white and then in the day in color. Kathleen McCarthy Gauss offers this interpretation of one of the color photographs, *The Santa Fe,* 1982: "a unique configuration of space, light, and events." She continues:

> A highly formalized balance is established between the nubby ground and smooth, blue sky, both neatly cordoned off along the horizon by red and white boxcars. The most reductive, minimal composition is captured. The train rolls along just perceptibly below the horizon, bisecting the frame into two horizontal registers. Yet, this is another illusion, for the train is in fact standing still.[23]

Gauss's treatment of this image mixes her descriptive observations with interpretive insights. She is content to leave this image with these observations and insights about its compositional arrangement and not to conjecture further.

SEMIOTIC INTERPRETATION   Roland Barthes's interpretation of the Panzani advertisement detailed earlier is an example of an interpretation that seeks more to understand *how* an image means than *what* it means. Bill Nichols uses a similar interpretive strategy to understand a *Sports Illustrated* cover published during the first week of football season when Dan Devine began coaching the Notre Dame football team. The photographic cover shows a close-up of the quarterback ready to receive a hike and an inset of Devine gesturing from the sideline. Nichols points out that the eyeline of the two suggests that they are looking at each other and that their expressions suggest that the quarterback is wondering what to do and the coach is providing him an answer. Nichols interprets the contrast between the large size of the photograph of the quarterback and the smaller photograph of the coach as signifying the brawn of the player and the brain of the coach. He surmises:

> This unspoken bond invokes much of the lure football holds for the armchair quarterback—the formulation of strategy, the crossing of the boundary between brain/brawn—and its very invocation upon the magazine's cover carries with it a promise of revelation: within the issue's interior, mysteries of strategy and relationship will be unveiled.[24]

MARXIST INTERPRETATION   Linda Andre provides a sample of the kinds of questions a Marxist critic might ask about an exhibition of Avedon's celebrity photographs:

> We might look at the enormous popularity of Richard Avedon's photographs at the Metropolitan Museum of Art as attributable as much to the public's hunger for pictures of the rich, famous and stylish—a hunger usually sated not by museums but by the daily tabloids—as to his photographic virtuosity. To broaden the focus even more, we might ask what kind of society creates

such a need—obviously one where enormous class inequalities exist and where there is little hope of entering a different class—and what role Avedon's pictures might play in the maintenance of this system.[25]

Andre explains that one of her attempts as a critic is to place photographs in the context of social reality—to interpret them as manifestations of larger societal developments and social history, as well as photography and art history.

INTERPRETATION BASED ON STYLISTIC INFLUENCES   Critics often explain or offer explanatory information about a photographer's work by putting it into a historical and stylistic context. In an introduction to the work of Duane Michals, for example, Anne Hoy writes that Michals's images "pay homage to the spare, realistic styles and dreamlike subjects of the Surrealist painters René Magritte, Giorgio de Chirico, and Balthus."[26] Such contextual information helps us to see the work of one photographer in a broader framework, and it implicitly reinforces the notion that all art comes in part from other art or that all artists are influenced by other artists' work. Such comparisons demand that readers have certain knowledge: If they do not know the work of Magritte, de Chirico, and Balthus, for example, then Hoy's interpretive claim will not have much explanatory force for them. If they do possess such knowledge, however, then they can examine Michals's work in this broader context.

BIOGRAPHICAL INTERPRETATION   Critics also provide answers to the question "Why does the photographer make these kinds of images (rather than some other kind)?" One way of answering this question is to provide biographical information about the photographer. In his introduction to the work of Joel-Peter Witkin discussed in Chapter 2, Van Deren Coke provided a lot of biographical information about the photographer.[27] In writing about the images, Coke strongly implies a cause-and-effect relationship between Witkin's life experiences and the way his images look. For instance, after relating that Witkin's family had little extra money, Coke says: "This explains in part why we find in Witkin's photographs echoes of a sense of deprivation and insecurity." For some critics, however, such a jump from an artist's biography to a direct account of his or her images is too broad a leap. Regarding Coke's claim, for instance, we could first ask to be shown that there is a sense of deprivation and insecurity in the work, and then we could still be skeptical that the reason, even "in part," is because Witkin's family had little extra money. There could be another reason or many reasons or different reasons or no available reasons why there is, if indeed there is, a sense of deprivation and insecurity in Witkin's photographs.

INTENTIONALIST INTERPRETATION   It is a natural inclination to want to know what the maker intended in an image or a body of work. So when critics interview artists, they seek their intended meanings for their work, how they understand their own photographs. Well-known photographers are frequently invited to travel and talk about their work in public, and sometimes they explain their intentions in making their photographs. An artist's statements are good sources of information from the artist's point of view about his or her work, for example, Lauren Greenfield's statement about her intent in making the exhibition and book *Girl Culture*:

> In this work, I have been interested in documenting the pathological in the everyday. I am interested in the tyranny of the popular and thin girls over the ones who don't fit that mold. I am interested in the competition suffered by the popular girls, and their sense that popularity is not as satisfying as it appears. I am interested in the time-consuming grooming and beauty rituals that are an integral part of daily life. I am interested in the fact that to fall outside the ideal body type is to be a modern-day pariah. I am interested in how girls' feelings of frustration, anger, and sadness are expressed in physical and self-destructive ways: controlling their food intake, cutting their bodies, being sexually promiscuous. I am interested in the way that the female body has become a palimpsest on which many of our culture's conflicting messages about femininity are written and rewritten. Most of all, I am interested in the element of performance and exhibitionism that seems to define the contemporary experience of being a girl. These interests, my own memories, and a genuine love for girls, gossip, female bonding, and the idiosyncratic rituals of girl culture, have fueled this photographic journey over the last five years.[28]

Although the views of the makers about their own work can and should influence our understanding of their work, those views should not *determine* the meaning of the work or be used as *the* standard against which other interpretations are measured. I will discuss the problems of intentionalism as an interpretive method later in this chapter.

INTERPRETATION BASED ON TECHNIQUE   Critics also provide answers to the question "How does the photographer make these images?" In answering this question, the critic may provide much interesting information about how the photographer works—his or her choice of subject, use of medium, printing methods, and so forth. Although these accounts provide useful information, they are descriptive accounts about media and how photographers manipulate media rather than interpretive accounts of what the photographs mean or what they express by means of the surface and beyond the surface. Interpretations usually account for how the photographs are made and then consider the effects of the making on the meanings.

Combinations of Interpretive Approaches

When critics interpret photographs, they are likely to use a hybrid of approaches rather than just one approach. For his analyses of photographs, Bill Nichols, for example, claims to draw on Marxism, psychoanalysis, communication theory, semiotics, structuralism, and the psychology of perception. A feminist may or may not use a Marxist approach, and Marxist approaches are many, not just one. A critic may also choose among approaches depending on the kinds of photographs being considered. Finally, a critic may consider one photograph from several of these perspectives at a time, resulting in several competing interpretations. This approach raises issues about the correctness of interpretations.

"RIGHT" INTERPRETATIONS

"Surely there are many literary works of art of which it can be said that they are understood better by some readers than by others."[29] Monroe Beardsley is an aesthetician who made this comment about interpreting literature. And because some people understand artworks better than others do, concludes Beardsley, some interpretations are better than others. If someone understands a photograph better than I do, then it would be desirable for me to know that interpretation to increase my own understanding. If someone has a better interpretation than I do, then it follows that better (and worse) interpretations are possible. In essence, not all interpretations are equal; some are better than others, and some can be shown to be wrong. Unlike Beardsley, however, the aesthetician Joseph Margolis takes a softer position on the truth and falsity of interpretations—the position that interpretations are not so much true or false as they are plausible (or implausible), reasonable (or unreasonable).[30] This more flexible view of interpretation allows us to accept several competing interpretations as long as they are plausible. Instead of looking for *the* true interpretation, we should be willing to consider a variety of plausible interpretations from a range of perspectives: modernist, Marxist, feminist, formalist, and so forth.

Although I will not use the term *true* for a good interpretation, I will use such terms as *plausible, interesting, enlightening, insightful, meaningful, revealing, original;* or conversely, *unreasonable, unlikely, impossible, inappropriate, absurd, far-fetched,* or *strained.* Good interpretations are convincing and weak ones are not.

When people talk about art in a democratic society such as our own, they tend to unthinkingly hold that everyone's opinion is as good as everyone else's. Thus, in a discussion in which we are trying to interpret or evaluate an artwork and a point of view is offered that is contrary to our own, we might say, "That's just your opinion," implying that all opinions are equal and especially that our own is equal to any other. Opinions that are not backed with reasons, however, are not particularly useful or meaningful. Those that are arrived at after careful thought and that can be backed with evidence should carry weight. To dismiss a carefully thought-out opinion with a comment like "That's just your opinion!" is intellectually irresponsible. This is not to say that any reasoned opinion or conclusion must be accepted, but rather that a reasoned opinion or conclusion deserves a reasoned response.

Another widespread and false assumption in our culture about discussing art goes something like this: "It doesn't matter what you say about art, because it's all subjective anyway." This is extreme relativism about art that doesn't allow for truth and falsity, or plausibility and reasonability, and that makes it futile to argue about art and about competing understandings of art. Talk about art can be verifiable, if the viewer relates his or her statements to the artwork. Although each of us comes to artworks with our own knowledge, beliefs, values, and attitudes, we can talk and be understood in a way that helps make sense of photographs; in this sense, our interpretations can be grounded and defensible.

There are two criteria by which we can appraise interpretations: correspondence and coherence.[31] An interpretation ought to *correspond* to and account for all that appears in the picture and the relevant facts pertaining to the picture. If any items in the picture are not accounted for by the interpretation, then the interpretation is flawed. Similarly, if the interpretation is too removed from what is shown, then it is also flawed. The criterion of correspondence helps to keep interpretations focused on the object and to keep them from being too subjective. This criterion also "insists on the difference between explaining a work of art and changing it into a different one."[32] We want to deal with what is there and not make our own work of art by seeing things not there or by changing the work into something that we wish it were or which it might have been.

We also want to build an interpretation, or accept the interpretation, that shows the photograph to be the best work of art it can be. This means that given several interpretations, we will not choose the ones that render the photograph insignificant or trivial but rather the ones that give the most credit to the photograph—the ones that show it to be the most significant work it can be.

The criterion of correspondence also allays the fear of "reading too much into" a work of art or photograph. If the interpretation is grounded in the object, if it corresponds to the object, then it is probably not too far removed from and is not reading too much into the photograph.

According to the second criterion, *coherence,* the interpretation ought to make sense in and of itself, apart from the photograph. That is, it should not be internally inconsistent or contradictory. Interpretations are arguments, hypotheses backed by evidence, cases built for a certain understanding of a photograph. The interpreter draws the evidence from what is within the photograph and from his or her experience of the world. Either the interpretive argument is convincing because it accounts for all the facts of the picture in a reasonable way, or it is not convincing.

INTERPRETATIONS AND THE ARTIST'S INTENT

Minor White, a photographer and influential teacher of photography, once said that "photographers frequently photograph better than they know."[33] He was cautioning against placing too much emphasis on what photographers think they have photographed. White placed the responsibility of interpretation on the viewer rather than on the photographer, in response to the problem in criticism of "intentionalism," or what aestheticians refer to as "the intentional fallacy."[34] Intentionalism is a faulty critical method by which images (or literature) are interpreted and judged according to what the maker intended by them. According to those who subscribe to intentionalism, if the photographer, for instance, intended to communicate x, then that is what the image is about, and interpretations are measured against the intent of the photographer. In judging photographs, the critic attempts to determine what the photographer intended to communicate with the photograph and then on that basis judges whether the photographer has been successful or not. If the photographer has achieved his or her intent, then the image is good; if not, the image is unsuccessful.

There are several problems with intentionalism as a critical method. First it is difficult to find out what the intent of the photographer was. Some photographers are unavailable for comment about their images; others don't express their intents. Several photographers would rather not have to make images *and* criticize them. As Cindy Sherman (see Plate 4 and Color Plate 1) has said, "I've only been interested in making the work and leaving the analysis to the critics."[35]

Some photographers are unaware of their intents when they photograph. Jerry Uelsmann (see Plate 10), for example, works very intuitively and spontaneously: "I don't have an agenda when I begin. I'm trying to create something that's visually stimulating, exciting, that has never been done before but has some visual cohesiveness for me, has its own sort of life."[36] He tells of how he made an image of a young woman, standing nude, presenting a glowing apple, and the picture now seems to him to be obviously an "Eve image." But at the time he made the multiply exposed photograph, he was unaware of this connotation:

> Because I concentrate so intensely on detail while I'm working, it wasn't really until the next morning that I recognized the obvious iconographic implications of the image that are so blatantly there. It seems impossible, in retrospect, that I didn't plan to do an Eve photograph. But at the time I was working the idea didn't enter my conscious thought.

Many photographers allow room for their subconscious in their work and unintended meanings that it may add to the work. Sandy Skoglund, for example, says that "one of the most captivating aspects of the ways I work is the subterranean content and consciousness that kind of leaks out, that I don't intend when I'm making art."[37]

Most important, perhaps, the interpretive task should be on the viewer and not on the photographer. By relying on or waiting for the photographer to explain his or her intents, we are abnegating our responsibility of interpreting what we see. For all the reasons given earlier, intentionalism is a flawed and weak critical method.

Some critics advocate that viewers should ignore photographers' statements of intent as irrelevant, but a less extreme position seems more reasonable. When expressed intents are available, we can consider them as part of the photograph's

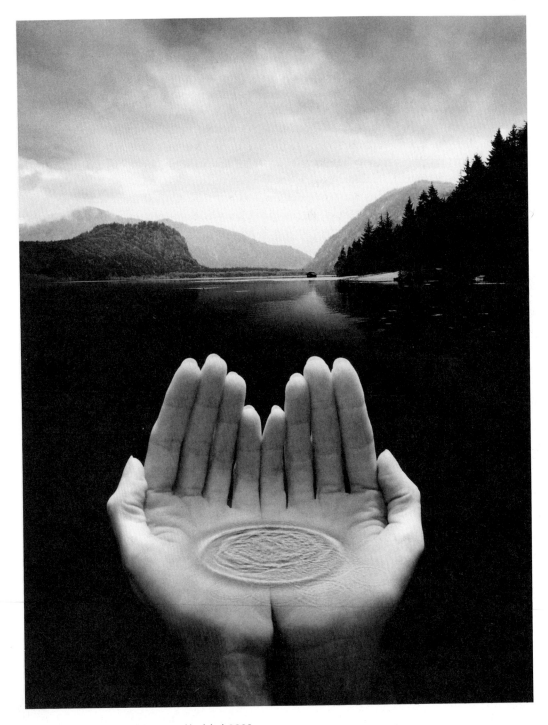

PLATE 10.   Jerry N. Uelsmann, *Untitled*, 2003.

causal environment and part of the evidence for interpretation. Some artists are very articulate about their work. Edward Weston has written two volumes of diaries, *The Daybooks,* which offer insights about him and his work. Nathan Lyons and Alan Trachtenberg have published valuable anthologies that include early photographers' statements about some of their photographs and photography in general.[38] In our highly mobile society, photographers frequently travel and speak about the intents of their work, which can increase our general understanding and appreciation of their photographs.

When a photographer does offer particular interpretations of specific images or general interpretations that apply to his or her work, that interpretation becomes one among many possible or actual interpretations. If the artist's interpretation is to be accepted as sound, it must adequately account for what is presented in the picture and conform to the standards of coherence and correspondence as must all interpretations. We should take an artist's interpretation as an argument and evaluate it on the same grounds as we do other interpretations that are offered. We should not consider an interpretation more privileged because it comes from the artist.

INTERPRETATIONS AND FEELINGS

Interpreting photographs, or responding to them in other ways, should not be solely an intellectual endeavor. As an art educator studying criticism has observed, "What *really* happens in art criticism relies heavily on that flash of insight based on gut feelings, life experiences, and perceptual information coming together just right."[39] Feelings provide important clues to learning about the content of an image. If we are aware that a picture evokes feelings in us, then we can identify them, acknowledge them, and try to decipher whether something in the picture triggers such feelings in us. Then we need to relate those feelings back to the image, perhaps through questions: What is it that I am feeling? Why am I feeling it? Is there a certain subject or form or a particular use of the media that I am reacting to? Being attuned to our feelings when viewing images is a way to get beyond the obvious, to begin to identify the connotations of images. As well as being a clue toward understanding and a possible starting point for interpretation, feeling is an appropriate result: After we perform careful critical analysis of an image or exhibition, our feelings about it may change profoundly.

INTERPRETATION, MEANING, AND PERSONAL SIGNIFICANCE

A distinction can be made between significance and meaning.[40] *Significance* is more personal than meaning. Significance refers to how a photograph affects us or what it means to us. *Meaning* is more objective than significance, referring to what the photograph is about in itself or what several people would infer or what can be made obvious to any informed viewer. A similar distinction between "meaning *in*" and "meaning *to*" helps the interpreter stay on track in presenting an interpretation of the photograph.[41] What a photograph means *to me* may not be what the photograph is about in itself. Personal significance and personal associations with photographs are valuable to each of us, but they may be too idiosyncratic, too personal, to be valuable to others who wish to understand more about the image itself. If our interpretations are too personal and too idiosyncratic, they become more about us and less about the image. Another way of saying this is that "if interpretation is not referenced to visual properties (in the image), discourse leaves the realm of criticism and becomes conjecture, therapy, reminiscence, or some other manner of purely subjective functioning."[42]

THE COMMUNITY OF INTERPRETERS

Ultimately, viable interpretations are those held by a community of informed interpreters that includes critics, artists, historians, dealers, collectors, and viewers. Interpretations, in the end, are a collective endeavor arrived at by a variety of people observing, talking and writing about, and revising their understandings of complex and dynamic images made by sophisticated image makers. Julia Kristeva pleads for an "ethics of modesty" for all interpreters—that is, that no one considers his or her perception as the only possible one.[43] Michael Parsons, an art educator, has written insightfully about the community of art interpreters:

> As we look at a painting, we presuppose the company of others who are also
> looking at it. We are imaginatively one of a group who discuss the painting
> because they see the same details, and can help each other to understand
> them. The painting exists not between the two individual poles of the artist
> and the viewer but in the midst of an indefinite group of persons who are con-
> tinually reconstructing it—a community of viewers.[44]

The community is corrective: It won't accept any interpretation unless the interpretation is sensible and contributes to knowledge; on the other hand, the community of interpreters disallows dogmatic and inflexible understandings because it knows that art objects are ultimately rich objects that are less than determinable and that our understandings of them will continue to shift, usually subtly but sometimes dramatically. By following the principles detailed in this chapter we can join in that dialogue, contribute to it, and benefit from it.

Types of Photographs

SINCE THE EARLY YEARS OF PHOTOGRAPHY, PEOPLE HAVE BEEN PLACING PHOTOGRAPHS IN CATEGORIES. In 1839, the year the medium was invented, photography was divided into its two oldest and most enduring categories when it was proclaimed to be both a science and an art.[1]

Another time-honored division from the early years of photography, and still in use but with different labels, divides photographs made as art into two groups, pictorialist and purist. More current terms for these divisions are "manipulated" and "straight." The division was antagonistic; at issue was the means of making photographs. In 1861 C. Jabez Hughes, a pictorialist, declared: "If a picture cannot be produced by one negative, let him have two or ten; but . . . the picture when finished must stand or fall entirely by the effects produced and not the means employed."[2] The straight aesthetic, however, would mandate that photographers use techniques considered "photographic" rather than hand-manipulated and "painterly." In 1904 critic Sadakichi Hartmann promoted straight photography: "In short, compose the picture which you intend to take so well that the negative will be absolutely perfect and in need of no or but slight manipulation."[3] About twenty years later Edward Weston reiterated the straight position, declaring "the approach to photography is through realism."[4]

Photography historian Beaumont Newhall, in his book *The History of Photography*, divides photographs into four stylistic trends: straight, formalistic, documentary, and equivalent.[5] He identifies Alfred Stieglitz, Paul Strand, Edward Weston, and Ansel Adams as paradigm examples of those employing a *straight approach* "in which the ability of the camera to record exact images with rich texture and great detail is used to interpret nature and man, never losing contact with reality." Man Ray and Lazlo Moholy-Nagy are identified with the *formalistic style,* which Newhall typifies as a means of isolating and organizing form for its own sake without the use of cameras and without a concern for the photograph. The subject matter is paramount in *documentary,* which is essentially a desire "to record without intrusion, to inform honestly, accurately, and above all, convincingly." The term *equivalent,* borrowed from Stieglitz, designates photographic metaphors, "charged with emotional significance and inner meaning," but which are "first of all, photographs." Newhall is not neutral about these categories and promotes the straight aesthetic and approaches that are considered uniquely photographic. He cites photographs made by Walker Evans and other photographers employed by the Farm Security Administration as documentary images. Stieglitz referred to his own photographs of clouds as *equivalents,* and Newhall mentions the photographic landscapes Minor White made as other examples of equivalents.

CATEGORIES OF PHOTOGRAPHS

In two of the photography exhibitions he has organized, John Szarkowski proposes categories through which we may view photographs. In the exhibition and subsequent book published in 1966 called *The Photographer's Eye,* he embraces photographs from both the art and science categories and identifies five characteristics that he considers unique to photography:

> The thing itself—photography deals with the actual.
> The detail—photography is tied to the facts of things.
> The frame—the photograph is selected, not conceived.
> Time—photographs are time exposures and describe discrete parcels of time.
> Vantage point—photographs provide us new views of the world.[6]

In 1978, with a traveling exhibition and in a book, Szarkowski proposed a breakdown for looking at photographs made since 1960: "mirrors and windows." Although he presents mirrors and windows as the two poles of a continuum between which photographs can be placed, he divides the photographs in the book and the exhibition into two distinct groups rather than placing them along a continuum. He aligns mirrors with the romantic tradition and windows with the realist tradition in literature and art:

> The romantic view is that the meanings of the world are dependent on our own understandings. The field mouse, the skylark, the sky itself do not earn their meanings out of their own evolutionary history, but are meaningful in

terms of the anthropocentric metaphors we assign to them. It is the realist view that the world exists independent of human attention, that it contains discoverable patterns of intrinsic meaning, and that by discerning these patterns, and forming models or symbols of them with the materials of his art, the artist is joined to a larger intelligence.[7]

Mirrors tell us more about the artist, and windows more about the world. Mirrors are romantically self-expressive, exhibit concern for formal elegance rather than description, are generally made from a close vantage point for simplicity by abstraction, and favor subject matter such as virgin landscapes, pure geometry, the unidentifiable nude, and social abstractions such as "the young." Windows are realistic explorations more concerned with description than suggestion that attempt to explain more and dramatize less and which usually deal with subject matter that is specific to a particular time and space, and they can usually be dated by evidence within the picture.

In the 1970s, Time-Life publications came out with a widely distributed series of books, the Life Library of Photography. One book of the series, *The Great Themes*, uses the following categories to cover photography: the human condition, still life, portraits, the nude, nature, war.

There are also subdivisions of categories. Sally Eauclaire, as the curator of a traveling exhibition of color photographs, wrote an accompanying catalogue, *The New Color Photography of the 1970s*. She divided the large category of recent color work into seven subsets: self-reflections, formalism, the vivid vernacular, documentation, moral vision, enchantments, and fabricated fictions. Estelle Jussim and Elizabeth Lindquist-Cock, in 1985, looked specifically at another category of photographs, landscapes, in *Landscape as Photograph* and subdivided that category into landscape as God, fact, symbol, pure form, popular culture, concept, politics, and propaganda. In *Fabrications: Staged, Altered, and Appropriated Photographs*, Anne Hoy divided recent photography into five categories: narrative tableaux, portraits and self-portraits, still-life constructions, appropriated images and words, and manipulated prints and photo-collages.

Categories are designed for different purposes, and they use various means to distinguish photographs. The Time-Life great themes are distinguished by subject matter and are easy to use. The pictorialist and purist, or straight and manipulated, categories attend to photographic procedure and resulting photographic form. They tend, however, to wrongly suggest that straight photographs are not manipulated. Newhall's categories are dated, and he no longer uses them. Szarkowski's photographer's eye categories and mirrors and windows also start with form and then ask us to consider how form affects meaning. They consider photography to be a unique medium. Hoy's and Eauclaire's divisions help us make sense of bodies of new work in specific, contemporary times, and Jussim and Lindquist-Cock's ask us to think about photographs with one subject matter, the landscape, throughout time.

NEW CATEGORIES

This chapter presents a new category system that incorporates the best of the categories just mentioned. It covers all photographs, art and nonart, family snapshots and museum prints. It is based not on subject matter or form but rather on how photographs are made to function and how they are used to function. This system is designed to help viewers think about photographs and especially to interpret them. It has six categories: descriptive, explanatory, interpretive, ethically evaluative, aesthetically evaluative, and theoretical. The categories have distinguishing characteristics, but photographs overlap them. It is the viewer's task to figure out in which categories a photograph fits and in which one or more it fits best. The categories are explained in the sections that follow, and examples of photographs are given for each.

These six categories are for sorting photographs, not photographers. Photographers tend to make certain kinds of images with some consistency, but they also may depart from their usual work. Most of Edward Weston's photographs fit within the aesthetically evaluative category, but his photographs that condemn destruction of the environment belong in the ethically evaluative category. Many of Barbara Kruger's images are about social issues and are ethically evaluative, but some are more specifically about how we as a society use images; these would overlap into the theoretical category.

Photographs may fit well in more than one category, and more than one category may apply to any single photograph. For example, all photographs, no matter how abstract, give relatively accurate descriptive information about the people, places, and objects they show. Thus, all photographs could fit the descriptive category. Most photographs also interpret what they present photographically because they are made by people with points of view, with understandings of the world, with passions. Thus, all photographs could be placed in the interpretive category. All art and all photographs are about other art in the sense that past art influences present art, and present art can always be read in the light of influences upon it. Thus, all photographs could fit in the theoretical category. Most of these placements, however, would be in a weak sense. To place a photograph into a category and show that it fits in a strong sense, we have to figure out what it does most, what it does best, or how it is most clearly being used.

Some photographs and photographic projects do fit accurately in more than one category and belong in more than one category in a strong sense. An example is the water tower project of Bernd and Hilla Becher. For years they have systematically photographed water towers in Germany and America and in 1988 completed a book of 223 of them, *Water Towers*. Of these photographs, Andy Grundberg writes that they are presented "with such detail and tonal fidelity that they tempt us to see them as uninflected transcriptions," but he goes on to explain that the photographs "are equally allied with the practices of Conceptual and Post-modernist art, since they erect typologies of form that challenge the traditional meanings of art, architecture, and photography."[8] These photographs, in Grundberg's understanding, would fit best in both the descriptive and the theoretical categories: They meticulously describe a class of structures—water towers—but in their style or, more accurately, their conscious denial of style, they also comment on art and photography. To see them only as descriptive photographs of water towers—not also as art about art—would be to misunderstand them.

Because the categories overlap, we can use them to see how any given photograph is descriptive, if and how it explains in any scientific sense, how it is inflected by the photographer's worldview, if it makes a value judgment of an ethical or aesthetic type, and how it may be commenting on or influenced by other photographs and artworks.

Often photographs made to be a certain type of photograph are later used as another type. NASA's space exploration photographs were certainly made as descriptive and explanatory photographs, but some of them were later used as ads for Mobil Oil and Tang orange drink. Advertisers moved them from a descriptive category to an ethically evaluative one, from fact to advertisement. The Farm Security Administration photographs, in their day, were generally accepted as "documentary" but are now understood to be "propaganda"; yesterday they would have been placed in the explanatory category, today in the ethically evaluative category. Many photographs not made as art are often shown as art: Photomicrographs, space exploration photographs, and studies of motion once made for science are published in coffee table books and hung on museum walls. Implications of category displacements such as these will be discussed in the next chapter, which considers how the context in which a photograph is seen affects its interpretation.

The most important aspect of these categories is that they are interpretive. That is, we must interpret a photograph before we can reasonably categorize it. As we saw in the previous chapter, to interpret is to figure out what an image is about and to build an argument based on evidence for the understanding we have of an image. We do not have to do much interpretation to sort photographs into piles according to whether they are landscapes, nudes, still lifes, or portraits. But we do have to put a lot of interpretive thought into determining whether a portrait by Diane Arbus is like a portrait by Joel-Peter Witkin or one by Richard Avedon and whether any one of these is like a portrait on a driver's license or one made at a Sears department store.

To place a photograph in one or more of these categories is to interpret it. Interpretations, as discussed in the previous chapter, are always open to counterargument. *Suburbia,* by Bill Owens, the groundbreaking book of 1970s suburbanites in California, would be placed in the explanatory category because it uses straightforward photographs of people who are aware of being photographed and who are cooperating with the photographer. It uses the people's own words for its captions. Owens claims that it is a documentary project, and it seems a project that attempts, in scientific fashion, to pictorially survey a suburban community. In *American Photography,* however, Jonathan Green writes: "Although Owens's work purports to be neutral and objective, his final pronouncement is much harsher. . . . His conservative anecdotal and reportorial style documents a visual environment unrelieved in its superficiality. For Owens, suburbia is beyond redemption."[9] Presumably, if Green were to use these categories, he would place *Suburbia* into the ethically evaluative group because he sees it as a condemnation of that which it portrays. If we were using these categories to discuss *Suburbia,* we would find ourselves in disagreement; and a friendly argument might ensue, but a very beneficial one, because deciding whether *Suburbia* is objective and neutral about what it presents or whether it condemns is essential to accurately understanding the book.

Photographs have been placed in the following categories without argument and without presentation of much evidence for their placement, mostly even without reproduction of the images, and you may think they have been placed incorrectly or inaccurately. You are invited to disagree and to provide evidence for more accurate placements. And although many photographers are mentioned in this chapter, certainly not all could be. The ones mentioned are thought to provide the clearest examples for explaining the categories and how they can be used. Those knowing the history of photography, including the immediate past, will recognize the photographers mentioned in the categories; those unfamiliar with the photographers may use the many names of artists and projects as a basis for browsing the library.

That is the point of creating these categories and for using them. Placing photographs in these categories demands interpretive thought and encourages interpretive agreement and disagreement. These categories have been designed to encourage and facilitate interpretive discussion; they are not meant to end discussion through pigeonholing, or automatic sorting. If they are used in this way, they are rendered useless.

DESCRIPTIVE PHOTOGRAPHS

All photographs describe in the sense that they offer descriptive, visual information, with more or less detail and clarity, about the surfaces of people and objects. Some photographs, however, are not meant to be more than descriptions, such as identification photographs, medical X-rays, photomicrographs, NASA space exploration photographs, surveillance photographs, and reproductions of artworks. Their photographers are attempting to accurately record subject matter, and in many cases these photographs are painstakingly produced to be accurately descriptive and to be interpretively and evaluatively neutral. An ID photograph attempts neither to express the sitter's personality nor to flatter the sitter's appearance but rather to accurately describe the sitter so that someone can match the photograph to the person.

In an elaborate descriptive undertaking in 1982, the Eastman Kodak Company, in collaboration with Musées de France Research Laboratory, meticulously reconstituted the Bull Room of the cave at Lascaux, France, for exhibition at the Grand Palais des Champs Élysées in Paris. The celebrated 17,000-year-old bison paintings on the walls of the cave at Lascaux had been closed to public viewing in 1963 to save them from environmental deterioration. Set designers used details from surveyors' photographs made with a pair of stereoscopic cameras to build contours of the cave walls. Twenty-five photographs of the bison paintings were taken with a photogrammetric camera and flash and were printed in a 1:1 ratio on Ektacolor paper. The prints were assembled as a flat mosaic under the direction of a physicist who ensured that they were fit together in such a way that distortions would be avoided when the photo mosaic was adhered to the contours of the overhanging, concave sides of the reconstructed cave walls. The print mosaic was placed on decalomania paper, separated from its Ektacolor base, and adhered to the artificial rock face and its myriad indentations. The cave paintings were accurately reproduced.

Descriptive photographs are very valuable to medical researchers. In early cancer research, pathologist Daniel Gould made an electron photomicrograph showing virus particles in a portion of cancer tissue (magnified 52,000 times) occurring naturally in a woolly monkey, and a virus particle budding from a cell membrane (magnified 201,000 times). Further studies of this virus provided the first views of certain basic molecular mechanisms in cancer. NASA photographs have provided us with astonishing photographs that describe phenomena that we could otherwise not see.

Manabu Yamanaka's *Gyahtei #17* (Plate 12) is one of a series of life-size photographs of old Japanese women in the nude. Yamanaka calls his descriptive project "Gyahtei," a Buddhist term that means "great age." Although descriptive in intent, Yamanaka's nudes are also influenced by his interpretation of Buddhist beliefs, showing "The last physical body of a human who is just vanishing away."[10] That the pictures are clinically descriptive does not preclude personal

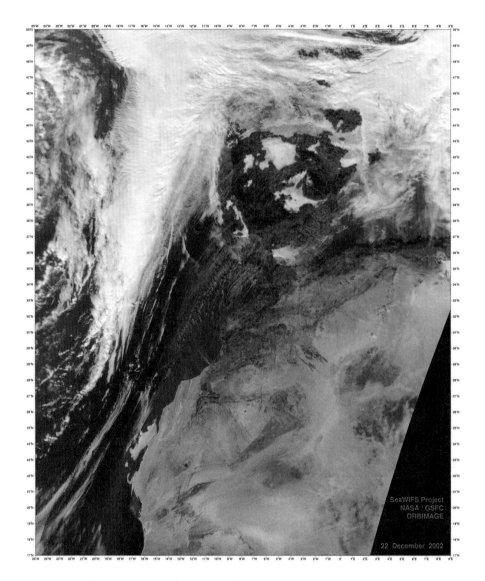

PLATE 11.   Dust storm over Morocco, Spain.
NASA/Goddard Space Flight Center, and ORBIM-AGE.

and social interpretations. About the "Gyahtei" series, Michael Amy wrote in *Art in America*:

> The tinges of desire which traditionally arise in us as we are confronted by a nude are replaced here by waves of empathy, both for these fragile subjects and, ultimately, for ourselves. The photographs give us the traditional genres

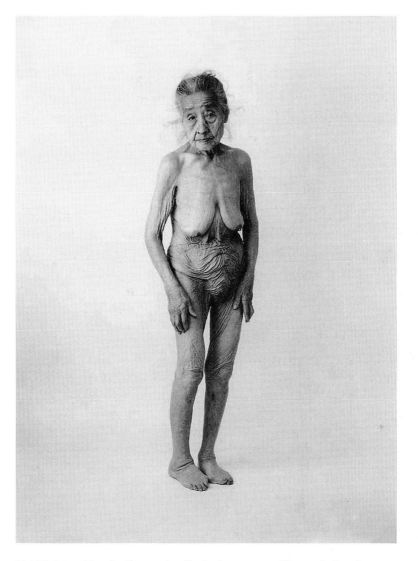

PLATE 12. Manabu Yamanaka, *Gyahtei #17,* 1995. Silver gelatin print,
68 × 31 inches.
Courtesy of the artist and Stux Gallery, New York City.

of the nude and the portrait repackaged as memento mori—reminders of
death. Most perplexing, perhaps, is how alien these bodies seem to us, who
are constantly exposed to the glorification of youth.[11]

An eleven-year-old shows the wonder that can be incited by descriptive NASA
space exploration photographs and the vast universe they reveal (Plate 13). After

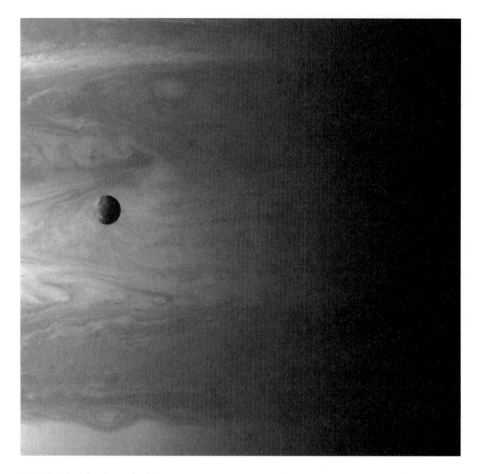

PLATE 13.   Io above Jupiter.
NASA/JPL/CICLOPS.

looking at such photographs, Sara Weschler answered the question, "Why is the Human on Earth?" with this response:

> I believe that there is, despite the fact that we humans have done so much damage to the world, a reason for our existence on this planet. I think we are here because the universe, with all its wonder and balance and logic, needs to be marveled at, and we are the only species (to our knowledge) that has the ability to do so. We are the one species that does not simply except what is around us, but also asks why it is around us, and how it works. We are here because without us here to study it, the amazing complexity of the world would be wasted and finally, we are here because the universe needs an entity to ask why it is here.[12]

EXPLANATORY PHOTOGRAPHS

The difference between "photographic descriptions" and "photographic explanations" is small, but there is enough difference between an ID photograph on a driver's license and Eadweard Muybridge's photographs of how animals and people move to merit separate categories. Photographs made by Muybridge in 1880 typify what I call *explanatory photographs*.

While employed as a photographic surveyor of the Pacific coast in the 1870s, Muybridge, an Englishman, met Leland Stanford, a railroad magnate, lover of horses, and founder of Stanford University. Stanford was engaged in an argument with a man named Frederick MacCrellish over whether a trotting horse ever had all four of its hooves off the ground at the same time. Stanford believed it did, MacCrellish did not, and they wagered $25,000. Stanford hired Muybridge to solve the issue and supplied him with whatever research funds he needed. Muybridge laid a track made of rubber to eliminate dust, hung a white cloth with numbered vertical lines as a backdrop to the track, and pointed twelve cameras at it. He designed the cameras so that they would be tripped in sequence when a horse broke a thread stretched across the track as it moved down the track. Muybridge's photographs showed all the different gaits of the horse, which further showed that in the midst of its walk, trot, and gallop, all four of its hooves were off the ground at the same time. Stanford won his bet, and to the chagrin of many artists, previously painted and sculpted representations of horses, from ancient times to contemporary, were shown to be inaccurate. Muybridge offered a visual explanation of how horses move. A question had been asked of him and answered by him through his invention of equipment and procedures that provided an explanation in photographs. He went on to refine his techniques and eventually, with the support of the University of Pennsylvania, made over 100,000 photographs of moving animals, including ostriches and baboons, and men, women, and children in a variety of movements and actions.

Physicist Harold Edgerton has photographically examined the characteristics of bullets in flight and other fast-moving objects with the stroboscopic equipment and technologies he invented for his photographic studies. By photographically stopping the action of bullets moving 15,000 miles per hour with strobe exposures of a millionth of a second, he has discovered that as a bullet strikes a hard object, the bullet liquifies for an instant, losing its shape as it compresses upon itself, and then solidifies again in shattered fragments.

During a twenty-five-year period, Edward Curtis produced a twenty-volume work with more than 2,000 images and anthropological notes about Native American culture as he witnessed it in the early part of the twentieth century.[13] In his photography career, which spanned eighty years, James Van Der Zee documented the Harlem Renaissance in the 1920s and 1930s and made thousands of photographs depicting African American culture in New York.[14] The work of these two men provides clear early anthropological and sociological examples of explanatory photographs.

Lauren Greenfield has three projects that clearly exemplify the explanatory category. Greenfield's *Fastforward* is a book of color photographs of wealthy teenagers growing up in very wealthy communities of West Los Angeles, contrasting them with counterparts in poor black and Hispanic neighborhoods in the central city. Greenfield's *Girl Culture* documents American girls and women in photographs of their social lives and private rituals, and includes quotations by the subjects.

Greenfield's film and exhibition of photographs, both called *Thin* (Plate 14), examines lives of young women with eating disorders. She spent six months working with the patients. A reviewer for TV Ontario wrote: "Unflinching and incisive, *Thin* is an emotional journey through the world of eating disorders that provides a greater understanding of their complexity, encompassing not just issues of food, body image or self-esteem, but also a mix of personal, familial, cultural and mental health concerns."[15]

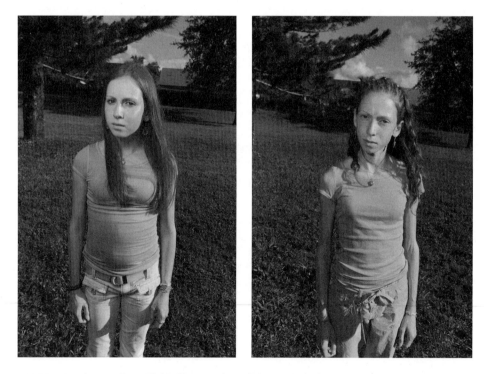

PLATE 14.   Lauren Greenfield, Aiva, 16, from Atlanta, Georgia at the Renfrew Center for the treatment of eating disorders. She entered treatment at 77 pounds, 69% of her normal body weight.

Lauren Greenfield/INSTITUTE.

Color Plate 3 is a clear example of work that fits comfortably into the explanatory category.

> While living in Wales in 2001 KayLynn Deveney noticed her older neighbor, Albert Hastings, outside his apartment watering the garden, going to the grocery store, and sometimes just watching the activity on the street. Deveney eventually began photographing Hastings's daily routines, and then she asked him to caption the images in a small notebook. The perspectives of photographer and subject intertwine: Hastings's commentary adds depth to the narrative suggested by Deveney's images, and in some cases provides an idiosyncratic interpretation of the depicted moment. Like the series more broadly, this diptych evokes both the patterns that make up Hastings's days and the small surprises that punctuate them. In the first image Hastings is ironing laundry just behind his hanging pajamas, while the second image reveals his clever use of a rubber band to prop up an ailing daffodil in a teacup.[16]

Cheng YuYang made a press photograph of the Xiayuan Temple in Sichuan Province about one month after an earthquake of a 7.9 magnitude hit Sichuan Province, a mountainous region in Western China, killing about 70,000 people and leaving more than 18,000 missing. It is a clear example of a descriptive or explanatory photograph. The photographer, however, named the photograph *Numen* (Plate 15), a Latin term referring to the power of a deity or a spirit that is present in places and objects. By naming it *Numen,* the photograph reinforces the central figure of the surviving Buddha and takes on an expressive quality of enduring calm and happiness even amidst a devastating earthquake. Explanatory photographs can have mystical connotations without being fictional.

Szarkowski's observation about windows applies to photographs in the explanatory category: Most explanatory photographs deal with subject matter that is specific to a particular time and place and that can be dated by visual evidence within the photograph.[17] Formally, these photographs usually use an angle of view that places the subject in a social context; they are usually printed so that details are not lost in tones that are too dark; and they favor a contrast range that can be duplicated clearly in the inks of offset printing.

Most press photographs can be placed in the explanatory category, but not all, because some go beyond explaining and also evaluate, condemning or praising aspects of society, and thus would fit better in the ethically evaluative category.[18] Press photographs that attempt neutral, objective reportings about persons, places, and events fit in the explanatory category. Explanatory photographs are often made to be reproduced in books, magazines, and newspapers. Susan Meiselas is one of the leading photojournalists of recent times. She has published several books including *Carnival Strippers, Nicaragua* and *Kurdistan,* both war reportage, and *Encounters with the Dani,* tribal people discovered in Indonesia in 1938.

Mary Ellen Mark is another acclaimed photojournalist whose work falls within this explanatory category. Mark has photographed for a variety of magazines and

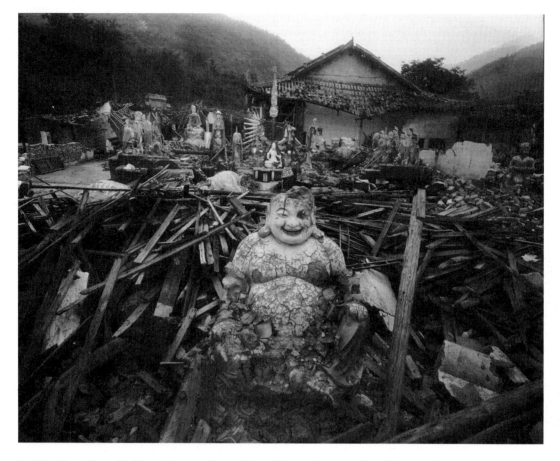

PLATE 15.   Cheng Yu Yang, *Numen, Hunan No. 1, Xiayuan Temple, City of Shifang, Sichuan Province,* June 2008.

© Cheng Yu Yang. Courtesy of M.R. Gallery, Beijing, China.

the *New York Times.* She has also produced books including *Ward 81,* about women in the psychiatric ward of Oregon State Hospital, where she lived for thirty-six days, and *Falkland Road,* about prostitutes in Bombay, with whom she stayed for three months. Mark also makes celebrity photographs, such as Color Plate 4. Most celebrity photographs would fit in this category including paparazzi's stolen images of the famous. According to critic Shelley Rice, Mark's work is rooted in "the particular, in the day-to-day struggles, rituals and relationships that make up a life, however heroic or tragic."

About Nan Goldin's *The Other Side,* 1993, critic Elizabeth Hess writes that it is "a visual exposition of drag culture" that Nan has explored since the early 1970s and adds that "there are few artists able to speak from and for a subculture."

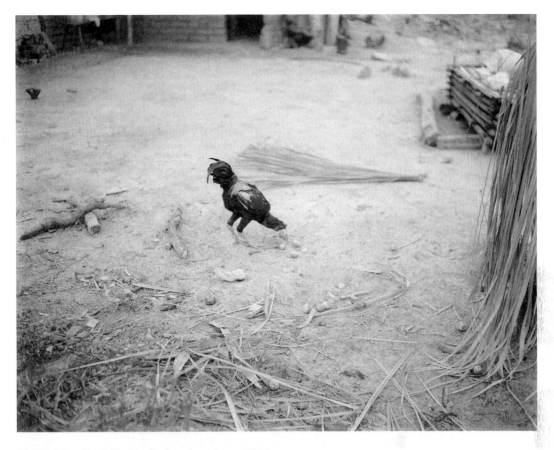

PLATE 16.   Fazal Sheikh, *To Cure Impotence,* 2001.
© Fazal Sheikh.

Hess credits Goldin with the ability to do this: "Goldin spent 20 obsessed years with transvestites, shooting queens in dressing rooms, hotel rooms, bathrooms, and other private places. She traveled to Berlin, Manila, and Bangkok, moving freely with the lives of her subjects in each location."[19] *The Devil's Playground,* published in 2004, is a collection of thirty-five years of work that begins in the 1970s. It includes images from the "Ballad of Sexual Dependency" in the 1980s; selected images from *The Other Side;* narrative sequences such as "57 Days," made in 2000; "Landscapes"; "Self-Portraits"; "Maternity, Heartbeat" made in 2001; and "My French Family" made from 1999–2001. Goldin's work (see Color Plate 5) fits within the explanatory category, and while it is candid, it is also affirmative of the people it shows.

Fazal Sheikh is a photographer and writer who documents refugee communities in ways that attempt to reveal the cultural and historical ties in some of the world's most remote places. Before making his photographs, he spends weeks living with the people whom he photographs and quotes. He made *To Cure Impotence* (Plate 16) in a remote, vast savanna-like region of Brazil where people farm poor land illegally. About the people, Sheikh writes:

> My main concern as a photographer is community . . . The ninety families in this community do not have title to the land they farm . . . they shared their feelings with me about place, rituals, and connections to the land, which they view with a kind of enchantment. . . . Through their voices, their faces, and their hands, they teach us about the landscape and how they survive. Theirs is a story of land lost, exile, and sanctuary.[20]

Katy Grannan's gallery interprets her work in the following way: "Grannan photographs subjects she calls 'new pioneers,' northern Californians who struggle to define themselves under the scrutiny of relentless sunlight. Grannan followed several individuals over the course of three years. The resulting series, 'The Westerns'

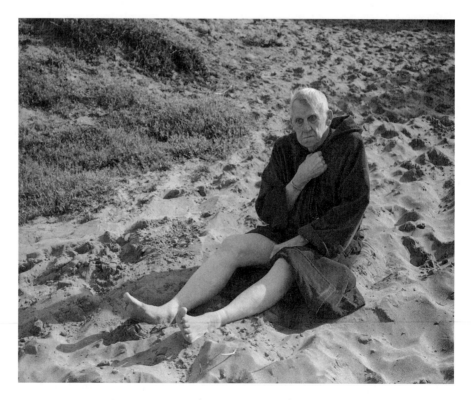

PLATE 17.   Katy Grannan, *Edward (with Prayer Beads), Baker Beach,* 2006. Color photograph.

© Katy Grannan. Courtesy of Fraenkel Gallery, San Francisco and Greenberg Van Doren Gallery, New York.

[Plate 17], explores the uneasy relationship between fixed photographic portraiture and her subjects' mercurial identities. The photographs are replete with ambiguity and contradiction: they are evidence of an invented unknowable self, confronting inescapable photographic description."[21] Given the images and the gallery's interpretation, no doubt informed by the artist, her series "The Westerns" would fit within the explanatory category.

In *Aperture* magazine, Philip Lopate writes about Sally Gall's "Crawl" series (see Color Plate 6): "Seen from a distance, hanging on the wall of a gallery, these enlarged photographs of nature are fetching, verdant, very (why not say it?) *pretty*. But closer inspection reveals something curious and perhaps unsettling: each picture has a bug in it. Or two. You don't always see the animal right away, because of course nature evolved in such a way as to make creatures merge with plant life." Gall prefers to make her prints large to bring us closer to the bug's point of view. Gall considers herself a realist and more: "I like photographing things that really exist, but making them look odder, slightly abstract, or surreal. . . . I sense nature is not a big part of most people's lives anymore. I want to show how nature can be nourishing, nurturing, not just for 'green' reasons but for aesthetic ones." Lopate concludes: "Gall has captured the profiles and postures of daddy longlegs, katydids, and caterpillars in the act of being themselves, and in doing so, has extended her already impressive photographic range in a manner that is surprising, fresh, imaginative, colorful, organic, and witty." Although these photographs are explanatorily accurate, they are more—pretty and witty—expanding notions of what explanatory photographs can be.[22]

To be accurately placed in this category, a photograph should provide visual explanations that are in principle verifiable on scientific grounds. Edgerton's photographs should provide valid data for other physicists, Goldin's photograph of her subjects that explore people living an alternative lifestyle ought to provide valid information for social scientists, and Gall's photograph of insects, although beautiful, ought to be of benefit to natural scientists. Whereas the claims to truth that explanatory photographs make should be verifiable (or refutable) with further evidence of a scientific type, photographs in the next category, interpretive photographs, cannot be verified or refuted with scientific evidence.

INTERPRETIVE PHOTOGRAPHS

Interpretive photographs, like explanatory photographs, also seek to explain how things are, but they do not attempt scientific accuracy, nor are they accountable to scientific testing procedures. They are personal and subjective interpretations, more like poetry than a scientific report. They are usually fictional and often use the "directorial mode" of photography defined by A. D. Coleman as one in which the photographer causes "something to take place which would not have occurred had the photographer not made it happen."[23] Photographers working directorially stage people or objects in front of the lens or intervene in real-life situations, directing the participants, or they do both. This tradition dates from the beginning of photography including photographs by Clarence White (1871–1925), F. Holland Day (1864–1933), and Gertrude Käsebier (1852–1934).

Interpretive photographs are closer to Szarkowski's mirrors than to his windows. They are self-expressive and reveal a lot about the worldviews of the photographers who make them. They are exploratory and not necessarily logical, and sometimes they overtly defy logic. They are usually dramatic rather than subtle and are generally concerned with formal excellence and good print quality. If a viewer questioned their claims, he or she would be hard pressed to find either confirming or denying scientific evidence. This is not to say, however, that interpretive photographs make no claims to truth or that they do not have truth value. Fiction can offer truths about the world.

Janine Antoni's *Inhabit* provides a clear example of an interpretive photograph by the artist's stated intent as well as its obvious construction. The artist says:

> *Inhabit* [see Plate 18] came to me first as a very simple image. I imagined that a spider had created its web between my legs. As I started to research the process of actualizing this image, things became complicated. Would a spider actually cooperate? How would I remain still in order to facilitate its weaving? After speaking with several entomologists, and learning about the extreme sensitivity of spiders to motion, I looked into getting a harness that would immobilize me. That led me to the world of harnesses, where I found a particular design that enabled me to be attached to a structure from many points on my torso. I realized that my body could be suspended in a way similar to a spider in its web. But I would need to build a cage around my legs in order to keep the spider in that particular area of my body. And it also became apparent that the spider would be too sensitive to build directly on my body due to body heat. It's worth mentioning that, from the beginning, I equated the spider and its web with my daughter, and myself, the mother, with the support structure. Suddenly I thought of turning the spider's cage into a doll's house, as a way of incorporating the spider into the photograph. I now have an image that is a web within a web, a house within a house.[24]

Rodney Graham's *Dance!!!!!* (see Color Plate 7) is a 10 by 12 foot color transparency mounted in a light box. It too is a clear example of an interpretive photograph. Art critic Nancy Princethal explains: "It shows two Wild West gunslingers menacing a top-hatted worthy played by the artist. One outlaw, seated atop a player piano—his partner is at the keyboard—points his gun at the victim's feet, which are lifted, as are his arms, in a cheerless jig. The slightly silly, or hysterical, extra exclamation points in the title enforce the impression that the familiar cinematic scenario is a kind of inside joke, but no one's laughing; the dancer is especially stone-faced. Though both his feet are off the floor, his expression and the crystal

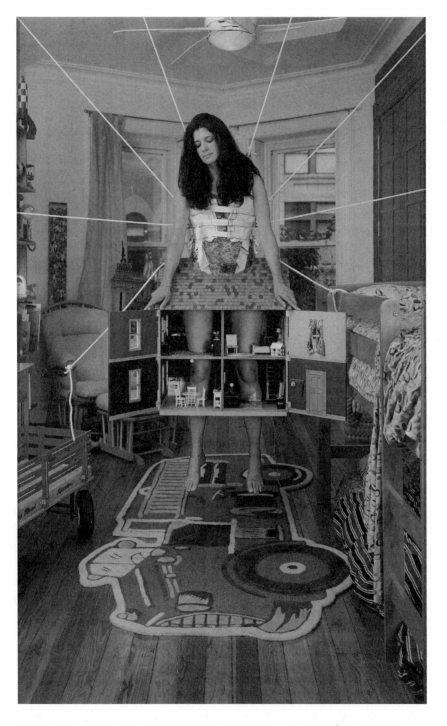

PLATE 18. Janine Antoni, *Inhabit*, 2009. Digital C-print, 116 1/2 × 72 inches. Frame: 119 11/16 × 75 1/8 × 3 inches.

Courtesy of the artist and Luhring Augustine, New York City.

clarity of every detail of his body (which must be in furious motion) make him look like he's standing still."[25]

Graham has put in historically accurate details such as spittoon, potbellied stove, and oil lamp. The photograph is fictional and belongs in the interpretive category. However, very importantly, like many other images in this category, *Dance!!!!!* is not made just for our amusement. It has political and moral implications and overlaps with the ethically evaluative category. Graham sees the image "as a reference to the abuses at Abu Ghraib, insofar as it shows two nameless men terrorizing a third for no apparent reason; the protagonists are poised on a slope that leads from humiliation to physical abuse and deadly assault."[26]

Jerry Uelsmann and Duane Michals (see Color Plate 8) are two photographers well known for their exploration of conflating fact and fiction in their work. Uelsmann combines many images into one in a seamless manner (Plate 10), and has been doing this in the darkroom since 1959 with traditional printing methods long before digital imagery and PhotoShop were available. The *Twentieth Century Encyclopedia of Photography* introduces Uelsmann's work this way: "Influenced by Surrealist ideology about dreams and the subconscious, Jerry Uelsmann is considered a master of the photomontage creating his private metaphoric statements in universes of his imagination . . . producing photographs in which reality and fantasy seamlessly merge into complex visual poetry. Process and idea remained simultaneously integral to the success of the final image, as he always stressed."[27]

Michals is famous for using narrative sequences of black and white photographs with his handwritten texts on them. He began making these in the 1960s and continues today. The *Twentieth Century Encyclopedia of Photography* opens its entry on Michals with this statement: "Self-taught in photography, Duane Michals has redefined photography by traveling a path unrestricted by the rules of the medium in order to explore its possibilities, always seeking expression and imagination rather than an adherence to specific, traditional forms. Michals is particularly known for his narrative sequences, in which he plays upon the cinematic aspect of photography."[28] Themes of imagination, mystery, and desire are major in his work (see Color Plate 8).

Jeff Wall (Plate 7), discussed in Chapter 3, and Gregory Crewdson, discussed in Chapter 2, also make work that fit within the interpretive category, and their work also is cinematic, especially Crewdson's.

In an interpretive project, Neil Folberg brings a Biblical narrative into the present by means of *Serpent's Chronicle,* a sequence of thirty-five photographs (see Color Plate 9). Folberg shows the events from the eye of the serpent: "The images have a direct romantic energy that speaks to our primal senses. *Serpent's Chronicle* is an interpretive narrative of events in the Garden of Eden from the viewpoint of a cunning observer; it is the Serpent's visual and textual record from that archetypal time until now."[29]

Carlo McCormick, writing in *Aperture* about "Travelers," interprets a fictional series of photographs made of snow-globes by Walter Martin and Paloma Muñoz (see Color Plate 10):

> Home is a dot on some map, but when you are not at home, wherever you are is also a place in and of itself. Call it out, or away; the designation doesn't determine the location. It is the absence of the material and social condition of being at home. To be not home is to occupy an ontological other space. It is this other realm that is conjured in the snow-globe sculpture photographs of Walter Martin and Paloma Muñoz: an exterior manifestation of the internal topographies of adventure, alienation, dread, discovery, and destiny that we, from our proverbial spot on the couch, have come to view as the greater world.[30]

Peter Galassi places Philip-Lorca diCorcia's series of photographs of heads begun in Times Square, New York City, in 2000 (see Color Plate 11) in the fictional category, even though for these photographs diCorcia selects anonymous subjects who are unknown to him, and photographs them surreptitiously and without their conscious cooperation:

> What began as a refreshing slap in the face of photographic realism (thanks, we needed that) has never lost its theatrical polish. But, as diCorcia's subjects gradually mutated from the intimate to the anonymous, from family and friends to Hollywood hustlers to passersby who rarely even notice that they have been photographed, his fictions improbably absorbed the weight and ambition of what some people still insist on describing as photography's more innocent documentary past. . . . As always, the mise-en-scène is rigidly defined. Except for choosing among the characters who unknowingly audition for his cast, however, the photographer is powerless to direct his actors. Even the instant of exposure, precisely dictated by the X on the sidewalk, is out of his control. diCorcia's old blend of fiction and fact has precipitated into extremes: absolute control and passive observation, cinematic drama and slice of-life realism. . . .[31]

Photographs by Robert ParkeHarrison (Plate 19) are clearly fictional and interpretive, but perhaps they should be placed in the following category of photographs that morally judge what they show. As Vicki Goldberg commented in the *New York Times,* ParkeHarrison "comes down on the side of lamentation but expresses it with an unusual combination of poetic license, laboriously constructed props and a wry and melancholy, vaguely allusive sense of myth. He appears in every picture, in a black suit and white shirt with no tie, a kind of Everyman or a minor employee of the universe, patiently, dutifully doing a job that's too big for him. That job is essentially to take care of a devastated Earth with inadequate equipment."[32]

Like all photographs, interpretive photographs need to be interpreted. Many of these photographs play with ambiguity and are open to a variety of readings. For example, Rimma Gerlovina and Valeriy Gerlovin (see Color Plate 12), the Russian émigré husband and wife team who make larger-than-life self-portraits, conjure several associations with their playful and ironic transformations of themselves: "beatific visions from medieval and Renaissance art, dadaist puns, poetic theories

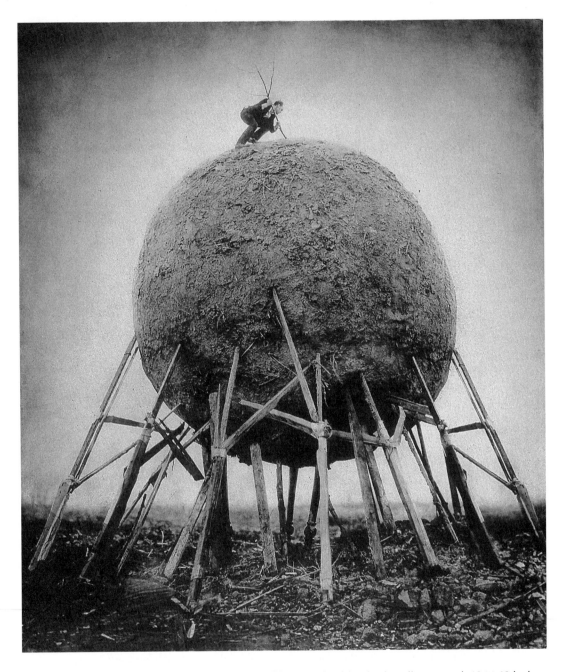

PLATE 19.   Robert ParkeHarrison, *Kingdom,* 2000. Photograph with mixed media on panel, 46 × 40 inches.
© Robert ParkeHarrison. Courtesy of Bonni Benrubi Gallery, New York City.

of paradox, Jungian images, graphics in the service of revolution, Russian constructivism, even the history of body art from ritual scarring to contemporary tatoos."[33]

ETHICALLY EVALUATIVE PHOTOGRAPHS

David Levi Strauss and Alfredo Jaar collaborated on a series of images called
"Lament of the Images" as a protest to the United States government from keeping us from seeing certain photographs from the war in Iraq. In one *Lament of the
Images* (see Plate 20) Jaar and Strauss submitted a composition for the Op-Ed page
of the *New York Times*. Strauss wrote the captions for the three missing images, in
his words, "to stand in for the many images the president had decided we should
not be allowed to see. In refusing to release more than two thousand images docu-
menting the abuse and torture of prisoners in Iraq and Afghanistan by U.S. military
and intelligence personnel, thereby reversing a previous agreement the government had made with the American Civil Liberties Union to release the images on
May 28, 2009." The *Times* refused to print Jaar and Strauss's piece. *Lament of the
Images* fits well within both the explanatory category and the ethically evaluative
category of photographs as political protest.[34]

Ethically evaluative photographs describe—some attempt scientific explanations, others offer personal interpretations—but most distinctively, they all make
ethical judgments. They praise or condemn aspects of society. They show how
things ought or ought not to be. They are politically engaged and usually passionate.

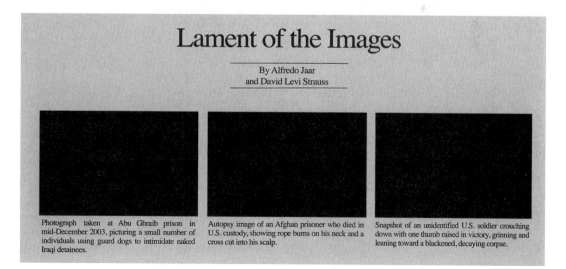

Lament of the Images

By Alfredo Jaar
and David Levi Strauss

Photograph taken at Abu Ghraib prison in mid-December 2003, picturing a small number of individuals using guard dogs to intimidate naked Iraqi detainees.

Autopsy image of an Afghan prisoner who died in U.S. custody, showing rope burns on his neck and a cross cut into his scalp.

Snapshot of an unidentified U.S. soldier crouching down with one thumb raised in victory, grinning and leaning toward a blackened, decaying corpse.

PLATE 20.   Alfredo Jaar and David Levi Strauss, *Lament of the Images,* 2009.
Courtesy of the artists.

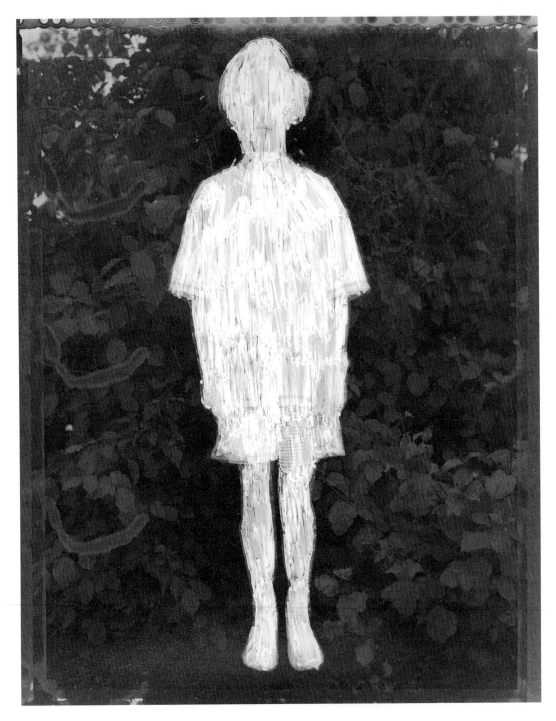

PLATE 21.   Wendy Ewald and Gerdien van Anen, *Gerdien's Portrait, the Netherlands*, 1997.
Courtesy of the artists.

Portraiture need not be limited to descriptive uses, and some portraits are clearly made in the service of improving social relations. For many years as part of her art in collaborative portrait projects, Wendy Ewald (Plate 21) has been working with children, many of whom have experienced physical and psychological violence and loss, helping them turn their experiences and dreams into interpretive and poetic photographic images, frequently accompanied by texts of their stories. She is committed to helping children around the world to recognize the worth of their own visions and themselves and has worked in remote villages in India, Colombia, Mexico, and the Netherlands.[35]

Carrie Mae Weems is an African American woman who combines written accounts and photographs that expose racial prejudice in society. She draws upon autobiographical accounts, oral history, racial jokes, and appropriated images, one of which shows a man and two women slaves stripped to the waist. According to Vince Aletti of the *Village Voice,* "One of the women—so angry, so belittled—glares at the photographer and, now, at us with a barely contained fury that needs no commentary." Weems also makes what she calls "gender stuff"—portraying "the tensions and the issues that exist between men and women, women and women, and women and their children."[36] Lorna Simpson uses metaphor, biography, and portraiture to resist racist acts of aggression, discrimination, and alienation. According to Deborah Willis, a curator of photographic exhibitions, Simpson combines large photographs with texts in museum installations dealing with black women as "survivors, protagonists, and victims" in "a society weighted with oppressive, repressive and consumer-oriented behavior."[37]

For about forty years, Alan Sekula has been photographing "social relations within an ascendant global economy," [38] or what he calls "the imaginary and material geographies of the advanced capitalist world." [39] In his exhibited and published textual and photographic works *Fish Story* and *Geography Lesson: Canadian Notes,* Sekula intends to raise these questions: "How does photography serve to legitimate and normalize existing power relationships? How is historical and social memory preserved, transformed, restricted and obliterated by photographs?"[40] According to critic Benjamin Buchloh, Sekula's project is one of critical realism that details the political and economic transformations caused globally by advancing capitalist rule. The work is also an effort to retrieve, through still photographs during an age of electronic media, memories of the factual, social, and political while capitalism continuously shifts, changes, and conceals them.

In "Polonia and Other Fables" (2007–2009), Sekula combines forty photographs taken in Poland and Chicago, a city with a large Polish population, with wall texts of anecdotes, jokes, and proclamations. Sekula contrasts human subjects and commercial rituals, including two photographs of pig farming, one of a Polish family farm (see Plate 22) and an aerial view of another that was owned by a collective

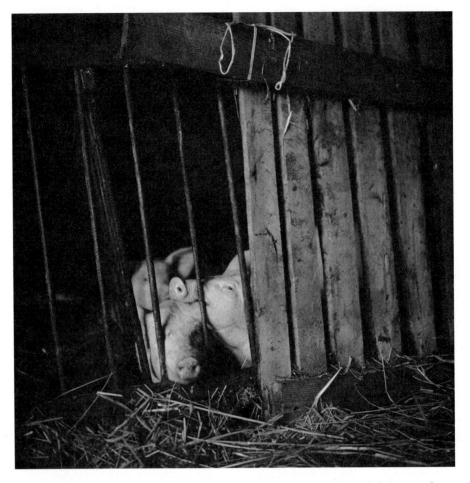

PLATE 22.   Allan Sekula, *Three pigs on family farm.* Nowa Huty, Poland, July 2009 from *Polonia and Other Fables,* 2007. Chromogenic print, 48 × 48 inches.
© Allan Sekula.

but has since been bought by an American multinational business known for its deplorable treatment of animals and dismal environmental record. The company denied him access to the farm, thus, the aerial view. Another photograph of a lone Polish trader at the Chicago Mercantile Exchange reveals very little about capital transactions. The social ills brought by late capitalism have long interested Sekula, and his photographs situate in the ethical category.

In fictional dioramas using dummies and dolls, Laurie Simmons explores the psychological landscapes of women consumed by home and family. Critic Nicholas Jenkins interprets Simmons's photographs of hybrids of objects and dolls' legs to be exploring sexual exploitation in that they suggest a perversely fascinating theater of humiliation and a sympathetic imagining of degradation and vulnerability.[41]

Color Plate 13 also shows female vulnerability in a fictional interpretive and ethically evaluative photograph by Gerald Slota and Neil LaBute. The two work collaboratively: Slota makes altered photographs, and LaBute composes texts for them. LaBute says Slota "doesn't seem to really 'create' them at all—that's too kind a word for it—he seems to dredge them up from their collective graves like some nineteenth-century figure digging by lamplight, only to take them home and desecrate them in private. Scrawling images on top of images, often tearing photographs to pieces or piercing them with scissors or whatever he can get his filthy hands on seems to be more like it. Gerald Slota's work makes me feel dirty, and that is as big a compliment as I can give the man." LaBute offers his interpretation of one particular image:

> There is a particularly creepy one that he sent to me late in the process that looked like a standard student photo from an old-time yearbook and into it he had stuffed a troubling image of an adult woman, fully laid out in some carnal pose. . . . If there is one picture of Gerald's that seems most representative of him and his work and our time together it could very well be this one for me—the purity of a childhood that is at the mercy of a leering adult and, unlike in fairy tales or our dreams, that child will soon be swept away and consumed by an unthinking, unfeeling world.[42]

Because of the look of the photograph, it's made-up text, and the duo's manner of working, this image fits within the interpretive category, and it overlaps with the ethically evaluative category because it suggests an evil scenario of sexual abuse.

Edward Burtynsky has devoted his career to photographing industrial incursions into the landscape. He understands the need for development and is also concerned with sustainability as humans radically transform the environment to satiate their collective appetite for goods and services. Color Plate 14 is one of a series of the construction of the Three Gorges Dam, the world's largest and most powerful hydroelectric dam built in China to generate electricity, control floods, and provide inland shipping. Burtynsky acknowledges "building mega dams in the 21st century has gathered much global criticism and is central to a growing debate. To make room for the Three Gorges Dam, approximately 1.13 million people must be relocated and their livelihoods challenged. It is the largest peacetime evacuation in history. Fertile agricultural lands and important cultural/historic sites will be found submerged under a vast reservoir. By 2009, 13 major cities, 140 towns and over 1,300 villages, along with 1,600 factories and mines and an unknown number of farms have vanished beneath its surface." Burtynsky acknowledges "the winners of this massive undertaking who include those who improved their standard of living and benefited from new housing and new opportunities. China's industries, hungry for electricity, also win. However, there are many who must face short-term hardship. For instance, farming families stand to lose much as their ancestral lands disappear, often without sufficient compensation. Farmers relocated to land parcels further uphill face the prospect of poor soil, steep slopes and erosion. . . . Environmental degradation, escalating costs and human rights concerns are the main issues entangling mega-dam projects."[43]

Chris Jordan also made a seemingly beautiful photograph he calls *Gyre* (see Color Plate 15). It is based on the famous image by Hokusai, *Wave off Kanagawa* (about 1829). However, Jordan constructed *Gyre* of 2.4 million pieces of plastic, equal to the estimated number of pounds of plastic pollution that enter the world's oceans every hour. All of the plastic in this image was collected from the Pacific Ocean. In *Gyre,* Jordan provides an example of a photograph that is hard to place. The original piece is 8 by 11 feet, but from a distance and when reduced in size in reproduction it does not show what it is made of. Without contextual knowledge of what it is made of, it looks like a copy of a famous work of art and thus might be a piece of conceptual art to be placed in the theoretical category. It also could easily be moved into the aesthetically evaluative photograph as a positive aesthetic statement. It overlaps the explanatory category and the ethically evaluative category, but is placed in the latter because it condemns what it pictures, namely, the pollution of the oceans by discarded junk. It would not be placed within the interpretive category because the image is scientifically accurate.

Iranian photographer Shadi Ghadirian, in the series *Like Everyday* (see Color Plate 16) explores tradition, women, and modernity. The picture shows what would appear to be women in full chador with household implements in place of their faces. Iranian women are not required to wear full chador in public, though many do for reasons of modesty, and they are not required in the home. Ghadirian's women with implements seem to comment on the absence of personal identity for women in Iran, and thus would tentatively be placed within the ethically evaluative category as protest statements. Such a placement, however, is not certain without more contextual information about the image, the intent of the photographer, and the uses to which the photograph is put, which we currently lack. For a more confident placement, or interpretation, contextual information is necessary.

Nina Berman provides a photograph that can be placed in the ethically evaluative category with some confidence: *Marine Wedding, Sergeant Ty Ziegel and Renée Kline* (see Color Plate 17). Berman made a series of photographs of wounded war veterans entitled "Purple Hearts." When asked in an interview if she intended the photographs to send an antiwar message, Berman replied: "I think this project humanizes the whole issue and I . . . hope it makes it more personal for people, so that when you think about the Iraq War, you're not thinking about slogans like 'Shock and Awe' or 'Mission Accomplished,' or the cartoonlike coverage; you're seeing real people."[44] Both the image and her statement about it is supportive evidence for placing this photograph in the ethically evaluative category.

AESTHETICALLY EVALUATIVE PHOTOGRAPHS

Other photographs make judgments, not about social issues but about aesthetic issues. The photographs in this category point out what their photographers consider to be worthy of aesthetic observation and contemplation. They are usually about the wonder of visual form in all its variety and how it can be rendered photographically. This is the kind of "art photography" most familiar to most people. Photographs in this category are usually of beautiful things photographed in beautiful ways.

John Szarkowski sums up some essential characteristics of this tradition in photography: "a love for the eloquently perfect print, an intense sensitivity to the mystical content of the natural landscape, a belief in the existence of a universal formal language, and a minimal interest in man as a social animal."[45]

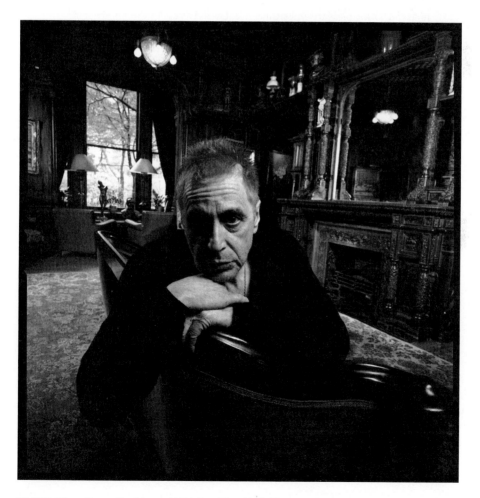

PLATE 23. Bruce Davidson, *Al Pacino, New York City*, 2002.
Bruce Davidson/Magnum Photos.

Photographic portraits (Plate 23) present challenges for placements within a single category. Portraits may be as simple as identification photographs, and fit within the descriptive category. All portraits present some explanatory content about their subjects and many add interpretive nuances to the persons they depict. Many portraits are meant to flatter the subject and would thus be placed in the aesthetically evaluative category.

In making her still lifes Laura Letinsky (see Color Plate 18) is informed by seventeenth-century oil painting as she explores tabletops:

> Pondering the perishable nature of all worldly things and the evanescence
> of sensual pleasures. Her still-lifes concentrate on the remains of the meal,
> focusing on half-filled glasses, discarded food and dirty silverware, and stained
> tabletops. She addresses the relationship between ripeness and decay, pleni-
> tude and waste, pleasure and sustenance. Letinsky's compositions are stark,
> using a soft palette of ivory linens and bright white surfaces set against pale
> and dark backgrounds. They contain a strong emphasis on diagonals and close
> croppings are used to frame the organized simple groupings.[46]

About her work, Letinsky says, "I want to explore the formal relationship between ripeness and decay, delicacy and awkwardness, control and haphazardness, waste and plenitude, pleasure and sustenance."[47]

The landscape is common subject matter for photograph in the aesthetically evaluative category. A critic writing about "Portfolio Brazil," a series of photographs by Mona Kuhn, says the artist "returned to her homeland Brazil in search of connections both past and present. It was a journey fuelled by an emotional desire to understand her relationship with the place where she had spent the first 20 years of her life. The allegories of returning to a homeland run deep and wide in human experience and have many varied expressions in arts, music, and literature. Kuhn's point of entry was photographic, a visual inquiry that . . . weaves together photographs of nature and people in a highly personal portrait of a place seen through the artist's eyes and imagination."[48] (See Color Plate 19) Thus, the critic would seem comfortable in placing the photograph within the aesthetically evaluative category.

Equisetum (Plate 24) by Catherine Wagner is one photograph from a series of large-scale photographs called "Morphology." She made it while an artist-in-residence for the California Academy of Sciences. For the image, she drew from the Academy's collections of specimens, photographing hundreds of plant species whose relatives existed during the Devonian Age, and organized them as graphic images. Thus, she decontextualized from descriptive specimen photographs and recontextualized them as elegant calligraphic gestures, similar to the linear "chalk board" paintings by Cy Twombly that fit within the aesthetically evaluative category.

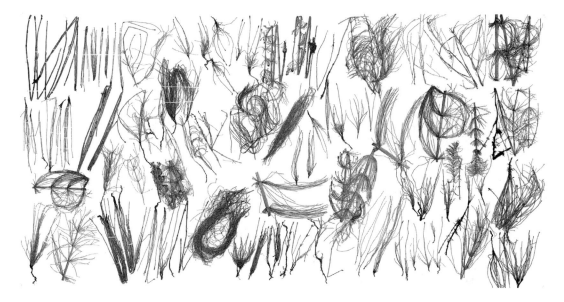

PLATE 24.   Catherine Wagner, *Equisetum*, 2008. Lambda print, 48 × 96 inches.
Courtesy of the artist and Stephen Wirtz Gallery, San Francisco.

The *Encyclopedia of Twentieth-Century Photography* identifies Mark Klett (see Color Plate 20) as "among the most accomplished landscape photographers in the ranks of twentieth century American photography. His unique photographs incorporate elements of a nineteenth century tradition, while critically examining many of the twentieth century's most poignant environmental concerns. Throughout his work, Mark Klett focuses on the experience of contemporary travelers in the American West, while demonstrating how that experience differs from the mythologized histories of this same land." Note Klett's use of triangles as a formal motif in Color Plate 20.

About Richard Misrach's stunning color photographs of natural spaces, Mark Johnstone writes "while they tell us something about the place, these pictures are also about what it means to transform experiences of the world into photographs."[49] Lynne Cohen (see Color Plate 21) has been photographing interior spaces devoid of people for more than thirty years. Her subject matter includes classrooms, health spas, military installations, laboratories, and waiting rooms. Because of her use of rigorous framing, consistent distant and point of view, lighting that puts things in relief, and color, her images look artificially constructed, but they are documents of actual spaces. In their straightforward starkness, Cohen's pictures imply social control through interior design and social engineering. Her subtly eerie images hint at subthemes of protection or concealment. Her work crosses from descriptive photography to a formal play between sense and nonsense, the ordinary and the strange, the real and surreal. They overlap categories of interpretation but can be comfortably placed within the aesthetically evaluative category.

Fashion photography would also fit within the aesthetically evaluative category. The photograph by Magnum photographer Christopher Anderson (Color Plate 22) provides a clear example of a photograph made for its exuberant color, dynamic patterns of shapes and textures, and the flamboyant movement of fabric and hair. The identity of the model is not provided because the photograph is not about her, but about the general look and feel of a trend in fashion.

Similarly, the identity of the model or models in Solve Sundsbo (Color Plate 23) is not important to the aesthetic use of their features which bear heavy eye make-up and startling contrast of red lips against very pale facial skin. The photograph also pushes the edges of what is aesthetically desirable in photographs by including and enhancing the "red eye" of the models. The flattening of the picture plane and placement of the nose borrows from traditions in Cubist painting.

Since the Ancient Greeks, comedy as well as tragedy has been a concern of aesthetics. Martin Parr is a British photographer with a sense of humor (see Color Plate 24) who is a member of the prestigious photo agency Magnum. Magnum describes his work:

> Parr began his formal training in the arts at Manchester Polytechnic in the early 1970s. There he explored his growing curiosity for the choices we make: from the clothes we wear, to the groups we associate with, things we buy and even the people we love. Parr's photographs tell stories of the ordinary moments in our lives that we never would imagine could be worth telling: he catches us while we are eating; during the mundane rituals of our commute, work or home life; in uncomfortable moments being a tourist so obviously out of place in a foreign land. Parr's satire portrays life as it appears to be: from scenes of overcrowded British seaside resorts, to iridescent cupcakes, to the many ironic and odd moments he finds in our lives. His photographs shine an excessively bright light on the everyday in our lives, at once penetrating and often unflattering. Parr at once challenges us to look at ourselves in unflattering ways while having a good laugh in the process. In that he triumphs.[50]

The aesthetically evaluative category also includes photographs that are made particularly because they are not beautiful. Larry Sultan, a photographer involved in California Conceptualism, explored photography as "more than just the modernist practice of fine-tuning your style and way of seeing." According to critic Randy Kennedy in the *New York Times,* the pictures Sultan exhibited were "a strange, stark, sometimes disturbing vision of a late-industrial world,"[51] like Color Plate 25, which is not a pretty picture conceptually or compositionally.

PLATE 25. Sarah Charlesworth, *Text,* 1994. Silver print, 20 × 24 inches.
© Sarah Charlesworth.

THEORETICAL PHOTOGRAPHS

This last category includes photographs about photography. These photographs comment on issues about art and art making, about the politics of art, about modes of representation, and other theoretical issues about photography and photographing. Prime examples are Cindy Sherman's photographs (Plate 4, Color Plate 1), mentioned in Chapter 2, with which she critiques how women are represented in different media.[52] They are photographs about films, photographs about photographs, art about art, and can be considered a visual type of art criticism that uses pictures rather than words. Joel-Peter Witkin's photographs about historical paintings and sculptures, also mentioned in Chapter 2, are clearly art about art (Plate 5).

Some photographers who work in this mode are concerned with aesthetic—that is, philosophical—issues not specific to photography. Sherrie Levine has photographically copied the work of such photographers as Walker Evans and Edward Weston, and painters Piet Mondrian and Egon Schiele, and exhibits them.[53] These appropriations have been understood to be attacks on such modernist beliefs as artistic genius, originality, the preciousness of the unique art object, and the expense of the art commodity.

Since 1977 Richard Prince has been systematically rephotographing photographic ads in magazines and exhibiting them in galleries.[54] Some of his works are rephotographs of the heads of male models, or their wristwatches, or the eyes of female models, presented as a series and without the advertising copy. By photographically clipping them from their contexts, he draws our attention to the visual conventions of advertising and scornfully mocks it. In 2004, Prince published *Women,* a collection of appropriated photographs of women, recycled male fantasies from images he found in magazines and then rephotographed, painted over, collaged, or broke down into fragments.

Sarah Charlesworth has devoted her artistic career to making photographs that would fit within the theoretical category, raising questions about the photograph's status as knowledge and its effects on its subjects and its viewers. About her work, critic Kate Linker writes that the core of Charlesworth's artistic enterprise is not so much about what photographs are or look like but what they do to all of us.[55] Writing about Charlesworth's photograph *Text* (Plate 26), Dave Hickey notes that beneath the white satin lies an open book, and through the satin, or on top of the satin or even printed on top of the photograph of the satin, there appear lines of text. Hickey says, "If reading a book, as the image implies, is to snatch the word-soaked satin off the page and carry it away, just what does one carry?. . .The question applies, as well, to the photograph."[56]

Many of the photographers who make theoretical photographs are very aware of and concerned in their picture making with the photographic medium itself, with what it does and does not do, how it pictures and to what effect. Andy Grundberg, in a catalogue essay about the work of Zeke Berman (Color Plate 17), writes that Berman's photographs carefully constructed in a studio are "sculptures squeezed into two dimensions."[57] On his Webpage, Berman says his "works reflect his long standing interest in visual cognition, optics and the intersection between sculpture, photography and drawing. The formal range of his work, and his sculptural use of materials is varied, original and idiosyncratic"[58] (see Color Plate 17).

James Casebere's eerie photographs (see Color Plate 26) are based on real and imagined architecture and range from state penitentiaries to Thomas Jefferson's Monticello home to current housing developments. Casebere constructs tabletop models with styrofoam, paper, and plaster, and photographs them, often as if they are flooded spaces.

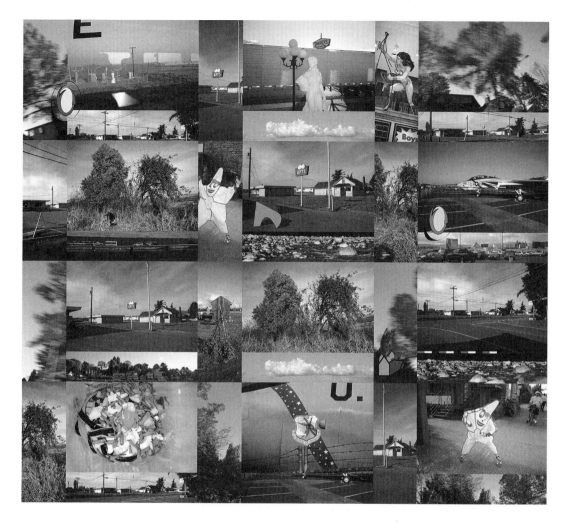

PLATE 26.   Paul Berger, *Warp and Weft: Figure, Tree* (detail), 2002. Iris print, 35 × 47 inches.
© Paul Berger.

For the past twenty-five years, Thomas Ruff has

redefined photography's conceptual possibilities, simultaneously capturing
and questioning the essence of photography as both a means and a tool for
visual experience. . . . Works in the *Cassini* series [see Color Plate 27] are
based on photographic captures of Saturn taken by NASA's Cassini-Huygens
Spacecraft, which launched in 2004 and completed its initial four-year mission
in June 2008. The spacecraft orbited around Saturn to provide the first in-
depth, close-up study of the planet and its domain, including its rings, moons,
and magnetosphere, the enormous magnetic bubble that controls its planetary

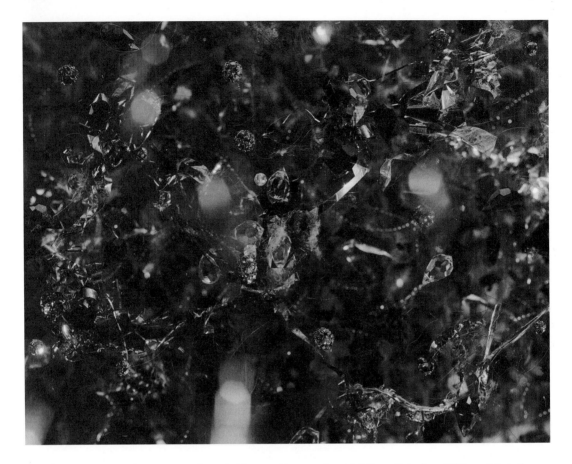

PLATE 27.   Carter Mull, *Untitled (reverie V)*, 2004. Type c print, 37 3/8 × 48 inches. Edition of 3 + 1ap. Original work in color.

Courtesy of the artist and Marc Foxx, Los Angeles and Taxter & Spengemann, New York City.

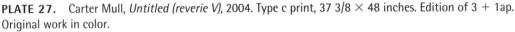

movement. Ruff acquired these black and white raw images from NASA's website, where they were broadcast directly from the spacecraft and made available for public download. Through computer manipulation, Ruff infused each gray-scale image with saturated color. The resulting chromogenic prints transform the originals into visual statements that both capture the sweeping enormity of planetary structures while still distancing themselves from concrete forms, evocative instead of abstract and minimalist compositions.[59]

Given the formal minimalist beauty of *Cassini 06* and his continued exploration of what the medium of photography can produce, this digital work by Ruff fits comfortably in the aesthetically evaluative category.

Rod Slemmons, director of the Museum of Contemporary Photography, Columbia College, Chicago, would likely place Paul Berger's digital photographic images (see Plate 26) in the theoretical category. Slemmons interprets Berger's images as asking these questions:

> How do we know what we know in a maelstrom of images specifically designed to confuse us and rob us of access to our own experience, opinions, and knowledge? How do we test the difference between information and knowledge when replication in the form of imagery is increasingly substituted for experience? . . . Berger has refused to forget, or ignore, that photographs that simplistically appear to be factual statements are really just flat, frame-bound, closed arenas of evidence that do not admit to anything without the introduction of the human eye, without human experience to support their abstract claims.[60]

According to his American gallerist, Thomas Demand (see Color Plate 28), the well-known and influential German photographer

> studied with the sculptor Fritz Schwegler, who encouraged him to explore the expressive possibilities of architectural models at the Kunstakademie Düsseldorf, where Bernd and Hilla Becher had recently taught photographers such as Andreas Gursky, Thomas Struth, and Candida Hofer. Like those artists, Demand makes mural-scale photographs, but instead of finding his subject matter in landscapes, buildings, and crowds, he uses paper and cardboard to reconstruct scenes he finds in images taken from various media sources. Once he has photographed his re-created environments—always devoid of figures but often displaying evidence of recent human activity—Demand destroys his models, further complicating the relationship between reproduction and original that his photography investigates. [61]

According to critic Liz Kotz, Walead Beshty and Carter Mull and other young contemporary image makers are interested in photography that results in "the exploration of photographic materiality and abstraction, partly as a response to our digital moment, with its endless vernacular proliferation of images," including those made by "everyman" with cell phones.[62] Beshty, for example, made the photogram reproduced as Color Plate 29 by cutting and folding a large sheet of light sensitive paper into a three dimensional form and exposing it to light a certain number of times in a darkened room. By working in the dark, the artist is conforming to predetermined parameters set up beforehand. In the image he is exploring "the interaction between light and time."

Carter Mull is "a maestro of the mundane . . . who inventively manipulates and shoots everyday items (torn magazines, broken glass, salt, human hair) to create trippy, color-saturated abstract images that mingle order with chaos. In some pieces elements are recognizable; in others they remain mysterious" (Plate 27). Mull, like Beshty, is primarily interested "material presence." Mull says, "The issue for me is trying to devise a new way of looking at photographs where the viewer can't escape the fact that the image they're seeing is constructed." Rather than pursue documentary images with the medium of photography, "Mull is all about distortion. He embeds materials so deeply in his work that they are utterly transformed, losing their original shape, context, or meaning." [63]

All of these photographs are placed within the theoretical category because each, in its own way, challenges accepted assumptions about photography. They are self-reflexive in regard to the medium that is ever shifting in production and uses.

Photographs and Contexts

I T IS DIFFICULT TO ACCURATELY PLACE A SINGLE PHOTOGRAPH OF UNKNOWN ORIGIN IN ONE of the six categories presented in the previous chapter. This is another way of saying that it is difficult for viewers to arrive at a trustworthy interpretation if they don't have some prior knowledge of the photograph: who made it, when, where, how, and for what purpose. This kind of information is *contextual* information, which can be either internal, original, or external.

INTERNAL CONTEXT

To consider a photograph's internal context is to pay attention to what is descriptively evident, as was discussed in Chapter 2, namely, the photograph's subject matter, medium, form, and the relations among the three.

Some photographs are understandable just by looking at them and thinking about what is shown in them. If we are familiar with the culture in which some photographs were made, we don't need to know much about the origin of the photographs to understand what they are about. The photograph by Bill Seaman that won the 1959 Pulitzer Prize for press photography is a good example of a photograph that is interpretable on the basis of what is shown in it.[1] At the bottom edge in the photograph's foreground is a crushed wagon on the pavement at an intersection of two streets in a residential neighborhood. In the middle ground of the photograph, about a third up from the bottom, there is a blanket or sheet draped over a small body shape. A policeman writing on a pad of paper stands next to the covered shape, and a medic is walking away from it. Some bystanders, women and children, are looking on from a distance. People in cars are also gazing as they pass by. We know by looking at the photograph and drawing upon our knowledge of draped body shapes, police officers, medics, crushed wagons, and fatal accidents, that the photograph is about a child who has been run over by a vehicle. We would readily and correctly place the photograph in the explanatory category.

We can also readily interpret many art photographs—any of Edward Weston's photographs of peppers or seashells, for example—by considering what is shown. When we see Weston's *Pepper No. 30,* 1930, we know that we are to attend to the pepper's form, to enjoy the twists of its sensuous curves, to note the lighting that makes it sculptural.[2] We understand that we are to appreciate the photograph as an aesthetic object rather than as a botanical illustration of an edible vegetable. We would readily and correctly place this photograph in the aesthetically evaluative category. This understanding depends, however, on some general knowledge of contemporary Western culture, especially on some familiarity with art of the twentieth century, abstraction, and the notion of art for the sake of art. But if we have gathered this knowledge, we can understand and appreciate *Pepper No. 30* based on what Weston shows in the photograph.

ORIGINAL CONTEXT

Although the Weston art photograph and the Seaman press photograph are understandable on the basis of what they show, many photographs are inscrutable without some information beyond that which can be gathered from simply observing the photograph. Photographs in the theoretical category depend on knowledge of art and the art world. Les Krims's *Making Chicken Soup* seems pointless humor if the viewer does not know that it is making fun of "concerned photography." Sherrie Levine's copies of Walker Evans's photographs would be completely misunderstood if the viewer didn't know that they were copies.[3] They are not labeled copies; they are titled "After Walker Evans," which casual observers probably would misunderstand to mean that they are "in the manner of" or "in homage to" rather than exact copies of Evans's photographs. Even if one knows they are copies, an uninformed viewer would still be perplexed as to why they are in a museum, why they are displayed as art. To be fully comprehended and appreciated, Levine's images require knowledge of Walker Evans and his stature in the history of photography, especially knowledge of postmodernist theory and its rejection of such notions as the originality of the artist, the preciousness of the original art object, and artistic genius. Levine's images are irreverent challenges to a prior theory of art. Such knowledge cannot be gathered by merely considering what is shown in the photographs.

Photographs made for the press also benefit from, and often depend on, knowledge of the contexts from which they merge. In 1972 Huynh Công Út, professionally

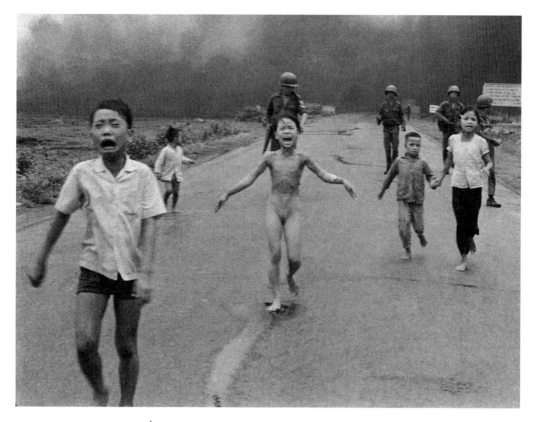

PLATE 28.   Huynh Công Út (Nick Ut), *Vietnam*, June 8, 1972.
Huynh Công Út/AP Images.

known as Nick Ut, made a horrifying photograph (Plate 28) that shows children, crying and screaming, and soldiers, fleeing with smoke behind them, running on a country road toward us.[4] The children are obviously traumatized. A young girl in the center of the frame is naked. Because of the evident pain of the children, this is a horrifying image. It is all the more horrifying when one knows that the children have just been sprayed with napalm from a jet above and that the girl is naked because she tore off her clothes trying to remove the burning jelly from herself. They were bombed by mistake. Although they were on the same side in a war, the pilot mistook the group as the enemy. The photograph itself reveals little. It is knowledge of the circumstances surrounding the making of the photograph that makes it more than a picture of traumatized children. The photograph has been credited with helping to stop American involvement in the Vietnam War.

Knowledge of context can also add richness to our understanding of easier photographs—those we can understand by looking at them. Photographs, by nature, are always swatches cut from seamless reality. They are segments, shot from close or afar, with a wide or narrow angle of view. By use of the viewfinder, photographers include and exclude. In a sense, all photographs are literally "out of context." They are out of a spatial context, and they are out of a temporal flow. They are one instant stopped in time. To understand and appreciate photographs, it is sometimes very useful to imaginatively put them back into their *original contexts,* to see what the photographer has done to make a picture, to study what was included, and how, and to imagine what was excluded and why. To consider their temporal element, we can try to see them as if they were one frame from a feature-length film. We can imaginatively consider what was physically available to the photographer at the time the exposure was made.

Knowledge of a photograph's original context includes knowledge of what was psychologically present to the photographer at the time the exposure was made. To consider a photograph's original context is to consider certain information about the photographer and about the social times in which he or she was working. The photographer's intent—what he or she meant to do by taking a photograph—can be revealing when it is available and can aid in our understanding of a photograph. Many photographers have written about their work. Julia Margaret Cameron, for example, has written very personally about her work in portraiture. Her revelations about herself add insight to her photographs. Knowledge of the photographer's biography can also reveal much about influences, personal and stylistic, on his or her work.

Original context includes knowledge of other work by the photographer. One close-up photograph of a gnarled green pepper might seem strange, but knowing that it is one of some thirty photographs of green peppers by the same photographer and that the photographer also made similar, close-up pictures of halved artichokes, cabbage leafs, toadstools, and halved and whole seashells, makes it less strange.

Knowledge of the work of other photographers, musicians, and writers, as well as knowledge of dance, painting, and sculpture, from the same period as the photographer in question may also provide considerable insight. Photographers do not work in social and aesthetic vacuums. Like all artists and all people, they are influenced by those around them and by their culture and cultural heritage. Knowledge of the history, the politics, and the religious and intellectual milieu of the period in which the photographer was working is important to a fuller understanding of a photograph. Much of the effect of Nick Ut's photograph depends on knowledge of Vietnam, the war, and napalm. Levine's photographs depend on knowledge of art history and art theory. Original context is history: social history, art history, and the history of the individual photograph and the photographer who made it.

EXTERNAL CONTEXT

External context is the situation in which a photograph is presented or found. Every photograph is intentionally or accidentally situated within a context. Usually we see photographs in very controlled situations: books, galleries, museums, newspapers, magazines, billboards, and classrooms. The meaning of any photo-graph is highly dependent on the context in which it is presented: How and where a photograph is seen radically affects its meaning. Gisèle Freund, a French scholar and photographer, relates how one of her countrymen's photographs was placed in various external contexts that radically affected its meaning.[5]

In 1953 Robert Doisneau, a French photojournalist, made one of several photo-graphs of French cafés, one of his favorite topics (Plate 29). In one café he entered, he was charmed by a man and woman drinking wine at a bar and asked if he could photograph them. They consented, and eventually the photograph appeared in *Le Point,* a mass circulation magazine, in an issue devoted to cafés illustrated with his photographs. He then gave this and other photographs to his agent. Some time later, and without the consent of Doisneau or the photographed man and woman, the café photograph appeared in a brochure on the evils of alcohol published by a temperance league. It had been sold to the league by Doisneau's agent. Still later, and still with-out the photographer's or the subjects' consent, and this time without the agent's knowledge, the photograph again appeared, this time in a French gossip tabloid that had lifted it from *Le Point.* It appeared with the caption: "Prostitution in the Champs-Élysées." The man in the photograph sued the tabloid, the agency, and the photographer. The court fined the tabloid and also found the agency guilty but acquitted Doisneau.

The presentational environments in which this café photograph appeared over-rode the content of the photograph and overdetermined its meaning in ways unfair to the photographer, the subjects, and the photograph itself, but that is the power of external context.

Since the 1950s, Doisneau's café photograph has appeared in other notable external contexts that have further changed how it is received. It frequently hangs in the Museum of Modern Art in New York, matted and framed under glass, with this label on the wall: "Robert Doisneau, French, born 1912, *At the Café, Chez Fraysse, Rue de Seine, Paris.* 1958. $11\frac{7}{8} \times 9\frac{3}{8}$." In this external context, it is not part of a popular magazine spread on cafés, it is not used to preach against alcohol, it is not titillating readers about prostitution; it is hanging as a work of art in one of the most prestigious museums in the world.

This photograph also appears in John Szarkowski's *Looking at Photographs: 100 Pictures from the Collection of the Museum of Modern Art,* with a one-page essay. Szarkowski interprets the photograph to be about the "secret venial sins of ordi-nary individuals," a sexual seduction:

> For the moment she enjoys the security of absolute power. One arm shields
> her body, her hand touches her glass as tentatively as if it were the first apple.
> The man for the moment is defenseless and vulnerable; impaled on the hook
> of his own desire, he has committed all his resources, and no satisfactory line
> of retreat remains. Worse yet, he is older than he should be, and knows that
> one way or another the adventure is certain to end badly. To keep his presen-
> timent at bay, he is drinking his wine more rapidly than he should.[6]

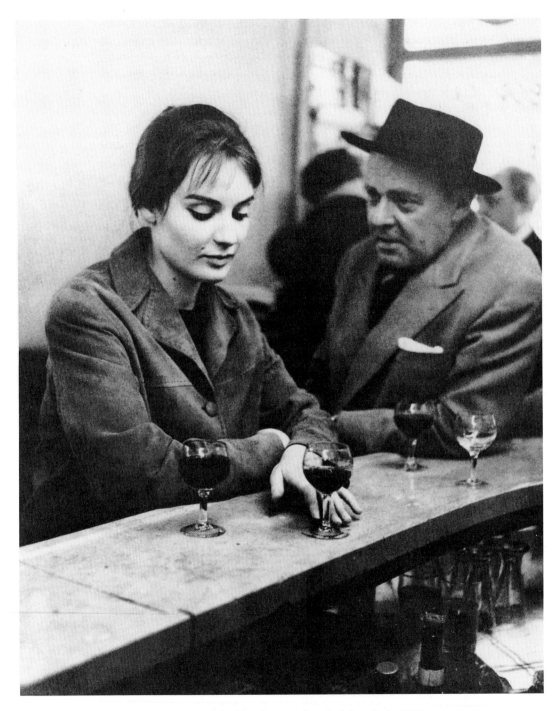

PLATE 29.   Robert Doisneau, *At the Café, Chez Fraysse, Rue de Seine, Paris*, 1958.
© Robert Doisneau.

Szarkowski backs his speculative understanding of the photograph with information from the photograph's internal context, or what is shown: The woman appears younger than the man, he appears to be gazing at her longingly, she looks more confident, and one of the two wine glasses before him is empty, although her two are nearly full. Although these observations do not automatically add up to an attempted seduction, Szarkowski argues for his interpretation and tries to convince us with evidence that his view is correct.

Szarkowski's treatment of the photograph is much more fair and reasonable than are those given it by the temperance league and the gossip tabloid: He lets his readers know that he is making an interpretation. The other two users ignore Doisneau's intended purpose of the photograph as part of a photo essay on cafés and impose their wills on the photograph to suit their purposes without warning the viewer about what they have done.

EXTERNAL CONTEXTS AND CONNOTATIONS

Doisneau's café photograph has appeared in at least six very different contexts, including this book. Each context strongly affects how the photograph is understood. These examples of one photograph in different external contexts illustrate how easily the meaning of a photograph can be altered, especially if text is added to it. Photographs are relatively indeterminate in meaning; their meaning can be easily altered by how they are situated, how they are presented.

Roland Barthes writes about the press photograph and how its meaning is heavily influenced by the publication that surrounds it, what he calls its "channel of transmission":

> As for the channel of transmission, this is the newspaper itself, or more precisely, a complex of concurrent messages with the photograph as the center and surrounds constituted by the text, the caption, the layout and, in a more abstract but in no less informative way, by the very name of the paper (this name represents a knowledge that can heavily orientate the reading of the message strictly speaking: a photograph can change its meaning as it passes from the very conservative *L'Aurore* to the communist *L'Humanité*).[7]

It is not hard to imagine the different connotations a photograph of a hunter beside a dead deer would receive in the United States if it were printed on the covers of both the *Sports Afield* and *Vegetarian Times* magazines.

Other writers have paid attention to how the art museum orients our interpretations of photographs, and some critics are especially concerned about the common museum practice of placing photographs not initially made as art into artworld contexts. Martha Rosler complains that the specific content of such photographs gets transformed into content about the artists who made them: "More and more clearly, the subject of all high art has become the self, subjectivity, and what this has meant for photography is that all photographic practice being hustled into galleries must be reseen in terms of its revelatory character not in relation to its iconographic subject but in relation to its 'real' subject, the producer."[8] She worries that the content of the photograph is erased with concern about the artist.

This concern is sometimes called the "aestheticizing" of photographs, and although the term is recent, the warning is as old as the 1930s when Walter Benjamin, the German Marxist critic, made a similar accusation. He complained that photography "has succeeded in turning abject poverty itself, in handling it in a modish, technically perfect way, into an object of enjoyment."[9] More recently, Susan Sontag has voiced concern that the cultural demand for aesthetically pleasing photographs has caused even the most compassionate photojournalist to satisfy two sets of expectations, one for aesthetic pleasure and one for information about the world. She argues that Eugene Smith's photographs of the crippled and slowly dying villagers in Minamata "move us because they document a suffering which causes our indignation—and distance us because they are superb photographs of Agony, conforming to Surrealist standards of beauty."[10] She makes similar claims about Lewis Hine's photographs of exploited child laborers in turn-of-the-century textile mills: Their "lovely compositions and elegant perspective easily outlast the relevance of the subject matter. . . . The aestheticizing tendency of photography is such that the medium which conveys distress ends by neutralizing it. Cameras miniaturize experience, transform history into spectacle. As much as they create sympathy, photographs cut sympathy, distance the emotions."

The point of these examples is that it is important to examine the context in which a photograph has been placed, whether that be a newspaper, a magazine, a billboard, or a museum gallery. When an editor captions a photograph, that editor is interpreting it. When a curator places a photograph in a museum, in a gallery, in a section of a show, under a heading such as "Mirrors," and with a label such as "Roy DeCarava, *Self-Portrait*, 1956, $10^1/_8 \times 13^{11}/_{16}$ inches, Museum of Modern Art, New York, purchase," that curator is interpreting it.[11] A caption or a placement of a photograph as part of a show may not be fully developed interpretations or reasoned arguments, but they are persuading us to understand an image in a certain way.

Sometimes curators' misplacements of photographs prevent accurate interpretations. In 1993, when selected to exhibit work in the prestigious Whitney Biennial, Pat Ward Williams submitted *What You Lookin At*, a large, 8- by 20-foot photographic mural with images and text. The images were offset photographs of African American men greatly enlarged so that the dot patterns of the offset images, when seen from a relatively close distance, are very apparent, almost obscuring the subjects of the photographs. When the images are seen from a close distance, the question the artist asks, "What you lookin at?" might be answered with thoughts about media representations of African Americans, specifically African American males. The images in the photo mural are very apparently, by the large dots, photographic reproductions, media representations. The Biennial curator, however, chose to display the mural in a window of the Whitney Museum facing a busy New York City street where thousands of pedestrians and motorists passed daily. From a distance viewers could not see the dots, just the subjects and text, African American males and "What you lookin at?" Rather than being asked to consider issues of photographic representations and rather than seeing an artwork sympathetic to the plight of African American males, viewers were instead confronted with a hostile image of African American males posing a threatening question. By the placement of the mural, the curator completely subverted the artist's intended message and precluded an accurate interpretation of the mural.

External contexts, or presentational environments, are forms of interpretation. As such, they, like all interpretations, ought to be evaluated for accuracy, fairness, reasonableness, and for their consequences.

INTERPRETATION OF BARBARA KRUGER'S *UNTITLED* ("SURVEILLANCE") WITH CONTEXTUAL INFORMATION

Following is an interpretation of Barbara Kruger's *Untitled* ("Surveillance"). The interpretation is based on internal, original, and external contextual information to show how context can be used to understand photographs.

"Surveillance" and Internal Context

This is a black and white photograph with words superimposed upon it—"Surveillance is your busywork" (Plate 30). A man is peering at us through a photographer's lupe, a magnifying device for closely examining negatives, contact prints, slides, and photographs. The lupe is a fixed-focus device, a cube, and he has it and his other hand against something, perhaps a pane of glass, a window, or a light table used for viewing negatives and transparencies. One of his eyes is closed, the other open. The light source is directly in front of his face, and it is harsh, revealing pores of skin and stubbles of whiskers. He looks to be in his forties or fifties. He is intent and, on the basis of the photograph, would be difficult to identify. The photograph in "Surveillance" looks dated, out of style, but vaguely familiar. It is dramatically lit and shot from a dramatic angle and distance—reminiscent of black and white Hollywood movies on late-night television, tough-guy cops-and-robbers movies.

The photograph is approximately square. It was shot either from a distance with a telephoto lens or from very close with a normal lens. Halftone dots are apparent—it is a halftone reproduction rather than a silver print made directly from a negative. The word *Surveillance* is larger than the other words, in black type

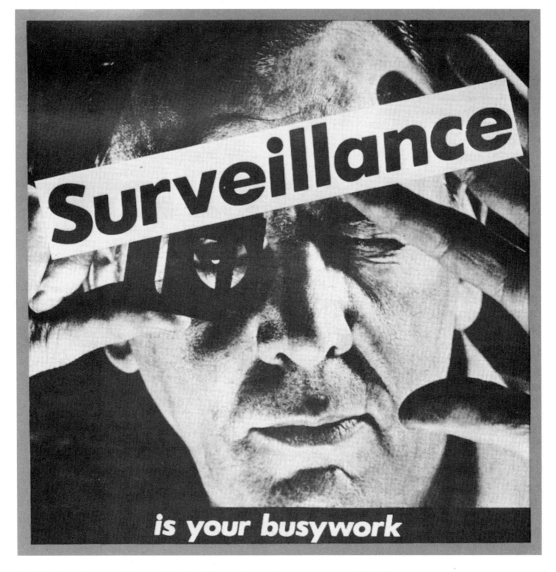

PLATE 30.   Barbara Kruger, *Untitled* ("Surveillance is your busywork"), 1983.
© Barbara Kruger. Courtesy of Mary Boone Gallery, New York.

on a white strip, pasted at a slight diagonal above the man's eyes. The phrase "is your busywork" is at the bottom of the image, in white type on a black strip. The words are a declaratory sentence. They are accusatory. "Surveillance" is associated with spying, sneakiness, furtiveness, unwholesome activities. "Busywork" is not something we want to be accused of doing—we have more important things to do with our lives. Someone is being accused by someone of something, and there is an urgency about the image.

"Surveillance" and Original Context

Barbara Kruger was 38 and living in New York in her Tribeca loft when she made the "Surveillance" image. She was born in Newark, New Jersey, in 1945, into a lower-middle-class, Jewish family. Her father was the first Jew hired by Shell Oil in Union, New Jersey, and the family was harassed by anti-Semitic phone calls during the year he was hired. She grew up in a black neighborhood, graduated from a competitive high school, and attended Syracuse University, where she was a straight-A student. She returned home after her freshman year when her father died and enrolled in Parsons School of Design in New York, where she had classes with Diane Arbus ("the first female role model I had who didn't wash floors 20 times a day"[12]). She also studied with Marvin Israel, an art director and designer who became her mentor. She lost interest in school after a year and began working for *Mademoiselle* magazine as a graphic designer and became its chief designer after a year. She began making fine art in 1969, quit *Mademoiselle,* but continued to work for Condé Nast publications as a designer on a freelance basis.

In the mid-1970s Kruger joined a group called Artists Meeting for Cultural Change and with the group read and discussed social and cultural theory by Walter Benjamin, Roland Barthes, Theodor Adorno, and other social critics of leftist ideologies. She socialized with a group of artists, including David Salle, Ross Bleckner, Eric Fischl, Ericka Bleckman, Barbara Bloom, and Mat Mullican. Marcia Tucker included Kruger's art, which were then stitched decorative wall pieces, in the Whitney Biennial exhibition in 1973. Kruger began writing poetry and had her first poetry reading in 1974. She could have carved out a niche as a painter but was more intrigued and challenged by her writing than her art making.[13]

Kruger began photographing and combining her writings with her photographs around 1975. She eventually winnowed her texts to short phrases or a single word on top of a single photograph; for example, over a picture of a woman with folded hands, wearing a pristine wool sweater, she placed the word *perfect* (1980). She also stopped making her own photographs and instead selected photographs from magazines and cropped and enlarged them. Most of the photographs she selects are posed or set up: "She does not work with snapshots, in which the camera itself suspends animation, but with studio shots, in which it records an animation performed only to be suspended."[14]

Kruger begins a set of new work with a "demi-narrative" in mind and selects photographs that might work with it. Once she has chosen her pictures she writes several different phrases, working from her notes, books, or a thesaurus. Writing the phrases and making them work in richly meaningful ways with the photographs is the hardest part for her. She plays with the words and pictures, relying on her experience and skill as a graphic designer. She crops, enlarges, and alters the contrast of the photographs in photostats and has the phrases set in different type sizes. After arranging a total image to her satisfaction, she sends it to a photo studio for enlarging and final printing. Her images are finally framed in bright red metal.[15]

In 1983 Kruger was again selected to participate in the Whitney Biennial and showed works similar to *Untitled* ("Surveillance is your busywork"), 1983. *Untitled*, 1981, for example, shows six men in tuxedos, with boutonnieres, laughing, as they pull at another man in a tuxedo. He appears to be laughing too. Where they are cannot be determined definitely, but it is probably a wedding reception, and he is probably the groom. "You construct intricate rituals which allow you to touch the skin of other men" is pasted over the photograph and to the right, in alternating white on black, and black on white segments, at slight diagonals.

A different *Untitled*, 1983, shows a short, clear glass with water, probably, and ten small pills on a cloth-covered surface, brightly lit from the above right corner. "You kill time" is printed over it, white letters on black strips.

A different *Untitled*, 1981, shows a baby's hand reaching for the finger of an adult hand. The photograph is contrasty, with an evident dot pattern, and starkly lit from the front. It is a close-up. The background is black. "Your every wish" is in small black type over the hands; "is our command" is in larger type at the bottom of the image. Still another *Untitled*, 1981, shows the familiar image of a mushroom cloud after the detonation of an atomic bomb. "Your manias become science" is emblazoned across it. "Your" and "science" are black on white and larger than "manias become," which are white on black. The succinctness of the phrase, and the black and white pattern, are reminiscent of a blinking neon sign. We can read it as "your science / manias become" or "manias become / your science" as well as "your manias / become science."

Thus, on the basis of these other images done by Kruger around the same time as "Surveillance," we know that it is not an abnormality, not an idiosyncratic image, but part of a larger, consistent body of work. The other images inform this one and vice versa. They all bear the same typeface, in strips. But the photographic images are different from one another and not cohesive. She has images of an atomic explosion, an adult's hand and a baby's hand, a wedding reception, and a glass of water and pills. The photograph of the mushroom cloud is an image embedded in public consciousness. All the photographs Kruger uses are somehow familiar. They are "appropriated" images, taken from mass culture. In pieces done in the mid-1980s after "Surveillance," she uses the technique of plastic lenticular double images usually associated with kitsch religious icons. In these, one image is visible from one angle and another appears as the viewers shift the pieces or their angle of view. Kruger's images are similar to the "rephotographs" of Walker Evans's work by Sherrie Levine and to Richard Prince's rephotographs of magazine ads. Kruger is working in the 1980s and 1990s, when postmodernist practice abounds, when many artists are using other images rather than making all images anew. Postmodernism questions the possibility and desirability of originality in art.

Kruger is very familiar with mass media images. She says: "I grew up looking not at art but at pictures. I'm not saying it's wrong to read art-history books. But the spectators who view my work don't have to understand that language. They just have to consider the pictures that bombard their lives and tell them who they are to some extent. That's *all* they have to understand."[16]

The phrases she writes, like the photographs she selects, also have a familiar ring to them (see Color Plate 30). They sound like advertising, but they are more terse and biting. Kruger says her work is "a series of attempts to ruin certain representations" in language and images by her use of photographs and text. She wants her work to expose and condemn stereotypes and clichés in advertising and throughout culture. Postmodernist practice is politically motivated. The phrase "your manias become science" over the image of the mushroom cloud is overtly political, resonant with controversial social issues in the 1980s concerning atomic energy, nuclear warfare, and global nuclear disarmament. In the 1980s many women artists became feminist in their ideologies and their art making. Barbara Kruger is known by her contemporaries as a feminist artist, and she acknowledges that she is a feminist, but she does not want to be tied to one feminist camp, saying that "there are a multiplicity of readings of what constitutes feminism."[17]

For an installation at the Mary Boone Gallery in New York City in 1994, Kruger used the floors, walls, and ceilings of the space to install large images and texts on the walls and bronze plaques in the floor. Stereo speakers filled the space with blaring sounds of voices delivering political and religious diatribes punctuated intermittently with cheers and sounds of anguish. The overbearing texts proclaimed, "Think like us," "Believe like us," "Pray like us," and in the window well of a skylight in the ceiling, "My God is better than your God." Another text declares:

> I slap you because it makes me feel good. I punch you because you deserve it. I burn you because you don't give me enough money. I mutilate you so you won't feel any pleasure. I want you to have my babies, because it shows how powerful and manly I am, and you want to do it because that is all you're good for.

If we interpret the images as political and feminist, they become sharper. The wedding-groom photograph, and the "you" in the phrase "you construct intricate rituals which allow you to touch the skin of other men," might now be read as an accusation by a feminist woman against men. Given that men are pictured, that they are in a ritual, and that men frequently exhibit fear of closeness with other men, it makes sense to interpret the image as accusing men. It is men, too, who have control of science and are responsible for inventing and using the atomic bomb. Probably it is they who are accused in the phrase "your manias become science" over the picture of the mushroom cloud. The "you" in the image of the pills and water with the phrase "you kill time" may be referring to women who kill time with sedating drugs, or the "you" may be addressing the pharmaceutical companies who make them, or the doctors, often male, who prescribe them for women, keeping women in a controlled state and contented by means of chemical sedation rather than through meaningful work. The 1994 installation is more overt in its expression of anger toward men, religions dominated by men which suppress women, and cultural practices which support the mutilation of women.

Kruger intentionally uses her pronouns in slippery ways: "With the question of You I say there is no You; that it shifts according to the viewer; that I'm interested in making an active spectator who can decline that You or accept it or say, It's not me but I know who it is."[18] When she lectures about her work, she is often asked what certain pieces mean, but she answers those questions of meaning generally and vaguely, placing the interpretive responsibility on the viewer. "Whenever they ask what a work means, I say that the construction of meaning shifts. And it shifts according to each spectator." She does admit, however, that she is "welcoming a female spectator into an audience of men." She also freely admits her desire for social change: "I want to make statements that are negative about the culture we're in," but she wants her images to be attractive "or else people will not look at them."[19] The changes she hopes for are toward "pleasure and tolerance."[20]

"Surveillance" and External Context

Barbara Kruger has placed her images in several different presentational environments and is acutely aware of the effect of external contexts on her work. She most often places her work in artworld situations, usually presenting them in galleries as fine art, under glass, in red metal frames, with expensive price tags. But she has also made works for marquees in subways in New York and electric signage for Times Square in Manhattan. In the winter of 1987 she placed eighty copies of a photograph, a pigtailed little girl looking admiringly at a boy's muscle, with the text "We don't need another hero," on billboards throughout England, Ireland, and Scotland. She saturated Las Vegas with fifty prominent billboards of twelve images. In 1985 she had "Surveillance is your busywork" enlarged for a billboard and displayed it in Minneapolis. "Your manias become science" has been reduced and printed on matchbook covers. Sometimes she uses newspaper ads to deliver her messages, and several of her images are available as postcards; other images are printed on T-shirts and sold in boutiques and department stores.

About the various means she uses to distribute her work, Kruger says: "The more visible I become in the artworld, the easier it is for me to place images outside the artworld in secular sites." She adds: "Why just do one thing? . . . Why just do posters? Or why just blow up pictures and put them in red frames for galleries? Why not do posters, do billboards, do the galleries?"[21]

Kruger sometimes targets very specific populations for her messages, and when she does, she may make significant changes to an existing piece. She has displayed "Your manias become science," for instance, in subways, and translated the phrase into Spanish. When she did, she changed the pronoun so that in Spanish "Your manias become science" reads as "*their* manias become science." This switch is an important clue to the meaning of this piece and her others. It is not Hispanics riding the subways of New York who possess the science and technology to militarily dominate the world. The Hispanic reader is addressed by the piece, but clearly it is not the Hispanic reader who is being accused.

The question of who is addressed and accused by her statements, particularly by her pronouns, is an essential question in viewing her work. Lynn Zelevansky writes in *Artnews* that "the voice generally seems to belong to a woman commenting bitterly on a male-dominated society."[22] About Kruger's use of language, Carol Squiers writes in *Artnews:* "The words strike out at you . . . provoking a variety of visceral responses—fear, disgust, denial. But the question remains, are you the victim or the victimizer? The position of the viewer remains ambiguous, shifting between gender roles and power positions, alternately active and passive, receptive and rejecting."[23] Craig Owens, writing in *Art in America,* agrees: Her particular uses of pronouns force the viewer "to shift uncomfortably between inclusion and exclusion."[24]

As an artist, Kruger has chosen to display her work in several different external contexts, but other people have also made choices about where her work belongs and have placed it in presentational environments of their choosing. Knowledge of some of these external contexts adds to our understanding of her work because by knowing these, we gain information about how others in the art world understand her work and how they situate it for the public and thus influence how it is understood by those who see it. Annina Nosei showed Kruger in 1981 in a group show titled "Public Address" with Jenny Holzer, Mike Glier, and Keith Haring. Hal Foster chose to unite and compare Jenny Holzer and Barbara Kruger in a feature article for *Art in America.*[25] He understands both artists to be addressing concerns about mass media and the art world through uses of language. Of both of them he says their "images are as likely to derive from the media as from art history, and whose context is as likely to be a street wall as an exhibition space." He sees both artists using language as a target and as a weapon. Both are "manipulators of signs more than makers of art objects—a shift in practice that renders the viewer an active reader of messages more than a contemplator of the esthetic."

Le Anne Schreiber writes in *Vogue:* "Kruger has been building a reputation as a sharp-edged, sharp-tongued, critic of the consumer society." Once a graphic designer, "she now uses her skills to unmask the hidden persuaders rather than to assist them."[26] Schreiber adds that Kruger "is the sworn enemy of cliché and stereotype, of those culturally reinforced images that tell us who we are and what we want." Lynn Zelevansky adds that "Kruger is one of a number of artists who quote commercial art, an inversion of the traditional relationship in which advertising utilizes the conventions and imagery of fine art because such connoisseurship denotes wealth, sophistication and intelligence."[27]

In an *Artforum* review of a 1984 show Kruger had at Annina Nosei Gallery, critic Jean Fisher contextually places Kruger's work in an area already mapped out by such artists as John Baldessari, Hans Haacke, and Victor Burgin, who were working in the 1970s with the relationship between word and photographic image. Fisher credits Kruger with adding feminist concerns, specifically concerns about inequitable divisions of labor according to gender.[28] In an *Artnews* review of another Annina Nosei Gallery exhibition two years later, John Sturman writes that "Kruger has become one of the leading feminist exponents of a form of contemporary photography that is grounded in the principles of mass communication and advertising."[29]

Fisher claims that Kruger's use of boldface type over images is reminiscent of design rooted in Russian constructivism and that her use of red frames reinforces the connection and suggests that the work is in the tradition of socialist propaganda.[30] Anne Hoy also thinks Kruger's style uses "the devices of Socialist propaganda to counter what she considers capitalist ideology, one agitprop against another," and that it evokes the photo collages John Heartfield made for the Communist workers' paper *AIZ* in the 1920s and the Soviet posters of the twenties and thirties.[31]

Two critics specifically mention Kruger's adroit use of humor. Shaun Caley writes in *Flash Arts*: "The pleasure of Kruger's text is the joy of the one-liner social commentary that throws the carnivalesque into perspective and capitalizes with a just amount of cynicism on the game of exploitation."[32] Carol Squiers thinks that Kruger's humor is dark humor: "Although Kruger's work is always leavened by and sometimes dependent on humor for its punch, it is usually humor of the blackly corrosive variety."[33]

Kruger was included in an exhibition titled "Playing It Again: Strategies of Appropriation" in 1985 along with several other artists who use images from the mass media to critique the daily onslaught of images created by those who control film, television, newspapers, and advertising. Her work was also selected for Documenta 8 in Kassel, West Germany, in 1987, by curators who wished to rescue all art from mere self-involvement: "Neo-Expressionism was about the relation of the artist to himself. Documenta 8 is about the relationship of art to society."[34] Documenta 8 was curated to be full of work with social themes, art which is socially engaged, and Kruger's work is seen by the curators to be an important exemplar of such socially engaged art. Anne Hoy includes Kruger in her book *Fabrications:*

Staged, Altered, and Appropriated Photographs, situating Kruger in the section "Appropriated Images and Words" along with such artists as Sherrie Levine, Richard Prince, Vikky Alexander, Sarah Charlesworth, and Victor Burgin. About these artists Hoy states that "their source remains mass culture and the power structure at its core."

Hoy also states that the appropriated photographs of artists such as Kruger, Levine, and Prince have generated some of the most complex and challenging critical writing we have on photography to date. In discussing Kruger's work in *Artnews,* critic Hal Foster refers to Friedrich Nietzsche, Bertolt Brecht, Walter Benjamin, and Roland Barthes, and in a feature article about Kruger in *Art in America,* Craig Owens appeals to the ideas of Jacques Lacan, Emile Benveniste, Roman Jakobson, Barthes, Michel Foucault, and Sigmund Freud. By appealing to the work of such scholars to make Kruger's work more understandable, critics Foster and Owens place her work in a larger intellectual arena and into an external context of progressive European thought.

Since 9/11, Kruger's "Surveillance" image has been especially relevant because of the tremendous increase of surveillance measures in the United States, Great Britain, and other Western nations. Airport surveillance has increased, and threat level is color coded according to perceived degree. The number of military satellites in use has increased, and drone aircraft fly throughout the Afghanistan and Pakistan.

BARBARA KRUGER'S *UNTITLED* ("SURVEILLANCE") AND THE CATEGORIES

We will now consider how Kruger's "Surveillance" fits in the six categories—descriptive, explanatory, interpretive, ethically evaluative, aesthetically evaluative, theoretical—and in which categories it fits best on the basis of what we have learned by examining its internal, original, and external contexts.

Descriptive Photographs

Although "Surveillance" shows a man from close range, it is not like an identification photograph, a medical X-ray, or a photomicrograph. The image of the man was probably not originally made to accurately describe the man or whatever he is engaged in doing. The way Kruger uses the image is not particularly descriptive either: She coarsens the image by adding contrast to it, severely crops it, and covers part of it with the word *Surveillance.* The photograph in "Surveillance" does describe, however, as do all photographs. It describes the man, portions of his hands, and the lupe he is looking through. It describes frontally by means of harsh lighting. And Kruger's use of the photograph is in a sense descriptive: She presents to us an image in circulation in the 1950s. She calls its qualities to our attention by selecting it, cropping it, labeling it with her phrase, framing it, and distributing it. But certainly this image is much more than a value-neutral description.

Explanatory Photographs

The text that Kruger uses, "Surveillance is your busywork," is not informational. The phrase sounds neither scientific nor objective but instead emotional and angry. Even though the man in the photograph might be doing something scientific or technological, the image of his doing it, especially with the phrase, is not explanatory in nature. It does not look like a Muybridge animal-locomotion study nor like a Bill Owens *Suburbia* photograph even though both *Suburbia* and "Surveillance" use pictures of people and words. In short, the image declares and accuses rather than explains.

Interpretive Photographs

"Surveillance," like all of Kruger's images, is her interpretation of the way the world is. It represents her worldview, her individual way of encountering and reacting to and picturing her experience in the world. It is her subjective view in her personally refined and highly identifiable style. It is clearly meant to persuade us to see the world as she does, and it uses photographic and linguistic rhetoric to do so. Although "Surveillance" is subjective and interpretive, it is informed by her knowledge of and experience in the world, her knowledge of art and political theory, and makes a claim to truth. Because it is an interpretive image, it asks to be thought about and considered seriously and not to be dismissed as "just Kruger's opinion."

Ethically Evaluative Photographs

There is a strong moral tone to the language in the image and negative connotations in the photograph of the man. The photograph is not at all flattering: It is spooky, in harsh light and deep shadows. Someone is being accused by someone of doing something wrong. "Surveillance is your busywork" is an ethically evaluative statement, a moral condemnation. The words and image mesh, reinforcing the condemnation.

Given the political nature of Kruger's work and her feminism, it seems likely that this image is directed at men, particularly white men who have and exert power over other people's lives. This image asserts that they control others through surveillance. Because of the photographer's lupe and the lighting that is probably from a light table, photography is the suggested means of their surveillance.

Surveillance is not a wholesome activity. It is sneaky business, a defensive and offensive activity directed at people who are declared enemies and suspect. Surveillance is usually engaged in by the military and police agencies and by those who have a lot of money, merchandise, and property. These are usually men, privileged by race, gender, and class. This image accuses them of sneakily watching over others to protect and maintain their privilege and status.

The surveillance that Kruger is addressing might also be men's voyeuristic surveillance of women for sexual titillation and gratification. Photography is widely used for pornography, the mainstay of *Playboy, Penthouse,* and other magazines, and for print and television advertising images that often exploit women. The man in the image could be a picture editor for a magazine or an art director of an ad agency.

Aesthetically Evaluative Photographs

In "Surveillance" Kruger uses a photograph that is harshly lit, visually compact, and shot from a close range that reveals stubbles of whiskers and pores of skin. It is not an appealing photograph of appealing subject matter.

Aesthetically evaluative photographs are sometimes made to comment negatively on the lack of aesthetic appeal in the world. This image by Kruger might in part be negatively commenting on the photograph of the man in "Surveillance" and perhaps on mass media, journalistic photography of the 1940s and 1950s. Because she so freely reproduces her work in so many different graphic formats, from matchbooks to billboards, and widely circulates them in large numbers, we can infer that the precious, one-of-a-kind, classical "fine print" is not a criterion of hers for her art. Because for her pieces she chooses photographs already existing in magazines and other sources, we can also infer that the originality of her photographic vision is not at issue. In her case it is not "the photographer's eye" that is paramount but rather the artist's mind. Most photographs that fit comfortably into the aesthetically evaluative category, such as much of the work of Edward Weston and Ansel Adams, exhibit concern for originality and fine printing and the photograph as a precious object, archivally processed, matted, framed, and under glass. Clearly Kruger, with her T-shirts and subway signs, is not concerned with such issues. In short, "Surveillance" does not fit well within this category, and this category does not inform us much about this image except to help us determine what the image is not about.

Theoretical Photographs

All images are about other images in the sense that images emerge from within a tradition. "Surveillance," like all postmodern images, is more directly about other

images. It quotes another image, appropriates it, and then transforms it by cropping, adding contrast, reproducing it, and especially by adding text. "Surveillance"
includes a photograph of an older photograph made by a photographer, probably
anonymous, other than Kruger. Kruger's "Surveillance" is about representations
generally and about photographs. Her use of others' photographs asserts again the
postmodern belief that there are enough images in circulation already and that
these need commentary. Kruger comments particularly on nonart images drawn
from popular media.

"Surveillance" also comments negatively on the use of photography as a means
of surveillance. By using the photograph of the man with the photographer's lupe,
Kruger, along with others, targets photography as a means of control, intimidation,
domination, and voyeurism.[35] The world is spied upon by satellites with cameras;
mug shots document criminals; suspected subversives in Third World countries are
surreptitiously photographed and their pictures filed for future reference; people
in protest groups in street demonstrations are frequently photographed by police
agencies; cameras patrol the aisles of department stores and the lobbies of banks;
and when we write a check in a department store, we are likely to be photographed
before the check is accepted. "Surveillance" connotes these practices.

THE INTERPRETIVE PROCESS: A SUMMARY

The process of interpreting photographs is complex, and there is no one way critics use to arrive at their understandings of images. In Chapter 3, for example, several general approaches or perspectives toward interpretation were mentioned with
examples quoted from critics: psychoanalytic, formalist, semiotic, feminist, Marxist, stylistic, biographical, intentionalist, and technical. Each of these approaches
has advantages and limitations. This list is not exhaustive, and some critics combine these approaches. Each of them could be tried to see how they fit an image
or how comfortably they fit the critic. What is most important to remember is that
interpreting a photograph is a matter of building a reasonable understanding based
on demonstrable evidence. Sound interpretations are not willy-nilly responses,
nor are they dogmatic pronouncements. They are reasonable arguments built by
critics, and they are always open to revision. Some interpretations are better than
others because they better fit the photograph, offer greater insight, and are more
compelling. Because there are so many critics with so many worldviews and ideological persuasions, there will be multiple interpretations that are reasonable and
compelling, even though different. Our lives are enriched by diverse interpretations of the same photograph.

In Chapter 4, we considered photographs according to the categories of descriptive, explanatory, interpretive, ethically evaluative, aesthetically evaluative, and

theoretical. These categories were introduced to emphasize that not all photographs are made as art nor presented as art and should not be interpreted solely as aesthetic objects. The categories are also a means of interpretation: If we use the categories, we have to consider how a photograph is functioning and what it is about. Placing a photograph in one or more categories demands that we interpret the photograph, not merely label it.

In this chapter, we have seen the importance of considering contexts—internal, original, and external—by using the example of the Doisneau photograph and its various placements and uses and misuses. These three contextual sources of information have been used to consider an image by Barbara Kruger; and based on the information gathered from these contexts, her "Surveillance" image was placed in each of the categories to further determine how it functions and what it might mean. The interpretive, ethically evaluative, and theoretical categories are the most helpful in understanding "Surveillance." The consideration of external and original contexts requires that we look beyond what is shown in the photograph. These contexts also reinforce the principle that interpretation is both a personal and a communal endeavor: It is usually possible and always wise to consider the views of other knowledgeable people when putting forth our own interpretations. Ultimately, it is a community of people knowledgeable about art and photography who formulate the meanings of images. In the short term, a critic is often the first one to formulate a meaning about an image, but in the long run, interpretation is a collective endeavor that includes the thoughts of a variety of people working from within a diverse range of perspectives.

The following list distills the material in this chapter and the two preceding chapters into several succinct principles for interpreting photographs. They are meant to be open ended and nondogmatic. Use them as reminders and guides for assessing extant interpretations and for offering new interpretations.

- All images require interpretation.
- SUBJECT MATTER + MEDIUM + FORM + CONTEXTS = MEANINGS.
- Images attract multiple interpretations, and it is not the goal of interpretation to arrive at single, exclusive meanings.
- Interpretations are persuasive arguments.
- Photographs are cultural rather than natural.
- Photographs should be seen as opinions.
- Photographs carry more credibility than other kinds of images and especially require interpretation.
- Photographs and photographers alter what they picture.
- To interpret an image is to respond to it in language.
- Feelings are guides to interpretations.
- People tend to look *through* photographs as reality rather than at photographs as social constructs.

- Photographs are made from light reflecting off of people, places, and objects in the world and thus have causal connections to what they show.
- Photographs are factual and fictional, factual and metaphorical.
- Photography is a subtractive medium, and the subject matter of a photograph is always cut from a larger context.
- Photographs are discrete instances excised from continuous time.
- Language accompanying a photograph can overdetermine the photograph's meaning.
- Photographs acquire meanings by how they are used.
- The critical activities of describing, interpreting, judging, and theorizing about photographs are interrelated and interdependent.
- Judgments of an image preclude alternate interpretations of that image.
- All images are in part about the cultures in which they emerge.
- All images are in part about other images.
- Interpretations imply the worldviews of interpreters.
- An interpretation ought to tell more about the image than about the interpreter.
- Any image will allow a limited range of interpretations.
- Meanings of images are not limited to what their makers meant them to mean.
- Interpretations are not so much *right* as they are more or less reasonable, convincing, informative, and enlightening.
- Some interpretations are better than others, and some are simply wrong.
- The objects of interpretations are images, not image makers.
- Interpretations can be assessed by their internal coherence, their correspondence to evidence, and their completeness.
- Interpretation is an endeavor that should be both individual and communal.
- The admissibility of an interpretation is determined by a community of interpreters and the community is self-correcting.
- Good interpretations invite us to see for ourselves and to think on our own.

Judging Photographs

Is It Good?

When critics criticize photographs, they sometimes but not always judge them. Contrary to popular belief, *criticism* and *judgment* are not synonymous terms. When critics do judge photographs, they usually praise them and sometimes fault them. Evaluation is different from interpretation. Judgments are statements about the worth or value of an image whereas interpretations are statements about the meaning of an artwork. How we interpret an image will influence our judgment of it, and how we judge it may influence what we think the image means. Both interpretations and judgments depend on description: factual statements about what is being interpreted or judged. If a critic inaccurately describes something, then the critic's interpretation or judgment is suspect.

To judge an image is to ask and answer questions such as these:

Is this a successful or unsuccessful image, and by what criterion?
By what criterion does this photograph seem to want to be judged?
By what criterion will I judge this image?
What reasons support a positive, negative, or mixed judgment?
Does the photograph's form and presentation support its intended meaning?
Is the photograph's aesthetic value sufficient, or must it also meet social criteria?
If it seeks to influence social change, is it effective?
Does it unwittingly or intentionally cause social harm?

There are also different kinds of judgmental foci, for example:

How might I help someone else appreciate this photograph?
If I do not think this a good photograph, why might others think it is good?
Is this photograph better than that photograph?
Is this the best photograph in the photographer's portfolio?
Is this a good use of photography?
How does this photograph compare with similar images in other media?
Is this photograph the best in the group exhibition?
Is the idea of an exhibition itself a worthy idea?
Is the theme of the show successfully realized through curatorial choices?

The judgmental statements that follow have been selected from published criticism, but without the context of the critics' fuller arguments in support of their judgments. Judgments, in their fullest sense, like interpretations, are persuasive arguments, and more than single declarative statements.

EXAMPLES OF JUDGMENTAL STATEMENTS

Positive Judgments

"Larry Fink, whose photographs typically involve the keen observation of small-scale social interactions, goes large with a series shot for *Vanity Fair* during the final months of the Hillary Clinton and Barack Obama primary campaigns [Plate 31]. His results include a number of very good images of the candidates in action and even more interesting behind-the-scenes views of the people drawn into their orbit, including staffers, Secret Service personnel, and fellow-citizens. Still, star power is hard to resist, and, in the best picture here, Obama gestures gracefully but forcefully at the edge of a roiling crowd, his poise thrown into relief by the frenzy." (*The New Yorker*)[1]

Positive judgments of photographs are frequent and easy to find when reading professional criticism. Examples follow.

"Henri Cartier-Bresson's fame is based on four decades of incomparable camera reporting . . . his genius lay in his recognition that unretouched reality was already tractable enough, that the world was most intoxicating when served straight up." (Richard Lacayo, *Time*)[2]

Cindy Sherman "is the first artist working in the photographic medium to have fully infiltrated the 'other' art world of painting and sculpture. . . . She has accomplished what other photographers have been pursuing for a century—true parity with the other two arts." (Lisa Phillips, *Cindy Sherman*)[3]

"The power of Lorna Simpson's work is founded on her ability to place powerful words and powerful pictures in the same ring and make their battle

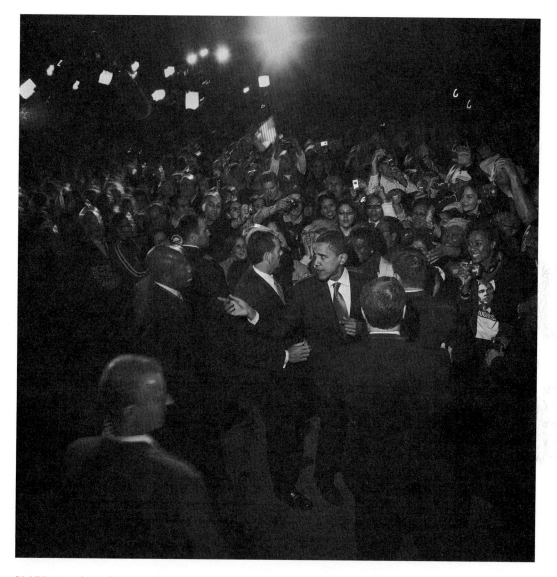

PLATE 31.   Larry Fink, the Obama campaign for *Vanity Fair* magazine, 2008.
© Larry Fink.

cooperative to her ends." (Rod Slemmons, Museum of Contemporary Photography, Columbia College, Chicago)[4]

"Using unerring tact and impeccable focus, Sarah Charlesworth sums up a generation's concerns with a whisper." (Kate Linker, *Art in America*)[5]

"This exhibition suggests that Martin Parr looks at people of all types as they are, doing what they believe is the best they can. What he captures is simultaneously touching and funny." (Janet Kopolos, *Art in America*)[6]

Negative Judgments

Judgments that disapprove of works are less frequent in published criticism than one might think. The following statements are examples of negative judgments.

"Richard Avedon's *In the American West* is 'fashion, not art.'" (Susan Weiley, *Artnews*)[7]

"Robert Heinecken has consistently failed to embody his concerns in anything but superficial ways." (Jonathan Green, *American Photography*)[8]

"Fully clothed or not, the women in Winogrand's photographs are victims of an obscene attention." (Arthur Danto, *Mapplethorpe*)[9]

Implied Judgments

Often critics suggest or imply judgments without coming right out and making an explicit positive or negative judgment. We infer their judgmental stances from the context of the entire piece of writing, particularly its general tone.

"Joel-Peter Witkin continues his work in the field of severed limbs and third nipples." (*New Yorker*)[10]

"Eugene Richard's record of his wife's fight with and death from breast cancer and his chronicles of inner-city drug users are harrowing and extraordinarily frank." (*New Yorker*)[11]

"The *Family of Man* universalizes the bourgeois nuclear family, suggesting a globalized, utopian family album, a family romance imposed on every corner of the earth." (Allan Sekula, *Photography Against the Grain*)[12]

Opposing Judgments

Critics frequently disagree with one another's positions on individual photographs, exhibitions, and individual oeuvres. Sometimes different critics may agree in their assessments, but for different reasons. Critics may use different sets of criteria for the same work and come to conclusions that match or contradict. Even using the same set of criteria, critics' appraisals may differ.

Diane Arbus is "one of the most remarkable photographic artists of the last decade." And she is "as rare in the annals of photography as in the history of any other medium—who suddenly, by a daring leap into a territory formerly regarded as forbidden, altered the term of the art she practiced." (Hilton Kramer, *New York Times Magazine*)[13]

Arbus's work "shows people who are pathetic, pitiable, as well as repulsive, but it does not arouse any compassionate feelings. . . . The insistent sameness of Arbus's work, however far she ranges from her prototypical subjects, shows that her sensibility, armed with a camera, could insinuate anguish, kinkiness, mental illness with any subject." (Susan Sontag, *On Photography*)[14]

Irving Penn is "a major talent, by most if not all standards, and at least arguably a genius, a maker of some of the most awesomely handsome photographs in the history of the medium." In Penn's photographs, "there is more pure sensual pleasure per square inch than can be found in the work of any other living photographer" and "anyone fortunate enough to see [his photographs] will find among them the most beautiful physical entities photography can produce." (Owen Edwards, *Saturday Review*)[15]

Irving Penn's "imperial eye can turn African villagers into caricatures and, when he transforms a motorcyclist from the Hell's Angels into a delicate study in gray, the eye is seduced—but the mind gags." (Mark Stevens, *Newsweek*)[16]

Comparative Judgments

Some judgments, but not all, are comparative. For example, when Lacayo calls Cartier-Bresson's photographs "incomparable," he has judged them against all other photographs. When Kramer writes that Arbus is "one of the most remarkable photographic artists of the last decade," he is comparing her favorably to all other photographers working in the 1960s.

JUDGMENTS AND REASONS

A judgment is a *what* that demands a *why*. Judgments, like interpretations, depend on reasons. Judgments without reasons are not particularly beneficial. To declare something "good" or "bad," "original" or "remarkable," without giving reasons as to why it is thought to be so is merely to offer a conclusion, and however well founded or thought out that conclusion might be, it is not very revealing or helpful if the reasons behind it are not offered in its support. The positive and negative conclusions about the work of various photographers previously cited have been quoted without the reasons the critics offered to support their judgments. But the critics who wrote them do have reasons, some of which follow.

When Hilton Kramer declared Diane Arbus to be "one of the most remarkable photographic artists," he offered several reasons, one of which was that Arbus invited her subjects to participate in her photographs and thus they "face the camera with patience and interest and dignity; they are never merely 'objects.'" Robert Hughes also provides several reasons supporting his admiration of Arbus's photographs: Her work is "very moving," and "Arbus did what hardly seemed possible for a still photographer. She altered our experience of the face."

Nevertheless, there is serious disagreement on Arbus's work. In a review of the same exhibition that Kramer and Hughes praise, Amy Goldin in *Art in America* specifically derides their views and claims that "for us her people are all losers, whether they know it or not. . . . Her subjects must not seem to feel too much, lest they destroy the delicate superiority we gain from knowing more of their vulnerability than they do. Nor can they be heroic; we must admire ourselves for respecting them."[17] Susan Sontag is also especially negative about Arbus's work and devotes a whole chapter to it in her book *On Photography*. Sontag argues that Arbus makes everyone look the same—that is, monstrous—and that she takes advantage of their vulnerability and their compliance, "suggesting a world in which everyone is an alien, hopelessly isolated, immobilized in mechanical, crippled identities and relationships."

In supporting Cindy Sherman's work (see Plate 4, Color Plate 1), Lisa Phillips argues that Sherman's use of photography for her content is an apt match: "To Sherman the secondary status of photography in the art world forms a perfect corollary to the status of women in a patriarchal society, and she uses each situation to question our assumptions of the other."[18] Deborah Drier also admires most of Sherman's work but expresses reservations about two pieces in Sherman's 1985 exhibition at Metro Pictures gallery in New York: "the bearded lady is saved from cliché only by the evidence of her wretchedness and the disgust engendered by the most horrid orifices erupting near her eye, and I could have lived without the girl-into-Miss Piggy trick."[19] In an introductory catalogue statement, the work of Robert Heinecken is praised because it "simultaneously questions and expands our notion of 'what is a photograph.'" But Jonathan Green rejects the work as "simplistic" and claims that in deviating from straight photography "Heinecken lost his way in a maze of pictorial alternatives."[20]

In important respects, critical judgments or evaluations are similar to interpretations or explanations. Both are statements that need reasons in their support; both are arguments that require evidence. Judgments without reasons are similar to opinion polls: They tell us that some people hold a certain position, but they fail to reveal why. If we are given reasons for judgments, we are better able to agree or disagree with them and thus further our own thought, discussion, and knowledge about photographs and deepen our understanding and appreciation of them.

Also, like interpretations, judgments are neither definitively nor absolutely right or wrong. Rather, judgments, like interpretations, are more or less convincing, persuasive, and compelling, depending on how well or poorly they are argued.

JUDGMENTS AND CRITERIA

Complete and explicit critical judgments have three aspects: *appraisals* that are based on *reasons* that are founded in *criteria*. Hilton Kramer's statement that Arbus is "one of the most remarkable photographic artists of the last decade" is an appraisal. Statements of appraisals are about the merits of the work being judged, that it is "remarkable," "strong" or "weak," "good" or "lacking." Reasons are statements that support an appraisal. One of the reasons Kramer provides for his positive appraisal of Arbus's work is that she gave her subjects dignity and never reduced them to objects.

Criteria are rules or standards for greatness upon which appraisals are ultimately based. One of Kramer's criteria for judging Arbus's work to be extraordinary is that it changed the history of the medium: She effected "a historic change in the way a new generation of photographers came to regard the very character of their medium."[21] In other words, Kramer is arguing that an artist is great if, among other things, her work positively affects the work of those around her and after her; Arbus's work has done this, and therefore her work is great.

Critics do not always, however, provide arguments for their judgments. Evaluations, particularly positive evaluations, are sometimes assumed to be obvious and not explicitly argued for. In a review in *Newsweek* of an exhibition by Henri Cartier-Bresson, Douglas Davis expends little effort defending the greatness of Cartier-Bresson's work.[22] He assumes that we are willing to accept its greatness and writes to give us more information about the man and his work. But he clearly implies positive evaluations throughout the review by using such phrases as "the king of photographers," "the master," and "his magnificent pictures."

Criteria are usually based in definitions of art and in aesthetic theories of what art should be. In published and casual art criticism, it is easy to find statements of appraisal. In casual art criticism, appraisals are abundant but reasons are rare and criteria rarer still. In published art criticism, reasons are usually offered but criteria can be difficult to locate. Sometimes they are hinted at or suggested, but it is not often that critics explicitly state their criteria. It is easier to find clear, though often complex, criteria in the writings of aestheticians, artists, and critics attempting to define what art is or what art should be. More often than not, in published criticism, criteria are implied.

In a *New York Times* review of a 1985 exhibition of then new work by Duane Michals, critic Gene Thornton offers clear judgments of Michals's photographs. Thornton opens his review by claiming that the work Michals exhibited was "as strong and moving as anything he has ever done."[23] Thornton was especially impressed with a sequence titled *Christ in New York*. Reasons for his praise of Michals's work and this sequence in particular come later in the review. Thornton explains that picturing Christ as a contemporary person is difficult and that Michals has done it convincingly, so much so that his visualization is the "most convincing one" Thornton knows. Thornton also praises Michals for his lyrical use of words accompanying his photographs. But Thornton's major reason for lauding Michals's work and especially his sequences is the quality of Michals's ideas: "Each was the visualization of a good idea, and good ideas are few and far between, especially good ideas that can be expressed in pictures." Thornton's review, then, offers clear statements of appraisal, that Michals is very good at what he does, and reasons for the appraisal—namely, that he works with difficult subjects convincingly, that his use of text is effectively poetic, and especially that his photographs are based on good ideas. Thornton never explicitly states criteria for his positive judgments of the work, but an implied criterion is that for a photograph to be effective it needs to be based on a good idea. As a critic writing an evaluative review, Thornton has done his job. He has provided clear judgments and has supported them with reasons based on implied and discernible criteria.

DIFFERENT CRITERIA

Critics judge photographs by many different criteria, most of which can be grouped into clusters derived from common theories of art: realism, expressionism, formalism, and activism.

Realism

Realism is one of the oldest theories of art, upheld by the ancient Greeks, backed by the authority of Plato and Aristotle, rejuvenated in the Renaissance, and upheld later throughout the history of photography. In aesthetics, realism is also referred to as "mimesis" and "mimeticism." In his exhibition and accompanying book *Mirrors and Windows,* John Szarkowski contrasts the realist tradition ("windows") in art and photography with the expressionist tradition ("mirrors"). He states that the basic premise of realism is that "the world exists independent of human attention, that it contains discoverable patterns of intrinsic meaning, and that by discerning these patterns, and forming models or symbols of them with the materials of his art, the realist is joined to a larger intelligence."[24] For the realist, because the world is the standard of truth, and because it is incomparably beautiful, the most noble goal of the artist is to attempt to accurately portray the universe in all its variations.

Paul Strand and Edward Weston are two historically prominent photographers who advocated realism in photography. Strand believed that the photographer ought to have "a real respect for the thing in front of him"—namely, reality—and that "the very essence" of photography is an "absolute unqualified objectivity."[25] Weston agreed: "The camera should be used for the recording of *life,* for rendering the very substance and quintessence of the *thing itself,* whether it be polished steel or palpitating flesh. . . . I feel definite in my belief that the approach to photography is through realism."[26]

Life magazine reaffirmed the primacy of realism in photography throughout its long and influential history. Henry R. Luce, founder and publisher, introduced the first issue of *Life* (November 23, 1936) with this statement:

> To see life; to see the world, to eyewitness great events; to watch the face
> of the poor and the gestures of the proud; to see strange things—machines,

armies, multitudes, shadows in the jungle and on the moon; to see man's work—his paintings, towers and discoveries, to see things thousands of miles away, things hidden behind walls and within rooms, things dangerous to come to; the women that men love and many children; to see and be instructed.

Realism is also upheld as a criterion by contemporary thinkers. In *The Photographer's Eye,* Szarkowski writes: "The first thing that the photographer learned was that photography dealt with the actual; he had not only to accept this fact, but to treasure it; unless he did photography would defeat him."[27]

Based on realist criteria, Charles Hagen judged a 1992 exhibition of nude photographs made by Lee Friedlander "challenging and ultimately thrilling" and "breathtaking in their acceptance of the facts of the scene." According to Hagen, Friedlander rejects idealized notions of women and instead concentrates on specificity: "body hair, bruises, dirty feet and sagging flesh in sometimes excruciating detail." Friedlander's "matter-of-fact nudes" are "intensely photographic, deeply voyeuristic in a way that only photography can allow." The exhibition is the last one curated by John Szarkowski before his retirement as curator of photography at the Museum of Modern Art in New York City, and Hagen acknowledges that the show affirms Szarkowski's criterion that photography should be "a means of discovery, of proposing new ways to see the world."[28]

Hilton Kramer summarizes realistic criteria in this statement:

> What we admire in the great modern photographers is, more often than not, the quick pictorial eye that wrests from this heterogeneous public scene an arresting conjunction of detail. . . . It is essential that the subject be "caught" from the outside, trapped, so to speak, in a given instant that can never be repeated. In that unrepeatable point in time, the photographer composes his picture, the quickness of his eye and the lightning sensitivity of his emotions joined in the flash of the shutter, and from that moment the reality of the subject inheres in the composition, for it can no longer be said to exist "out there."[29]

Traditional photographic realists also advocate certain techniques as proper and reject others. Realism is closely associated with "straight photography," some of the principles of which Sadakichi Hartmann articulated in 1904:

> Rely on your camera, your eye, on your good taste and your knowledge of composition, consider every fluctuation of color, light and shade, study lines and values and space division, patiently wait until the scene or object of your pictured vision reveals itself in its supremest moment of beauty.[30]

Both Strand and Weston advocated realistic criteria and the straight approach in making photographs. Strand held that the photographer should express reality "through a range of almost infinite tonal values which lie beyond the skill of human hand . . . without tricks of process or manipulation [and] through the use of straight photographic methods."[31] Weston derided photographs that relied on soft focus (what he called "dizzying out of focus blurs"), textured printing screens and papers, and handworked photographs as "photo-paintings" and "pseudo-paintings."[32] Minor White and Ansel Adams continued the straight, realistic tradition in photography they inherited from Strand and Weston. White wrote: "I have heard Edward Weston say that he strove to eliminate all accidents from his work and I copied his striving. . . . I now see like a lens focused on a piece of film, act like a negative projected on a piece of sensitized paper, talk like a picture on a wall."[33] Dorothea Lange had these words, quoted from the empirical philosopher Francis Bacon, hung on her darkroom door: "The contemplation of things as they are, without substitution or imposture, without error or confusion, is in itself a nobler thing than a whole harvest of invention."[34] Ansel Adams devised the zone system of exposure and development to enhance the abilities of the straight photographer.

Expressionism

Expressionism, or expressivism, is also time honored in photography but is not as old as realism in the history of art theory. Its basic premise is a respect for the individuality of the artist and the potency of the artist's inner life as vividly expressed in visual form. Expressionists believe the artist's intense experience is the basis of art making and that viewers should judge art according to the intensity of the feelings it provokes in them. They emphasize the artist rather than the world; and for expressionists, intensity of expression is more crucial than accuracy of representation.

The term *expressionism* is more common in the literature of art and aesthetics than in photography. The term *pictorialism,* however, is common in photography, and the pictorialist movement in photography fits within expressionistic criteria. Pictorialism preceded straight photography, which was a reaction to pictorialism. Pictorialists upheld photography to be art and strove to have it as honored as painting. In their struggle, they often mimicked the subject matter and stylistic conventions of the paintings of their day. For example, under rugged wind-twisted junipers, a guardian angel consoles a woman in *The Heart of the Storm,* circa 1912, a photograph made in California by Anne Brigman that looks like a charcoal drawing. Pictorialist images often used soft focus, textured paper, hand touching with brushes, allegorical stories, costumes, and props; and sometimes they were collaged images made from several negatives. The end was art and the means were whatever the photographer could use to attain that end. C. Jabez Hughes stated the pictorialist position in 1861:

> [The] photographer, like an artist, is at liberty to employ what means he
> thinks necessary to carry out his ideas. If a picture cannot be produced by one
> negative, let him have two or ten; but let it be clearly understood, that these

are only means to an end, and that the picture when finished must stand or fall entirely by the effects produced, and not by the means employed.[35]

Many pictorialists were particularly influenced by the paintings of Turner, Whistler, Degas, and Monet. The pictorialist tradition includes such historically influential photographers as Alvin Coburn, F. Holland Day, Frederick Evans, Gertrude Käsebier, Alfred Stieglitz, Edward Steichen, and Clarence White. Stieglitz championed the movement in *Camera Work* and Gallery 291. Pictorialism declined by the mid-1920s and was largely overtaken by the "straight" aesthetic, but interest in pictorialist aesthetics and techniques ("manipulated photographs") emerged again in the 1970s, and the tradition vigorously continues today. The Starn twins, for example, intentionally and obviously undermine the realistic look of the photographic medium, insisting on

> the material life of their medium, images on paper; for they are determined to undo the scientific look usually associated with photography's techniques of laboratory precision, cleanliness, impersonality. The fact and the illusion of accident and of the handmade are everywhere. Fragments are scotch-taped together; edges are furled and torn; black tape defaces images; photographic surfaces are crumpled or, at times, seen through the transparency of ortho film; push pins pierce ragged holes into paper and wall; frames look haphazardly chosen in shape or style.[36]

Formalism

Formalism is an aesthetic theory of the twentieth century. It is closely associated with modernism and is rejected by postmodernists. Formalism insists on the autonomy of art—that is, "art for art's sake"—and on the primacy of abstract form rather than references to the physical or social world.

Formalism is a theory of art—it should not be confused with a concern for form in art. All art, realistic and abstract, representational and nonrepresentational, has form. All artists, whether they be realists, expressionists, postmodernists, or of some other aesthetic persuasion, are concerned with form. Both straight and manipulated photographs have form. Expressionists want form that is vividly engrossing; realists strive for form that is consistent with immutable laws of nature; instrumentalists seek form that will effect social change.

The theory of formalism upholds the sovereignty of form and considers subject matter and references to religion, history, and politics aesthetically irrelevant, or "nonartistic," concerns. Art should be judged by its own criteria—that is, by whether or not it embodies "significant form." Roger Fry and Clive Bell, the originators of formalism in the 1930s, unfortunately did not, perhaps could not, specify criteria for formal excellence.[37] Their influence was in denial: Art should not be judged by its narrative content, historical references, psychological associations, emotional connotations, or imitation of objects and surfaces.

Although formalism supports abstraction, nonrepresentational imagery, and minimalist art, it is not limited to these. Representational painters such as Poussin and Cézanne are highly regarded by formalists because of their harmonious organization of trees, hills, or figures. That the subject matter happens to be fruit in a bowl or a sun-bathed hillside is not of interest. If Picasso's *Guernica,* for example, is to be honored, it is because of its superb formal organization; its references to the horror of war and the suffering of victims, for formalists, are aesthetically irrelevant.

Formalism and modernism gave rise to concern for the individuality of media, the uniqueness of a medium, and the distinct visual contributions different media could make. Straight photography came of age during the period of formalism and modernism and in turn influenced it. Edward Weston, for example, was concerned about identifying what the medium of photography did best or did uniquely and then made photographs according to these distinctions. *Group f/64,* founded in 1929 by Weston and including Ansel Adams and Imogen Cunningham, strove to make pictures that were "photographic" rather than "painterly." Thus, these photographers abhorred handwork and soft focus and championed crisp focus with a wide depth-of-field.

Formalism also influenced art criticism. Just as references in artworks to real-world concerns were considered aesthetically irrelevant, criticism that relied on history or biography or the psychology of the artist was also eschewed as aesthetically irrelevant. Context was ignored. In *Aperture,* founded in the 1950s by Minor White, photographs were presented as the sole matter on pristine white pages; information about photographer, title, date, and so forth, was put in the back of the magazine so as not to distract from the image itself. The art object itself, and only the art object, was the locus of critical attention. Formal description of the object itself, in painstaking detail, became paramount in art criticism.

Activism

"It was never our intention to curate an exhibition on the basis of conventional criteria—that is, work selected as *rarest, most unique, formally most inventive,* or *technically most polished.*"[38] This statement, based on a social view of art, is from an exhibition catalogue, *AIDS: The Artists' Response,* by Jan Zita Grover and Lynette Molnar, the curators of the exhibition of the same name. Activists reject the notion of art for art's sake and instead embrace art for life's sake. They are concerned with the consequences of art. Activist criteria hold that art is in service of causes that go beyond art itself, goals larger than "significant form," originality, and unique artistic expression. Artwork made about AIDS has generated debate that centers on the conflicting criteria for art and illustrates how activist criteria operate in judging art.

Michael Kimmelman states a social criterion in a *New York Times* article about art about AIDS: "The goal is not to produce museum masterpieces but to save lives, by whatever means at an artist's disposal."[39] Kimmelman sees several artistic shortcomings in some activist art about AIDS: Some of it is "dictatorial," and it can be simpleminded and "condescending" and "even counter-productive in its eagerness to provoke," and most of it will not last except as a relic of an era. But he defends the work by arguing that "most of these works don't pretend to be great art in the way traditional art historians use that phrase. To be heard above a roar of misinformation and in the face of so much indifference, shouting may be necessary."

Activist criteria play themselves out in reaction to Nicholas Nixon's photographs of people with AIDS exhibited in 1988 at the Museum of Modern Art in New York. Nixon photographed the final months of life of several AIDS patients. The photographs were clearly meant to elicit sympathy: "I hope my pictures humanize the disease, to make it a little bit less something that people see at arm's length."[40] For the most part his photographs were received positively by critics. But they also produced very hostile reactions on instrumental grounds from activist critics. One stated that "personally, I think the only proper response to these photographs is to walk into museums and rip them off the walls."[41] Those who critiqued the Nixon photographs objected that they made people with AIDS look like freaks, and sickly, helpless, fatalistic victims, barely human. Robert Atkins, a critic for the *Village Voice,* bitterly complains about photojournalism's penchant for the exotic and melodramatic. If an editor of a popular magazine has a choice between using a photograph of a person with AIDS shopping in a supermarket or a photograph of a person with AIDS being fed intravenously in the hospital, the editor will likely choose the more dramatic hospital photograph because it will sell more magazines. Thus, Atkins argues, we have received mostly "negative" rather than "positive" images of people with AIDS.[42] During Nixon's Museum of Modern Art exhibition, gay activists distributed leaflets that demanded images of "vibrant, angry, loving, sexy, beautiful" people with AIDS, "acting up and fighting back."

Activist criteria, then, encourage an examination of art based on social, moral, and economic purposes of art, how art is used in society, and its consequences. Instrumentalist criteria insist that art is subservient to, rather than independent of, social concerns.

Other Criteria

The preceding criteria are not exhaustive. Originality, for example, is a commonly used criterion. Hans-Georg Gadamer describes his reaction when he faces a new and creative element in a work of art:

> I simply am not able to keep on walking. Time comes to a stop. I no longer
> know how much time I've spent in reading the work, and I don't know how

long the things I have read will continue to remain alive in me. The experience of something new throws you off at first into sort of a state of confusion. I find myself in a dialectic relationship with what I have seen. When I see something new, it opens my eyes, both with respect to what I have already seen and with respect to what I will later see.[43]

Specific criteria such as originality, craftsmanship, and good composition are usually subsumed by larger clusters of criteria. Specific criteria may be in conflict with the larger and more inclusive criteria of realism, expressionism, formalism, and activism identified previously. Originality, for instance, might not be important to an instrumentalist critic who is interested in raising consciousness about sexism and racism in society: If the image is effective in improving society, whether it is derivative or original will likely be considered irrelevant.

There are other cautions about using specific criteria. The criterion of originality can only be used with confidence by someone who knows the history of photography and who has seen a very wide breadth of contemporary work. What seems original for a newcomer to photography might well be an established practice in the medium.

Craftsmanship is a time-honored criterion that seems easy to apply, but a well-crafted image for an expressionist might be different from a well-crafted image for a realist: A "dizzying out of focus blur" for Edward Weston might be a dynamic, innovative expression for Duane Michals. A good print for a formalist might be a waste of silver for an instrumentalist because the photograph lacks social content. A feminist critic would likely reject a photograph that encourages violence toward women no matter how well composed, well crafted, or original the image.

CHOOSING AMONG CRITERIA

Each of these sets of criteria is appealing, and deciding among them is difficult. There are some alternatives. We can let the work influence the criteria by which it will be judged. Such a decision presumes an interpretation; and based on our understanding of an image, we would choose criteria that are most favorable to the image. A formalist image would be measured against formalist criteria, a realistic image by mimetic standards. This is a pluralistic acceptance of art. Such a stance gives primacy to the art and keeps viewers open to a variety of artforms. But some types of art may be unacceptable to some critics, and a viewer might want to adhere more rigorously to a particular set of criteria that are consistent with his or her aesthetic or moral beliefs. The pluralist runs the risk of being wishy-washy.

We can accept a particular set of criteria and apply them to all art, whether the criteria fit the art or not. The risks here are dogmatism and rigidity of experience. The risk of a very narrow range of acceptance is particularly great for a naive viewer who has not had much exposure to the variety of artforms. If a viewer adheres strictly to a set of realistic criteria, for example, much art of the world and of our times will be dismissed.

A viewer who has carefully and thoughtfully sampled many kinds of art, however, may want to champion certain kinds of art and dismiss others. Some activist critics, including feminists and Marxists, take an informed and narrow stance about art they critically uphold and art they vehemently reject.

We can mix criteria and insist that an expressionist image adhere to certain non-negotiable formalist criteria, for example. But some criteria are incompatible, even contradictory. It would be logically inconsistent to adhere to both formalism and activism: Art is either autonomous or heteronomous, transcendent or subordinate to other values.

Different criteria illuminate different aspects of a work of art. All of the preceding criteria can be applied to a single photograph in order to draw attention to its different aspects. Trying different criteria can also broaden our critical perspective, allowing us to see an image from multiple points of view. By knowing different criteria, we have more standards of excellence to apply to photographs; and through them we may find more to appreciate in a photograph.

DIFFERING JUDGMENTS

Because there are different criteria for judging art, inevitably there are different judgments of the same work of art. Major exhibitions and new showings of prominent photographers' work receive multiple evaluations from a variety of critics. Sometimes critics agree that the work is good, but they may find it good for different reasons and by different criteria. Sometimes critics disagree over the worth of the work, with some upholding it and others rejecting it. Such disagreements can happen when critics use different criteria to judge the same work and when critics hold the same criteria but differ in their decisions about how the artwork holds up to scrutiny under those criteria.

Different evaluations of the same exhibition are interesting to read and compare because they show that critics' evaluations of the same work can vary, sometimes considerably. The different reasons that critics offer in praising or faulting an exhibition are valuable and stimulating because they give us several alternative viewpoints to consider in forming our own critical decisions about the work in question.

JUDGMENTS ARE ARGUMENTS

Critical judgments, like interpretations, are arguments. Evaluating a photograph or an exhibition requires formulating arguments. Not all judgments are equal. Judgments, like interpretations, are more or less convincing depending on how they are argued. Judgments are not so much right or wrong as they are reasonable, convincing, or enlightening. Critical judgments themselves can be judged according to whether or not, and how well, they increase our understanding and appreciation of artworks. Evaluative arguments are always open to dispute and invite counterarguments. Seeing how critics differ in their appraisals of an artwork is one of the aspects of criticism that makes it interesting and informative.

That critics disagree, however, does not warrant the claim that evaluative judgments are totally subjective and "mere opinions" or that all critical appraisals are equally legitimate. Critical judgments are arguments with reasons, and these arguments can be looked at objectively and then be evaluated. We can choose among judgments, reasons, and criteria and agree with some and disagree with others in reasoned ways. The most convincing judgments are better grounded and better argued.

REAPPRAISALS

Judgments, like interpretations, are not conclusive, definitive, and final pronouncements. Judgments can and do change. "The Family of Man," a major exhibition that traveled internationally, was curated in 1955 by Edward Steichen of the Museum of Modern Art in New York. It is the most successful photography show in history if measured by attendance and audience appeal; and it was generally unchallenged by critics in its time. More recently, the show has been written about extensively, reappraised, and harshly judged by several writers, including John Szarkowski, Allan Sekula, and Jonathan Green.[44] In 1984 Marvin Heiferman curated a new show, "The Family of Man: 1955–1984," at P.S.1 in New York. This new show was based on the original 1955 exhibition and rebuked it. Heiferman's exhibition was visual art criticism of Steichen's exhibition.

Revisionist history and criticism are about revising past interpretations and evaluations of works. Some historians and critics are deeply concerned that art by women, for instance, has been unfairly ignored or given too little critical attention. These historians and critics are attempting to right the wrongs of past scholarship by rediscovering lost work, reinterpreting it, and reevaluating it, showing that it deserves a more prominent place in history.

JUDGMENTS AND PREFERENCES

Critical judgments are different from preferences. Preferences do not require reasons, and preferences are rarely disputed. Critical judgments, however, do require reasons and do invite counterargument because their consequences are important. Also, statements of preference tell us more about the person making the statements than about the object in question. When engaging in criticism, we are seeking to find out about the art object, not about the persons engaging in criticism. More bluntly, whether someone *likes* the photograph is not particularly relevant; what is relevant is whether or not someone thinks it is good or bad and for what reasons.

Strategically, it can be beneficial to begin to formulate our judgments of photographs based on strong, immediate responses of liking or disliking them. Carrie Rickey, an art and film critic, chooses, when she can, to write only about works she feels passionately about. She uses her strong personal reactions to films or art as motivation to write, but she transforms these reactions into argued positions. To engage in responsible criticism, we need to transform preferences into judgments that are based on more than personal likes and dislikes. A strong, personal, positive or negative reaction to a photograph can be critically valuable if we decipher reasons for reactions, try out the reasons, and begin to posit criteria for what we consider to be good in a photograph.

The distinction between preferences and values can be personally liberating because the distinction allows us to dislike certain things even though it is understood that they are good and to like and enjoy certain things even though it is understood that they are not particularly worthwhile from a critical standpoint. John Corry utilized the distinction between preference and value in his review of *Hollywood Wives* for the *New York Times*. From the outset, he refers to this made-for-television movie based on a best-selling novel as "trashy" but also admits that "this critic enjoyed it."[45] He says it is not the kind of movie one would recommend to friends but that "everyone watches stuff like this, anyway, and then pretends they haven't seen it." In his review, he thoroughly explains the movie's flaws, but with some sarcasm he humorously concludes that "trashy fun is trashy fun, and if you want to be uplifted you can always read a book." As an informed critic, Corry knows the difference between the value of quality drama and his occasional preference for the fun of enjoyable entertainment, and in this case he opts for the latter.

INTENTIONALISM AND JUDGMENTS

The flawed critical method of "intentionalism," discussed earlier in relation to interpretation, also comes into play in evaluation. A critic can evaluate a photograph according to whether or not it meets the intent of the photographer: If the photographer tried to do x, and succeeded in doing x, then the photograph is good. But this is a weak method of critical judgment. As was said earlier, photographers do not always make public their intents. Also, because a photographer makes a photograph that matches his or her intent does not make it a good photograph. The intent itself may be weak. There are also cases when a photographer tries to make one kind of picture but ends up with another that may be as good as or better than the photographer intended.

It is beneficial for photographers to carefully consider what it is they intend to express and to consider whether they have achieved their intents and whether their intents are worth achieving; and it is appropriate for teachers to critically consider students' intents. But critics ought to work with the images photographers make, not with the minds of the makers.

THE OBJECTS OF JUDGMENTS

The objects of critics' judgments are individual photographs, portfolios, exhibitions, the entire life work of a photographer, movements, styles, and historical periods. Critics usually criticize new work but occasionally reevaluate older work that has already received critical attention, especially when it is presented in a new exhibition.

Whenever possible, critics work with original objects, not reproductions. Some photographic works printed in offset that look like reproductions are not. Tony Mendoza's *Stories,* for example, is a book, and critics have properly evaluated it as a book, not as a bound set of reproductions. If the photographs from the book are exhibited, then they become the objects for judgment. Similarly, *The Deerslayers,* by Les Krims, is a limited edition, offset portfolio, not a set of inexpensive reproductions substituting for more expensive, original silver prints. The offset folio ought to be judged as an offset folio. It would be inappropriate and unfair, however, to critically appraise photographs made for exhibition on the basis of reproductions.

JUDGMENTS OF ROBERT MAPPLETHORPE'S PHOTOGRAPHS

Robert Mapplethorpe's exhibition, "The Perfect Moment," 1989, caused considerable and consequential controversy when it opened in Cincinnati, Ohio, and his work continues to receive critical commentary and new exhibitions. *Aperture* magazine reports on two symposia in 2009.[46] The Whitney Museum of Art showed Mapplethorpe's early Polaroids from the 1970s in 2008:

> The Whitney's show of nearly a hundred Polaroids by Robert Mapplethorpe includes some of the artist's best work, much of it on exhibit for the first time. Taken between 1970 and 1975, when Mapplethorpe was in his twenties, these little pictures anticipate virtually all of his signature subjects: sex, beauty, celebrity, fetishism, elegance. They're the work of a photographer testing his eye, yet there's nothing tentative and nothing tossed off. Because

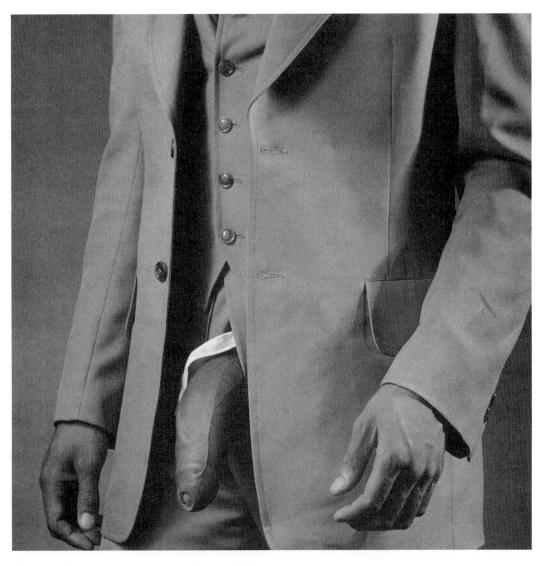

PLATE 32.   Robert Mapplethorpe, *Man in Polyester Suit,* 1980. Gelatin silver print.
© The Robert Mapplethorpe Foundation. Used with permission Art + Commerce.

the Polaroid encourages spontaneity and a certain amount of self-indulgence, many of Mapplethorpe's most revealing images are of himself and close friends, including his constant companion Patti Smith and his mentor/lover Sam Wagstaff. Aside from a few double exposures, however, his experimentation is largely a matter of exploring his range—from portraiture to still-life—and refining his style, which never strayed far from classic modernism.

The sophistication of this style is apparent early on, and, whether his subject is Marianne Faithfull or a tangle of bondage gear, it's at its most intimate and seductive here.[47]

Following is a synopsis of critical commentary on Mapplethorpe's work.

In 1993 a newspaper reporter wrote that "an exhibit of the works of photographer Robert Mapplethorpe is breezing through Europe this year, with barely a whisper of discontent. Yet, at the Beaux-Arts Palace, there is no escaping the pictures of oral sex, homosexual fondling, bondage and sadomasochism lacing the prints of pristine flowers and ornate portraits."[48] In Brussels the exhibition was sponsored by the city government, and in Denmark it was sponsored by Unibank, the nation's largest bank. The show was also seen without controversy in Hamburg; Venice; Stockholm; Lisbon; Barcelona; Turku, Finland; and Turin, Italy.

In Cincinnati on April 7, 1989, however, as 1,000 protesters chanted "Gestapo, go home!" sheriff's deputies and Cincinnati police officers closed the Contemporary Arts Center where Robert Mapplethorpe's photography exhibition, "The Perfect Moment," had just opened. A grand jury indicted the museum and its director on obscenity charges: pandering obscenity and illegal use of a child in nudity-related activity. Six months later a jury delivered an acquittal in the landmark obscenity case.

Prior to the Cincinnati ordeal, the Corcoran Gallery of Art in Washington, D.C., canceled its scheduled exhibition of "The Perfect Moment," an exhibition partially funded by the National Endowment of the Arts. The decision to cancel came amid some furor over another piece of art financed by the endowment, Andres Serrano's *Piss Christ,* a large Cibachrome of a plastic crucifix submerged in the artist's urine.[49] Controversy about these photographs still lingers, and debates continue about the desirability of federal government support for any art, particularly art that many find controversial. About the controversy, arts advocate Schuyler Chapin wrote, "Congress, art critics, enraged civil libertarians, religious fanatics, pro- and anti-censorship groups—all are having a field day, leaving the arts communities in defensive positions."[50]

Hilton Kramer's and Grace Glueck's Views of Mapplethorpe's Work

On two consecutive Sundays, the *New York Times* published two opposing articles about the controversy, the first by Hilton Kramer, who argued against government funding of art like that of Mapplethorpe.[51] The following Sunday, Grace Glueck defended the funding of Mapplethorpe's work, and work like it, and opposed the Corcoran's cancellation of the exhibition.[52]

In the following pages, Kramer's and Glueck's arguments are presented for and against the Corcoran's decision to cancel the Mapplethorpe exhibit. We will also consider various critics' judgments of Mapplethorpe's work, looking for reasons for their judgments and the implicit or explicit criteria on which they based their judgments.

Kramer is dramatic in his refusal to even describe the work in the show: "I cannot bring myself to describe these pictures in all their gruesome particularities, and it is doubtful that this newspaper would agree to publish such a description even if I could bring myself to write one." Clearly, his lack of description is a negative judgment of the work—he suggests that it is too disgusting to merit the dignity of language. Glueck has less difficulty in describing the contents of the exhibition:

> The Mapplethorpe show is a retrospective of the artist's work that contains images depicting homosexual and heterosexual erotic acts and explicit sadomasochistic practices in which black and white, naked or leather clad men and women assume erotic poses. Along with these photographs are fashionable portraits of the rich and trendy, elegant floral arrangements and naked children—images that might not necessarily be considered indecent if viewed singly but that in this context seem provocative.

Other potentially offensive pictures that neither critic mentions in detail are a man urinating into another's mouth, a close-up of a fist and forearm penetrating an anus, the handle of a bull whip protruding from the artist's rectum, and a close-up of mutilated male genitals. Glueck admits that some of Mapplethorpe's photographs are offensive: "Homosexuality is a subject that has deep emotional resonance for many people. For some, the show was certainly distasteful." But she argues that art is sometimes "hideous, even depraved," and cites Goya's painting of cannibalism and Picasso's explicitly erotic paintings and etchings, all of which are firmly enshrined as art. She asserts that the public does not want to be "saved" from viewing them and, likewise, that the public should not be "saved" from viewing Mapplethorpe's work.

In defending Mapplethorpe's work, Glueck adheres to expressionist criteria: "Artists are important to us, among other reasons, because of their ability to express what is deep or hidden in our consciousness, what we cannot or will not express ourselves." She argues that his photographs are art by appealing to an institutional definition of art; namely, they are art because those who know about art honor them as art: "Whatever one thinks of Mapplethorpe as an artist—and there are critics on both sides—his images are intended as art, presented as such and are judged to be art by those qualified in such matters. They have been chosen by well-established art institutions." Finally, she argues that "museums are traditionally the neutral sanctuaries—entered voluntarily by the public—for this expression. What we see there may not always be esthetic, uplifting, or even civil, but that is the necessary license we grant to art."

Kramer, however, strongly objects to the use of taxpayers' money to support art that flaunts standards of decency and civility: "Or, to state the issue in another way, is everything or anything to be permitted in the name of art? Or, to state the issue in still another way, is art now to be considered such an absolute value that no other standard—no standard of taste, no social or no other standard—is to be allowed to play any role in determining what sort of art it is appropriate for the Government to support?" He clearly is rejecting the autonomy of art. He also supports the public's right to have strong influence in decisions about art that is supported by their taxes. He argues that there was no public outcry about the exhibition of Mapplethorpe's photographs in private commercial galleries, but there was when taxpayers' money was to be used in their public display.

He identifies what he finds so offensive about some of the Mapplethorpe photographs. For Kramer, it is not that they depict male nudity. He asserts that no one has made a fuss about Minor White's male nudes on display at the Museum of Modern Art in New York City. What he finds so offensive in Mapplethorpe's images is "so absolute and extreme a concentration on male sexual endowments that every other attribute of the human subject is reduced to insignificance. In these photographs, men are rendered as nothing but sexual—which is to say homosexual—objects." But for Kramer, these are not the most troubling: "That dubious honor belongs to pictures that celebrate in graphic and grisly detail" a sadomasochistic theme. "In this case, it is a theme enacted by male homosexual partners whom we may presume to be consenting adults—consenting not only to the sexual practices depicted but to Mapplethorpe's role in photographing them." Kramer also finds it extremely offensive that Mapplethorpe made these pictures as a sympathetic participant.

Kramer argues that "to exhibit photographic images of this sort, which are designed to aggrandize and abet erotic rituals involving coercion, degradation, bloodshed, and the infliction of pain, cannot be regarded as anything but a violation of public decency." He goes on to argue that the images are pornography and, as such, have a right to exist, but belong in a private, not a public, realm. He also grants them the status of art: "I know of no way to exclude them from the realm of art itself. Failed art, even pernicious art, still remains art in some sense." He argues that "not all forms of art are socially benign in either their intentions or their effects," and when the government supports this kind of art, opposing citizens have a right to be heard, not to deny artists freedom of expression, "but to have a voice in determining what our representatives in the Government are going to support and thus validate in our name."

The *New York Times* published several letters of response to the articles by Glueck and Kramer. One response defending Mapplethorpe's photographs was from Veronica Vera, an artist and a model in one of the sexually explicit photographs in the exhibition: "I see them as debunking the whole idea of pornography—helping society to get rid of that self-hating concept that ghettoizes sex, that implies that some parts of our sexuality are too unspeakable to mention, too private to be public."[53] Two arts administrators wrote: "Attempts to insure that artwork supported by public funds conforms to the beliefs held by some deny the cultural plurality of our country and infringe on the freedom to express different views through artistic creation."[54] Many of the letters objected to any censorship of the arts, but others applauded the Corcoran's decision and Kramer's position.

Other Critics' Views of Mapplethorpe's Work

Most published criticism of Mapplethorpe's photographs (Plates 32 and 33) was positive with some reservations. Kay Larson, writing for *New York Magazine*, doesn't hesitate to describe Mapplethorpe's images: "Some are very hard to look at: men in leather and chains, sometimes hung upside down, often subjected to grim and tortuous sexual indignities."[55] She cites one particular example of a difficult photograph (see Plate 32): "*Man in Polyester Suit* is the kind of picture you could warn your children against: Out of an anonymous, unzipped fly comes a brutally surprising penis, like the life force erupting in the midst of a Victorian garden party." In addition to acknowledging the troublesome nature of the photographs, she puts her emotional reactions into language: "The shock of Mapplethorpe's images is a belly flop into dark ice water. You reexperience the sexual uproar and physical mystery usually concealed behind the zipper."

Before explicitly praising the photographs, which she eventually does, Larson offers her interpretation of them. She puts them in a context of other photography, social documentary photography and formalist photography: "He's an unsparing observer of the lower depths, like Weegee; he's a classicist enraptured with perfect form, like Edward Weston." Her main interpretive claim, however, is that Mapplethorpe aestheticizes all that he sees: "A Mapplethorpe photograph is a voluptuous visual experience, an ecstasy of details, from the erotic terrain of dark belly skin to the hair on the stem of a swollen, testiclelike poppy bud." She explicates further: "Mapplethorpe pursues a state of ferociously aestheticized desire—directed not just at men he is interested in but at all beautiful surfaces, whether skin or marble. Love, which might make room for the less than beautiful, is not part of this horizon." Ultimately, she praises the work because "he has caught the spirit of his times with uncanny accuracy and crushing honesty."

Stephen Koch's understanding of Mapplethorpe's photographs is consistent with Larson's.[56] Writing in *Art in America,* Koch explains that "Robert Mapplethorpe is an esthete. . . . Mapplethorpe is devoted to artifice: he brings an exceptionally gifted graphic intelligence to his photographs in order to render what he sees as part of a kind of esthetic utopia, formed from his own tastes and identity." Koch accepts the work as "phallus worshipping, homosexuality, transvestism, sadomasochism, racial fetishism," and explains:

> From flowers to phalluses to whips and chains and unhappy Manhattanites
> trussed up on torture racks, Mapplethorpe carries his audience step by

probing step deeper into his utopia of anonymity, testing not only the audience's willingness to follow, but also the power of his own exceedingly elegant graphic imagination to reconcile the audience (and his own eye as an artist) to the shameful and nasty preoccupations which rule in that realm.

Most of Koch's feature article on Mapplethorpe's work is interpretive rather than judgmental, but the article is clearly complimentary. Koch praises the work because it elegantly and convincingly pursues a utopian aesthetic world and because Mapplethorpe is working within an artistic tradition with other aesthetes and "holds an important place in that company."

Stuart Morgan has also written a mainly interpretive article in *Artforum* on Mapplethorpe's work.[57] It, too, is positive and complimentary, but in it he expresses reservations:

> Harder to tolerate is the easy passage from, say, flowers to people. We accept that flowers are placed in pots, but what are we to make of an event such as the pose of a nude male on a pedestal, like an object?. . . a procession of comparatively unknown young men, often black, whose relationship to the photographer and to the web of other sitters brings up issues of power, of master and slave. This is the aspect of the work that has bothered viewers more than any other; the black man posed as an object, a person who serves the purposes of another.

Andy Grundberg provides a characteristically reserved overview of Mapplethorpe and the controversy surrounding his imagery, but Grundberg, too, is ultimately positive in his appraisal.[58] In a 1988 *New York Times* review of Mapplethorpe's exhibition at the Whitney Museum of American Art, Grundberg places Mapplethorpe's work in historic context: "Like scores of photographers before him—Lewis Hine, Brassai, Weegee—Mr. Mapplethorpe chose to depict a subculture seldom photographed before, or at least seldom seen in the contexts of fine-art photography. In his case, the subculture is a sado-masochistic, male homosexual one." Grundberg also provides some recent historical context: "Roundly condemned 10 years ago as unsuitable viewing for adults, much less children, it has since been admired, collected and valorized by Susan Sontag, Holly Solomon, the late Sam Wagstaff, and other influential cultural figures." Grundberg especially admires Mapplethorpe's mastery of the photographic surface and manner of presenting subject matter: "The conjunction of perfect technique and perfect form gives his photographs a rarefied beauty that would seem anachronistic were it not for its obvious contemporary appeal."

Grundberg provides other critics' views in his own review by citing the essays from the catalogue that accompanies the Whitney exhibition. Grundberg presents Richard Marshall's understanding that equates Mapplethorpe's vision with abstract, formal considerations and idealized beauty; Ingrid Sischy credits the photographer

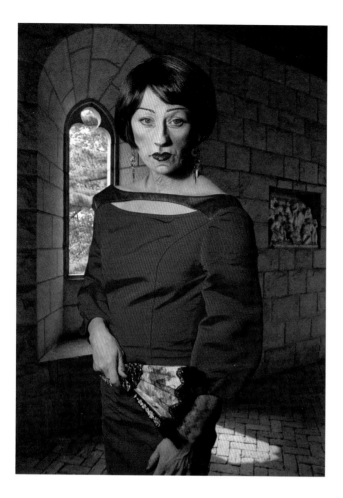

COLOR PLATE 1. Cindy Sherman, *Untitled,* 2008. Color photograph, 85.25 × 58 inches (216.5 × 147.3 cm).

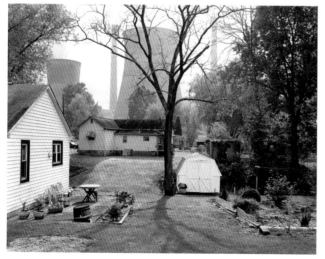

COLOR PLATE 2. Mitch Epstein, *Amos Coal Power Plant, Raymont City, West Virginia,* 2004.

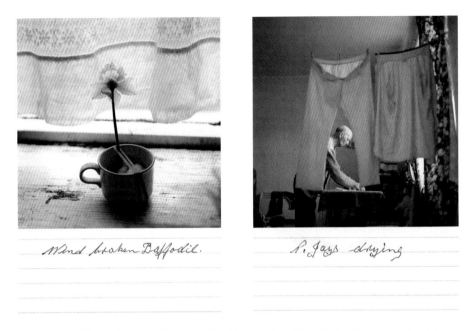

Wind broken Daffodil.   *P. Jays drying*

COLOR PLATE 3. KayLynn Deveney, *The Day-to-Day Life of Albert Hastings.* Ink jet print, 11 × 14 inches. 2 images. Princeton Architectural Press, 2007.
© KayLynn Deveney.

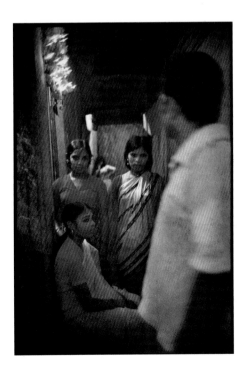

COLOR PLATE 4. Mary Ellen Mark, A brothel hallway, from *Falkland Road*, 1981.
© Mary Ellen Mark.

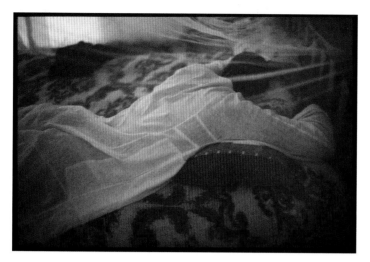

COLOR PLATE 5. Nan Goldin, *Jabalowe under His Mosquito Net, Barat, Luxor, Egypt,* 2003. Cibachrome, 20 × 40 inches.

© Nan Goldin. Courtesy of Matthew Marks Gallery, New York.

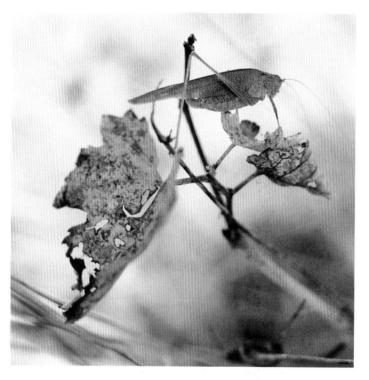

COLOR PLATE 6. Sally Gall, *Study for a Roman Fresco,* 2007. 30 × 30 inches.

Courtesy of Sally Gall and the Julie Saul Gallery, New York.

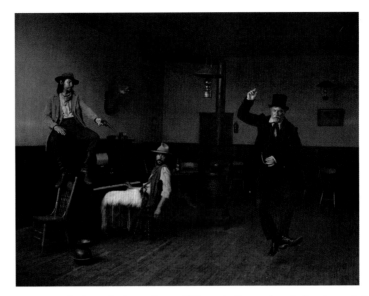

COLOR PLATE 7. Rodney Graham, *Dance!!!!!,* 2008. Two painted aluminum lightboxes with transmounted chromogenic transparencies. Each: 106 1/2 h. × 68 × inches (270.5 × 340.4 × 17.8 cm). Edition of four and one Artist's proof.

Courtesy of Donald Young Gallery.

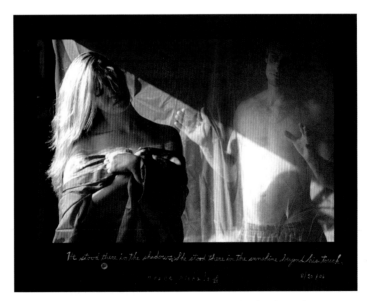

COLOR PLATE 8. Duane Michals, *He stood there in the shadows,* August 20, 2006. C-print with hand applied text, 11 × 14 inches.

Courtesy of the artist and Pace/MacGill Gallery, New York City.

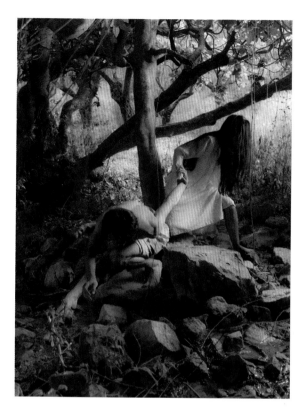

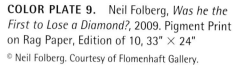

COLOR PLATE 9. Neil Folberg, *Was he the First to Lose a Diamond?,* 2009. Pigment Print on Rag Paper, Edition of 10, 33" × 24"

© Neil Folberg. Courtesy of Flomenhaft Gallery.

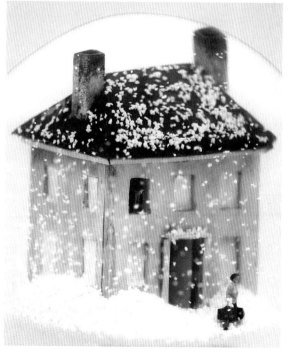

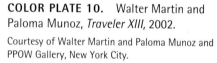

COLOR PLATE 10. Walter Martin and Paloma Munoz, *Traveler XIII,* 2002.

Courtesy of Walter Martin and Paloma Munoz and PPOW Gallery, New York City.

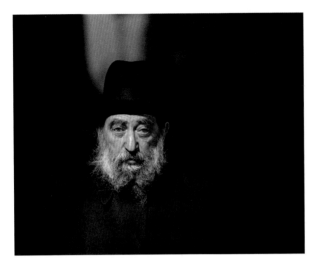

COLOR PLATE 11. Philip-Lorca diCorcia, *Untitled (Rabbi)*, from the series *Heads*, 2000. 48 × 60 inches.

© Philip-Lorca deCorcia. Courtesy of David Zwirner Gallery.

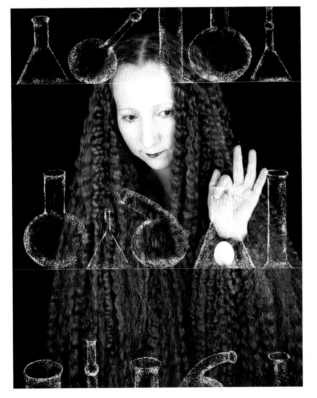

COLOR PLATE 12. Rimma Gerlovina and Valeriy Gerlovin, *Mini Lab*, 2003. C-print.

© Rimma Gerlovina and Valeriy Gerlovin.

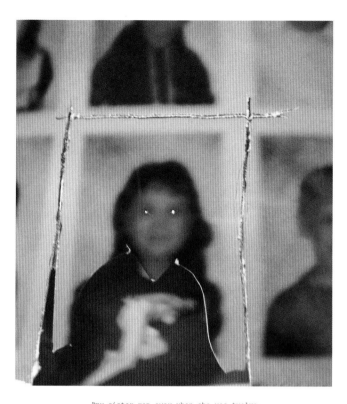

"my sister ran away when she was twelve.
we found her again when she was twenty.
i'm pretty sure it's her, anyway."

COLOR PLATE 13. Photo by Gerald Slota. Text by Neil LaBute, *sister*, 2009. Archival pigment print, 18 × 22 inches.

Courtesy of the artists.

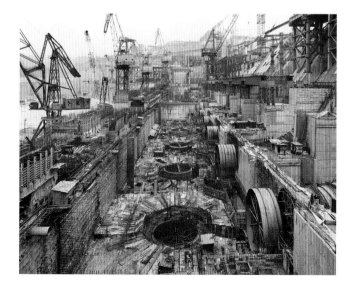

COLOR PLATE 14. Edward Burtynsky, *Dam #6, Three Gorges Dam Project, Yangtze River*, 2005.

© Edward Burtynsky. Courtesy of Hasted Kraeutler, New York / Nicholas Metivier, Toronto.

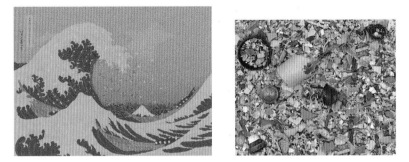

COLOR PLATE 15. Chris Jordan, *Gyre*, 2009. Depicts 2.4 million pieces of plastic, equal to the estimated number of pounds of plastic pollution that enter the world's oceans every hour. All of the plastic in this image was collected from the Pacific Ocean. 8 × 11 feet in three vertical panels.

© Chris Jordan. Courtesy of Kopeikin Gallery.

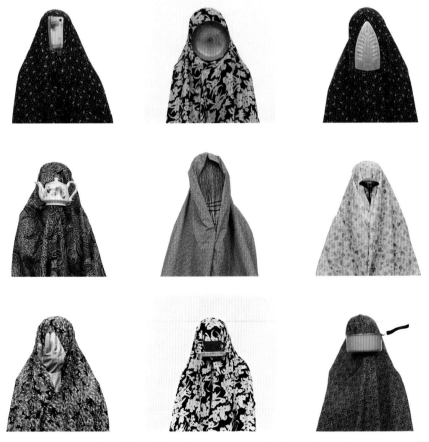

COLOR PLATE 16. Shadi Ghadirian, from the series *Like Everyday*, 2002.

Courtesy of the artist.

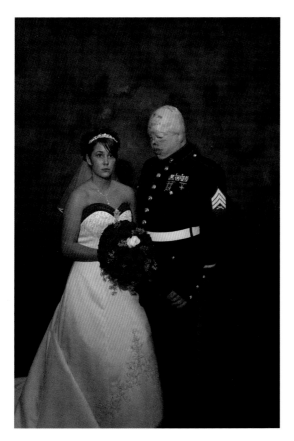

COLOR PLATE 17. Nina Berman, *Marine Wedding, Sergeant Ty Ziegel and Renee Kline,* 2006.

© Nina Berman/NOOR.

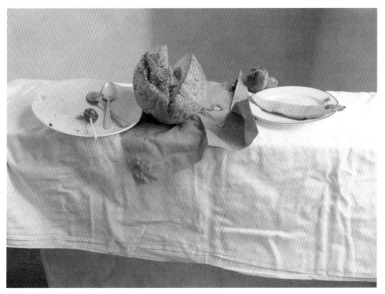

COLOR PLATE 18. Laura Letinsky, *Untitled, I did not remember I had forgotten (#54),* 2002. Chromogenic print, 22 3/4 × 30 7/8 inches.

© Laura Letinsky, Courtesy of the artist and Yancey Richardson Gallery.

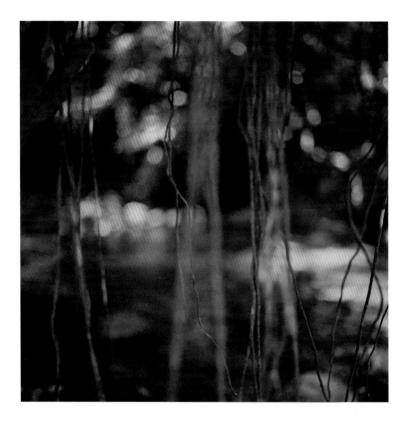

COLOR PLATE 19. Mona Kuhn, *Jungle Roots,* 2009. From the monograph *Native*, published by Steidl. Chromomeric print.

Courtesy of the artist, www .monakuhn.com.

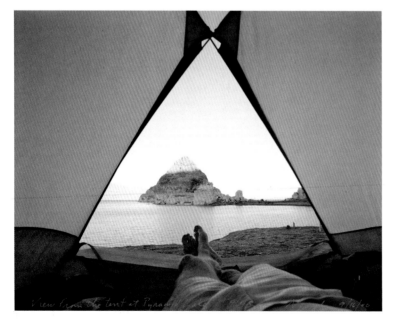

COLOR PLATE 20. Mark Klett, *View from the tent at Pyramid Lake, Nevada,* 7:45 a.m., September 16, 2000. Pigment inkjet print, 23 × 29 inches.

Courtesy of the artist and Pace/ MacGill Gallery, New York.

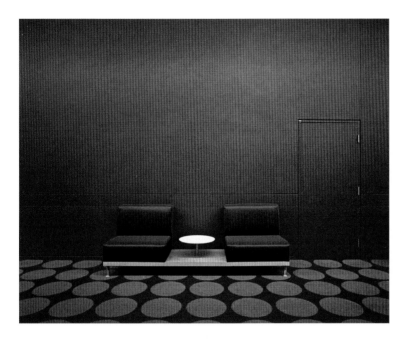

COLOR PLATE 21. Lynne Cohen, *Untitled (Red Door)*, 2008. Digital C-Print, 50 × 60 inches.

Courtesy of the artist and Olga Korper Gallery, Toronto.

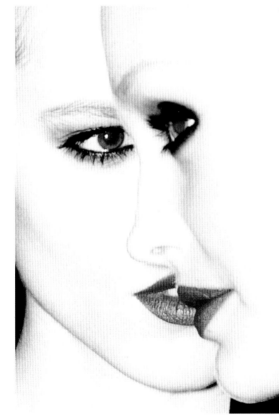

COLOR PLATE 22. Christopher Anderson, from Zac Posen fashion show, New York City, February, 2008.

Christopher Anderson/Magnum Photos.

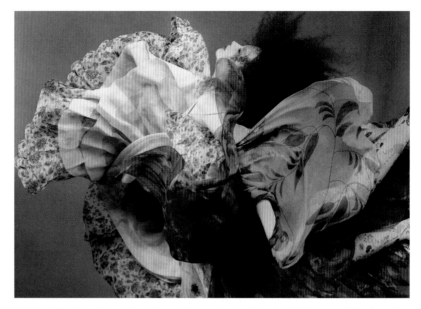

COLOR PLATE 23. Sølve Sundsbø, fashion photo, March 2004 issue of *V* magazine.
© Sølve Sundsbø/Art + Commerce.

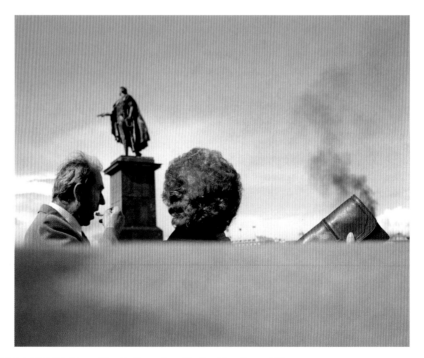

COLOR PLATE 24. Martin Parr, *Stockholm, Sweden,* 1992.
Martin Parr/Magnum Photos.

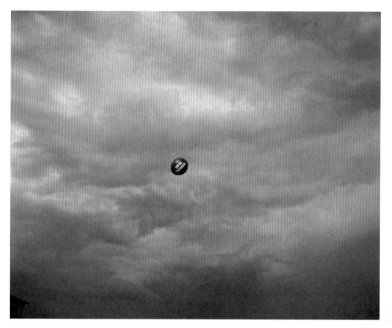

COLOR PLATE 25. Larry Sultan, *New Homes, Inland Empire*, 2008. Chromogenic print, 53 × 62 inches.

Courtesy of the artist and Stephen Wirtz Gallery, San Francisco.

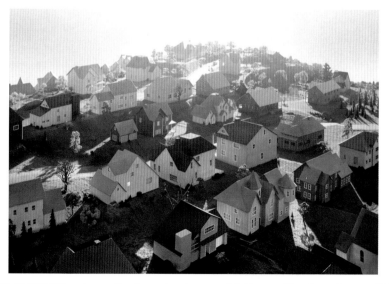

COLOR PLATE 26. James Casebere, *Landscape with Houses (Dutchess County, NY) #1,* 2009. Framed digital chromogenic print mounted to Dibond, framed: 74 × 104 1/2 × 3 inches (188 × 265.4 × 7.6 cm). Edition of 5 with 2 APs.

Courtesy of the artist and Sean Kelly Gallery, New York City.

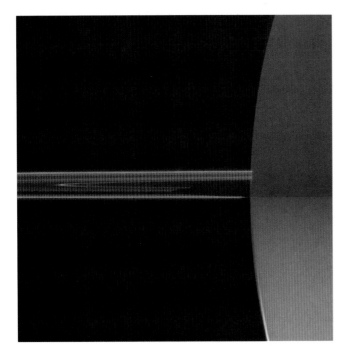

COLOR PLATE 27. Thomas Ruff, *cassini 06,* 2008. Chromogenic print, 42.72 × 42.72 inches. Edition of 6.

© Thomas Ruff. Courtesy of David Zwirner Gallery. Artists Rights Society (ARS), New York.

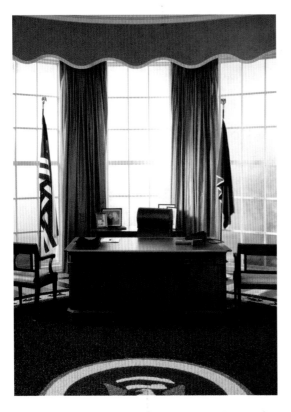

COLOR PLATE 28. Thomas Demand, *Presidency I,* 2008. C-print mounted on plexiglass, 122 × 87 3/4 inches (310 × 223 cm).

© Thomas Demand 2010/Artists Rights Society (ARS), New York/VG Bild-Kunst, Bonn/Image Courtesy Matthew Marks Gallery, New York.

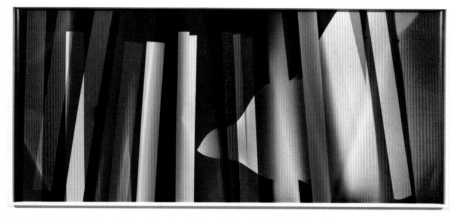

COLOR PLATE 29. Walead Beshty, *Three Color Curl, CMY/Four Magnet: Irvine, California, January 3rd 2010.* Fuji Crystal Archive Super Type C, color photographic paper. 51 1/4 × 122 1/4 inches. Photo by: Fredrik Nilsen.

Courtesy of the artist and Regen Projects, Los Angeles.

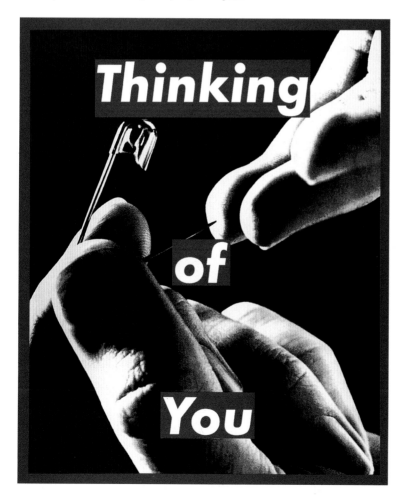

COLOR PLATE 30.
Barbara Kruger, *Untitled (Thinking of You),* 1999–2000. Photographic screen print on vinyl, 123 × 101 inches.

© Barbara Kruger. Courtesy of Mary Boone Gallery, New York. Whitney Museum of American Art, New York City. Purchase, with funds from the Katherine Schmidt Shubert Purchase Fund.

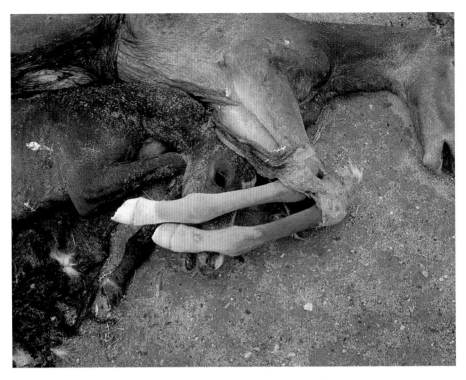

COLOR PLATE 31. Richard Misrach, *Dead Animals #79*, photograph, 1987.
Courtesy of Fraenkel Gallery, San Francisco, and Pace/MacGill Gallery, New York City.

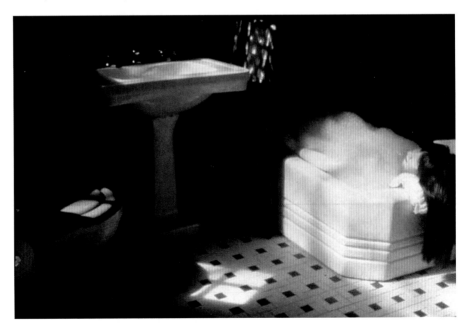

COLOR PLATE 32. Laurie Simmons, *Black Bathroom*, April 6, 1997. 30 × 40 inches.
Courtesy of Laurie Simmons and Sperone Westwater Gallery, New York City.

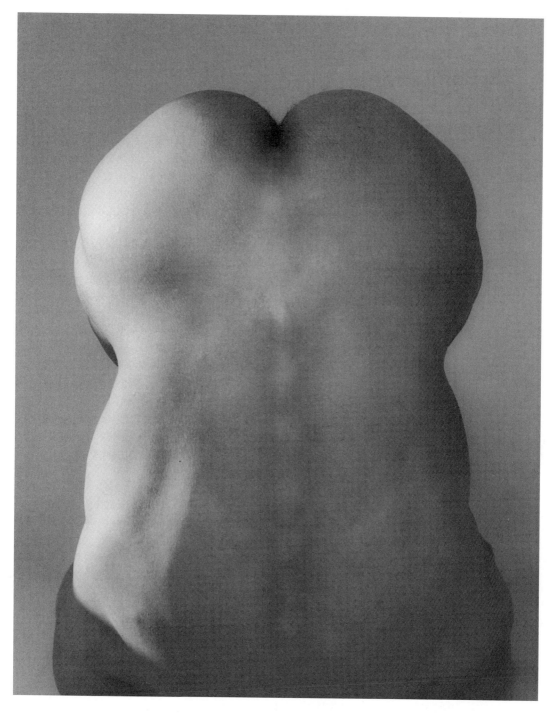

PLATE 33. Robert Mapplethorpe, *Raymond*, 1985.

© The Robert Mapplethorpe Foundation. Used with permission Art + Commerce.

with transgressing borders and foraging in areas of renegade subject matter; and Richard Howard persuades us that Mapplethorpe balances forces that uplift with those that pull down. Grundberg agrees with Sischy's "observation of the disruptive power of Mapplethorpe's work. . . . His pictures do serve to rupture the conventions of polite esthetic discourse." But he finds it difficult to accept that Marshall "can manage to talk about pictures of men bound in leather and chains in purely formalistic terms."

Thus, Grundberg criticizes the criticism of Mapplethorpe and adds to the criticism by concluding that Mapplethorpe's work is about style. Grundberg argues that style has its own substance and that Mapplethorpe has shown us that "the world is comprehensible through the mediation of taste but not by the imposition of moral values. This is the real and quite remarkable message of his pictures, and it makes them central to the issues of our times."

In another article, following the furor over Serrano's photograph and the Corcoran's cancellation of the Mapplethorpe exhibition, Grundberg took a stronger position and wrote in the *New York Times*: "Mr. Serrano's now-notorious image of a crucifix floating in a field of yellow can be interpreted as an attempt at exorcising the artist's Roman Catholic upbringing. . . . It is a work of art in part because it is so uncomfortable to look at, and because it bears the stamp of authentic conflict."[59] He defended Mapplethorpe's work this way: "[His] work is predicated on trespassing the boundaries of conventional mores. That trespass is, one could say, the ultimate subject of his art, and it makes even his most unsettling images something more than pornography."

Ingrid Sischy in the *New Yorker* and Arthur Danto in an essay published with a recent comprehensive collection of Mapplethorpe's photographs, offer defenses of Mapplethorpe's sexual photographs based in part on truth and knowledge.[60] Danto declares the sadomasochistic homosexual photographs to be "disclosures of sexual truth." Sischy writes that "the content of his most controversial work has an informational usefulness. The pictures provide views of sexual activities that are a puzzle to many people. He makes up for sex education most of us didn't get." She continues:

> Of the subject of sex, it's as though Mapplethorpe had picked up a shovel, not a camera, and dug up what was buried. His most infamous imagery—the all-male S & M pictures—has angered many, including homosexuals who believe that these dark scenarios weaken the argument that homosexuality is as healthy as heterosexuality (and who remind us that sadism and masochism are not unknown in the heterosexual world).

Sischy acknowledges that "the pictures are inarguably upsetting; but upsetting is no reason for banishment."

Writing from a gay perspective, critic and photographer Doug Ischar expresses appreciation for some of Mapplethorpe's photographs, especially because they provide "representational visibility" for gays, "constructing a productive gay presence in contemporary art, that keeps us visible," countering "a long tradition of homosexual invisibility." He cites as examples of representational visibility three of Mapplethorpe's self-portraits: him "butch in leather," "fem in heavy makeup," and in "full drag":

> I like and respect these pictures a lot. I like what they do to a genre, portraiture, that has been so unkind and useless to queers and gay men by being unable to recognize and index our invisible difference; by sparing for history only a few of our stars.
>
> What these pictures do together is refill the portrait of a man with everything that's not supposed to be there: makeup, dress-up, ornament, pleasure in these; femininity, taunting defenselessness, contempt for maleness, woman.[61]

CONCLUSION

Judgment presupposes interpretation, and interpretation presupposes description. We need an understanding—hopefully a defensible and convincing understanding—of what a photograph is about before we judge it. This does not mean, however, that the process of judgment can never be the starting point. It is counterintuitive and somewhat unnatural to walk into a gallery and to describe, and describe only, before we form a judgment. It is more likely that we first judge whether or not we even want to take the time to carefully describe and interpret the work. But a judgment without the benefit of an interpretation is irresponsible.

Ratings without reasons are also irresponsible. Many judgments are tossed about casually in conversation with passion and finality but with no reasons provided or requested. Responsible judgments can and should be argued, not pronounced.

Critics write persuasively, perhaps especially when they are trying to convince us of the worth or worthlessness of an artwork or an exhibition. If we really love something or someone, we would usually like to convince others important to us to share our positions or at least understand and accept them. Passionate critical writing can be very good critical writing and very engaging to read.

Finally, issues of theory overlap with issues of critical judgment because criteria for judging art are so tightly linked to theories of art—or what one believes art is or should be. If a critic is arguing about whether the government should fund "offensive art," he or she is probably engaged in theorizing about art and the role of art in society rather than, or in addition to, judging the art in question. Theory is the topic of the next chapter.

PRINCIPLES FOR JUDGING PHOTOGRAPHS

The following principles for judging photographs are offered as a summary of the important points made in this chapter and as a guide to making judgments and to assessing judgments already made. This set of principles is meant to be open ended and nondogmatic. Its purpose is to stimulate further thought about the complex activity of judging images.

- APPRAISALS + REASONS + CRITERIA + JUDGMENTS.
- Judgments are different from preferences.
- Judgments, interpretations, and descriptions are interdependent.
- Judgments, like interpretations, should be persuasive arguments.
- Some judgments should be taken more seriously than others.
- Judgments consist of appraisals with reasons in support of those appraisals.
- Judgmental appraisals and reasons are based in criteria.
- Some criteria can be combined while others are mutually exclusive.
- Solid judgments depend on accurate descriptions and informed interpretations.
- Feelings guide judgments.
- Photographs, not photographers, are the objects of judgments.
- Judgments, like interpretations, are communal decisions, and the community is self-corrective.
- Judgments, like interpretations, should be personal as well as communal.
- Judgments should tell more about the work being judged than about the person doing the judging.
- Judgments of photographs are usually based on worldviews broader than aesthetic views.
- Different judgments are beneficial because they highlight different aspects of photographs that we might otherwise overlook.
- Judgments, like interpretations, should invite us to decide for ourselves and continue on our own.

Photography Theory
Is It Art? Is It True? Is It Moral?

T O THEORIZE IS TO OFFER ANSWERS TO BIG QUESTIONS AND TO CRITICALLY EXAMINE answers to those questions. A theory is a set of (hopefully) coherent and non-contradictory principles and beliefs about something that aids understanding and directs practice. Religions, for example, can be thought of as different theories offered to explain mysteries of existence: How did we get here? Why are we here? Is there a purpose to our existence? Why is there suffering? What happens when we die?

Theories, like religions, offer competing explanations of phenomena. Some theorists (realists or essentialists, for example) believe that theories strive to be absolutely true and immutable; other theorists (pragmatists, for example) are less concerned with the absolute truth of a theory and are more interested in how well the theory solves current problems or answers certain questions.

We all have assumptions and beliefs about phenomena, and these add up to theories. Many of the theories that we hold are implicit, and we may not be aware of them. Upon analysis we can make our theories explicit and then examine them to better know ourselves, what we believe, and why we do certain things. We may find that we hold a coherent and consistent set of beliefs or that our beliefs are arbitrary, inconsistent, incomplete, or contradictory.

Individuals develop theories, but if those theories remain private, they have limited social impact. When groups of people share theories, they become socially consequential.

Any single phenomenon or set of phenomena can be explained, more or less adequately, by a number of different theories. When phenomena are addressed from different theoretical perspectives, many different theoretical answers result. Some people are satisfied with single theories as adequate explanations for whatever engages them; others employ different theories depending on what they are examining and what questions they are answering. Multiple theories of the same phenomenon, like multiple interpretations and judgments of a single photograph, can offer a diversity of views that some find enlightening and stimulating; others, however, prefer the confidence that can come with adhering unwaveringly to a single theory.

Theory and practice are productively circular. Bits of information influence theory, and theory places bits of information within a larger account. A surprising datum or an unexplained phenomenon can cause an adjustment or revision of an existing theory, and a newly conceived theory provides a fresh new way of understanding old data.

We usually want to explain the unaccountable things we experience. A benefit of theories is that they can be used to guide behavior, offering principles for what to do, what not to do, and why. Theories can also provide clarity in a complex world, add stability to what might otherwise be a chaotic existence, and suggest ways to think about solving newly emerging problems.

PHOTOGRAPHY THEORY AND PRACTICE

Who needs theories of photography? Do photographers? Critics? Curators? Collectors? Historians? Photography teachers? Theories of photography guide practices, and practices of photography influence theory, but are theories necessary? Photographers could make images for random reasons or no reason at all; critics could criticize photographs based on their idiosyncratic impulses; collectors could collect whatever suits their fancy and budget at any given moment; historians could canonize any image they liked for any reason or no reason; and photography teachers could teach whatever they individually believed their students should know about the medium and perhaps show some randomly selected images from the past or ignore photography history altogether.

When criticizing a particular exhibition or the work of a photographer, critics sometimes interject theoretical points. For instance, while reviewing the work of Irving Penn, Owen Edwards writes: "The purpose of the still life is to allow us time to contemplate the beauty of objects by holding them aloof from time."[1] Edwards's statement is theoretical because it is a large claim about a group of images, still lifes. He is attempting to elucidate all still lifes by stating what he thinks is their purpose.

In the opening paragraph of a review of the photographs of John Coplans, Andy Grundberg states: "Unlike other methods of representation, including drawing and painting, photography cannot claim to be an art of line, stroke, or touch."[2] His claim is theoretical. It is about photography in general, as a means of representing. He distinguishes photography from painting and drawing. Grundberg states the claim in the service of his review of Coplans's photographs, and he builds on the claim throughout the review, partly as a literary device and partly as a means to illuminate the photographs of Coplans that he is considering.

Sometimes critics set out to write more fully developed theory. A. D. Coleman wrote an influential theoretical article in 1976, "The Directorial Mode: Notes Toward a Definition."[3] His article is theoretical because its purpose is to define an approach to photography, one that he termed "directorial." In addition to recognizing this mode of working, naming it, defining it, and identifying its practitioners, Coleman discusses how directorial photography differs from other ways of working photographically and its relation to differing theories of photographic art. This article and the ideas in it are now established and may seem self-evident, but they weren't until Coleman articulated them in his writing.

Some critics consistently write from a theoretical point of view because they are more interested in photography generally than in individual photographs or individual photographers. They seek to know about photography as a cultural phenomenon and to understand how photographs are used in a society and how they affect the society. Allan Sekula's writings about photography are critical and historical investigations consistently dealing with theoretical problems he identifies and addresses from a particular concern, namely, "a concern with photography as a social practice."[4]

Edward Weston, Paul Strand, and August Sander are notable examples of photographers who have written theoretical pieces that define what photography is and what it does best. Weston and Strand pointedly implemented their theories in their photographs and significantly influenced all the photography that followed. Victor Burgin, Martha Rosler, and Allan Sekula are three contemporary photographers who write theory, embody their theories within their work, and influence other image makers through their writing, exhibiting, and teaching.

All historians of photography are influenced by their theories of photography—by their assumptions of what a photograph is, which photographs are the most important to consider, and which ones could be ignored. Beaumont Newhall has been faulted by others for too narrow a view of photography and for diminishing the contributions of those who favored approaches to photography other than the straight approach.

Curators build new theory and influence accepted theory. John Szarkowski offered shows to certain photographers but not others by choosing which photographs to purchase for the museum and which to accept from donors and by conceptualizing, organizing, and circulating exhibitions. One such exhibition and accompanying book of the same name, *The Photographer's Eye*, was introduced in 1966. The exhibition is an attempt to provide in language and by means of photographic examples a definition of photography. In *The Photographer's Eye,* Szarkowski investigates what photographs look like and attempts to explain why they look the way they do. His concerns are with photography in general, and he uses individual photographs to explicate and illustrate his understanding of photography.

Theory affects the teaching of photography in colleges and universities. It largely determines where departments of photography are located (perhaps within departments of journalism, visual communication, or art); when it is offered within art departments, theory determines whether photography is taught separately or in conjunction with painting, drawing, and printmaking, or as a lens-based medium with film and video. Theory also determines, in part, whether photography is taught as art or as journalistic communication, whether commercial photography is included, and whether the history of photography is taught as part of art history in history of art courses, or apart from art history as a distinct discipline and by a historian of photography.

It is not difficult to find people working within fields of photography who say or imply that they are proud to be uninterested in and uninformed by theory. During a visiting lecture at a college with a sole faculty member teaching photography, most students who had successfully completed Photography I and II acknowledged to me that they had not heard of or seen work by Henri Cartier-Bresson, John Coplans, Rimma and Valeriy Gerlovin, Emmit Gowin, Barbara Kruger, Annie Leibovitz, Robert Mapplethorpe, Joel Meyerowitz, Sally Mann, Duane Michals, Nic Nicosia, Irving Penn, Andres Serrano, Cindy Sherman, Lorna Simpson, Sandy Skoglund, Mike and Doug Starn, Jock Sturges, Carrie Mae Weems, William Wegman, Hanna Wilke, and Joel-Peter Witkin. Their instructor held an implicit theory of photographic education that enabled him to ignore recent photographic history and to concentrate solely on teaching photographic technique.

There are, however, benefits to being informed by and contributing to photography theory. Theory can be interesting in itself. Theory certainly influences practice of what images are made, written and talked about, shown, collected and preserved, and taught. Theory also influences what photographs are ignored. In many senses, understanding or appreciating *any* photograph is impossible without being able to place it within some kind of theoretical context. A snapshot or home video of a baby's first step depends on an implied and loose "theory" of human development that includes recognition and celebration of notable stages of development. It is not possible to adequately understand and appreciate many art photographs without an understanding of the intellectual milieu from which they emerged: Discussions of Cindy Sherman's photographs in Chapter 2 (see Plate 4, Color Plate 1) and Barbara Kruger's images in Chapter 5 (see Plate 30, Color Plate 30) are examples of the necessity of knowing theory to appreciate images.

This chapter could be the first of the book rather than close to the end of the book: Theory pervades all thinking about photography—its history, criticism, making, and teaching. Theory is placed here because the book proceeds from simple to complex critical procedures in the order of describing, interpreting, evaluating, and theorizing. This sequence is suited to teaching criticism because it moves from easier to more difficult ideas. We can now refer to earlier examples of photographs and criticism used in the book with a new eye toward theoretical presuppositions embedded in those photographs.

Disagreements over photographs and exhibitions already cited in this book are based in disagreements about underlying theories of photography. The disagreements have usually been based on theories larger than whether something is an "aesthetically pleasing" photograph. Two extended examples of disagreements based in competing theories about photographs are contained in Chapter 2 about Richard Avedon's exhibition "In the American West," and in Chapter 6 about Robert Mapplethorpe's exhibition, "The Perfect Moment." The disagreements are at times harsh and heated, but very importantly, all of the critics in disagreement over the value of the works of the two photographers agree that the photographs in question are traditionally good photographs in the sense that they are well made, exquisitely composed, and beautifully presented. Indeed, the contested photographs have been shown in art museums around the world. All of the critics agree that the photographs are *art*, but that they are art is insufficient for some critics to designate them *good* art.

The critical disagreements are not over "beauty," a traditional concern of philosophical aesthetics. For some critics the photographs are not "real," or "true," or "ethical." Recall that Douglas Davis in *Newsweek* partially objects to Avedon's photographs of the West because they look like they are "documentary" (real) but they are actually "highly contrived" (unreal). William Wilson in *Artforum* clearly understands the photographs to be "fiction," not caring if they are "real," and not caring if they are "true" documents. He enjoyed them as fictional art, holding that fiction presents its own kind of truth. For Richard Bolton in *Afterimage,* the photographs exploit the subjects and are thus deemed morally reprehensible.

Hilton Kramer, writing about Robert Mapplethorpe's photographs in the *New York Times,* knew of no way "to exclude them from the realm of art," but nevertheless, for him, Mapplethorpe's photographs of sadomasochistic gays are socially "pernicious." Years after the exhibition, the photographer's death, and the initial controversy, Mapplethorpe's photographs continue to raise ethical concerns of a different sort for some in the artworld. Again the objectors do not deny the photographs the status of art, but they see them as raising ethical concerns regarding race. Carrie Mae Weems and Glen Ligon, both African American photographers, question Mapplethorpe's use of black males as subjects. Lauri Firstenberg talks about both artists' work in *Only Skin Deep: Changing Visions of the American Self.* In a work of her own, Weems appropriated Mapplethorpe's *Man in a Polyester Suit* to make the statement that "his images of a sexualized black body can be read as a kind of postmodern extension of the colonial archive."[5] Ligon appropriated ninety-two images of Mapplethorpe's that use blacks as subjects and wrote critical comments on the borders of the Mapplethorpe photographs. Ligon's "linguistic intervention produces an alternative to an exhausted mode of representation linked to racial and sexual difference."[6] Again, these critiques by Kramer, Weems, and Ligon are not on aesthetic but ethical and political grounds.

In these varied examples of critical stances toward two bodies of work, Avedon's and Mapplethorpe's, we see expanded criteria and different concerns at play, concerns broader than traditional aesthetic concerns. Weems and Ligon consider the ethical implications of Mapplethorpe's photographs, and their stances are informed by aspects of psychoanalytic theory (the photographic fetishization of the black male body); postcolonial theory (the disempowering of one group by a more powerful group); queer theory (the disadvantaging of someone on the basis of sexual preference); multicultural theory (the "othering" of some because of their skin color); and feminist theory (turning the human subject into an object through variations of the male photographic "gaze"). In Chapter 2, Davis implicitly questions the *ontological status* of Avedon's photographs (What are they?) and their *epistemological status* (Are they true?), and Bolton questions their *ethical consequences* (Are they socially harmful?). These concerns are more inclusive regarding photography than its *aesthetic status* (Is it art?).

Ontology, epistemology, aesthetics, and ethics are each branches of philosophy, and each has a bearing on how we think about photographs. *Ontology* is a branch of philosophy that examines questions of being and essences of things; *epistemology* is an examination of knowledge, truth, and beliefs; *aesthetics* is an examination of the nature of art and related topics; and *ethics* involves concerns about moral good. These branches of philosophy are not in themselves theories, but theories arise from them, or questions about photography can be designated as ontological, epistemological, aesthetic, or ethical questions. The remainder of this chapter uses these four branches of philosophy (ontology, epistemology, aesthetics, and ethics) to organize, explain, and examine theoretical problems raised by photographs and those who think about photographs.

ONTOLOGICAL CONCERNS: WHAT IS A PHOTOGRAPH?

Photography grew up with claims of having a special relationship to reality and thus to truth. In 1839, Dominique François Arago, in preemptively claiming the invention of photography for France, positioned photography as both a science and an art. Photography is thought to be scientific, as well as artistic, in large part because of how a photograph is made: The photograph is seen as having a unique and automatic connection to reality. A photograph is a chemical recording of light reflected off some person or thing in the real world onto a light-sensitive material. Contemporary photographer Adam Fuss puts this definition into practice very literally in his *Untitled* photogram of two rabbits and their entrails that he laid directly onto color paper to make an indexical image of the rabbits that is caused by the rabbits. The real-world connection of photography has significance for some photographs: Kenneth Jarecke's photograph of a burned Iraqi soldier and Richard Misrach's *Dead Animals #79* (see Color Plate 31 according to Color Art MS.) are striking examples—these things *did happen.* Likewise, the explicit and graphic photographs that Robert Mapplethorpe made of sexual activities among males infuriated some because of their real-world connection: The images cannot be denied as imaginary concoctions by those who are bothered by them. Pornographic images cause similar reactions.

A photograph has what C. S. Peirce, the American pragmatist philosopher interested in sign systems, called an *indexical* quality: That is, a photograph is a sign that is caused by what it shows. William Henry Fox Talbot, the Englishman who stabilized previously fleeting images obtained by the camera obscura, referred to the camera as "the pencil of nature" and published a book of that title of his images and writings in 1852. The pencil of nature is different from the pencil of the artist: The camera, in Talbot's view, allowed nature to directly inscribe an image onto paper without an interfering and fallible human hand.

Roland Barthes, in the last book he wrote before his death in 1981, *Camera Lucida: Reflections on Photography,*[7] declared photography to be "a magic, not an art." He theorizes about photography in a very personal manner: "Now, one November evening shortly after my mother's death, I was going through some photographs." He reflects upon a single photograph of his mother as a young girl, standing in a garden. He wanted "to learn at all costs what Photography was 'in itself', by what essential feature it was to be distinguished from the community of images." The magic of photography, for Barthes, is that the photograph emanates beyond reality and authenticates the past existence of what it represents. Its power of authentication exceeds its power of representation. He declares the essence of photography to be "that which has been"—"what I see has been here."

Barthes explains that photography is different from other systems of representation because the thing that is photographed has really been there. In painting or writing, however, the things to which the words or strokes refer are not necessarily real. But in photography, because of the way photographs are made, because photographs result from light reflected from objects to light-sensitive material, he "can never deny that the thing has been there."

In opposition to Barthes and earlier writers, Joel Snyder insists that photography is no more privileged than painting or language in getting us to the "really real." He argues that we have falsely come to believe that the camera gives us privileged access to the world because of our ignorance of the historical developments in the invention and refinement of photography. The camera was invented to match the ways of picturing developed by Renaissance artists—namely, drawing in Western, Renaissance perspective. The standards for rendering developed by Renaissance artists are invented, not natural; they are conventions for depicting the world. Snyder points out that cameras themselves have been made to conform to standards of Renaissance painting: The round lens of the camera obscura that "naturally" creates a circular image was modified by Renaissance painters and draftsmen to a rectangular format to meet traditional expectations for paintings and drawings.[8]

Digital Images and Ontology

Digital images are being realized in many ways by many people including the millions who snap pictures from their cell phones. A traditional photograph can be scanned, whereby it is translated into a numerical code, fed into a computer, and seen on a computer screen. The digitized photograph is now made up of *pixels*—tiny squares arranged in a grid. The pixels can be changed one by one or in groups. Changes in color, brightness, and contrast can be made instantly, and parts of the photograph can be deleted or repeated ("cloned"). The dimensions of the image can be altered, its edges expanded or cropped, and other images can be incorporated into it.

Digital photographs can also be made directly by means of digital cameras, eliminating the step of scanning. Both types—scanned analog photographs and photographs made with digital cameras—are lens based. They, like traditional photographs, depend on light reflecting off surfaces in the real world. Virtual images, however, are also possible; that is, images that are totally constructed mathematically in the computer to simulate the structure and light of photographs made by cameras. Virtual images have no chemical or lens-based necessary connection to the real world, although they are often made to look like they do because they are carefully constructed to simulate traditional photographs.

Fred Ritchin, picture editor for the *New York Times* from 1978 to 1982, describes computerized pictorial alteration as

> translating a photograph into digital information (a numerical code that can be read by the computer) by using a device called a scanner. An image then appears as the sum total of many tiny squares, called pixels, or picture elements, each of which represents information as to the brightness and color of that sector of the image. Once digitized, an image can be subtly modified pixel by pixel. The entire image can be altered in a variety of ways: colors can be changed, the apparent focus sharpened, some elements can be taken out, and others replicated. The process also allows for the original images to be combined with another.[9]

The enhancement of photographs through digital means is increasing rampantly. Plate 34 shows what can be done, and how seamless the results can be. Lauren Collins writes:

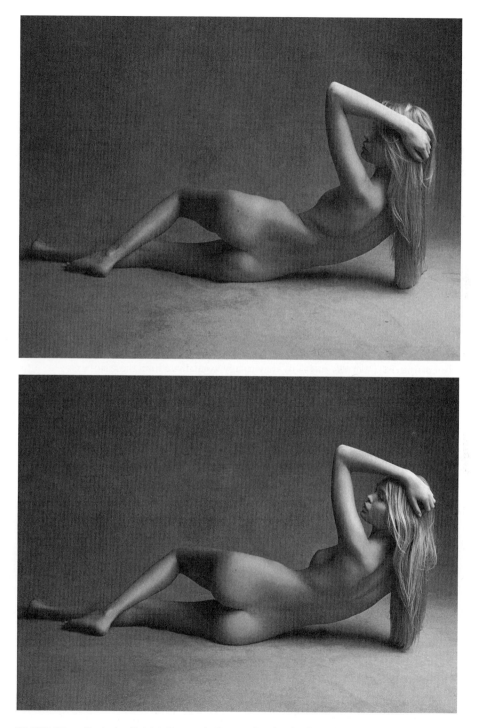

PLATE 34.   Photo by Patrick Demarchelier, realization by Pascal Dangin.

© Patrick Demarchelier. Realization by Pascal Dangin. Courtesy of Pascal Dangin, box, New York.

Pascal Dangin is the premier re-toucher of fashion photographs. Art directors and admen call him when they want someone who looks less than great to look great, someone who looks great to look amazing, or someone who looks amazing already—whether by dint of DNA or MAC—to look, as is the mode superhuman. . . . In the March issue of *Vogue* Dangin tweaked a hundred and forty-four images: a hundred and seven advertisements (Estee Lauder, Gucci, Dior, etc.), thirty-six fashion pictures, and the cover, featuring Drew Barrymore. . . . *Vanity Fair, W, Harpers Bazaar, Allure,* French *Vogue,* Italian *Vogue, V,* and the *Times Magazine,* among others, also use Dangin. Many photographers, including Annie Leibovitz, Steven Meisel, Craig McDean, Mario Sorrenti, Inez van Lamsweerde and Vinoodh Matadin, and Philip-Lorca diCorcia, rarely work with anyone else."[10]

Eighty employees of his company Box Studios occupy a four-story warehouse in Manhattan. Box Studios also retouches film.

Martin Lister, a British theorist of cultural studies who is especially interested in photography and communication, explains the difference between traditional (optically and chemically based) analog photographs and new digital images this way:

Traditionally, images have been analogue in nature. That is, they consist of physical marks and signs of some kind (whether brush marks, ink rubbed into scored lines, or the silver salts of the photographic print) carried by material surfaces. The marks and signs are virtually inseparable from these surfaces. They are also continuously related to some perceivable features of the object which they represent. The light, for instance, cast across a rough wooden table top, becomes an analogous set of tonal differences in the emulsion of the photograph. A digital medium, on the other hand, is not a transcription but a conversion of information. In short, information is lodged as numbers in electronic circuits. It is this feature of digitization which has meant that images can now exist as electronic data and not as tangible, physical stuff.[11]

He continues with the significance of the difference:

The material basis of the chemical photograph, the photographic emulsion, is a granular structure of silver halides dissolved in gelatin and spread onto a plastic or acetate base. This emulsion holds the nearest thing there is to a photographic "mark": the tiny light-sensitive grains of silver, the constituent bits out of which an image is configured. This material basis of the photograph has long been industrially produced. It is put in place by workers in the factories of Kodak, Ilford, Fuji or Agfa. The individual photographer has never had access to this level of signification, except to control the degrees of contrast which various intensities of light reflected from an object in the real world bring about within this granular field.[12]

New digital technologies now grant the photographer unprecedented access to this previously inaccessible level of information and signification (silver halides, for example). The randomly granular field of the chemical photograph is now reconfigured into a precise numeric code, and the image can be changed by altering, adding, or removing pixels.

With traditional photographs, by some theories such as Barthes's, we can be certain that something was in front of the lens that optically reflected light onto a chemical light-sensitive surface held in the camera; that is, that something in the real world existed when the photographer intervened and took the picture. In this sense, something preexists the photographer's intervention in the forming of an image, and this fact is the foundation of beliefs and epistemological claims that the photograph grants us a privileged access to the real world and to truth that other media, such as painting and writing, do not have.

The introduction of photography in the 1830s was accompanied by dire pronouncements about the death of painting. At the end of the 1980s, when new digital technologies became available to photographers, prophecies and pronouncements of the death of photography were abundant, for example: "The advent of this new technology is changing the very nature of photography,"[13] computer imaging practices signal "the end of photography as we have known it,"[14] bringing in "a new era of artistic exploration,"[15] and causing "a transformation in the nature of visuality."[16] Such claims are epistemological in nature.

EPISTEMOLOGICAL CONCERNS: ARE PHOTOGRAPHS TRUE?

Does traditional photography get closer to the truth than do painting and other forms of representation? Do digital images falsify knowledge and undermine belief in photographs? These questions, around which theory has been built, receive different answers. This discussion is sometimes called the *ontological debate* because it has to do with the philosophic nature of the photograph—its ontological status (what a photograph is) and what follows from how one conceives of a photograph. In an ensuing *epistemological debate*, theoretical claims and counterclaims are made about the knowledge that photographs can or cannot bear and about photographic truth and falsity. The differing answers can be grouped into two major theoretical stances, one realist and the other conventionalist.

Realist Theory

In 1839, Arago promoted photography on the basis of its "exactness," its "unimaginable precision," and faithfulness to reality.[17] Daguerre himself wrote that "art cannot imitate [the daguerreotype's] accuracy and perfection of detail,"[18] and Edgar Allan Poe, an early enthusiast of the medium, wrote "the Daguerreotype plate is infinitely (we use the term advisedly) more accurate in its representation than any painting made by human hand."[19] Poe also attributed to photography "a more absolute truth" than ever before possible with pictures. For these thinkers, photography was scientific as well as artistic.

Photographic aids to seeing had been under development since the Renaissance. Around 1839 when previously fleeting photographic images were finally fixed and made permanent by chemical means, Europeans were in the midst of an enthusiastic search for scientific knowledge of both the natural world and the social world. Photography grew up with the new science of sociology. The guiding epistemological theory was positivism, which would have us believe that the methods of natural science can be directly applied to social science. As British art critic John Berger wrote in 1982:

> The camera was invented in 1839. Auguste Comte was just finishing his *Cours de Philosophie Positive*. Positivism and the camera and sociology grew up together. What sustained them all as practices was the belief that quantifiable facts, recorded by scientists and experts, would one day offer man such total knowledge about nature and society that he would be able to order them both.[20]

Positivist investigators pursued facts—empirically verifiable and measurable—which would yield certain knowledge that was believed to be unbiased by the subjectivities of observers. Positivism was a supposedly disinterested and rational method of inquiry that assumed there was an external reality that could be neutrally observed by a detached observer. Within the intellectual milieu of positivism, photography was assumed to be the new scientific instrument that would itemize objective truths. As Allan Sekula wrote in 1986, "For positivism, the camera provides mechanical and thus 'scientifically' objective evidence or 'data'. Photographs are seen as sources of factual, positive knowledge, and thus are appropriate documents for a history that claims a place among the supposedly objective sciences of human behaviour."[21]

CREDIBILITY AND PERSUASIVENESS   Regardless of what a person thinks about the nature of photography, whether it is more accurately thought of as a unique medium or as a medium of conventions it shares with other media, most critics agree that photography is accepted by the public as believable. "People believe photographs," Coleman wrote in 1976,[22] and Andy Grundberg reiterated the point in 1989: Photography "is the most stylistically transparent of the visual arts, able to represent things in convincing perspective and seamless detail. Never mind that advertising has taught us that photographic images can be marvelous tricksters: what we see in a photograph is often mistaken for the real thing."[23] People have inherited a cultural tendency to see *through* the photograph to what is photographed and to forget that the photograph is an artifact, made by a human. The assumed credibility of the photograph is due to the optical and chemical relationship of the photograph to the thing photographed, to its dependence on a mechanical device, the camera, and its reliance on Western realism, especially the perspectival way of seeing that was developed and codified by artists during the Renaissance.

Photographers are well aware of the aura of credibility the photograph has that other media of representation do not share. Jacob Riis and Lewis Hine, for example, wrote and made photographs in the cause of social reform and knowingly used the medium of photography to give their writings more credibility. Hine stated, "The average person believes implicitly that the photograph cannot falsify," but he was quick to add, "you and I know [that] while photographs may not lie, liars may photograph."[24] Although Hine knew that photographs could lie, he also knew that the photograph was more persuasive and effective than the journalistic hand-drawn illustrations common in the early 1900s. Paul Strand, a student of Hines's, believed in the realism of photography but took the idea into an aesthetic direction, namely, the straight aesthetic discussed in Chapter 6. Strand declared that the "very essence" of photography is "absolute unqualified objectivity."[25] This position, in due course, was furthered by Edward Weston, Ansel Adams, and many others of the straight aesthetic.

A belief in the trustworthiness of the photograph was fostered by the news media, especially *Life* magazine in the 1930s–1950s, when it was influential in society and in journalism. Gisèle Freund, photographer and writer about photography, claims "what gave so much credibility to it [*Life*] was its extensive use of photographs. To the average man, photography, which is the exact reproduction of reality, cannot lie."[26] She explains, "few people realize that the meaning of a photograph can be changed completely by the accompanying caption, by its juxtaposition with other photographs, or by the manner in which people and events are photographed." Recall from Chapter 5 how Doisneau's photograph of a Paris bar was variously and severely altered by texts that accompanied it. The electronic news media today rely on the credibility of the images recorded by cameras.

Advertisers have long been knowingly using photographs because of their credibility. David Ogilvy encourages his colleagues in his book *Confessions of an Advertising Man* to use photographs: A photograph "represents reality, whereas drawings represent fantasy, which is less believable."[27]

Susan Sontag comments cuttingly on such uses of photographs:

> A capitalist society requires a culture based on images. It needs to furnish vast amounts of entertainment in order to stimulate buying and anesthetize the injuries of class, race, and sex. And it needs to gather unlimited amounts of information, the better to exploit the natural resources, increase productivity, keep order, make war, give jobs to bureaucrats.[28]

No writing or painting can give Barthes the certainty of photography: "Photography never lies: or rather it can lie as to the meaning of the thing . . . never to its existence." Barthes's method of building theory is phenomenological. His writing in *Camera Lucida* is in the first-person singular, and he draws upon his direct experience in looking at photographs. The following quotation elucidates his interesting and insightful subtheory of portraiture, which he derives from his experiences of being photographed:

> In front of the lens, I am at the same time: the one I think I am, the one I want others to think I am, the one the photographer thinks I am, and the one he makes use of to exhibit his art. In other words, a strange action: I do not stop imitating myself and because of this, each time I am (or let myself be) photographed, I invariably suffer from a sensation of inauthenticity, sometimes of imposture (comparable to certain nightmares). In terms of image-repertoire, the Photograph (the one I intend) represents that very subtle moment when, to tell the truth, I am neither subject nor object but a subject who feels he is becoming an object: I then experience a micro-version of death (of parenthesis): I am truly becoming a specter.[29]

Another contribution to theories of realism is the concept of "transparency." Kendall Walton, an aesthetician, identifies transparency as a unique and distinguishing characteristic of the medium of photography.[30] In Walton's account, photography is special and significant because it gives us a new manner of seeing—a manner of "seeing through" photographs to the thing photographed. He is not claiming that the photograph gives us the impression or illusion of seeing reality but rather that the photograph allows us "to see things which are not in our presence" and that "the viewer of the photograph sees, literally, the scene that was photographed." In an argument similar to Barthes's, Walton argues that because the photograph is caused by objects in the photograph, it allows us to see what was there. Paintings are not necessarily caused by what they depict. In cases of doubt about the existence of things painted, we have to rely on the painter's vision of what was seen; regardless of what the photographer believes, however, the photograph shows what was before the lens. For Walton, photography is unique because photographs are transparent.

Photographs continue to be powerfully persuasive. Both Susan Sontag and Abigail Solomon-Godeau have commented on the credibility and resulting political power of the photograph in relation to American abuse of Iraqis held at Abu Ghraib prison in Baghdad in 2004. American soldiers, with personal digital cameras, took unauthorized photographs of Americans abusing Iraqis, and these photographs eventually found their way into the news media, creating international outrage and national embarrassment. Solomon-Godeau comments: "Appalling and politically devastating as [the photographs] are to the White House and the military, their authenticity is unquestioned. The belated release of these pictures has yielded what seems the unimpeachable truth (photography's original PR claim) that American soldiers have sexually humiliated and tortured their Iraqi captives."[31] Written reports of the atrocities, however, had circulated for more than a year, and the government of the United States ignored them before the photographs became public. Sontag comments:

> The pictures will not go away. That is the nature of the digital world in which we live. Indeed, it seems they were necessary to get our leaders to acknowledge that they had a problem on their hands. After all, the conclusions of reports compiled by the International Committee of the Red Cross, and other reports by journalists and protests by humanitarian organizations about the atrocious punishments inflicted on "detainees" and "suspected terrorists" in prisons run by the American military, first in Afghanistan and later in Iraq, have been circulating for more than a year. It seems doubtful that such reports were read by President Bush or Vice President Dick Cheney or Condoleezza Rice or Rumsfeld. Apparently it took the photographs to get their attention, when it became clear they could not be suppressed; it was the photographs that made all this "real" to Bush and his associates. Up to then, there had been only words. . . . [32]

Conventionalist Theory

Theoretician Joel Snyder is one scholar among many who disagrees with realist theories of photography:

> The notion that a photograph shows us "what we would have seen had we been there ourselves" has to be modified to the point of absurdity. A photograph shows us "what we would have seen" at a certain moment in time, from a certain vantage point if we kept our head immobile and closed one eye and if we saw things in Agfacolor or in Tri-X developed in D-76 and printed on Kodabromide #3 paper. By the time all the conditions are added up we are positing the rather unilluminating proposition that, if our vision worked like photography, then we would see things the way a camera does.[33]

Snyder agrees that photographs seem like natural phenomena, but they are not, and he directs our attention to how we came to think of photographs as natural phenomena.[34]

Snyder and coauthor Neil Allen Walsh point out some common conventions operant in supposedly realistic photography. In photographing a horse running, for example, photographers ordinarily choose one of three conventions. By keeping the camera stationary and using a slow shutter speed, they render the horse blurred and the background stationary. By panning the camera on the horse as it runs, they render the horse sharp against a blurred background. By using a fast shutter speed and stationary camera, they freeze both horse and background. Each of these pictures, the authors argue, might seem natural enough to us now, but they remind us that photographers had to invent these ways of conveying motion in their still photographs and that we had to learn photographers' conventions for representing motion so that we could understand their photographs.[35]

Snyder's conventionalist arguments owe much to the theories of Ernst Gombrich and Nelson Goodman. Gombrich writes about the history of art to reveal how different people in different cultures and time represent the world and understand those representations. Goodman is a philosopher interested in the different ways we represent our world through symbol systems such as graphs, maps, charts, and paintings. Both Gombrich and Goodman argue that pictorial realism is culturally bound. That is, what was realistic for the ancient Egyptians is not realistic for us; and perhaps more important, our version of realism, to which we are so accustomed as convincingly realistic, would not be decipherable to ancient Egyptians. Styles of representation, realistic and otherwise, are invented by artists and draftsmen in a culture, and then learned by viewers in that culture. Styles of picturing are made up of invented codes that become conventional. Realism, for Goodman, is a matter of a picture's codes being easily decipherable, readily readable. Ease of information retrieval from a style of picturing is mistaken by a culture for pictorial accuracy because the viewers are unaware of the representational system within their own culture; they are too familiar with it to notice it. A style becomes so easily readable that it seems realistic and natural—it seems to be the way the world is.

Geoffrey Batchen, following Michel Foucault's philosophical methodology of identifying the origins of ideas and practice—the archeology of ideas—examines the origins of photography, especially the intellectual context in which photography came to be. Batchen acknowledges the realist claims of the early inventors, such as Daguerre's 1839 description of photography as a process that "consists of the spontaneous reproduction of the images of nature reflected by the means of the Camera Obscura," and Talbot's claim, also made in 1839, that through photography "objects delineate themselves without the aid of the artist's pencil."[36] While recognizing early photographers' claims that Nature herself was making the images by means of cameras, Batchen reminds us of the aesthetic concerns of early practitioners with how nature was represented. By means of visual devices, "protophotographers," as Batchen calls them, for many centuries were attempting not merely to reproduce reality but to visually improve it, to make it "picturesque."

Batchen reminds us that Daguerre was a professional artist. As a teenager he sketched landscapes and later worked as an assistant in making large historical paintings, and exhibited paintings and drawings of his own. Talbot was also well versed in the picturesque aesthetic of that time. Artists and leisurely travelers of the period walked the countryside and made drawings, and when Nature herself was not sufficiently picturesque, they used machines to enhance her beauty, including a portable camera obscura and a more portable device called the *camera lucida* that was invented in 1801. The camera lucida was a mirrored device that made nature look reminiscent of landscapes painted by Claude Lorrain. It diminished details in favor of prominent features of a scene, toned down colors so that they looked like colors in varnished paintings, bent trees so that they better composed a particular view, and allowed the photographer to hold both foreground and background in focus, achieving pictorial integrity.

Talbot's mother hired landscape designers to give the Talbot's land ideal picturesque scenes. Batchen quotes the Reverend William Gilpin as an influential contributor to ideas about the picturesque who published travel books on the topic. Gilpin defined the *picturesque* as "expressive of that peculiar kind of beauty which is agreeable in a picture." Gilpin also said, "I am so attracted to my picturesque rules, that if nature gets it wrong, I cannot help putting her right."[37] Thus, the camera provided not a *real* way of seeing, but a *conventional* way of seeing, using conventions that adhered to the aesthetic of the picturesque, popular at the time.

Photographic Truth

DIGITAL IMAGES   The introduction of computer technology into photographic practices is cause for alarm to realists because they see it as threatening the reality base of photography, which for them is the optical and chemical relationship between the camera and what it photographs. If the photograph's reality base is compromised, realists fear that the photograph's truth value is weakened or lost altogether. For conventionalists, the introduction of computer technology into photography is not alarming but merely a continuation of practices that artists and photographers have invented and used throughout history to make expressive photographs.

Adrian Piper is a philosopher and an artist who uses lens-based images in her work, and she ruminates on the special nature of the photograph and its ability to accomplish what other media cannot (a realist position) while acknowledging how images are conventionally constructed:

> They have a kind of transparency that other media don't have. Although there are obviously all sorts of choices that go into what ends up in the photograph, and there are all sorts of ways in which it can be manipulated. Even given all you can do with changing the photographic image using Photoshop, I still think that there is a directness of reference to the thing that is photographed. It's less mediated by individual idiosyncratic choices about how to render—all of those things—than other media.[38]

Piper's thoughts offer a calming and balanced view of computer technology and photography: There is something special about the photograph's relation to what is photographed even when that information is adjusted with Photoshop.

By means of computer-enhanced photographic technologies, we can see "distant planets, the inside of a beating heart, a molecule that is a concept, and we can move through buildings which have not been built."[39] Scientists invested in scientific truth don't fear computer-enhanced images; they use them. Astronomers, for example, make digital images by using charge-coupled devices (CCDs). These light-sensitive chips produce small regions of electrical charges when struck by light. The light-induced charges can be read as an image and can be greatly enhanced with the aid of a computer. CCDs are much more sensitive to light than is film: A two-minute exposure with a CCD is equivalent to a thirty-minute exposure with conventional film. CCDs provide images of 16 million pixels, 4,000 by 4,000 square, and have replaced photographic film in professional astronomy. A new camera tested in 1999 increases the 16 million pixels of CCDs to over 67 million pixels. It has a field of view larger than the moon. The camera, a wide-field imager (WFI), uses a mosaic assembly of CCDs linked to computers and telescopes, sometimes located in different parts of the world, and renders images with levels of detail exceeding by a factor of 10,000 what the naked eye is able to see.[40]

Messier Grid Map, by astronomer Paul Gitto (Plate 35), is a composite of 110 CCDs of celestial objects in the Northern Hemisphere that he made from dawn to dusk on the first day of spring with a CCD camera and a telescope. The images replicate a handwritten list of objects made by Charles Messier, an eighteenth-century French astronomer. Gitto's grid, based on Messier's astronomical catalogue, has eleven rows and ten columns in numerical order, beginning in the upper left with Ml, the Crab Nebula, and ending in the lower right with MHO, a small elliptical galaxy in Andromeda. The image was made not to be reproduced in a book or to hang on a gallery wall but to be displayed on the Internet as an interactive image that coexists with the other 109 images to which it is linked. [41]

CCDs are enhanced electronically so that features of objects that could not be seen otherwise are made visible through a range of operations called *image processing*. These extensive operations are not possible with film. The CCD camera first subtracts electronic noise—unwanted electrons caused by factors other than light hitting the chip material—from the image. Usually, a number of images of the same object are taken and electronically merged into a single calibrated image that then undergoes further processing. The processes are designed to reveal or hide, sharpen or soften, lighten or darken, and color different facets of the image's details otherwise hidden in the electronic data. Using an unsharp mask, one can also enhance small- and medium-scale detail; log scaling enhances weak signals by increasing the pixel values of the fainter pixels; histogram equalization makes the brightness of all the pixel values the same. These image-enhancement processes combine art and science to turn digital data into images of scientific value and aesthetic beauty.

Journalists are now widely using digital technologies and, as they have since photography became available, continue to rely heavily on photographs to report

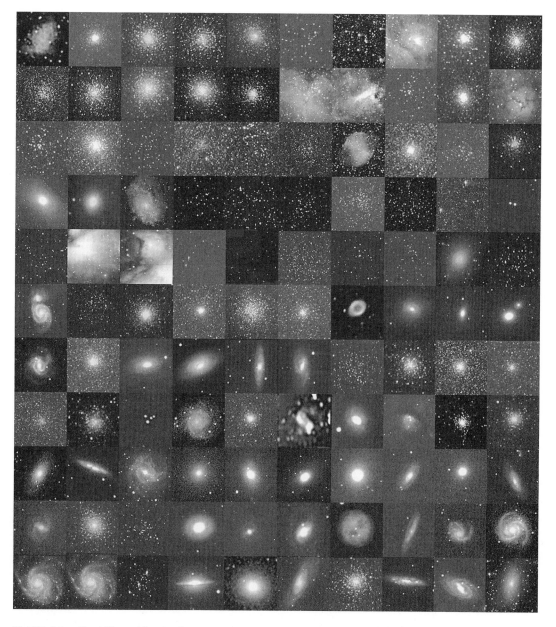

PLATE 35. Paul Gitto, *Messier Grid Map*, 1999.
© Paul Gitto, The Arcturus Observatory.

on the world. Credibility is paramount for journalists, and whereas they have enjoyed the assumed credibility and authority of photographs in the past, they are aware that the possibilities of misusing digital processes can undermine society's implicit trust in the photograph. With the relative ease of manipulating photographs through computer technology, their fears of false but credible and influential images being circulated are justified. The digital photograph is a mathematical formula that can be modified by simply adjusting the formula. Some digitized photographs presented and accepted as journalistic or evidentiary photographs pose threats to photographic veracity.

A newspaper editorial quoted a former head of photography for State Farm Insurance Company who claimed, "What you can do in a darkroom is 2 percent of what Photoshop is capable of doing." The editorial noted that many police departments have switched to digital photography because of lower cost and higher efficiency but expressed worry over how easy it would be to digitally manipulate evidence. The editorial was prompted in part by the release on the Internet of a digitally doctored photograph in 2003 that showed presidential candidate John Kerry on a speaker's platform with Vietnam antiwar activist Jane Fonda in an attempt to smear the candidate in the eyes of veterans.[42]

Two older journalistic examples are now notorious. On the February 1982 cover of *National Geographic,* editors visually shifted two pyramids closer together to better fit the vertical format of the magazine; *Time*'s cover, June 27, 1994, about the arrest of O. J. Simpson for the murder of Nicole Simpson and Ronald Goldman, featured a digitized version of the Los Angeles Police Department's mug shot of Simpson. *Time*'s illustrator, however, darkened Simpson's skin (dark skin implies more guilt than light skin?) to the outrage of many readers who interpreted the manipulation to be racist. The ability to convincingly alter photographs undermines image authentication in courts of law, the enforcement of missile-verification treaties, and other documentary uses of photographs.

Colin Jacobson, editor of the book *Underexposed: Censored Pictures and Hidden History,* an exposé of censored and distorted photographs, shows many examples of digitally altered photographs.[43] In 1993, for example, Somalis dragged a dead American soldier through the streets of Mogadishu. The soldier was clothed only in his underpants that revealed a part of his genitals. When *Time* published the photograph, the editors digitally covered that detail.

In 1991 the National Press Photographers Association (NPPA), aware of emerging technology that enables "the manipulation of the content of an image in such a way that the change is virtually undetectable," adopted the following principle of photographic ethics: "As journalists we believe the guiding principle of our profession is accuracy; therefore, we believe it is wrong to alter the content of a photograph in any way that deceives the public." The Nature Photography Association, however, does not have "any principle so strong," and instead embraces "poetic license." In 1996, exposés in the *Denver Post* and the *Seattle Post-Intelligencer* revealed that Art Wolfe fabricated photographs in his nature book, *Migrations:* "In about a third of the book's images the wildlife—caribou, zebra, geese, greater sand-hill cranes—had been digitally enhanced, and some had been digitally cloned and multiplied."[44]

ANALOG MANIPULATIONS   Examples of manipulations of photographs prior to digital technology are plentiful in the history of photography. Manipulations of two kinds are available: altering the subject matter before photographing it to suit the photographer's purposes and distorting photographic negatives or prints after initial exposures have been made.

Regarding the alteration of subject matter, consider, for example, F. Holland Day's photographs of the crucifixion of Jesus, such as *Christ with Mary and Saint,* made in 1898, available through the Library of Congress. Certainly, Day's crucifixions and other fictitious pictorialist images by him and others are not deceptive in intent nor result, but they point to a historical tradition of altering subject matter and prints for expressive purposes. Henry Peach Robinson's tenets of pictorialism, expressed in his book *Pictorial Effect in Photography: Hints on Composition and Chiaroscuro,* first published in 1869, advise practitioners of pictorialism to imitate paintings by England's Royal Academy of the Arts for themes and subjects as well as techniques. Robinson's recommended techniques include "selecting, arranging, rejecting, and rearranging elements to produce a pleasing result . . . if necessary by assembling models, props, and costumes, and by combination printing, and montage paste-up."[45]

Edward Steichen photographed Hawaiian hula dancer Tootsie Steer as part of an advertising campaign for the Matson cruise line in 1941. Steichen constructed his version of an "authentic native": Steer recalls that Steichen sought out dramatic natural backdrops, and that he instructed her to stop cutting her hair, to clip her nails, and to stop using nail polish.[46]

Kenneth Brower, a journalist who specializes in ecological issues, began accompanying nature photographers when he was twenty-one. Brower assisted renowned nature photographer Eliot Porter, then age sixty-four, on the Galapagos Islands, "helping to lug Porter's 4 × 5 camera and tripod up volcanoes, rowing dories in tough surf, and hunting meat, like Robinson Crusoe, on various islands. . . . It was one of the best times of my life."[47] On that particular journey, Brower met former Disney cameraman Tad Nichols and British nature photographer Alan Root, who along with Porter exchanged stories of work in the wild, specifically, fake nature photographs.

Porter was a purist and was opposed to changing the environment to photograph it but did uncomfortably admit that he occasionally moved a stone or feather or piece of driftwood to improve a picture. John Rohrbach, custodian of Porter's collection at the Amon Carter Museum, showed Brower a photograph of Porter "hacking away at a cactus to get a picture of a roadrunner nest." Paul Strand was also a purist, but Rohrbach has prints in which Strand drew in manholes or etched out people to balance his compositions. In the 1970s, Ansel Adams began removing "random clouds" in *Moonrise, Hernandez, New Mexico,* 1941, one of the most acclaimed photographs of the twentieth century, made within the realist, straight aesthetic.

Root told Brower the story of how one *Life* magazine cover came about, made by one of his colleagues. An editor in Manhattan imagined a photograph of a leopard and its kill in a tree backlit by a setting sun. "The photographer set off in quest of this vision, traveling the East African savanna for weeks with a captive leopard, killing antelopes, draping the carcasses in the branches of various thorn trees, and cajoling the leopard to lie proudly on 'the kill', a tableau that the photographer shot against a succession of setting suns."

Nichols told about working on Disney's movie *The Living Desert,* most of which was shot on a huge table, set up in a sound stage. For the film's famous sequence of lemming suicide, Disney workers bulldozed lemmings off cliffs. Brower recalls how Disney filmmakers made a documentary of a hawk killing a flying squirrel: "Assistant grip stands on tall stepladder with pouch of flying squirrels. Grip tosses squirrels—unpaid rodent extras—skyward one by one, as in a skeet shoot, until trained hawk, after dozens of misses, finally gets it right."[48]

CENSORSHIP   Colin Jacobson shows many examples of willful distortions of truth through censorship of photographs. He defines censorship as:

> A disturbing concept, usually referring to the act of someone in authority who prevents us from reading or hearing certain words or seeing certain images. By implication, it can also mean we are persuaded to accept phony material as genuine or consider a distorted context as the supposed truth.

Regarding such overt forms of control, he also asks these rhetorical questions about less obvious means:

> How often have government-inspired visual messages persuaded the populace not to be alarmed at certain threats to its health or welfare? How many times have editors banned the use of a disturbing image, not on the basis of its journalistic significance but because it might upset the sensitivities of their readers? How often has a vocal and influential minority in society dictated to the majority what may be looked at in culture and the arts? How many family picture albums have glossed over the mysterious woman standing behind Uncle Arthur? [49]

Jacobson provides hundreds of photographic examples in *Underexposed* of censored or altered images and notes that publishers engage in insidious forms of self-censorship by alleging that the public wants to be entertained rather than over-whelmed with harsh reality. *Underexposed* cites the example from the 1980s of the *London Observer*'s pulling a magazine cover image by Sebastião Salgado of a severe drought in Mali on the pretext that it might disturb readers "enjoying themselves on the beach during August Bank holiday." The paper replaced Salgado's image with a fashion photograph. Similarly, during the Vietnam War, the *New York Times* suppressed photographs of Buddhist monks setting themselves on fire in protest to the war. The editors feared that such shocking images might cause readers to cancel subscriptions.

During the first Gulf War, according to Jacobson, the *Observer* in London was one of the only publications to publish a gruesome photograph of an incinerated Iraqi staring sightlessly in death from his destroyed truck. The *Observer*'s editor was inundated with protests for publishing the photograph. Jacobson observes, "The Gulf War was presented to the world as a squeaky-clean technological mas-terpiece and the public were not encouraged to associate computer controlled, laser-directed weapons with subsequent human carnage."[50] Kenneth Jarecke, the photographer who made the image, objected, "the whole US press collaborated in keeping silent about the consequences of the Gulf War and who was respon-sible."[51] In an introductory essay in *Underexposed*, Harold Evans asserts, "when authority moves to suppress it is usually an indication that they have little confi-dence in their actions—precisely the moment when a more informed debate can avert catastrophe."[52]

On June 4, 1989, Magnum photographer Stuart Franklin photographed a pro-testing man in Tiananmen Square standing in front of an approaching column of tanks. It is one of the most widely distributed images of China in recent years. *Time* magazine's editors chose the protestor, the "unknown rebel," as one of the "top 20 revolutionaries and leaders of the twentieth century." However, to suit the political agenda of the democratic West over Communist China, the photograph was shown with little contextual information so as to clearly imply the brutality of the Chinese regime. In his book *Photojournalism and Foreign Policy*, David D. Perlmutter says that the tanks maneuvered around the yelling protestor, but he blocked their moves and ultimately jumped on the front tank, trying to persuade the driver to turn back. His friends ran out and pulled him away.[53]

AESTHETIC CONCERNS: IS PHOTOGRAPHY ART?

The question of whether photography is art, which was once hotly debated, especially in the 1960s and 1970s, is no longer salient. The question has been answered pragmatically by institutional consensus: Most art museums now house photographic collections. The J. Paul Getty Museum in Los Angeles, for example, bought nine private collections, 65,000 photographs, in 1984, for an estimated

$20 million. Even cursory samplings of the world's major art festivals and biennials readily reveal the predominance and importance of photography and other lens-based media in contemporary art today. The assertion that photography is clearly accepted as art today does not, however, explain how or when it came to achieve this status.

Andy Grundberg, independent scholar and former photography critic for the *New York Times,* offers a distinction between photographers who make art and artists who make photographs, each group with its own history.[54] According to Grundberg, the two parallel histories began in the middle of the nineteenth century, when photographers advanced photography as an artform, and when some artists—that is, painters and sculptors—openly embraced the camera as an aid to their artmaking. Photographers of the time based their photographs in a realist aesthetic, reproducing the natural world. Artists, notably Edgar Degas and Pierre-Auguste Rodin, used the camera and were influenced by photographs, yet they thought photographs did not merit the status of art because, in their view, the camera was incapable of utilizing imagination.

During the advancement of modern art in the first half of the twentieth century, painters and photographers pursued similar aims and mutually influenced one another, although they were reluctant to admit it because modern art theory held that each medium should be independent and self-sufficient. Paul Strand was indebted to Pablo Picasso and Georges Braque, but referred to his work as "pure" photography. Charles Sheeler, friend of Strand, made both paintings and photographs, but downplayed his photographic activity to increase the aesthetic and economic value of his paintings. Man Ray collaborated with Marcel Duchamp, and Henri Cartier-Bresson was highly influenced by surrealism.

Photographers who were making art photographs in the 1940s and 1950s either stood with or fought against the dominant photographic aesthetic of the time, articulated by Alfred Stieglitz, who asserted that photographic meaning was metaphoric, and that photographers' thoughts and feelings were best expressed when they were embedded in "pure" straightforward photographic technique. At that time, abstract expressionism and the New York School of painting were at their apex, and photographers such as Minor White, Paul Caponigro, and Aaron Siskind made abstract photographs with meanings that were as free floating as those attributed to abstract paintings. Photographs could be as otherworldly and mysterious as abstract paintings. About the same time, Grundberg points out, some photographers, most prominently Walker Evans and Robert Frank, turned to social-documentary photography as a new model of how photography could influence American culture and contribute a new kind of art. Later photographers in this tradition, notably Diane Arbus, Lee Friedlander, and Gary Winogrand, came to be known as "street photographers."

The Museum of Modern Art was one of the few, and the most prestigious, of American art museums to first collect photographs as art. It embraced both metaphoric and realist photographs. The department was founded by Beaumont Newhall, David McAlpin, and Ansel Adams in 1940, and Newhall was its first curator and grew in prestige and importance under the direction of John Szarkowski, who like Stieglitz, held the modernist and formalist belief that photography was unique among media and fundamentally different from painting, and that photography should be based in the pure use of cameras and photographic materials.

As examples of more recent artists (that is, painters and sculptors) who make photographs, Grundberg points to Robert Rauschenberg and Andy Warhol, who made paintings by silk-screening photographic images onto canvases. Rauschenberg and Warhol, eschewing abstraction, favored photographs for their representational subject matter. Other artists in the 1960s and 1970s also chose photography, film, and video in revolt against abstraction and the ideas that art is self-generated and self-expressive. In Grundberg's view, photography (and performance, installation, mail art, and collaborations with dancers) represented artists' turns toward social content in their artmaking.

While Rauschenberg and Warhol were silk-screening photographic images onto canvases, in 1963 Ed Ruscha published 400 numbered copies of *Twentysix Gasoline Stations,* a book straightforwardly picturing gas stations on Route 66 between Los Angeles and Oklahoma City. This and other photographic and painterly works by Ruscha were first seen as West Coast versions of pop but are now recognized as works of conceptual art, exemplifying, in Grundberg's words, "seriality, procedural rigor, and the documentary nature of photographic information."[55] Grundberg includes other recent artists with similar attitudes and strategies who used photographs: Dan Graham, Robert Smithson, Sol LeWitt, Mel Bochner, Joseph Kosuth, Hans Haacke, Vito Acconci, Bruce Nauman, Douglas Huebler, Gordon Matta-Clark, Ana Mendieta, Robert Cumming, and William Wegman. Art photographers Bernd and Hilla Becher, Lewis Baltz, and Martha Rosler make photographic art that is serial and reliant on documentary photographic information.

In the 1970s photography received much critical attention, specifically in Susan Sontag's series of articles begun in 1973 that eventually were published as *On Photography* in 1978. *October,* a theoretical journal of art, devoted an issue to photography in 1978. The writings on photography by European authors such as Roland Barthes, Jean Baudrillard, Walter Benjamin, and Michel Foucault became available in English. According to Grundberg,

> Much of the critical attention to photography was directed at its functional role in contemporary culture, and to its instrumental role in forming that culture. In other words, photographs were recognized as both reflections and producers of the world in which we live. The commonplace idea that photography's documentary abilities allowed it to objectively reproduce social reality (as in, for example, the practices of photojournalism and portraiture) was replaced by the conviction that its fictive capabilities (as in, say, advertising and fashion photography) allowed it to create a false sense of reality,

a replacement reality that obscured and/or obviated what was really real. Baudrillard's term for this condition was the simulacrum—roughly, a world in which representations of things, not the things themselves, ruled.[56]

By the end of the 1980s, photography was at the center of art discourse and postmodern practice, placed there in part by the photographic work of Sherrie Levine, Cindy Sherman (see Plate 4, Color Plate 1), Richard Prince, Barbara Kruger (see Plate 30, Color Plate 30), Sarah Charlesworth (see Plate 25), Laurie Simmons (see Color Plate 32 according to Color Art MS.), and James Welling, artists who in their different ways "posited a world in which all experience was mediated by lens-produced images." Thus, roughly between 1970 and 1990, photographs became fully integrated with other forms of contemporary art.

Grundberg's account of how photography came to be art is largely an institutional account and an extended application of what is known as the Institutional Theory of Art, authored primarily by aesthetician George Dickey. That is, a work of art is an artifact that has conferred upon it the status of being a candidate for appreciation by an institution, namely, the art world.[57] The institution that Grundberg focused upon in his account of how photography became art is the Whitney Museum of American Art and the photographs it collected between 1940 and 2001.

Meanwhile and nearby, another institution, the Museum of Modern Art, was also defining art photography by its collecting practices. Before the 1990s, the Museum of Modern Art had not given an exhibition to John Baldessari, Gilbert & George, David Hockney, Robert Mapplethorpe (see Plates 32, 33), Richard Prince, Laurie Simmons, William Wegman (cover), Joel-Peter Witkin (see Plate 5), Cindy Sherman, Barbara Kruger, Sherrie Levine, or Mike and Doug Starn (Plate 36). These artists had widespread support in other museums, such as the Whitney, but had not been conferred museum status under the curatorial, intellectual stances of John Szarkowski.[58] Theory influences curatorial practice, and curatorial practice influences theory.

Underlying the curatorial decisions of the Whitney and the Modern are competing arguments of an aesthetic nature about how photographs should be made and how they should look. In a 1987 review of a Cindy Sherman exhibition (see Plate 4, Color Plate 1), Eleanor Heartney wrote in *Afterimage*: "These days, we seem to prefer our art obedient to theory."[59] The critic partially attributed Cindy Sherman's rise to fame to its relevance to current theory: It fit well into feminist-poststructuralism. If theory remains influential today, it was also true of photography in the past, but under different rubrics, terms, and theories. Alfred Stieglitz, for example, exhibited in Gallery 291 and published in *Camera Work* only those photographers whose work fit his theory of photography and political agenda for photography. In the 1920s Edward Weston accused pictorialist photographers of not making "photographs" but of making "pseudo-paintings,"[60] images that by Weston's aesthetic were neither good photographs nor good paintings.

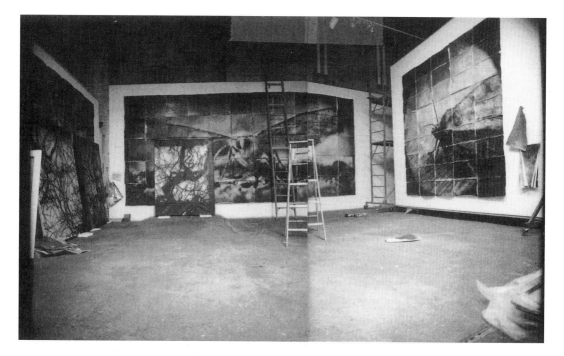

PLATE 36. Mike and Doug Starn, *View of Mike and Doug Starn's Studio, July 2003.*
© Mike and Doug Starn/Artists Rights Society (ARS), New York.

When writers theorize about the aesthetics of photography, they generally attempt to define what photography is—that is, what it should be and how it should best be considered. Most definitions of art try to persuade us to view art in a certain way and to make certain kinds of art. New definitions are often put forth in reaction to prior definitions. Definitions of photography may be given in a sentence. In a catalogue essay to an exhibition, Max Kozloff, for example, writes, "A photograph, with its two-dimensional surface, is the inert, flattened light trace of certain external maneuvers that once occurred."[61] He offers this definition of photography, almost in passing, in his development of another thought.

Allan Sekula opens an article with this sentence: "Suppose we regard art as a mode of human communication, as a discourse anchored in concrete social relations, rather than as a mystified, vaporous, and ahistorical realm of purely affective expression and experience."[62] His definition is clearly meant to be persuasive. That is, he wants the reader to accept photography as a "mode of communication anchored in concrete social relations." His definition is in opposition to a definition of photography as art, which he dismisses as "mystified, vaporous, and ahistorical affective expression." In the remainder of his article, "Dismantling

Modernism, Reinventing Documentary (Notes on the Politics of Representation)," Sekula explains his definition, argues for its acceptance, and offers examples of photography that fit within it.

Some definitions of art, or photography, take the length of a book to fully explicate. Such books are Aristotle's *Poetics*, Arthur Danto's *Transfiguration of the Commonplace: A Philosophy of Art,* Susan Sontag's *On Photography,* and Roland Barthes's *Camera Lucida: Reflections on Photography.*

Some photography writers consider definitions of photography to be too narrowly aesthetic and have broadened the definition of photography by which photographs they have chosen to examine: For example, Sally Stein has attended to the photography and layout of women's magazines; Carol Squiers has examined the photography of annual corporate reports; Allan Sekula has written about French police photography; Louis Kaplan has critically examined the "living photographs" of American flag motifs by Arthur Mole during World War I; and Geoffrey Batchen has explored nineteenth-century photography objects such as photographic jewelry, cased daguerreotypes, and decorated albums.

Writers who theorize about photography are not inquiring about a particular photograph, although they use particular photographs for examples. They are exploring photography in general, attempting to answer how it is like and how it is different from other forms of picturing. These long-standing questions that have received many different answers are typical theoretical questions: What is photography? Is photography art? What are the consequences of calling photography "art"? Is photography different from painting? Does photography get us closer to reality than does painting? What does photography do best? Can a photograph be value neutral?

Theories can be partial, incomplete, and fragmented. We move through the world with such theories and may not be cognizant of them until questioned about them. Such theories are probably better understood as assumptions rather than theories about reality, life, art, and photography. Whether consciously held or not, assumptions and theories affect how we make photographs and how we understand them. The theories of our teachers, whether fully developed or a loosely held set of assumptions, certainly influence the way they teach about photography, the way we learn about photography, and the kinds of photographs we are encouraged to make. In 1985 Abigail Solomon-Godeau critiqued educational consequences of modernist photography theory on the college education of photography students:

> The teaching of photography tends to be cordoned off from what goes on in the rest of the art department. So while young painters are reading art magazines and as often as not following developments in film, performance and video, photography students are reading photography magazines, disputing the merits of documentary over self-expression, or resurrecting unto the fourth generation an exhausted formalism that can no longer generate either heat or light.[63]

Douglas Crimp took critical issue with the New York Public Library in 1975 when it took a look at all its books containing photographs and discovered several books that were illustrated with old photographs by now famous photographers. These books had been catalogued under various topics, such as history, geography, and science. Based on the ontological position of photography and its newly acquired special status, the administration formed a new department of photography and appointed a librarian to oversee the department. Books on the Civil War that contained photographs by Timothy O'Sullivan and Alexander Gardner, and books on Egypt with photographs by Beato, have all been recatalogued under the single category of "photography." Douglas Crimp wrote an essay objecting to the recataloguing.[64] He argued that the decision was a misguided one in that it was based on the new economic value photographs received because of their newly acquired status as high art. Crimp argued that recataloguing the books under "photography" changes the content of the books from history and geography and science to art and to photography. He fears on epistemological grounds that an accurate understanding of the books will be befuddled by their new label and that their contents will now be restricted to a limited understanding of them as aesthetic objects: "What was Egypt will become Beato, or du Camp, or Frith; Pre-Columbian Middle America will be Desiré Charnay; the American Civil War will now be Alexander Gardner, Timothy O'Sullivan, and others. . . . The horse in motion will be Muybridge, while the night of birds will be Marey . . . urban poverty and immigration become Jacob Riis and Lewis Hine." He is arguing against defining, in words and in practice, all photographs as "art."

Richard Woodward titled an article he wrote in 1988 "It's Art, but Is It Photography?" His title is ironic: Earlier debates about whether photography was an artform were finally answered in the affirmative, but with the acceptance into art museums of all kinds of photographic imagery, questions arose about what constituted a photograph. Postmodernists tend not to care about whether an image is "truly photographic" or not, but modernists who want to maintain distinctions about media and their individual uniqueness, would be concerned. Thus, Woodward, embracing a modernist perspective, writes, "It isn't clear anymore how photography should be valued or looked at, where within our museums it should be exhibited—even what is or is not a photograph."[65]

There are consequences in the art market to positioning images as photographs or as artworks. Charles Desmarais, former director of the California Museum of Photography, said in 1988, "I'm not sure why it is that when you call yourself a photographer you charge $300 for a picture, but if you're an artist its OK to ask $3,000 or $30,000."[66] At that time, David Hockney's large photo collages, sometimes produced in editions of twenty, were priced between $10,000 and $60,000. A Barbara Kruger billboard piece then sold for $30,000. A photograph by the Starns could earn $50,000. Hockney is known as a painter, and Kruger and the Starns are promoted by their galleries as artists, not photographers. Their prices for single images were well above the price of a single photograph by living photographers, which were then much closer to the $300 figure. Discrepancies continue between prices for what are identified as "photographs" versus prices of photograph images designated as "artworks." Woodward, in a 2004 article, cites the discrepancies between auction prices for a photographic artwork by Gregory Crewdson ($41,825) and a photograph by Joel Sternfeld ($3,600).[67]

Modernism and Postmodernism

Modernism in art and photography is a small part of a much larger era known as *modernity,* temporally ranging from the Enlightenment (about 1687 to 1789) to the present. Early modernity is characterized intellectually by a belief that science would save the world and that, through reason, a foundation of universal truths would be established. Through the use of science and reason, which yield "truth," political leaders thought they could produce a just and egalitarian social order. These beliefs fed the American and French democratic revolutions. The major movements and events of modernity are democracy, capitalism, industrialization, science, and urbanization. Modernity's rallying flags are freedom and the individual.

There is no discrete beginning of postmodernity, but some scholars look at the student revolution in Paris in 1968 as its symbolic birth. Postmodernists react against modernism: Postmodernity does not simply temporally succeed modernity; it largely rejects it, and *antimodernism* may be a clearer term for the wide-ranging phenomenon of postmodernism. The French postmodernist writer Jean-François Lyotard explains the difference between modernism and postmodernism:

> Even though the field of the postmodern is extremely vast, and even though the word can sometimes be applied to things that are diametrically opposed to one another, it's based fundamentally upon the perception of the existence of a modern era that dates from the time of the Enlightenment and that has now run its course; and this modern era was predicated on a notion of progress in knowledge, in the arts, in technology, and in human freedom as well, all of which was thought of as leading to a truly emancipated society: a society emancipated from poverty, despotism, and ignorance.[68]

Postmodernist social critics object that modernists fell far short of producing a just and egalitarian society, faulting modernists for producing the suffering and misery of peasants under monarchies, and later the oppression of workers under capitalist industrialization, the exclusion of women from the public sphere, the colonization of other lands by imperialists for economic and religious reasons, and ultimately the destruction of indigenous peoples. Postmodernist artists and photographers draw on these social themes in their work. Recall Barbara Kruger's work, for example, discussed in Chapter 5 (see Color Plate 30 and Plate 30).

Postmodernists are much less optimistic than modernists about the possibility of progress and our ability to positively affect the future, and they are much more skeptical about freedom of the individual and the power of reason to solve social problems. Michel Foucault, the late French cultural critic who has profoundly influenced postmodern thinking on such diverse disciplines as criminology, philosophy, and literary criticism, argued that knowledge is power that is too often used by a powerful few to impose their ideas of what they consider to be right and true on a weaker majority.

Jacques Derrida, the influential French postmodernist who uses deconstruction as his critical methodology of analyzing "texts," explains his sense of deconstruction and text:

> To deconstruct a "text" (a term defined broadly enough to include the Declaration of Independence and a Van Gogh painting) means to pick it apart, in search of ways in which it fails to make the points it seems to be trying to make. Why would someone want to "read" (defined equally broadly) like that? In order to experience the impossibility of anyone writing or saying (or painting) something that is perfectly clear, the impossibility of constructing a theory or method of inquiry that will answer all the questions or the impossibility of fully comprehending weighty matters, like death.[69]

For Derrida and other postmodernists, deconstruction guards against the modernist belief: "a belief that has led to much violence—that the world is simple and can be known with certainty. It confronts us with the limits of what is possible for human thought to accomplish."

Postmodernists see all kinds of things as texts, including photographs, and insist that all texts need to be read critically. For postmodernists, *a text* is different from modernists' notion of *a work*. A work is singular, speaking in one voice, that of the author or maker, which leads the reader to look for one meaning, presumed to be the author's. A postmodernist text, however, implies that any piece of literature or work of art is not the product of a free and unique individual but rather a field of citations and correspondences in continual permutation in which many voices speak, blend, and clash. For postmodernists many readings (interpretations and understandings) of a text are desirable—no single reading can be conclusive or complete. Further, reading should not simply be seen as consumption but as production. Reading is "a productive activity, the making of meaning, in which one is guided by the text one reads, of course, but not simply manipulated by it; [one should] perceive writing as an activity that is also guided and sustained by prior texts. The writer is always reading, and the reader is always writing."[70]

Using examples from daily experience familiar in 1988, Todd Gitlin, a sociologist, offers a list of persons, places, and things he considers postmodernist and in need of critical readings, including Robert Rauschenberg's silk screens, Warhol's multiple-image paintings, and Sherrie Levine's photographs of "classic" photographs.[71]

Structuralism and *poststructuralism* are coexisting and opposing ways of making meaning of the world. Both influence current theory about photography and criticism. Structuralism is modernist in the sense that structuralists, in their search for underlying codes, systems, or structures, believe they can attain ultimate truths about the world and social interactions. Claude Levi-Strauss, for example, developed structuralist anthropology to uncover systems embedded in social codes. He sought scientific truths. Poststructuralists, such as Derrida, are skeptical of any ultimate truths, believing that truth is historically dependent and always partial. Thus, structuralism is modernist, and poststructuralism is postmodern.

The poststructuralist text is an elaboration of the structuralist's notion of the sign: "Every meaningful action—wearing a necktie, embracing a friend, cooking a meal—is meaningful only to the extent that it is a sign in some interpretive code."[72] Recall from Chapter 3 how Roland Barthes deciphered the interpretive code of a photographic print advertisement for a tomato sauce.

Postmodernists who are influenced in their beliefs by Jacques Lacan, the French psychoanalytic scholar, are also wary of the notion of a self. René Descartes's dictum, "I think therefore I am," expresses an Enlightenment foundational belief in the existence of a unified rational being. Later, existentialists such as Jean-Paul Sartre proposed that "existence precedes essence"—that is, individuals are free and undetermined. James Hugunin, a photography critic, summarizes Lacan's theory of the self, which strains against modernist notions:

> For Lacan, the Self is not the unitary ego of the Cartesian *Cogito ergo sum.* That sense of a unitary Self is, according to Lacan, an illusion, an effect of ideology; rather, the subject only exists as if it were a unitary subject. It is actually a misrecognized Self formed from an idealized image which it forms of itself in the mirror of the idealized Other, be that one's family, Big Brother, or cultural forms of reflection like film, television, and literature.[73]

This theory of the self, not coincidentally, is very similar to critics' interpretations of what Cindy Sherman (see Plate 4, Color Plate 1) has fashioned with her self-portraits discussed earlier in this book. Modernists place the individual at the center of the universe; postmodernists decenter the individual and claim that the self is an effect of language, social relations, and the subconscious.

Modernity and postmodernity imbue all aspects of society and are apparent in its cultural forms, including fiction, architecture, painting, and popular culture. This chapter, however, is particularly interested in distinctions between modernist and postmodernist manifestations in photography. Modernism in art is known for such tenets as these: a superior attitude toward and opposition to popular culture;

an emphasis on high art and its superiority to the crafts; an objection to art as entertainment; an insistence on its own self-sufficiency and transcendency ("art for art's sake"); a belief that art primarily refers to other art rather than to the social world; a desire to be judged by formalist criteria and how the artwork furthers the history of art; a disregard for context in interpretation; a preoccupation with the purity of a medium ("flatness" in painting, for example);[74] a rejection of narrative content as appropriate for serious art; a belief in the individual genius of the artist; a desire for originality; a thirst for the new; and reverence for the precious, unique art object.

MODERNISM AND PHOTOGRAPHY   Modernism in photography is known for theoretical positions parallel to the modernist positions given earlier for painting and sculpture, namely formalism, as discussed in Chapter 6. Modernist photographers believe that art photography is different from and superior to commercial photography. For several decades, color photographs, popular in mass media, were considered trivial by the photographic art community, and black and white was held to be serious. Modernists hold fashion photography in lower esteem than art photography; Richard Avedon and Irving Penn still fight, whether they need to or not, to be recognized as artists. The commercial work of Diane Arbus and Duane Michals, for example, has not been treated equally with their art photography. *Life* magazine offered copious context for its photographs through captions and articles, whereas *Aperture* magazine during the same years, under the editing of Minor White, did not even publish the name of the photographer under an image so that contextual information would not distract from aesthetic and spiritual contemplation of the image. The modernists' desire to have photography a pure medium has fueled debates throughout the history of photography, with Edward Weston, for example, rallying against what he derogatorily called the "pseudo-paintings" of photographers who visibly hand-brushed their emulsions. John Szarkowski's defining characteristics of photographs as the thing itself, the detail, the frame, time, and vantage point[75] sought to make the medium unique and especially different from painting. Modernists favor symbolist rather than narrative photographs, and realism over instrumentalism. Modernists believe the straight photograph to be the embodiment of what photography does best. Modernist prints are precious, signed, numbered, and archivally processed.

Photographers Alfred Stieglitz, Paul Strand, Edward Weston, Imogen Cunningham, Minor White, and Ansel Adams, historian Beaumont Newhall, and curator John Szarkowski are preeminent modernists in photography. Szarkowski for twenty-five years had a major role in shaping modernist theory in art photography. According to Woodward, Szarkowski "is one of the great figures of American art; and the Museum of Modern Art has shown a longer, deeper regard for the art of photography than any institution in the world."[76] Woodward credits Szarkowski with cutting "the photograph's ties to journalistic themes and captions and letting work stand on its own, without relying on subject matter for its importance." Letting the work "stand on its own" is a modernist theme, that of transcendency and independence; letting the work stand on its own "without relying on subject matter" is also a modernist tenet that looks to form rather than subject as the important element. For more than twenty-five years, Woodward adds, Szarkowski has "done more than anyone to analyze how a photograph differs from any other kind of art." Szarkowski's analysis is a typically modernist project, one of sorting characteristics of photography from those of painting and other media, to establish its uniqueness.

Michael Köhler, in *Constructed Realities: The Art of Staged Photography,* a book he edited in 1989, offers these principles of modern photographic practices:

> Modern Photography—Basic Aesthetic Principles
> 1. The camera artist should find, and not invent, his subjects.
> 2. He should make no alterations of any kind to the segment of reality chosen.
> 3. In taking the photograph, he should attempt to render things as "objectively" as he finds them, i.e. clearly and sharply and true to both form and detail.
> 4. No manipulations of the exposed negative are permitted in the darkroom.
> 5. Prints should be of the highest technical perfection and contain a rich range of grey tones. Prints are not to be manipulated.
> 6. The creative achievement of the camera artist consists in his choice of motifs and their photographic depiction as determined by the selection of camera view, focal length and exposure time. All affectations of "painterly" or "graphic" effect diminish the realistic quality of the photograph and are therefore to be avoided.[77]

For some, modernism is not a thing of the past but is still very much in the present, as evidenced by a 2004 exhibition by the J. Paul Getty Museum in Los Angeles, "Photographers of Genius at the Getty," organized by Weston Naef, the founding head of Getty's huge photography collection of nearly 70,000 images. While postmodernists generally deny the concept of "genius," Naef embraces it: "This collection was founded on the idea that there are certain very great makers of photographs who are able to repeat their superlative performance over and over again, and for whom mastery of craft is essential."[78]

Modernism in photography has its own tradition different from the tradition of fine art. Modernism in photography and in fine art are based on the same beliefs, but the photographic community, desiring to have photography accepted as a legitimate and respected fine art on a par with painting, defensively developed its own history books, its own departments in universities, its own journals, and favored educational separatism from other artists at the same time it was seeking acceptance in the art community.

That photography has been accepted as art is a "dubious reward," in the view of Solomon-Godeau:

> Today art photography reaps the dubious reward of having accomplished all that was first set out in its mid-nineteenth century agenda: general recognition as an art form, a place in the museum, a market (however erratic), a patrimonial lineage, an acknowledged canon. Yet hostage still to a modernist allegiance to the autonomy, self-referentiality, and transcendence of the work of art, art photography has systematically engineered its own irrelevance and triviality. It is, in a sense, all dressed up with nowhere to go.[79]

POSTMODERNISM AND PHOTOGRAPHY   Köhler contrasts modern photographic practices with these principles of postmodern photographic practices:

> Post-Modern Photographic Practice—Basic Aesthetic Principles
> 1. The photo artist must invent his subject, or more precisely fabricate it; mere finding is no longer enough.
> 2. What methods he employs in doing so are entirely his own choice. Either he makes the effort to arrange, construct or stage his subjects before the camera, or he uses pictures produced by others as points of departure for his own.
> 3. All exposure techniques are acceptable; the choice is a function of the particular intentions of the individual artist.
> 4. All manipulations of negatives and prints are not only permitted but welcome. The more imaginative, the better.
> 5. Technical finesse in the production of negatives and prints is allowed, but does not represent a binding standard for the quality of a piece of work. Demonstrative technical dilettantism itself can be a successful pictorial strategy.
> 6. The creative achievement of the photo artist is measured according to his ability to undermine the traditional claim of the camera image to "truth," "objectivity" and "realism"—and to give it the character of an "autonomous" pictorial object instead.[80]

Postmodernism, in the views of Solomon-Godeau and other postmodernist photography critics, has rightly replaced modernism. Jan Zita Grover writes: "Individual genius, the object as unique and precious, art as the new, the violate (yet the pearl beyond price) had run smack into a highly persuasive, hugely pervasive mass culture that obscured the differences between original and reproduction, high and low art, entertainment and information, art and advertising."[81]

Both statements by Solomon-Godeau and Grover reiterate principles of modernism that they reject: the autonomy, self-referentiality, and transcendence of the work of art, "individual genius, the object as unique and precious, and art as the new." Those who embrace postmodernist theory generally recognize that art exemplifies the political, cultural, and psychological experience of a society; they are aware of and refer to the previously hidden agendas of the art market and its relation to art museums, dealers, and critics; they are willing to borrow widely from the past; they have returned to the figurative in art; they embrace social content over aesthetic form, and a plurality of styles.

Walter Benjamin is an early influential figure whose writings have become central to postmodernist practices and to photography's centrality in postmodernism. A German cultural theorist, Benjamin in the 1930s wrote two essays on photography that are frequently cited by recent theorists, especially those of postmodernist and leftist persuasions: "The Work of Art in the Age of Mechanical Reproduction" and "A Short History of Photography."[82] In these essays, Benjamin stresses aspects of the photographic medium different from those that Strand and Weston were emphasizing in the United States. While Strand and Weston herald the honesty of the medium and the infinite detail of the negative and the beautiful photographic print, Benjamin stresses that, unlike the painting, the photograph is infinitely reproducible. Photography could also reproduce the painting. So while modernists were promoting the precious image, Benjamin's notions suggested possibilities for a mass-produced image in the age of mechanical reproduction.

Photography is at the center of postmodernism. As Woodward wrote in 1988, "In the last few years, as neo-conceptualism—an art of ideas, riddles and barbed queries in which the inner life of the artist is irrelevant—has replaced neo-expressionism in critics' conversation, photography has moved from the margins toward the center of the art world's interests."[83] With an implicit nod to Benjamin's thought, Woodward cites reproduction as photography's main contribution to postmodernist practice: "Unlike a painting, a photograph is an infinitely reproducible image. (Paintings can be reproduced only by means of photography.) A photograph is also readily adaptable: It can be blown up, shrunk, cropped, blurred, used in a newspaper, in a book, on a billboard." Similarly, Solomon-Godeau lists the formal devices "seriality and repetition, appropriation, intertextuality, simulation or pastiche" as the primary means of such artists using photography in 1985 as John Baldessari, Victor Burgin, Hilla and Bernd Becher, Dan Graham, Sarah Charlesworth, Barbara Kruger, Louise Lawler, Sherrie Levine, Richard Prince, Cindy Sherman, Laurie Simmons, and James Welling.[84]

Postmodernism is not immune to criticism. Some fear that postmodernists' ridicule of a search for truth fosters a cynical nihilism, and others fear that postmodernists' emphasis on the impossible, on what we cannot know, threatens to leave us paralyzed and unable to react to the world's injustices.[85] Susan Sontag, for example, when faced with war, devastation, suffering, and death in 2003, writes angrily about the "fancy rhetoric" and the "radical cynical spin" she associates with the writings on reality of two French writers: "Guy Debord, who thought he was describing an illusion, a hoax, and of Jean Baudrillard, who claims to believe that images, simulated realities, are all that exists now." The ravages of wars make Sontag reject postmodernist assertions that everything is mere spectacle and all that we have are representations.

> To speak of reality becoming a spectacle is a breathtaking provincialism. It universalizes the viewing habits of a small, educated population living in the rich part of the world, where news has been converted into entertainment. . . . It assumes that everyone is a spectator. It suggests, perversely, unseriously, that there is no real suffering in the world. But it is absurd to identify "the world" with those zones in the rich countries where people have the dubious privilege of being spectators, or of declining to be spectators, of other people's pain, just as it is absurd to generalize about the ability to respond to the sufferings of others on the basis of the mind-set of those consumers of news who know nothing at first hand about war and terror. There are hundreds of millions of television watchers who are far from inured to what they see on television. They do not have the luxury of patronizing reality.[86]

Digital Images and Aesthetic Concerns

The technology that forms the digital image is intrinsically different from the chemically based photographic image. The digital image exists as numerical information and does not necessarily have to be represented as a physical entity. The computer stores and processes information, such as an image, as a set of instructions known as *binary code* and displays it on a screen. This code, like a light switch, operates in two states, on and off. The use of binary code allows the digital image to be easily manipulated and stored.[87]

Examples of aesthetic uses of digital technology in the production of expressive images abound: See, for example, "The digitally liquid, melting imagery" made by Jeremy Blake for a DVD called *Planet Waves*. The DVD is a posthumous visual tribute with narration to Ossie Clark, a British fashion designer to "swinging London" in the 1960s and 1970s who was murdered by his lover in 1996. According to critic Edward Leffingwell, Blake's "9-minute loop morphs through photographically derived, computer generated and hand-painted images evoking the pharmaceutically enhanced ups and downs of Clark's fast-lane life."[88] The critic tells us about the digital making of the imagery as part of its aesthetic and resulting expressivity and sees no need to further discuss ramifications or implications of the digital process.

Similarly, when Sontag interprets Jeff Wall's digital image of Russian soldiers in Afghanistan (see Plate 7), she feels no need to discuss its technical production or go into the ramifications of it being a digital rather than a traditional photograph. She does tell us that the photograph is fictional, clearly an important bit of contextual information, much more important, in her thinking, than telling us the details of how the photographer constructed the image. Sontag gives more import to its meaning and effect.

Although Wall's fictional image could have been made by photographic means other than digital technology, many photographic expressions are uniquely possible because of digital technology, and many artists are exploring the expressive and conceptual possibilities of digitized imagery.

Andreas Gursky enhances his large-scale photographs through digital means. Generally, his photographs appear to be realistic and unmanipulated. Looking at them, many would likely not know that they are digital and enhanced. The images are aesthetically crisp and detailed with loads of information. Most viewers knowledgeable about photography do know that they are digital images, but the information does not seem to be essential to their understanding of Gursky's expressions. If viewers are not aware of digital manipulations in Gursky's photographs, no harm is likely to follow.

One of Gursky's images, *Stockholder Meeting, Diptych,* is two large panels of digitally convened figures that represent a meeting of many executives from large and influential German corporations. Upon close inspection, one can eventually determine that the scene could never exist in reality. As described by critic Edward Leffingwell, the image shows "a rapt and ghostly audience that fans out in seats ranked along the diptych's base. Their lines of sight lead upward to a disconcerting central mass of snow-encrusted granite. Assembled groups of corporate leaders seated at long tables are ranged above the audience as though set into the mountain or suspended in surrealistic space." The assembled executives seem to wait for some "corporate benediction so the business of their convention might begin. Their names appear before them on plaques. A cheerless row of decorative geraniums extends along the base of one section, and ferns along another. Corporate logos hover like Pentecostal tongues in a cloudless sky above."[89] Whether one is aware of the technology Gursky used to make the image seems irrelevant. Seeing that it is a fabricated image suffices to know that it is fiction with an expressive purpose. The important expressive point is that of a fictional metaphor and not how it was made.

Computer technology allows artists to make new images and statements, unavailable without such technology. For the past twenty-five years, Thomas Ruff has "redefined photography's conceptual possibilities, simultaneously capturing and questioning the essence of photography as both a means and a tool for visual experience." . . . Works in the *cassini* series (see Color Plate 27) are based on photographic captures of Saturn taken by NASA's Cassini-Huygens Spacecraft, which launched in 2004 and completed its initial four-year mission in June 2008. The spacecraft orbited around Saturn to provide the first in-depth, close-up study of the planet and its domain, including its rings, moons, and magnetosphere, the enormous magnetic bubble that controls its planetary movement.

Ruff acquired these black and white raw images from NASA's Website, where they were broadcast directly from the spacecraft and made available for public download. Through computer manipulation, Ruff infused each gray-scale image with saturated color. The resulting chromogenic prints transform the originals into visual statements that both capture the sweeping enormity of planetary structures while still distancing themselves from concrete forms, evocative instead of abstract and minimalist compositions.[90] Given the formal minimalist beauty of *cassini 06* and his continued exploration of what the medium of photography can produce, this digital work by Ruff fits comfortably in the aesthetically evaluative category.

SOME CONCLUSIONS ABOUT DIGITAL IMAGES   Any manipulation of a photograph carries with it concerns that are aesthetic, ontological, epistemological, and often times, most importantly, ethical. Cases of intentionally made and obviously manipulated (digitally and otherwise) art photographs are generally not problematic. As we have seen, especially in Chapter 2 on description, how a photograph is made may be of interest in itself to some and, more importantly, may have implications for how the photograph is interpreted and judged. Similarly, one can gain aesthetic insight and appreciation through technical knowledge of darkroom montages made by Jerry Uelsmann (see Plate 10).

Overtly manipulated images by Crewdson, Uelsmann, and a host of others contemporarily and historically are not controversial on ontological, epistemological, or ethical grounds; however, some thinkers do engage these photographs on aesthetic grounds. Recall that Edward Weston rejected some photographs as pseudo-paintings, and Richard Woodward judges Joel Sternfeld's photographs to be superior to Crewdson's because although they both rely on similar subject matter, Sternfeld's are "real," and Crewdson's are cinematically constructed (Plate 37).

Ontology, epistemology, and ethics seem to suffer significantly when some photographs are presented and received as straightforward documents but in fact are highly but invisibly altered in significant ways. When Art Wolfe digitally cloned and multiplied caribou, zebra, geese, and greater sandhill cranes in his photographic nature book, *Migrations,* he changed what viewers thought to be reality—"How many sandhill cranes were there!?" He offered false information about the real world, which deceives those who look at the pictures as if they are accurate nature photographs when, in fact, they are not. Had Wolfe clearly announced that he was aestheticizing nature by altering it with computer technology, his photographic practice would probably not have aroused anger and resentment. Thus, a key question is not so much "Is the photograph digital?" but "How does it alter the world and our knowledge of it and with what consequences?"

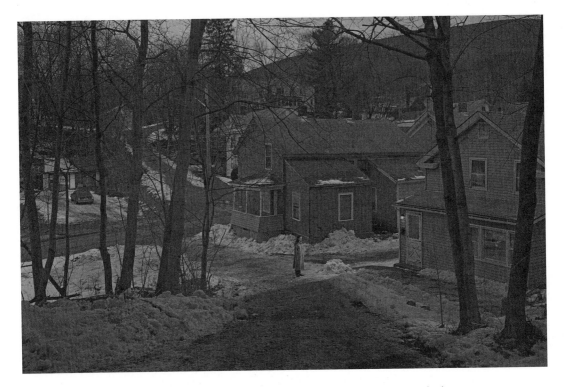

PLATE 37.   Gregory Crewdson, *Untitled, Winter,* 2006. Inkjet color print, 57 x 88 inches.
© Gregory Crewdson. Courtesy of Gagosian Gallery.

The next section offers careful considerations of ethical concerns in photography. It explicates a wide variety of theories of knowledge and aesthetics that affect how all photographs, digital and otherwise, are made, understood, and judged.

ETHICAL CONCERNS: ARE PHOTOGRAPHS MORAL?

Many photography and cultural critics raise concerns about ethical and unethical behaviors of photographers and the moral and political consequences of photographic images and the uses to which they are put. Socially minded critics, for example, have disparagingly linked photography with hunting and the camera with the gun. In *On Photography,* Sontag argues that "a camera is sold as a predatory weapon. . . . Just as the camera is a sublimation of the gun, the photograph is a sublimated murder." She began articulating these thoughts in 1973, and thirty years later, her apprehensions continue to be justified. Read, for example, the following account in *American Photo* of how photographer Scott Cosman made a photograph of two celebrities that he sold to *Us Weekly* for $50,000 with expectations that it would subsequently generate around $200,000 globally. Note the unabashed and uncritical enthusiasm of the *American Photo* writer (emphases added):

> When Associated Press reported that Cameron Diaz had broken her nose surfing in Hawaii, Scott Cosman, co-owner of the Los Angeles-based Flynet picture agency, dispatched a photographer to *snap the injured starlet. The shooter tracked* Diaz to the Kahala Mandarin Oriental Hotel on the island of Oahu and found out that her boyfriend, pop star Justin Timberlake, was there too. After making a few discreet images of the hot couple, he called Cosman with the news. Cosman hopped the next flight to Luau Land and joined in on *stalking* Diaz/Timberlake who got wise to their pursuers and proceeded to check out of the Oriental. Cosman *tracked them* to the very beach where Diaz had originally broken her nose—"I had a feeling they'd be there," he says—and *set up to shoot.*[91]

Photographers also show constraint, based on their personal moralities and sensibilities, in what they do *not* photograph. Nan Goldin, for example, passed up an opportunity to photograph her friend David Wojnarowicz as he lay dying of AIDS in 1992:

> He was lying on the bed. He had pearls on. He was holding them up in his hands, [and] he was describing something. Then his eyes were closed and he would be quiet. I loved him. He was a beautiful man, very tall and very skinny. I have some beautiful pictures of him. But it didn't feel right in my stomach. We weren't in the same reality at that time. Do you know what I mean? Have you ever taken LSD? He was hallucinating from dying. I don't know what medication he was on. I'm sure he was on some kind, to help him die without too much pain.
>
> All the people that I photographed dying of AIDS gave me their consent, but I never asked Dave. I know that he liked my work; in his book I'm one of the first people that he thanks. I don't know. I didn't want to hurt him, even if he wasn't 100 percent conscious.[92]

Rankin Waddell, a photojournalist who happened to be in New York City on September 11, 2001, decided not to photograph the destruction of the World Trade Center:

> I was uptown in a hotel, and my agent phoned me and said, "A plane just got into the WTC." I didn't realize the enormity. I was like, "I'm sleeping. I'll speak to you in a minute," and then I woke up and I saw on the news the second [plane] going in. So I realized what was happening 30 blocks away from me. In my heart I thought, "Should I go and document it?"

> I didn't go out and photograph it. I didn't want to. I guess it was strange,
> in a way; so many people did. For me it was such a horrific thing, and I didn't
> want to have anything to do with it. I didn't want to mediate it in any way,
> to document it in any way, deal with it like that. I wanted to deal with it
> personally.
> I thought, "My experience of this is not going to be through
> photography."[93]

This last section of this chapter deals with ethical concerns by introducing, with examples, theoretical perspectives that are centrally engaged in such concerns: Marxist theory, feminist theory, multicultural theory, queer theory, and postcolonial theory. None of these perspectives is a single theory (there are many feminisms, for example), and each theory is informed by the others.

Marxist Theory and Ethical Photography

Allan Sekula criticizes photographic postmodernism as a "cynical and self-referential mannerism," which he calls "a chic vanguardism by artists who suffer from a very real isolation from larger social issues."[94] Sekula instead embraces a critical social documentary in his own photography and his writing: "I am arguing, then, for an art that documents monopoly capitalism's inability to deliver the conditions of a fully human life." He adds:

> Against violence directed at the human body, at the environment, at working
> people's ability to control their own lives, we need to counterpose an active
> resistance, simultaneously political and symbolic, to monopoly capitalism's
> increasing power and arrogance, a resistance aimed ultimately at socialist
> transformation.[95]

Sekula discusses his own work and the work of Philip Steinmetz, Martha Rosler, Fred Lonidier, and Chauncey Hare in 1983 as working against the strategies of "high art photography." These photographers, like the postmodernists, refuse to treat the photograph as a privileged object and instead use it as an ordinary cultural artifact. They add language to their photographs to "anchor, contradict, reinforce, subvert, complement, particularize, or go beyond the meanings offered by the images themselves."

Their work is also very different from "liberal documentary work." Sekula writes:

> For all his good intentions, for example, Eugene Smith in *Minamata* provided
> more a representation of his compassion for mercury-poisoned Japanese
> fisherfolk than one of their struggle for retribution against the corporate pol-
> luter. I will say it again: the subjective aspect of liberal esthetics is compassion
> rather than collective struggle. Pity, mediated by an appreciation of "great
> art," supplants political understanding.[96]

Sekula is arguing for political understanding of the corruption of capitalism and then radical change. Mere compassion, through art photography, is not enough, and worse, it distracts understanding and deflects rage. He insists that "the expressionist liberalism of the find-a-bum school of concerned photography" is not a solution.

Critic James Hugunin groups the thinking of Sekula, Rosler, and Lonidier with Marshall Mayer, Steve Cagan, Connie Hatch, Victor Burgin, Carole Conde, and Karl Beveridge under the term "Marxist Realism."[97] Hugunin differentiates these Marxist realists from "traditional documentary" or "concerned photography" in the tradition of Lewis Hine, Eugene Smith, and Roy DeCarava. According to Hugunin, traditional documentary photography is based on (false) assumptions that the photograph represents a one-to-one correspondence with reality that is nearly accurate and adequate and that the photographic image is capable of conveying information, needing language only as a verbal aside. Traditional documentary photographers position the viewer as a receptive subject taking in the objective information of the world through the photograph.

Another traditional (false) assumption is that the photograph is transparent; that is, it hides its own ideology and presents itself, and is easily received, as the thing itself. Marxism and postmodernism reject these assumptions of traditional documentary as naive and posit that traditional, humanistic, concerned photography makes social comments that merely evoke sympathy rather than encourage resistance. Further, photography deals with surface appearances, and surfaces obscure rather than reveal the actual complex social relations that underlie appearances.

Victor Burgin insists that when Marxist cultural theory is applied to photography theory, it "must take into account the determinations exerted by the means of representation upon that which is represented."[98] Through his writing and photographs, Burgin is interested in determining how representation affects what is represented. Part of his project is to make visible the ideologies that are operant within society and that are reinforced by all images, including photographs. Marxist cultural theory sees ideology as a system of representations, including images, myths, and beliefs, which exist in a society at a certain historical time and have a role within the society; these representations act on men and women by a process that escapes them. Burgin credits the women's movement for initially and continually critically examining how women are represented and exposing the detrimental consequences of those representations.

Feminist Theory and Ethical Photography

An anonymous, early Guerrilla Girl set the context for feminism in the art world: "In 1984, the Museum of Modern Art opened with an international painting and sculpture show. There were 166 people in that show, and only about 16 were women—so that was 10 percent or less, and we knew we were in deep shit. So we started the Guerrilla Girls" (Plate 38). The women took on the gorilla, the animal, by wearing great hairy masks and waving bananas, and *guerrilla,* the term referring to freedom fighters' actions. The name works imagistically—the angry gorilla image combined with the female body. They use humor strategically: "I think there is something very empowering, and also very positive, about targeting people with a lot of humor and addressing issues that we have a vested interest in—not apologizing for it, but being very open about it." One of the women (they are all anonymous to protect themselves from reprisals) says that "to actually change the system is so unbelievably complex that at this point, our interest is in getting women more access to it. So that's our attitude about change, as opposed to breaking down the system."[99]

Two key ideas propel feminist theory: *Sex* is different from *gender,* and feminism is instrumental. *Sex* refers to the physical features that make us female or male or some combination of the two and *gender,* to the cultural ideas of what it is to be a man or a woman. According to Sally McRorie, a scholar of feminist theory in aesthetics and art education, genders are the political constructions of what it means to live in a world where we are not merely human but always man or woman.[100] Genders are several. Genders are socialized (recall *Thin* by Lauren Greenfield). Gender is how a culture expects and tries to ensure that men act a certain way and women another, or a gay man this way and a lesbian that way. Of course, there are many ways one could act, but cultures specify which ways one *should* think, feel, and behave if one is of a certain sex. Genders are usually hierarchically constructed: Power, usually male, would have it be that it is better to be male than female, masculine than feminine, "straight" than "queer." According to McRorie, gender is a meta-level phenomenon—it is something to think about, not just something we do on a nonconscious level. As we become more conscious of behavior, our judgments change, and our conscious acts also change. Gender in a hierarchical society can be very constraining. In a nonhierarchical society, gender might merely be a matter of choice (Color Plate 32).

Feminism is instrumental, in that to be a feminist is a political choice, a choice toward action to resist and to change the status quo. One is not born a feminist, but rather, one chooses to become one. All women are not feminists, and all women do not make feminist art; nor do all feminists make feminist art, although feminists refuse to believe that art and politics are separate.

Solomon-Godeau reveals how feminist theory is concerned with how women are represented: "Central to feminist theory is the recognition that woman does not speak herself: rather, she is spoken for and all that that implies: looked at, imagined, mystified and objectified."[101] Barbara DeGenevieve, a feminist photographer committed to changing oppressive representations of women (and other minority groups) in society, writes:

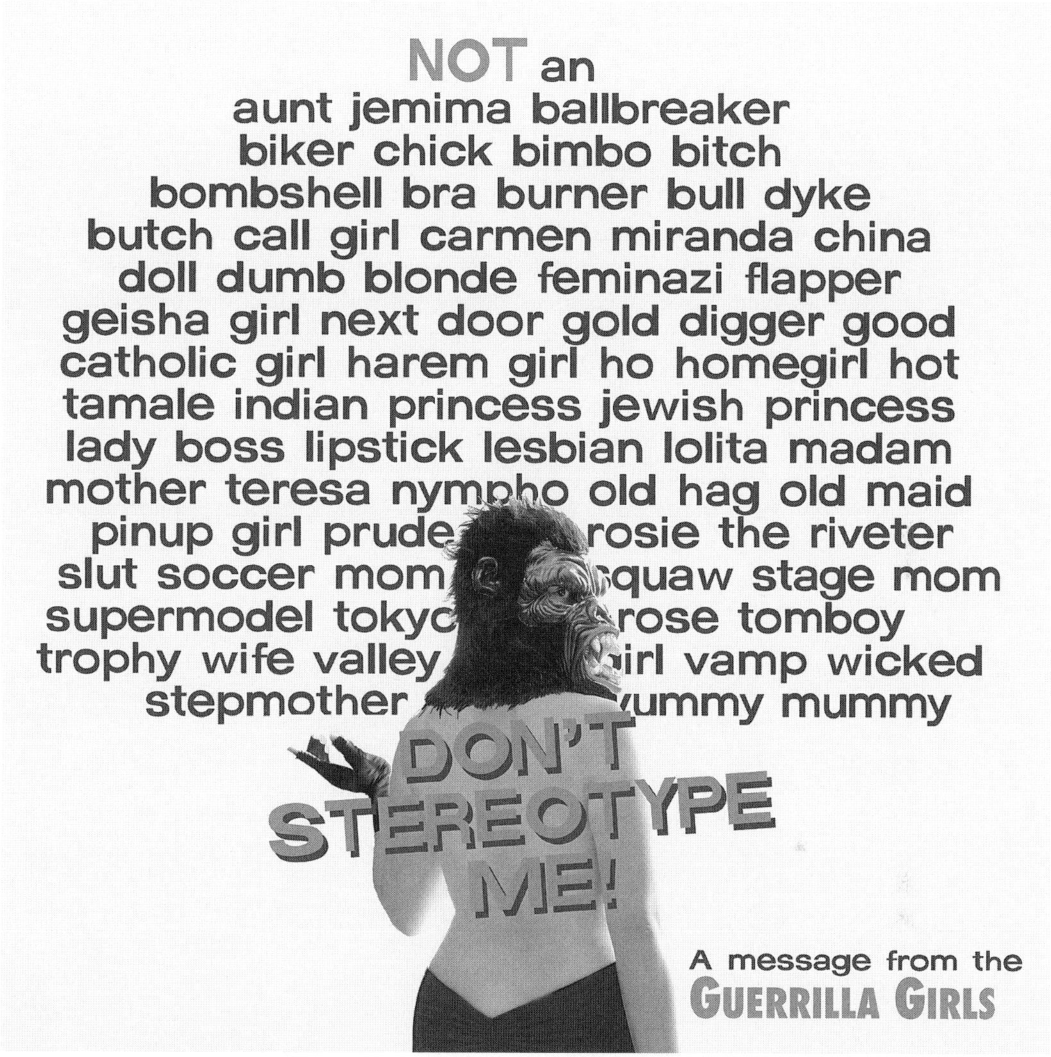

NOT an
aunt jemima ballbreaker
biker chick bimbo bitch
bombshell bra burner bull dyke
butch call girl carmen miranda china
doll dumb blonde feminazi flapper
geisha girl next door gold digger good
catholic girl harem girl ho homegirl hot
tamale indian princess jewish princess
lady boss lipstick lesbian lolita madam
mother teresa nympho old hag old maid
pinup girl prude rosie the riveter
slut soccer mom squaw stage mom
supermodel tokyo rose tomboy
trophy wife valley girl vamp wicked
stepmother yummy mummy

DON'T STEREOTYPE ME!

A message from the
GUERRILLA GIRLS

PLATE 38. Guerrilla Girls, T-Shirt Transfer, 2003. From *Bitches, Bimbos, and Bailbreakers: The Guerrilla Girl's Illustrated Guide to Female Stereotypes, Penguin,* 2003.

© Guerrilla Girls, Inc. Courtesy www.guerrillagirls.com.

Photographic images carry ideological messages which cumulatively shape the culture's ideas, values, and attitudes. They are the bearers of cultural mythologies. If we see enough pictures of a certain type (women being brutalized by men, minorities as ghetto residents) we can conclude that such imagery is valuable to the culture. Especially, if certain aspects of society are not represented, it is most likely due to the fact that no importance is given to them or that they have a negative value for the culture (vulnerability in male sexuality, nonstereotypical images of women and people of color).[102]

Griselda Pollock and Deborah Cherry, two feminist art historians, make a related point about how women have been positioned in fine art: "Representing creativity as masculine and circulating Woman as the beautiful image for the desiring male gaze, High Culture systematically denies knowledge of women as producers of culture and meaning."[103] Solomon-Godeau explains how feminist theory in 1985 is embodied in the work of two feminist artists who use photography: Silvia Kolbowski and Vikky Alexander. Both deal directly with images of women in the fashion industry. Both appropriate fashion imagery in mass circulation sources to subvert them. Kolbowski exposes how the fashion image constructs the female as different, as other, and therefore estranges and oppresses her by making her the voyeuristic object of the male gaze. When fashion imagery is presented for women, the female viewer must project her own sexual identity as existing by and for the eyes of men.[104] In her work, Alexander exposes how women in fashion imagery are presented as ritual objects and as commodities. In Solomon-Godeau's analysis, "By de-naturing such images, Alexander unmasks them." About these two artists, and others like them, Solomon-Godeau concludes:

> Differences in emphasis, tactics and degree of appropriation notwithstanding, Alexander, Kolbowski, Kruger, Levine and Prince are artists whose concerns are grounded in the cultural, the political, the sexual. Viewed individually, collectively, or as sample representatives of postmodernist art practice, their work contrasts vividly with parochialism, insularity, and conservatism of much art photography.[105]

Feminist production in writing or art making, however, is not restricted to how women are represented. On an image appropriated from *Newsweek* of two policemen dragging a pro-choice woman away from a rally, Lynette Molnar superimposes these words: "Keep your self-righteous right wing fundamentalist Christian male laws off my body." The image is about two feet by three feet, an assemblage of color photocopies, and was made as a placard for street demonstrations to oppose Right to Life demonstrators who are attempting to repeal laws that allow abortion. Molnar's work is socially activist, direct, and accessible to a wide audience; it is intended for the street rather than the museum. Feminists in the field are also working to achieve full participation in the art world, including equality in arts funding and representation in galleries and museums, and to improve the number and status of women on photography faculties. An allied project is the recovering of lost and unknown women artists in history, exemplified by Naomi Rosenblum's *A History of Women Photographers*. In art criticism, some feminists have interjected a personal voice and style of writing and have eschewed the notion of objectivity— Lucy Lippard's activist criticism discussed in Chapter 1 is one clear example.

In a critical view through a feminist lens, Laura Cottingham summarily credits feminist photographers and scholars for restructuring our sense of photographic representation by their "claiming the personal as political, rewriting the art-historical canon against the patrilinear unwriting of female contributions, introducing autobiography, reclaiming craft and domestic labor, and centralizing female subjectivity against the universalization of male experience."[106]

Multicultural Theory and Ethical Photography

Multiculturalism is a social reform movement developed in the early 1960s in the United States out of the civil rights movement as a means for reconstructing society to make it more equitable and just for all individuals. According to Patricia Stuhr, a theorist of multiculturalism especially as it can affect education, multiculturalists advocate a social reconstruction that provides everyone with the means to be more responsive to the social, political, and economic conditions of the times and to issues of power and disenfranchisement associated with diversity.[107] The theory behind this reform movement provides people with theoretical and practical means to construct and implement changes that question the dominant ideology and provide hope for establishing a more equitable and just society. Multicultural theorists do not have a single answer, comprehensive model, or single set of prescriptions. Rather, they encourage people to learn to look at their own historic and contemporary cultural traditions, which include aesthetic visual production, and the cultural constructions of others from a critical perspective, with the understanding that what has been socially learned can also be unlearned or changed by individuals if they deem it just and necessary to do so.

Stuhr acknowledges that rights and blame are often attributed to cultures; however, a culture doesn't have rights or deserve blame because it does not act—people, within a culture influenced by global events and media, act. Getting people to think critically about their own and their group's actions and whom they are empowering or disenfranchising through their personal lives, community affiliations, actions, and work includes making and interpreting the meanings of visual culture. Multiculturalists identify and deal with cultural complexity and issues of power associated with social affiliations and aspects of personal, national, and global cultural identities. Multiculturalists foster social skills and actions that help individuals participate in shaping and controlling their present and future lives, in a socially and environmentally responsible manner, through the production and interpretation of visual culture. The notion of visual culture, in itself, seeks to remove photography from the rarefied air of fine art and place it within a larger context of the communicative world.

Richard Dyer, attending to race in a multicultural society, believes that "racial imagery is central to the organization of the modern world."[108] Because race in itself refers only to some insignificant geographical or physical differences among people, Dyer argues that it is *images* of race that are significant. The most powerful social position is one of being "nonraced," or simply human, without a racial qualifier; that is, to be white. White people have made themselves nonraced by continually "racing" others. Dyer offers these commonplace examples:

> The sense of whites as nonraced is most evident in the absence of reference to whiteness in the habitual speech and writing of white people in the West. We (whites) will speak of, say, the blackness or Chineseness of friends, neighbors, colleagues, customers, or clients, and it may be in the most genuinely friendly and accepting manner, but we don't mention the whiteness of the white people we know. An old-style white comedian will often start a joke: "There's this bloke walking down the street and he meets this black geezer," never thinking to race the bloke as well as the geezer. Synopses in listing of films on TV, where wordage is tight, nonetheless squander words with things like: "Comedy in which a cop and his black sidekick investigate a robbery," "Skinhead Johnny and his Asian lover Omar set up a launderette," "Feature film from a promising Native American director," and so on. . . . This assumption that white people are just people, which is not far off saying that whites are people whereas other colors are something else, is endemic to white culture.[109]

White people claim to speak for humanity; raced people are allowed to speak only for their own race. In imagery in books, magazines, newspapers, advertising, television, and films, whites are predominant, central, and standard: "Whites are not of a certain race, they're just the human race." Dyer's point of racing whites is to "dislodge them/us from the position of power, with all the inequities, oppression, privileges, and sufferings in its train, dislodging them/us by undercutting the authority with which they/we speak and act in and on the world."[110]

Using Dyer's insights, Coco Fusco, artist and writer, asks why Richard Avedon titled one of the photographs in his *In the American West* book and exhibition "Unidentified Migrant Worker," while he named most of his other subjects. Fusco makes the point that the pictured man seems to be Mexican. He appears in the photograph bare-shirted and dripping wet. She further asks, "Are we to see him as a degraded version of an ethnic type, a 'wetback'?" She suggests that the "imprimatur of the auteur," Avedon, precluded these questions, although a similar image in another context would likely draw objections.[111] Fusco along with Dyer points out that cowboys were crucial to the construction of white masculinity in the United States, but the dominant cultural representations of cowboys in Hollywood westerns are as white men, often with Indian scouts and these representations obscure the widespread presence of black, Native American, and Mexican cowboys, and the Mexican origins of cowboy culture. So do Marlboro cigarette ads featuring cowboys, and so do Richard Prince's critical renditions of these ads.[112]

Nicholas Mirzoeff, a scholar of visual culture, makes a similar point about the frequent imaging of some subjects over others in Edward Steichen's famous and immensely popular exhibition "The Family of Man" that debuted at the Museum of Modern Art in 1955 and then toured worldwide. Africans were photographed half-naked while hunting with spears, carrying water, or storytelling around a fire; that is, Africa is "primitive" and the West is "cultured." In Mirzoeff's view, Steichen also used photographs to assert American values and political superiority as universal truths, especially in the midst of the cold war being waged against the USSR. Steichen, for example, juxtaposed a photograph of a Soviet woman harvesting wheat by hand with an aerial view of a group of large, mechanical combine harvesters reaping an immense field of wheat in America. American technological superiority, and by implication, cultural superiority, was made visible to all who saw the exhibition.[113]

Mirzoeff also offers many examples of how photography was used in the United States in the service of slavery and racism. Lynching was a ritualized spectacle of extended torture and murder by fire or hanging. Photographs of lynching freely circulated as postcards for the entertainment of whites and the terror of blacks. In 1878, in Custer County, Nebraska, art photographer H. M. Hatch made stereographic slides of the lynchings of Ami "White" Ketchum and Luther H. Mitchell, guilty of trying to become homesteaders, and sold slides of their mutilated bodies for thirty-five cents each or three dollars a dozen. The "culture of spectacular lynching" was further aided by the invention of easy-to-use Kodak cameras introduced in 1888. In 1916, in Waco, Texas, photographer Fred A. Gildersleeve sold photographs for ten cents each of Jesse Washington's burning body and its burning corpse dragged through the streets.[114]

On the other hand, Sojourner Truth, the African American abolitionist and defender of women's rights, also used photography, but as a means of resistance to oppression. She traveled the country giving impassioned speeches during the years between slavery and emancipation and supported her work by selling photographs of herself giving speeches and leading rallies. She was one of the first to realize that charisma could be photogenic.[115]

Linda Weintraub considers Lorna Simpson's photographs to be a continuation of the discourse begun by Sojourner Truth:

> Simpson's work reveals that a century-and-a-half later, she is still reckoning with the after-effects of the struggle between the master and the slave that Sojourner Truth fought to vanquish. Simpson embodies the lingering effects of racism. Instead of celebrating the vitality of black culture, she focuses on such dehumanizing aspects of black experience as living in urban redevelopment

projects or standing in line at unemployment offices. In addition, she conveys the psychological toll of racism by assuming the artistic stance of the outcast. Simpson's suppression of individuality [in her photo works] suggests the consequence of exploitation, marginalization, and prejudice.[116]

Many believe that the effects of the past are present today.

Kobena Mercer asks of Robert Mapplethorpe's photographs of black gay males in *Black Book* (recall Chapter 6), "do the images undermine or reinforce racial stereotypes?" Mercer's initial reaction in 1982 when he and his friends began circulating the book was to see it "as a kind of illicit object of desire, albeit a highly problematic one."

> We were fascinated by the beautiful bodies, as we went over the repertoire of images again and again, drawn in by the desire to look and enjoy what was given to be seen. We wanted to look, but we didn't always find what we wanted to see: we were shocked and disturbed by the racial discourse of the imagery, and above all, we were angered by the aesthetic equation that reduced these black male bodies to abstract visual "things," silenced in their own right as subjects, serving only to enhance the name and reputation of the author in the rarefied world of art photography.[117]

Some twenty years later and after much reflection, Mercer changed his views of *Black Book*. Although he previously argued that the images were harmfully stereotypical because they positioned the photographer as the white male subject over the black object, Mercer then realized that Mapplethorpe practiced as a gay artist himself, and that

> In social, economic, and political terms, black men in the United States constitute one of the "lowest" social classes: disenfranchised, disadvantaged, and disempowered as a distinct collective subject in the late capitalist underclass. Yet in Mapplethorpe's photographs, men who in all probability came from this class are elevated onto the pedestal of the transcendental Western aesthetic ideal. . . . The subaltern black social subject, who was historically excluded from dominant regimes of representation—an "invisible man" in Ralph Ellison's phrase—is made visible within the codes and conventions of the dominant culture whose ethnocentrism is thereby exposed as a result.[118]

Queer Theory and Ethical Photography

Catherine Opie investigates aspects of community, making portraits of many groups including members of the lesbian, gay, bisexual, and transsexual community. Holland Cotter describes her as "best known as a portraitist . . . an insider and an outsider: a documentarian and a provocateur; a classicist and a maverick; a trekker and a stay-at-home; a lesbian feminist mother who resists the gay mainstream;

an American—birthplace: Sandusky, Ohio—who has serious arguments with her country and culture."[119] Her work is informed by "queer theory" (see Plate 39).

Teresa de Laurentis coined the term "queer theory" in 1989 and traced the historical path of terms that move from homosexual to *gay,* to *gay and lesbian,* and then to *queer.*[120] The term *queer* is meant to cover lesbian, gay, bisexual, and transgendered persons, sometimes abbreviated and identified in "queer literature" as LGBT. Lesbians, gays, bisexuals, transgendered persons, and others who embrace queer theory, pridefully and defiantly use the term *queer* to reclaim it from its historically derogatory meaning.

Queer theory emerged from literary and cultural criticism in the academic community in the mid-1980s and was influenced especially by feminist theory and French philosophers Jacques Derrida and Michel Foucault.[121] It grew out of the gay liberation movement of the 1970s, which struggled to build a safe place for sexual minorities in the United States and Europe. Queer theorists, however, demand more than liberation: They aim to "destabilize cultural ideas of normality and sexuality and terms like *hetero-* and *homosexual* which have been used to oppress people who don't conform to the Western ideal of monogamous heterosexual marriage."[122] Their ultimate goal is to provide people the freedom to create their own sexualities.

Like the deconstructionist Derrida, queer theorists analyze texts—most anything, including novels, television programs, and photographs—"with an eye to exposing underlying meanings, distinctions, and relations of power in the larger culture that produced the texts."[123] Their analyses disclose complicated cultural strategies that attempt to regulate sexual behavior by defining notions of what is "normal" and "deviant in order to repress those who challenge sexual norms or who do not conform to socially privileged gender roles of straight men and women."

Some people of gay and lesbian persuasions accept queer theory but do not want to use the term *queer,* thinking it too burdened with hurtful negativity from the past. For example, the gay pride parade in San Francisco has been renamed the gay/lesbian/bisexual/transgender parade to include the diversity implied by the term *queer.* Some scholars who are interested in gay rights and issues do not accept queer theory: Rictor Norton, for example, holds an essentialist, body-based view that gays are basically different from straights, that gays are a minority population that exists in all times and spaces.[124]

Queer theorists, however, believe that one's sexual identity is in part or wholly constructed by society and culture, and they reject general sexual terms and categories such as "woman" or "homosexual" as overly simplistic and restrictive social constructs of behavior and desire. They argue that sexuality is largely influenced by social discourse and practice; therefore, verbal language and visual images are significant and in need of critical deconstruction. Queer theorists strive to understand "societal hostility towards homosexuality. It is concerned with the power

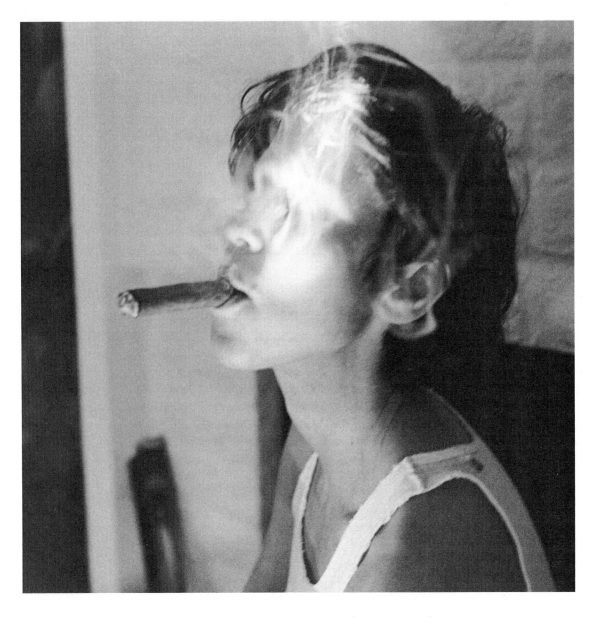

PLATE 39.   Catherine Opie, *Amy,* 1996. Inkjet print, 8 × 8 inches (20.3 × 20.3 cm). Edition of 8.

© Catherine Opie. Courtesy of Regen Projects, Los Angeles.

of heterosexual privilege; it is concerned with understanding the ways in which a hierarchy of sexual values and sexual power is constructed."[125]

De Laurentis writes that male homosexuality and female homosexuality are

> social and cultural forms in their own right, albeit emergent ones and thus still fuzzily defined, undercoded, or discursively dependent on more established forms . . . interactive and yet resistant, both participatory and yet distinct, claiming at once equality and difference, demanding political representation while insisting on its material and historical specificity.[126]

David Halperin says, "queer is by definition whatever is at odds with the normal, the legitimate, the dominant."[127] In their activism, queer scholars and activists work to overcome "heteronormativity," a societal given that privileges heterosexuality and punishes homosexuals as deviant.

Socially active groups who use imagery to confront mainstream politics and practices that discriminate are ACT UP (AIDS Coalition to Unleash Power), Gran Fury, DIVA TV (Damned Interfering Video Activist Television), and LAPIT (Lesbian Activists Producing Interesting Television). Gran Fury is a collective of AIDS activists founded in New York City in 1988, who make and use art for social change. The following excerpts are from their position statement. They collectively make artwork that confronts the political and social underpinnings of the AIDS crisis. They attempt to increase awareness of social prejudices that result in inequities of class and race. They explore the politics of power and the economic conditions that contribute to the health care emergency. Gran Fury places its graphic images on buses and subways, billboards, and posters. Their graphics are often disguised to resemble the advertising that people are accustomed to seeing in these locations.

> People are influenced by what they see. Public images and public words, from advertising to the arts, are groupings of cultural ideas. Every package design, every building advertisement we glance at is, to some extent, propaganda. . . . Inserting our message into public spaces is one of the ways of influencing public debate in this country. That is why we "advertise" our political ideas, why we choose to project them in public spaces. Art is only important to us insofar as the techniques of art help to attract and hold the viewer's attention. The seductiveness of well-turned phrases or good graphics can speak by using the "look" of authority. The message, which is the true content of our work, is what is most important to us. . . .[128]

Regarding aesthetic theory, perhaps the single most revealing statement in Gran Fury's proclamation is their criterion for art: "Art is only important to us insofar as the techniques of art help to attract and hold the viewer's attention." This statement is a clear example of an activist criterion.

In recent photography history, a key queer image is *Untitled (Falling Buffalo),* (Plate 40) made by David Wojnarowicz, who died of AIDS in 1992. Wojnarowicz

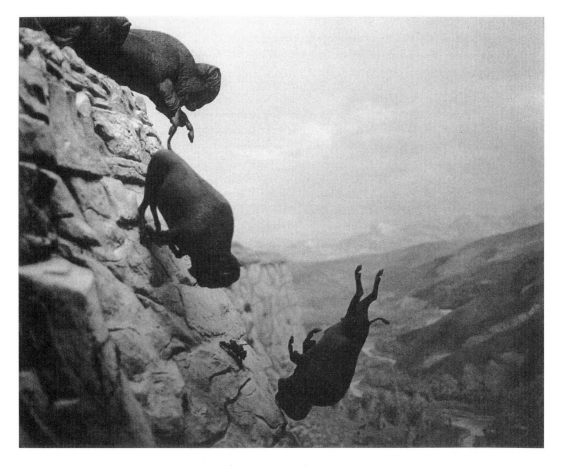

PLATE 40.   David Wojnarowicz, *Untitled (Falling Buffalo)*, 1988–89. Gelatin silver print, 27 1/2 x 34 1/2 inches.

Courtesy of the estate of David Wojnarowicz and PPOW Gallery, New York.

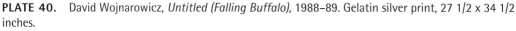

was an important presence in the New York City art scene because of his openness about his HIV condition and his public debates, provocative political writing, and multimedia images about lack of health care and ineffectual AIDS policies. His self-examinations of his life as a gay artist showed the profound effect AIDS had on gay life and culture and the portrayal of gay men.[129] In an interview, Wojnarowicz reflected on the metaphoric impact of the falling buffalo he saw and photographed in a museum of history:

> The buffalo thing is a small part of a large diorama in the Natural History Museum in Washington, and I was shocked when I turned the corner and came face to face with this diorama. It had a lot of connections to things I

had learned when I was a child, because I grew up in mostly rural towns in Jersey that were just being developed for suburban tract housing. I felt very alien in those communities because the communities were alien in themselves. Most people wouldn't go beyond the edge of their lawn and had no interest in interacting.[130]

Postcolonial Theory and Ethical Photography

Colonialism (sometimes called "cultural imperialism") is a policy of control wherein one power exerts its military, economic, religious, or cultural domination over an area or people. Colonizers exacted tribute, goods, and wealth from the colonized and restructured the colonized peoples' economies to ensure a continual flow of resources, human and natural, between the two. In the years 1500–1900, Europe colonized all of North America, South America, Australia, most of Africa, and much of Asia by sending settlers to populate these lands or by taking control of existing governments. Peoples and lands were colonized for a variety of reasons: economic exploitation of the colony's natural resources, creation of new markets for the colonizer, and extension of the colonizer's way of life beyond its national borders. The Spanish and Portuguese established colonies in the Western Hemisphere in the fifteenth and sixteenth centuries, the Dutch colonized Indonesia in the sixteenth century, and Britain colonized North America and India in the seventeenth and eighteenth centuries. British settlers later colonized Australia and New Zealand, and Africa was rigorously colonized in the 1880s. By the time of the First World War, European nations "owned" about eighty-five percent of the world. The colonial era ended gradually after World War II: For example, India became independent in 1947, Egypt in 1954, the Congo in 1960, Uganda in 1962, and Kenya in 1965.

As a country colonized by Britain, the United States might be considered a post-colonial country, but it is also seen as a colonizer because of its genocidal policies toward Native Americans; its enslavement of Africans between the seventeenth and nineteenth centuries; its possession, after the Spanish-American War, of Puerto Rico, Cuba, the Panama Canal, the Philippines, and Hawaii; and its present position of dominant power in world politics.

Some scholars position African American studies within postcolonial studies:

> African-American studies concerns itself primarily with the examination of the customs and culture of its people, namely Black Americans of African descent, who were forcefully brought to America between the seventeenth and nineteenth century because of America's colonization of their homeland; the "dark" continent of Africa. Arguably the most significant investigation within post-colonialism at present, African-American studies tackles issues such as the effects of imperialism on identity and racial boundaries, ethnicity, marginality and the authenticity of literary and oral records of history.[131]

Coauthors Christine Roth and Cary Henson explain the concerns of postcolonial theorists:

> Postcolonialism examines the impact of the economic, cultural, and political colonization of Asia, Africa, and the Americas by the United States and the countries of Europe. Major concerns in postcolonial studies include 1) how the native populations were destroyed, oppressed, or otherwise transformed by the process of colonization itself; 2) how those populations struggled to achieve freedom from the colonial forces (hence, "post"colonialism); and 3) how the effects of colonialism continue to be felt in both the colonized and colonizing nations.[132]

Some scholars argue that the effects of colonization can never be overcome and that *postcolonial* is an inadequate and misleading term. Tim Spurgin offers this broad overview of some mutual concerns of postcolonial scholars who are engaged in many different theoretical approaches and concerns:

- an interest in the experience of being colonized and living under—either by accommodating or resisting—foreign rule;
- an interest in the experience of, and in the discourses and rhetorics used when, seeking freedom from colonial rule;
- an interest in the aftermath of the struggle for independence—which is to say, the experience of "post-coloniality";
- and, perhaps most importantly, an interest in issues of identity.[133]

The academic field of postcolonial studies has been growing since the 1970s. It is influenced by and influences many theoretical perspectives, including Marxism, feminism, queer theory, and postmodernism. Edward Said's book, *Orientalism,* published in 1979, is one of its earliest and most influential texts.[134] In that book, Said, a Palestinian American literary critic, carefully and persuasively explains and critiques how Western thinkers (nineteenth-century "Orientalist" scholars) constructed vast expanses of the world, including Asia and the Middle East, as "the Orient."

Said's critique revolves around the theme of knowledge as power. Believing that an effective conquest required knowledge of those conquered, Western scholars translated into English the writings of authors from "the Orient." The Orient became the studied, the observed, the sensual passive object; Orientalist scholars were the active subjects. The Orientalist scholars essentialized—made real—a self-serving and totalizing image of all the diverse people of Asia and the Middle East. Westerners constructed the Orient as biologically inferior, culturally backward, strange, and unchanging; feminine and weak, awaiting Western male dominance. In Said's words, Orientalism "not only degrades its subject matter but also blinds its practitioners." Said does not deny differences between "the West" and "the Orient," but insists that a scholar must study smaller culturally consistent

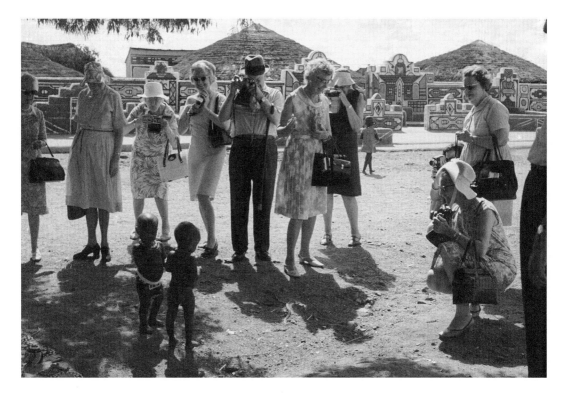

PLATE 41.   Ed van der Elsken, American tourists photographing children, no date.
Courtesy of Nederlands Fotomuseum.

regions, rather than totalizing peoples, and allow the subjects to tell their own narratives.[135]

Anandi Ramamurthy, a British postcolonial cultural critic, is especially interested in issues of photography, colonialism, and power. She writes, "During the nineteenth century, the camera joined the gun in the process of colonization." The early years of photographic inventions coincided with expansions of European empires through colonization of peoples and countries. Some ideologies of photography were counterpart to ideologies of colonialism, and those histories affected how we mentally and visually picture others: "The camera was used to record and define those who were colonized according to the interests of the West." Postcolonial scholars explore such issues as the unequal relationship of power of the white photographer over the colonized subject, who was usually of color. The "Other" is seen and photographed as submissive, exotic, and primitive. By means of such photographs, "the European photographer and viewer could perceive their own superiority. Europe was defined as 'the norm' upon which all other cultures should be judged. That which was different was disempowered by its very 'Otherness'."[136]

Eroticized photographic representations of Others were made to serve anthropological, geographical, and economic interests. The Belgian company Kasai, for example, hired photographers to explore the Congo, looking for resources and markets. The French developed a new genre of photography, exotic and erotic postcards of Algerian women taken by French studio photographers during the colonization of Algeria. Their constructed sexual visions of Algerian women suited European fantasies. Ramamurthy sees such commercial images of women as perversely apt for the colonial times with continuing influence today (emphasis added):

> Colonial power could be more emphatically represented through gendered relations—the white, wealthy male photographer versus the nonwhite, poor female subject. These images, bought and sold in the thousands, reflect the commodification of women's bodies generally in society. They are also part of the development of postcard culture which enabled the consumption of photographs by millions. The production of exotic postcards also brought photographs of the "Empire" and the non-European world into every European home. It was not only the photographs of non-European women which were sold: landscape photographs, which constructed Europe as developed and the non-European world as underdeveloped, were also popular. *These colonial visions continue to pervade contemporary travel photography, not only through postcards, but also in travel brochures and tourist ephemera.*[137]

In a self-portrait (Plate 42), Renée Cox reclaims the severely "othered" native body by inserting her own body into the colonial discourse of the exhibition of native bodies as freaks of nature in the West as exemplified in the Hottentot Venus. In 1810 a young woman from South Africa, Saarjite Baartman, was brought to Europe and placed on display naked in a cage at Piccadilly, England, and in France, for over five years. The fascination was the woman's large buttocks. After her death at age twenty-six, Baartman's body was dissected and her genitals were cast in wax in the interest of studying "primitive sexuality." An anatomist presented Baartman's dissected labia to the Academie Royale de Medecine as physical proof of African women's "primitive sexual appetite."[138]

CONCLUSION

Theoretical questions receive different answers as do interpretive and evaluative questions. Theorizing about photography, like interpreting and evaluating photographs, results in conclusions that are more or less enlightening, more or less informative, more or less helpful in making photography, photographs, and the

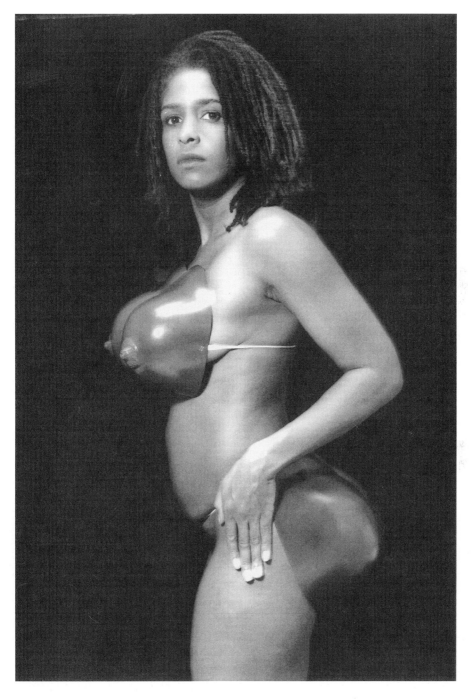

PLATE 42. Renée Cox, *HOT-EN-TOT*, 1994. Gelatin silver print, 20 x 16 inches.
© Renée Cox. Courtesy of Robert Miller Gallery, New York.

world understandable. Theories or theoretical points, like interpretations and evaluations, are offered, considered, and accepted, rejected, or modified. Some are dismissed as misguided; others are saved and mulled over and altered over time through rational argument. Theoretical debates and conflicting views contribute to an ongoing, interesting, and informative dialogue about photography and photographs that enlivens the viewing of photographs as well as their making. Theories of photography are important and valuable, even if they are sometimes contradictory. They are important because they affect practice. They are valuable because they help us understand more about photography and photographs and increase our understanding and appreciation of the medium, individual pictures, and the world. Different theories also allow us to enter the minds of others and may contribute to sympathetic understandings of differences among people. Knowing some of the issues and theoretical assumptions allows us to join the discussions and to be better informed about what we are doing when making and criticizing photographs.

Writing and Talking About Photographs

STUDYING *CRITICIZING PHOTOGRAPHS* SHOULD WELL EQUIP YOU FOR WRITING AND TALKING about photographs and the issues they raise. The book identifies four major questions, and many elaborations and revisions of these questions, that can be asked of any photograph: What do I see here? What is it about? Is it good? Is it art? Answering any of these questions will give you something significant to write about and to talk about when looking at photographs made by professionals or made by you and your fellow students.

Criticizing Photographs examines the work of professional critics and scholars as models for deepening your thoughts and furthering your talk about images. This chapter puts theory and professional practice more directly into your hands.

WRITING ABOUT PHOTOGRAPHS

To write well, you need to want to write. Choose a photograph, a book, or an exhibition that interests you and about which you care. You may be interested because you like the work or because you object to it. You may be intrigued for reasons you haven't yet identified or because the work appeals to you but you don't yet feel you understand it. If you don't care about the work, you will have difficulty writing about it. If you have been given an assignment in which you are not interested, think of an alternative and comparable assignment that does interest you, and ask your instructor if you may switch. If permission is not granted, the burden will be on you to find motivation, and you might even start your paper with reasons for your reluctance about the assigned topic.

Observing and Taking Notes

Study the photograph or exhibition intently, and jot down notes as you reflect on the work. Be sure your notes are complete. If they are not, you may have to return to the gallery, library, or Internet to get what you could have obtained during the first visit. Be sure your notes are accurate, especially when consulting written material. Sloppy note taking can result in unintended plagiarism, which is using another's ideas or words as if they were your own. When taking notes, enclose another author's words in quotation marks, and carefully cite all bibliographic information: author, title, publisher, place of publication, publication date, page numbers. If you use another's words in your writing, you must put them within quotation marks. If you use another's ideas but not the person's exact words, you must still credit the source of the idea within the text or in a footnote. Plagiarism, whether intended or not, is illegal and can have serious consequences.

Obtain a writer's style manual. An instructor, academic department, or publisher may have a preferred style. If a style manual is not specified, choose one from a bookstore and follow it. Style guidelines, such as *The Chicago Manual of Style, Modern Language Association Handbook, The Elements of Style,* and others provide you with information on good writing, how to footnote and construct bibliographies, and other technical matters, and they provide consistency. Latest editions of these references will include information on conducting and citing electronic research. Without a style guide, you will be unnecessarily and inefficiently inventing your own style, and it will not have the internal consistency of established guides.

To learn more about the photographs you will write about, follow the activities of description, interpretation, and evaluation. Describe the subject matter and note the presentational environment of the work or its external context. Are you writing about one piece or a show? Where did the one piece originate; why is it being shown here and now? If it is a show, who organized it, and why? Are there useful statements by exhibiting artists or the curator? Recall what you know about the photographer and the time and place the photograph was made. This external information will inform your interpretation of the work.

While you are observing a photograph and deciding what to write about, listen to your feelings and determine what in the work has triggered them. Remember that feelings are guides to describing, interpreting, and judging images. Reveal your feelings in your writing, identifying how the image affected you. Match the emotional tone of the image with the emotional tone of your writing.

Freely write down phrases and words that come to mind; the more phrases you write now, the fewer you will have to construct later. Afterward you can arrange them logically and discard the irrelevant. Allow yourself the time to set aside your work for a while and come back to it later to check your initial reactions. Write down new thoughts. Decipher why you care about the work, and determine what you want someone else to know about it and your reaction to it.

Quick-Writes and Careful-Writes

A nonthreatening way to begin writing anything is to do a *quick-write*. That is, put your pencil to paper, or fingers to keyboard, and write quickly about a topic for a short but determined amount of time—five minutes, eight minutes, twenty minutes. Do not judge your writing, just write. Do not censor your thoughts. Do not worry about spelling or grammar. If you cannot think of the right word, leave a blank and keep going. Do not stop until the time is up.

You will find that you do have something to say. You will find that one of your ideas generates another and it, another. A whole class can write quick-writes about the same photograph or body of work and then read them all out loud, again, without apologizing for what was written or correcting or judging. All these quick jottings form a rich storehouse of first ideas upon which the group can build in an ensuing discussion, or in further and more careful individual writing, now with proofreading and editing encouraged.

Following are some five-minute quick-writes by college students about *Intirely*, a Polaroid photograph made by William Wegman (Plate 43). The first is by Susannah Van Horn when she was a beginning master's student in art education.

—her teats stand out—female dog
—why a dog (a female one) in a tire
—the tire is stretched into an egg shape—female trying to cope with the egg surrounding her
—children surround you and consume your life once the "egg hatches"
—she looks worn out—going through the motions of life—keeping the wheels turning even though her happiness is at stake,
—she looks like she has to struggle to stay within the confining roles of being a female in society
—tail which dogs use to show their emotions is not visible—assume it's between her legs
—the lighting on the dog is such that the buttocks is a highlight—front half in low light
—why am I standing in the circle—the tire—the lines that define me—I must break out—how—my head is stuck—I'm a futuristic car—a freak sideshow

The following quick-write is by Sarah Arruda, a first-year master's student studying art education to become a certified art teacher.

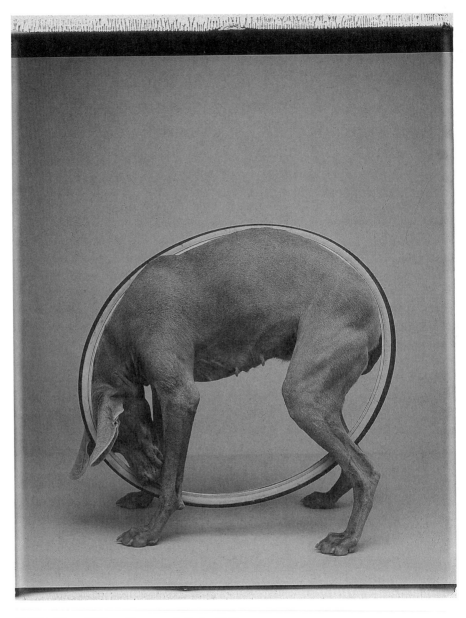

PLATE 43.   William Wegman, *Intirely,* 1990.
© William Wegman.

All-encompassing, almost feral life
The dog's body forms to the tire, they appear as one, then there is a
    disruption—the legs—they break the circle
Do the legs represent birth? Breaking free of something
Light source from above & the left
Very obedient dog to hold that position
Looks like motion—the way the dog is bent forward or coming to a halt
Strength or breaking out to stand tall
<u>Conformity</u>

This last quick-write is written by Kelly Helser, an art teacher.

There is a brown dog—not gray—Weimaraner? Inside of a bicycle tire.
She is caught inside of it as the tire is going between her legs, over the center of her
    head, down her spine.
Her head is pointed down within the squeezing tire and feet on the floor.
She looks like she is braced for action like she will roll herself.
Looks to be a playful image as a dog commonly chews on things like tires but this
    one has control of her.
She would like to escape but can't.
There is no beginning or end. How did she get there? Animal rights people would
    not like this! But I don't think she is in danger.
Now it makes me think of a baby in the embryonic sack. The way she is completely
    encircled by this tire. It is like a cross section of the womb.
The feet are the only things sticking out.
Themes: wanting to break free but stuck in a cycle—master/slave—formal
    qualities—circle of life

After hearing many of the quick-writes voluntarily read aloud, a discussion
ensued. Then the students were given an overnight assignment to compose a careful-
write about *Intirely*. That is, they were to review all that they first thought about the
image, and all that they heard from their classmates, and to compose a finished and
polished paragraph about the image. Susan Michael Barrett, an art museum educator, wrote this careful-write about *Intirely*:

Head down, tail up.
    She's encircled entirely in tire.
    So she thinks. Hey, your limbs are free! Tell me lady with your head down,
what are you doing? Are you having fun or are you stuck in a tire trap? If you
are trapped, who is holding you? Oh, you are not held, you want to stay to
play. Why? Hey, try this: just move your head an insy-bit. You'll have it—
freedom. Do you want it? You do? You want it? Well then do something. Take
that inch. Why don't you? You don't want freedom? Oh, I see. It is more fun
head down and tail up? No? What, bark up, I can't hear you! You can't see up

with your head down and up might be less and more. I know about you, she you, you don't know what to do with freedom. You are she and you don't have to be in the tire. You can BE the tire, the wheel. See, you can go, can't you? Go grrrrrr!

Students' Interpretive Writings

The following student paper is a good example of a primarily interpretive paper that uses descriptive information as needed to inform readers and to support the writer's understandings of the work. Kendra Hovey wrote it when she was a continuing-education student, equivalent to a first-year master's student, taking courses for personal enrichment. Her undergraduate degree is in philosophy. She wrote the paper while taking a course in photography criticism from the author, using this book. Kendra's paper is in response to an assignment for a two- to three-page interpretive paper on a contemporary photographer. The assignment specified that the students' audience was the university community, including both freshmen and professors, many of whom would not be previously aware of the work of William Wegman.

REVIEW: William Wegman   KENDRA HOVEY

A nude female model lounges seductively on a chair. Captured in a photographic print, her sultry eyes glance sidelong at us. This is not Marilyn Monroe or Linda Evangelista, but a new singular beauty with a singular name—Battina. Not just another French model, Battina is a creature of Germanic heritage. She is recognized by her dark features, smooth and shiny hair, slender legs, floppy ears and that ever so prominent snout. This bird is a bird chaser. Beautiful Battina is a Weimaraner, of the genus canine. A dog.

William Wegman is the prankster behind the camera, and pictures bearing his signature contain some of the funniest visual jokes available on photographic material. This one, titled *Lolita. With Battina*, amuses by portraying the *Playboy* prototype in the body of a dog. Wegman's canine models also roller-skate, watch TV bedside, mimic a Stonehenge arch, and engage in a number of other anthropomorphic activities. The images poke fun. They are playful and comical. The incongruity of a dog exercising on a stationary bike solicits laughter, but it is the seemingly self-aware expression of the dog that adds another dimension to this work. Humorous and silly it no doubt is. But boundary breaking it also is. Wegman, in presenting the normal with an element of the ridiculous, is creating an opening for us to *rethink* the normal. His whimsical images mock rationality; they extend and reinterpret common thinking.

In Wegman's photographs it is not just the dress or the surrounding props that bring to life these unlikely scenarios, but the expression of the model and the title that serves to define that expression. A cocked head looks ponderous in *Stills from a Spelling Lesson (Reel 4). With Man Ray.* A sideways stare is read as a forlorn glance in *Arm Envy. With Alexander Edwards and Fay Ray.* In Wegman's photographs the dogs look as if they know what they are doing. The title acknowledgments, "With Man Ray" and "With Battina" for example, give credit to the model's role as actor. They almost ask us to imagine Battina "losing character" when the spotlights are turned off and Wegman says "Relax, we're done for the day." We can imagine it, but we don't believe it. Likewise, though we don't know whether or not Man Ray is pondering we doubt he is pondering how to spell. Fay Ray may be forlorn but it is not Alexander Edwards' arms that she covets. Knowing this, we create a distinction between identity and imaging; it looks like this but it is really something else. Importantly, this is a distinction that is often blurred when looking at photographs. Recognizing this distinction becomes a challenge to our perceptions, as if these images are saying "OK, so you don't really believe this is real, but why are you so ready to accept the reality of other images?"

The piece *Frog I Frog II. With Man Ray* directly questions this distinction between identity and image, or put differently, it comically mocks the assumptions of the real. On one side of the frame is a frog, smallish, green, and perched on a lily pad. Sitting across is Man Ray with bug eyes and green flippers. The title refers to both as frogs of some kind. But we are likely to identify one as a dog dressed as a frog and the other as a frog. The frog, though, may be a frog or it may be a plastic replica of a frog, all we really know is that it is a frog-looking image on Polaroid material. The portrayal of Man Ray as a frog is, of course, absurd and we are not led to question his identity but the absurdity combined with the mimicry does ask us to question other assumptions of authenticity. Wegman's images ask us to take a second look at our accepted notions about the world.

A number of Wegman's photographic images contain references to photography. Tri-X is a brand of film; it is also the title of one of his pieces in which the word is ascribed a different meaning as three dogs stand with their legs crossed forming three Xs. Another piece is titled *Matted (Diptych). With Fay Ray.* In a reference to the standard method of presenting photographic prints Fay Ray stands with four paws firmly positioned on the four corners of a door mat. Other images use standard scenes of photographic attention—the portrait, the studio baby picture, and the fashion shot. Accurate or not, photography has a reputation for being authentic. Early on the camera was referred to as a machine that would allow nature to paint itself. Wegman uses this realistic medium to turn a derisive eye on our common notions of the real, and at the same time mocks our common notion of the real-ness of photographic imaging.

Recall or refer to Chapter 3 of *Criticizing Photographs,* which includes Roland Barthes's analysis of an ad for Panzani spaghetti products. Barthes's analysis uses two signifying practices: denotations and connotations. Barthes's schema can be applied to all images, and it is a powerful means of interpreting photographs.

Building Visual Interpretations

A class of undergraduate students in a criticism course built visual interpretations of photographs by Cindy Sherman. First they discussed a wide variety of Sherman's photographs available to them in reproduction.[1] Each member of the class was handed a postcard reproduction of a Sherman work, ranging from her Film Stills to her later color work made in the 1990s. Each of about twenty students, one by one, described the image they were handed and told what they thought it was about. A general discussion of Sherman's work and its relevance to societal concerns ensued. Then the class went through a pile of current women's magazines and tore out images of women that they thought corresponded conceptually and visually to Sherman's photographs. Ultimately, they matched one magazine photograph with one of Sherman's photographs, in a series of diptychs that they pinned to a wall. This interpretive exercise resulted in a visually striking temporary exhibition that put Sherman's work back into the social milieu from which it emerged—pictorial representations of women in visual culture and particularly in mass media.

Making Personal Meaning

Imaginatively becoming part of an image and writing about the image from that point of view can draw the writer and readers into an image in personal and compelling ways. Following is a response to a class assignment that asks the writer to assume *someone or something* in the image, and write about the image from that point of view in first-person singular. Jean Giacolone, a master's student and art teacher, wrote as if she *were the skin of the woman* pictured in *Identity Could Be a Tragedy* by Maria Magdalana Campos-Pons (Plate 44). The artist is Cuban and is of African descent.

> I have been given too much importance in the world. I wrap this woman, warm her, and cool her. I expand with her every breath. The color I give her is from a Mendelien lottery—a toss of the protein dice. She is sometimes so proud of my flawless surface and other times I feel if she had a zipper she would step right out of me, and leave me on the floor. Would she then be freer, less conflicted? I glow for her. Be proud of your heritage.
>
> If I am your identity I am only the beginning—the wrapper. When you covered me, were you mocking me or paying homage to the origin of our brown-ness? Because you are not looking at me, I do not feel beautiful or celebrated. Have I passed the rite? Am I more acceptable to you now? I want to come to terms with me. "Could" is the operative word you have scratched into me with your nail. I will not take the fall for this—I am not your tragic flaw.   JEAN GIACOLONE

For an assigned class paper to interpret one work of a living photographer, master's student Greer Pagano selected a multimedia installation by Carrie Mae Weems, *The Hampton Project,* Williams College Museum of Art, 2000. The visual impetus for the project was a series of photographs of Hampton University, a historically black college, taken in 1899 by the photographer Frances Benjamin

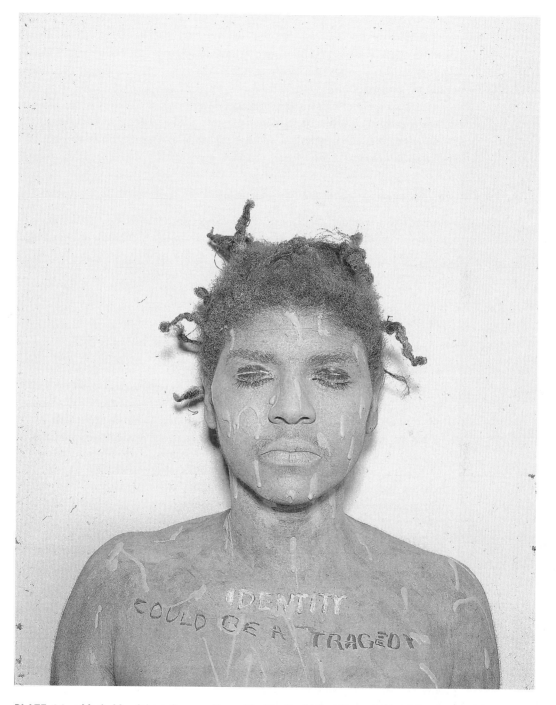

PLATE 44.   Maria Magdalena Campos-Pons, *Identity Could Be a Tragedy,* (detail from triptych), 1996. Color Polaroid, 20 × 24 inches.

Courtesy of the artist and Schneider Gallery, Chicago.

Johnston, a white woman. The photographs made by Johnston provided Weems with the opportunity to investigate a historic moment in time and to bring together Johnston and herself—two artists, two women at opposite ends of a century of different races and political perspectives. *Aperture* published a catalogue in tandem with *The Hampton Project.*[2]

In her paper, Greer presented a thorough description and history of the project, including published critical commentary about it. She concluded her paper with thoughts on what the installation and her investigation meant to her and her life. That section follows.

Personal Implications of *The Hampton Project*   GREER PAGANO

I came to know about *The Hampton Project* and Carrie Mae Weems through one of my fellow students. We both teach the course Ethnic Arts: A Means of Intercultural Communication, a general elective, entry level writing course for undergraduates at Ohio State. Over the past year we have been discussing how we teach the art of African American women. We have been asking our students and ourselves how we approach the artwork of women of other cultural experiences and ethnicities. How do we share a story that is not our own? What kind of investigations into personal and cultural identity do we undergo? Where do we begin to connect with another person? Leading discussions about the artwork of African American women was a challenge for us, two white women. We were apprehensive, given our backgrounds, our European ethnicities. How do we initiate dialogue and stimulate our students to search out meaning in the creative production of artists like Aminah Robinson, Faith Ringgold, Alison Saar, and Carrie Mae Weems?

My investigation of Weems's work has been an exciting process and has engaged my interests on both personal and professional levels. My students are not typically well informed about art. They are often skeptical about and unmotivated to discuss visual images. As an instructor, I have benefited from the fact that Weems actively calls out to her viewers and encourages dialogue about race and ethnicity. More importantly she goes beyond skin color to explore larger issues of human relationships, gender roles and identity, universal power struggles, and the critical role of representation. Weems says she is "committed to radical social change—that's the reason that themes of social relations recur in my art practice . . . Any form of human injustice moves me deeply . . . the battle against all forms of human oppression keeps me going and keeps me focused."

Weems's installation asks viewers to question the role of images in discussions of race, education, and violence, using Johnston's Reconstructionist era photographs in juxtaposition to contemporary imagery. Weems challenges her viewers to consider the role of photography as protest, social commentary, and as an educational site of transformation where viewers can reclaim the learning process for themselves and can begin redescribing the past in order to tell an honest story from multiple perspectives.

The Hampton Project addresses issues of identity and race within an educational context. The work bears witness to a past time and questions the effects of Hampton University's original mission and purpose. Weems uses Hampton as subject matter but pushes the envelope to confront and question the purposes and the results of forced assimilation, the replacement of one set of traditions and values for another, and the implicit hierarchy of race, class, and gender.

Weems, by appropriating Johnston's work and juxtaposing it with her own repertoire of images, confronts their original purpose. The installation becomes a critique of the concept of objective documentation and a site of questioning the role of photography. In light of this nation's history of slavery and human rights abuses, Weems asks us to consider the role of photography, as documentation, as protest, and as social commentary.

By having students look at and talk about Weems's work I sincerely hope to lead them into a discussion of how they see, how they label, how they name, and how they judge the "other." Weems uses personal narrative that complements and completes her photographs. I believe this methodology of personal narrative and investigation to be an excellent model for the construction of meaning. Using Carrie Mae Weems's work, students can be encouraged to investigate the interaction of text and image. What is meaningful about their combination? What do the students see in the work? Can they write their own narratives inspired by the photographs? Can Weems's vision connect with the student at a personal level? Is there an issue of family, of responsibility, of frustration about their education that allows a student to see beyond race and bridge differences, to find communal concerns through story telling and personal interpretation of images?

As I think about a future career as a museum educator, I want to better understand how to create an effective and positive museum experience. I believe in museums that allow the visitor to construct meaning using her or his own voice. *The Hampton Project* is an example of an artwork that demands dialogue and questions the authority of images. I believe the museum and the classroom can be sites of debate and discussion about the world in which we live. *The Hampton Project* can be a visual tool and inspiration to those who want to take part in a process of understanding history and a redescription of our world in a more equitable and honest manner.

Judging Photographs

If you are judging the work, be clear in your appraisal and offer reasons for it. Your criteria for judging work ought to be implicitly available to your reader if not explicitly stated. Remember that criticism is persuasive writing. Be persuasive by offering reasons and evidence in support of your interpretations and judgments and in your use of language. It is easy to be persuasive with someone who already agrees with your positions. Are your argument and manner of stating it persuasive enough to cause readers who oppose your positions to stop and reconsider their positions?

After seeing reproductions of *The Perfect Moment* by Robert Mapplethorpe, students at the university of North Texas responded to the work in brief paragraphs. These are first drafts quickly written in class.

Some of the works of Mapplethorpe were uncomfortable to look at as taboos and private parts and erections of male sexual organs are exposed in the bright open. The sexual tension was too strong for me to calmly analyze the quality of the artwork. The photographs are bold, fierce, aggressive, provocative, and pungent. They taste spicy and salty as I'm looking at them and the subject matter is too heavy for me to want to further investigate them—Chiai Li, Senior, Art Major

Immediately I feel like a pervert viewing his show. It feels like I should be at home with my boyfriend watching this art before sex as foreplay. I have no qualms with Mr. Mapplethorpe's art; it should not be censored, however, society has conditioned us to shame, which I think is unfair. I love it! Too bad Mr. Mapplethorpe has passed away, because "controversial" art always gets the best of me. Good form, good content, good message, I love it. Any pragmatic art that gets viewers talking is worth the effort of the artist, which I think Mapplethorpe successfully achieved—raising more awareness towards controversial issues.—McKenna McLean, Senior, Art Education Major

These photographs exhibited skill in technique, composition, and concept. While personally I'd prefer not to see some of the images, I only speak for myself, and this is a personal preference. I don't feel like the images should be banned and face legal action. I feel that offense taken by works of art is relative and varies from person to person. What type of art people prefer to look at is a personal decision.

My moral-, legal-, preference-issues aside, I feel that the images created a cohesive whole, and the concept of explicitly displaying the human body and the social and sexual taboos surrounding it was very clear and well executed. In addition, I feel that even the pieces I personally prefer not to see bring to light a world that is too often unexposed.—Anonymous Art Major

When he wrote the following paper, Eric Pickerill was an undergraduate majoring in art education at Ohio State University. He wrote the paper in an art criticism class in response to an assignment that asked students to judge the work of an artist of their choice, an exhibition at a local gallery, or at the art museum. The class had seen slides of *The Perfect Moment* and discussed Robert Mapplethorpe's photography. During the class discussion, Eric held and defended a minority position and later wrote this paper. I admire Eric for voicing his convictions, especially while faced with strong objections from his peers, and chose his paper as an example of good critical writing by a student because it is committed, forcefully argued, reasonable, and clearly expressed. This was the third assigned paper in that course; the first had been a generally descriptive paper, the second, an interpretive paper.

Judging the Work of Robert Mapplethorpe   ERIC PICKERILL

Robert Mapplethorpe has created a new paradigm in the art world. He has torn down the walls of art and gone where no one has gone before. He has brought his images to society, and his images challenge the values and morals our society tries to uphold. I am referring to and judging only one aspect of Mapplethorpe's work—his most controversial photographs containing sexually explicit subject matter.

Mapplethorpe presents this work in a manner that is confusing to the viewer. He presents his sexually confrontational images in the pristine settings of galleries and art books. His photographs are very concerned with composition and form. In his photograph *Self-Portrait,* 1978, he has centered himself in a room, and shows a hardwood floor leading to a wall. He has draped a box on the floor with a white sheet. He has placed his left foot on the box and his other foot on the floor. Mapplethorpe's body leans forward towards the wall and away from the camera and extends to the right where his face looks to the camera and the viewer.

Mapplethorpe is obviously concerned with composition and form because of the lack of any distracting elements in the portrait and the presentation of the subject matter in an aesthetically pleasing manner: The lines of the floor lead to the main subject, who is manipulated with light, casting shadows that enhance the formal excellence of the composition.

Although the description so far is "clean," Mapplethorpe confuses the viewer by manipulating the subject matter to depict a sado-masochistic act. Mapplethorpe wears leather chaps with a cutout seat and no pants underneath. He is also wearing a leather vest and boots. In his right hand he holds a bullwhip that protrudes from his anus and hangs to the floor.

Mapplethorpe has made a new paradigm in art by confronting society with images such as this one. His photographs are very pleasing formally in their making and presentation, but his subject matter often is of situations found in pornographic and sado-masochistic settings, such as magazines sold in adult bookstores. Because he presents his photography with formal excellence, we might say "It is art," but because his photography is often of sexually explicit images, we might say, "It is pornography."

By bringing his images to the public, Mapplethorpe has caused controversy over this very issue: Are they art or pornography? Whichever they are, and they may be both since there is disagreement between one viewer and the next, Mapplethorpe has been successful in furthering the progress of moral decay. This has even been exemplified while writing this paper. Having the Mapplethorpe photograph in front of me, I have become immune to its subject matter, although when I first saw it, I was horrified at its explicit sexuality.

This decline in morality is brought about by immersion. The decline is witnessed in the effects of Mapplethorpe's self-portrait on the public through immersion.

This portrait is shocking at first, but then I become consumed with the argument of art versus pornography, and after studying both the subject matter and form of the photograph, I become immune to what it shows.

The criteria for my judgment, that Mapplethorpe's images have furthered moral decay, are based in the root condition of humankind, forenamed "the sin condition." This condition is a separation between the living God, who is perfect and moral, and humankind, who is imperfect and immoral. This morality and perfection of God is witnessed in humankind's inability to meet God's standards; it is through the law of God that humankind becomes conscious of sin, for apart from this law, there is no sin. As this law reveals sin and immorality, it also stimulates it, because it is a natural tendency in humans to desire forbidden things. Therefore, we understand how Mapplethorpe's photographs have furthered moral decay because we are shocked, surprised, and drawn even closer to look into his images.

It took a little over ten minutes for my moral judgment to be tinted by Mapplethorpe's self-portrait. This portrait, along with others of his photographs, is among his most controversial. This is because it places society in a position of decision. Should America let its people be immersed in Mapplethorpe's images, which further moral decay?

Writing Criteria Statements

Try writing your own criteria for art or photography: By doing this, you can learn a lot about your own values for art, photography, and life. With a respectful nod to the biblical tradition, a class of students in a photography criticism course was assigned to write ten commandments of photography. Each commandment was to be a single idea, clearly expressed, so that another person could apply it to photographs. The commandment was to be expressed in positive or negative terms, using this form: "A good photograph shall (or shall not). . . ." The commandments should be sincere and held to be true by the writer.

After everyone spent sufficient time writing the commandments, everyone shared their lists. The group then considered whether a given commandment was too broad or too narrow, and clear enough to apply it to photographs. Most students had a difficult time coming up with ten. Here are some samples the class thought more or less successful as succinct, clear, and usable criteria statements:

A good photograph shall not contribute to violence. —Paula DiMarco
A good photograph shall not contribute to the degradation of women or people of color. —Paula DiMarco
A good photograph shall not expose a person's vulnerability without the consent of the person. —Paula DiMarco
A good photograph shall not be boring. —Erroll Wilson

A good photograph shall inspire internal discourse and may inspire external discourse. —Kendra Hovey

A good photograph shall be a tool to reach an end goal. —Lela Mendoza

A good photograph shall communicate a difficult to describe feeling or an intellectual idea. —Kendra Hovey

A good photograph shall provide the viewer with an experience of interest. —James Sampsel

A good photograph shall reveal something about the intentions of its maker. —Candace Feck

The students then tried to apply individual commandments (criteria) to an array of photographs, testing whether the criteria were clear and able to be applied. They also tested whether they still believed in their own criteria once they saw them put into practice. They found some criteria to be too subjective—for example, that a photograph not be boring.

Further problems with criteria became apparent. For example, some sets of criteria were inconsistent or held contradictory criteria. Some individual criteria could be applied to some kinds of photographs but would disallow other kinds that the writer thought were good. Thus, some revised their first set of statements to be more inclusive of different types of photographs. Predictably, some students had criteria with which other students disagreed, just as professional critics use competing and sometimes contradictory criteria in judging work.

The criteria-writing assignment challenged students to reconsider both their own work as photographers and their responses as viewers of others' photographs. Importantly, they realized that people write criteria and that criteria are not handed down from above by a god of aesthetics. The assignment also motivated students to look for hidden or implicit criteria for judging photographs that their classmates or professional critics employ when they make judgments. Once the students made the critic's implicit criterion explicit, they could better decide whether to (1) accept the criterion and the judgment on which it was based, (2) reject both the criterion and the judgment, or (3) accept either the criterion or the judgment but not both.

Four Student Views of *Immediate Family* by Sally Mann

The following four student papers are about Sally Mann's *Immediate Family* (Plate 45). The papers are in response to assignments in different classes that asked for judgments of Mann's work. In class the participants saw the photographs in the book *Immediate Family* and later had the pictures available to them for individual viewing. During the class discussion, they understood that some people find the work controversial. When she wrote the following paper, Anne Quilter was a returning student, an undergraduate senior in art education studying to become an art teacher. She is also a mother of five children.

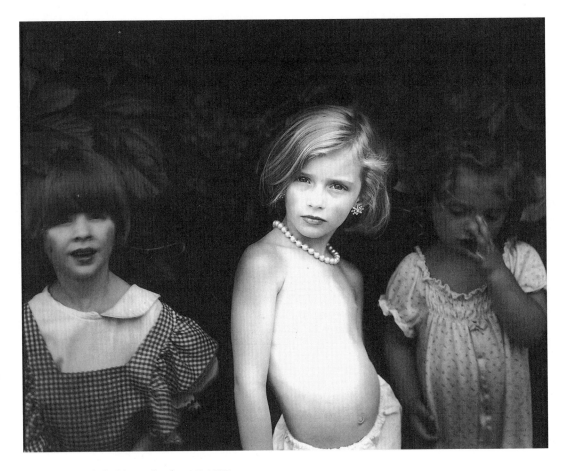

PLATE 45.   Sally Mann, *Jessie at 5*, 1987.
© Sally Mann. Courtesy of Edwynn Houk Gallery, New York City.

Sally Mann's Immediate Family   ANNE QUILTER

Childhood spins far too slowly for those growing through it and much too quickly
for us facilitating the process. Hurled into the world from the whirling dervish ride
after just a few short years, youthful adults face the incongruities of a sometimes
not-too-nice-society with only those messages of trust, integrity, and autonomy
that we, as parents, caretakers, and educators, manage to convey. When one of
these memos gets soiled, ripped, chewed, the child's perception of how the world
works becomes distorted. Sally Mann in *Immediate Family* shreds her own children's notions about worthy societal values by exploiting both their innocence,
and their trust in her with the publication of their portraits in the nude.

    This work chronicles the ordinary lives of her three young children as they go
about the business of childhood-playing, sleeping, eating—coupled with those

extra-ordinary moments in each child's life such as trips to the hospital emergency room. Given the common quality of these occurrences, the photographs in themselves would not be disturbing, but rather, touching looks at some of childhood's sweetest memories. The children's nudity, coupled with their provocative poses, however, presents a disturbing reality of childhood sexuality pushed and provoked to the surface by an unkind, unthinking, adult world.

In *Candy Cigarette,* Jessie mimics a sophisticated Hollywood starlet's pose with her right arm casually supporting her left which holds a cigarette. Her look of wanton defiance denies her tender grade school age. This same attitude repeats in *Jessie at 5* where the young girl poses with just a string of pearls about her neck. Childhood nudity itself doesn't necessarily disturb, especially if the innocence of the child is protected, but the air of blatant sexuality in Mann's work defiles all hope of guiding children safely through puberty with caring, responsible feelings about themselves and others.

Hayhook distresses me the most. Pre-pubescent Jessie hangs, nude, from a hayhook while a spattering of clothed adults loiter in the area. Her lithe little body, stretched out like a plucked chicken in the butcher's window, looks suspiciously like it is about to be abused. This might not be the intent at all, but even the hint that it might possibly be makes me wonder why Mann would ever shoot such a pose of her young daughter. Emmett, Mann's young son, fares no better at escaping his mother's probing camera lens. In *Popsicle Drips* his nude front torso becomes the entire focal point of the photograph. Here, so-called popsicle drips smear only his groin, exposed so delicately yet publicly flaunted. The drips a child endures while sucking a popsicle usually run down the arms, chin and neck, so it's hard to imagine this photograph as anything but a contrived view designed to shock and titillate.

Virginia at 3 shows the little naked girl leaning provocatively against a bed. Her demeanor is sullen and pouty, with a "dare me" look in her eyes. Little-ones do act this way, but usually a teddy bear or toy truck accompanies the look, not a rumpled bed.

Sally Mann exploits her young children's trust in her judgment as the parent and does them no favors publishing this collection of casual moments of their childhoods. The photographs, technically and artistically, are just so-so. The lighting is unimaginative; the compositions are ordinary; and the focus in several photographs blurs. Even the subject matter itself would not be controversial—if left in the protection of the family photo album. Paying her children to pose and then publishing prematurely, before her children are of age, sends the wrong messages about the value of children and their privacy.

Megan DiRienzo, a master's student in museum education at the University of North Texas, holds a contrasting view to that of Anne Quilter. She had not read Anne's essay when she wrote the following.

Reflections on *Immediate Family*   MEGAN DIRIENZO

Looking at Sally Mann's photographs made me reflect on conversations I overhear and participate in about how children in the 21st century are becoming overtly sexual much too quickly without any understanding of the adult, and arguably trashy and dangerous behaviors they are mimicking. Even though I do think that entertainment media is more often than not unnecessarily sexually charged, I don't think this has as much bearing on the behavior and stylistic experiments of little girls as society would like to think. Blaming the media for exposing our youth to overtly sexual young figures, (Mylie Cyrus and the Britney we all knew and loved from the earliest part of the 21st century come to mind), seems to me as cover for a stranger and maybe darker side of young children that we are afraid to acknowledge and examine. Are we a society filled with perverts and weirdos from which our children need to be protected, or are we a society pre-occupied with suppressing our own natural and innate sexuality fearful of the idea that we ourselves might indeed be the perverted and sick ones that we work so hard to expose and persecute.

Sally Mann's photographs were taken in a remote farm in southwestern Viriginia far removed from the influence of popular media like television, music, and movies. Somehow though, her children end up in poses that in a strange, innocent way radiate notions of sexuality and maturity that many in society argue to be inappropriate. But, what childcare worker or mother has not seen a child writhing around on the floor in the same position as the child in Mann's photograph, *Dirty Jesse?* These photos are not perverted, but rather reflective of a certain, strange characteristic that all children express as they grow up. Mann's daughter, Jessie, a frequent subject in the photographs, illustrates this idea when she states, "I also think she [my mother] brought out a certain sexuality in children that nobody wants to talk about." This statement suggests that her behavior was natural and innocent, uninfluenced by her mother, setting, or other outside forces. It also gets to the heart of the controversy in Mann's photos which document a very personal level of comfort with the awakening sexuality in her children as they grow up. That process is personal, parents are the ones who witness it first, watching their children grow from babies into puberty and to strange adolescents and all the way through to mature adults. Sally Mann has captured and shared that strange stage of late adolescence in her daughter Jessie, where puberty and mature sexuality are lurking in the shadows, but innocence and sweet naivety of childhood still hold sway. Mann pulls viewers into the intimate world of the family, forcing them to deal with their own reactions to the dark, strange, and innocent experience of childhood and budding sexuality.

When she wrote the following paper on *Immediate Family,* Rina Kundu was a master's student majoring in art education and the history of art and was enrolled in a course on photography criticism that used this book.

Sally Mann's *Immediate Family*   RINA KUNDU

Sally Mann's photographs are stunning. Twenty-five beautiful, 8 × 10 inch, black and white photographs line the wall of an exhibition space. Their vitality is instrumental in pulling the viewer into a world—an intimate world of the *Immediate*

Family—where Mann's children romp, play, pose, and pretend. The tensions are there as well because it is a complex world where children grow up. It is about their relationship with their mother.

Mann's photographs of her children, Jessie, Virginia, and Emmett, reveal a mother's gaze. She takes pride in the delicacy of their youth, captured before her camera. The obvious lack of self-consciousness among the unclothed children, as they play, reveals a non-traditional, but healthy atmosphere. Mann captures the spontaneity of their nakedness as they read, skate, and sleep. Often, her gaze turns to concern as she records the everyday mishaps that make up a child's life— bloody noses, cuts, bruises, and bed-wetting. The pictures express a mother's love and fear—and they are always carefully crafted.

Sally Mann makes pictures. She uses a large format camera, and she aestheticizes her compositions by contrasting tonal values, utilizing soft-focus, framing her subjects, and creating arresting juxtapositions. In *Sunday Funnies* the light from an open window dances across the children's bodies, creating interesting patterns against the shadowed recesses of their curves. In *Kiss Goodnight* the blurred focus and strong light produce an image of sketch-like quality, all of which add to the delicately tender moment. In *Jessie at 5* the child is framed between two friends, and her body creates a bold S-curve. Lastly in *Night-blooming Cereus,* soft, full blossoms are juxtaposed against the immature breasts of a child. Mann's interest in craft makes these photographs dynamic and vital, pulling the viewer in to examine the deeper implications of their content.

A child's world is never wholly innocent. They imitate and model themselves after adults. Mann captures these unsettling but compelling moments in her story. The photographs reveal the bridging of childhood and adulthood. Virginia and Jessie often pose as if they were fashion models; they wear make-up and jewelry, and they copy adult behavior. This unsentimental look into role-playing culminates in *Candy Cigarette,* where seven-year-old Jessie holds a candy cigarette between her fingers and poses provocatively. Although these pictures are disturbing, they are an unsparing depiction of the real world of children, not some idealized version.

Not all the pictures are a social document of children growing older, but some are allegorical in nature. *Popsicle Drips, Hayhook,* and *The Terrible Picture* allude to the pain of the Crucifixion—the contortion, the elongation, and the stillness. They are, indeed, striking images, but they also reveal Mann's ultimate control over her children. She takes over. The children no longer posture to imitate commercially packaged heroes; they are positioned. The allegorical scenes have nothing to do with a child's life; however, they do reveal a mother's control. Thus, even the process of image making draws our attention to the child's world—the nature of a child's relationship with his mother.

Although Mann's images are breathtakingly beautiful, their significance lies in their social content. Through her subjects and her process, Mann captures the psychological relationship between parent and child. Her gaze is loving and concerned, she allows her children to role-play, and she also takes control. *Immediate Family* is ultimately an ongoing story between a mother and her children, captured here for just a moment. The photographs draw our attention because they are not a sentimental view of children but a real relationship between an artist and her subject. Children are not altogether innocent; they model their behavior after adult figures. A mother watches as her children grow up, and she will learn that she must negotiate control.

At the time he wrote the following short essay, Terry Hermsen, a doctoral student, was immersed in study of Martin Heidegger (1889–1976), the influential existentialist philosopher. In his response to *Immediate Family,* Hermsen insightfully brings together his own lived experience as a father, a careful viewing of Mann's photographs, and key ideas from Heidegger to offer a sympathetic interpretation and defense of the work.

Heidegger, Childhood, and Sally Mann   TERRY HERMSEN

Studying Heidegger recently, I have come to see art, the way he does, as the conduit between what he calls "earth" and the human "world" that we make as we draw from earth our sustenance and civilization. Earth, however, remains hidden and not quite sayable ("continually self-secluding," as he puts it). It is all the **givens** of life—our birth, our death, our not-quite-chosen bodies, and on into rocks, fields, ozone, stars. . . . We like to pretend we are in control, that we understand our connection with earth. That's an illusion, Heidegger claims, and a sad one that robs us of our true sense of being. Art, he says, takes us back to *being,* to that marvelous meeting of earth and world, that charged and mysterious convergence.

I think Sally Mann's photographs in *Immediate Family* trouble people so much BECAUSE they tap so strongly into what Heidegger suggests art is supposed to do: bring the essences of earth back into our ever-easily-contained consciousness. In this case, the aspect of "earth" they bring back to us is the uncontrollable nature of childhood and its roots in the "mess" of the unconscious, the body, and physical presence. The power of these photographs for me is that they bring up, sometimes beautifully, other times in a troublesome way, often both, what a visceral struggle childhood is. Bloody noses, wet diapers, groans, bad moods, difficulties in sleeping, and the heat of the summer. I know it's rural Virginia, a particularly sweltering place in summer—but that swelteringness is present in many localities, if we don't wipe it away with the blandness of air-conditioning. Naked children's bodies no doubt is the stated reason many people object to these photos. But I wonder if the deeper reason could partially be: that we don't want to confront the realities of the physicality of childhood. We as Americans have put this off so well—with malls and pruned yards and the reserving of sexuality for TV and magazines. To have it brought back to us—especially in such nonprettified or sentimentalized directness—is unnerving. Balthus, as Barrett points out, painting young, provocative girls is one thing: we can write it off to a certain perversion in the artist's imagination. Sally Mann comes back to us with "representations of a LIFE actually lived," if seemingly more real because of her medium. She asks us so deliberately to re-consider what it means to have a body, to be torn between innocence and curiosity. That's hard to face. She does then what Heidegger would have her do: bring these realities of 'earth' back to us in a way that nothing but art CAN do. So we might fight those realizations. But we're the wiser for having seen them, through her photographs, afresh.

How does this affect me in a personal way? I guess because I've raised one daughter—struggling like crazy to keep her time connected to something more powerful and earth-bound than malls and highways and magazine images. And though I think we "made it through" together, so that she knows the hyperrealism of our culture without being sucked into its false seductions, I wonder what will happen to children coming up now, when the representational powers of the media are that much stronger. I have two adopted children from Guatemala now, 2 and 4 years old, and I wonder even more about them. I see them exploring their bodies, I see (even more than I did the first time around) how the nature of bodies and moods and physicality shape and drag at them daily, moment by moment. Mann's photographs remind me: this is the way it is . . . don't fight it, let the physicality be, find ways to let them be even MORE a part of the earth. American society will counsel otherwise: it will try to make everything seem pretty and easy and disconnected from troubled notions below the surface. There's another way to live, one truer, maybe less refined, but more connected to what "earth" is still left us, what much of the rest of the planet lives with every day. I think there's even more joy there, than in our overly-pruned lives. I go back to Mann's photographs to remember.

Writing Metacritically

Metacriticism is the criticism of criticism. Most of this book is metacritical: It looks at how and what critics do when they write about photographs. The following paper is in response to the fourth and final paper assigned in a criticism course taught by the author: "Select a contemporary artist of your choice, find three critics who have written about the artist, and metacritically analyze their writings in ten double-spaced pages."

When he wrote this, Brent Hirak was a graduate student of art education at the University of North Texas as well as a professional photographer. He chose the photographer and critics for his essay that follows in answering this question: How do professional critics respond to the work of Nikki Lee, the Korean photographer who inserts herself into different social groups by changing her identities? (See Plate 46.)

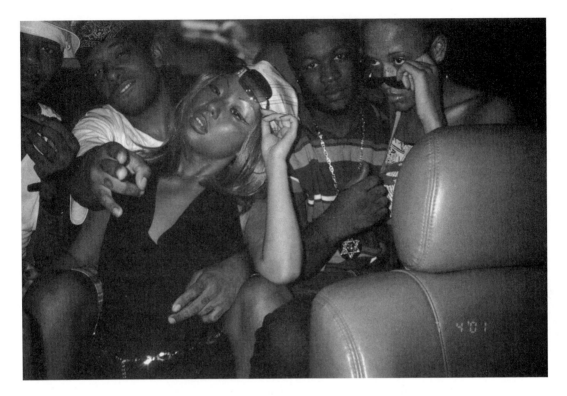

PLATE 46.   Nikki S. Lee, *The Hip Hop Project (1)*, 2001. Fujiflex print. Original work in color.

© Courtesy of Nikki S. Lee and Sikkema Jenkins & Co., New York.

Nikki S. Lee Reviewed   CHARLES HIRAK

When I first saw Nikki S. Lee's work, I got it, pretty quickly, or so I thought. I noticed the 'look,' the aesthetic: subjects were posing and therefore had a particular kind of face, one that was practiced; images were taken with a cheap camera and so details were blurred; the photographer placed subjects directly into the middle of the frame—these images were not composed, they were snapshots. I noticed that the central character of each image was the same woman. I studied her clothes, her use of makeup and body language, and soon was passing judgment on her performance within each scenario, on how well she fit in. Finally I began to wonder about how she gained entry into these groups, as the photographs didn't look forced. I projected myself into some of her images and was thereby extremely uncomfortable. I told myself that these were articulated fictions, the documentation of role-play, and evidence that a young Korean girl can become any kind of stereotype. How do professional critics engage with her work?

Jerry Saltz in the *Village Voice* begins by tracing a sketch of the East Coast art scene and setting Lee just on its border. He highlights her age, 29 at the time, and mentions though she is barely a year out of art school, that her bibliography is "ample," and that she is prominently featured in the current issue of *Artforum*. He seems to question her status (or the nature of a field which allows such artists to enter) by asking, "Are we turning British? Is it youth, girls, photography?" The state of photography, in his mind, has changed: "Photography now vies for attention with painting, video, and installation. The art-fashion boundary collapse is complete: Ads look like art, and many artists ape ads." He continues " . . . every picture, good or bad, is this finished, shiny phenomenon," and that " . . . photography is easy: anyone can take a picture, though not necessarily an interesting one." Why does he begin this examination in this way?

He structures a laundry list of "so-called girl photographers with their girl subjects," which includes Dana Hoey, Anna Gaskell, Jenny Gage, Katy Grannan, Mallerie Marder, and Justine Kurland (who is featured along side Lee in his review.) He ties the list to Yale, but subverts the status of institutions by suggesting that schools are always "moving in and out of zeitgeist," and noting that Lee emerged from the "not-as-hot NYU photo department." He binds Lee's strategic attributes to the "dressing-up" of Cindy Sherman and the "snap-shotiness" of Nan Goldin, but places her outside that canon by suggesting "she wasn't forced into her pictures in the same way the others were." For Saltz, Lee's photography is only a "tool" and "Her photos are nothing special, one looks pretty much like the next. They lack the drama, color, and intensity of a good Goldin. . . ." He deconstructs the formal elements to help marginalize the images, and asserts: "Her weakness is to be found in the very blandness of her photographs. There isn't enough undertow or tension to keep you engaged; too often you spot her, check out her "costume," and move on. The part of you that wants to see more still wants to see more."

If there is an enclave (Lee classifies them by function, ethnicity, or locale: "Lesbian," "Skateboarder," "Latino," "Ohio") that a performer can insert her into and document, then there is also a territory that we might call 'Art World,' within which an artist remains situated. Jerry Saltz positions himself as a gatekeeper in this world by simultaneously defining its parameters and noting whether the artist performs well within them.

By placing aesthetic as well as oeuvre into a margin, he allows for an emphasis on what her images might embody inside a practice: "Lee is a copycat, an egomaniac, and an aviator of a fluid identity. She's here because otherwise she wouldn't be. Her pictures are simply documents strange and sometimes wonderful parrotry." He continues, "What's so creepy, and what makes this her best series [the Yuppie Project], is not how Lee blends in, but how she stands out. It's like she's a glockenspiel in the middle of the John Tesh song . . ."Strengths." Lee is a ventriloquist of everyday life, a voice thrower, or an echo; her work is a piece of psychological feedback that reminds us how terrifyingly chunky the melting pot is."

For Saltz, the strength of Lee's work lies inside a capacity for a performance defined against its own stage. Like the work itself, his critique focuses on the social discourses within she performs. As gatekeeper Saltz has the choice to remain unsympathetic. Gilbert Vacario, the curator of the Institute of Contemporary Art in Boston, has a different goal.

Like Saltz, Vacario structures a categorization for the artist. But instead of juxtaposing her as a dislocation against other female photo artists, he situates Lee into a broader grouping:

> That's so Warholian. I think Andy Warhol said, "I'm a deeply superficial person." But your work does have a relationship to Pop Art, which is another level of your work that hasn't been touched on much, and also to the notion of celebrity. Even if it isn't something you set out to achieve in these photographs, your personality—the Nikki S. Lee personality—inevitably comes through, even though in your work you seek to integrate yourself into these different situations and groups. And when you look at a large body of work a viewer begins to develop a relationship with Nikki Lee. Again, it's similar to watching a movie star. You begin to identify with that person over time and repetition.

If Saltz gingerly scoots her to some periphery, then Vacario situates her inside a tradition, into a self-created ceremony: Lee's persona is emergent and relational, progressively recognizable, through circumstantial familiarity. Lee responds this way: "Changing myself is part of my identity. That's never changed. I'm just playing with forms of changing. My work is really simple, actually. I wanted to make evidence, as John Berger calls it. It does feel like I have a lot of different characters inside and I was curious to understand these things. I want to see some sort of evidence that could be all those different things." As Lee performs, and as her performance is documented and subsequently viewed, awareness of a particular kind of social construct blossoms. This is as much a comment about the viewer as it is about the artist or the documents. Vacario asks, "So what you're saying is that one's self is always understood in relation to that which surrounds you?" Lee understands it this way:

> That's the underlying concept: other people make me a certain kind of person . . . when I show the work, I prefer putting a lot of photographs together. If I showed just one project or one photograph, people probably don't get what I'm doing. He can't have one without the others—they're all connected. The Punk Project has to be with The Yuppie Project, The Lesbian Project, and other projects—that's what makes The Punk Project really look punk. The projects support and define one another. I don't necessarily see a sequence in my work, and my images don't have an order, but people can make up their own story when they see my work.

Through dialogue, Gilbert Vicario and Nikki S. Lee explore her aesthetic by discussing what her work is not. Lee: ". . . it's not about Nan Goldin's work, you know, going from bathroom to bedroom" and "you don't usually take pictures of yourself when you're crying, right? Look at Richard Billingham's work or Wolfgang Tillman's. But actually they make those things up." and "What does it mean to go deeper? Taking pictures when you're emotional or sorrowful, or having sex? I just want to have really boring snapshots—people just standing in front of a camera taking pictures with a smile."

Vacario is also interested in nationality, how it relates to ethnicity and to exoticness, and the degree to which the artist becomes active or passive within the various situations within which she practices. His most important question focuses upon the nature of her participation in and among groups. He asks if it is "formal progression" or something that enables the artist to "fully realize or authenticate" self within a specific social context. Form or content? Lee's response sidetracks his question/observation and instead the dialogue turns to the logistics of her practice and observations about specific attributes of the subcultures she investigates. Through dialogue between artist and curator we are given a unique vision into the location of meaning making. Here creator and created echo ideas to expand persona and gain depth. Vacario guides the dialogue but focuses his comments and response to the artist's lead.

Ben Davis, writing for *Artnet* roughly 5 years after the Vacario interview, plays the part of an apologist, explaining, defending, and noting the detractors. He calls it "likable late-late-model 80s phototheory; art." But his review focuses mostly upon Lee's hour-long film, which debuted that month at the Museum of Modern Art. He ties the film to earlier efforts and suggests that it is ". . . not so much an extension of the themes of her previous projects as it is a kind of gentle corrective to them." Like the others, he explores a connection with Lee's past work and "the complexities of identity theory." But Davis questions the validity of her work in this realm. How, he asks, can the categories she chooses to perform within be compared in any real way? He suggests that such comparison "represents a simplified, cardboard picture of social reality, not an exploration of its richness." He names the film's use of "mild irony," a characteristic which he also attributes to the artist: "The cumulative effect of the film is that the mutable self that Lee has become famous for illustrating is depicted as the logical product of a certain posturing type of art world, full of self marketing and disingenuousness." Finally, he questions the phenomenon of using her work as a vehicle to explore the "complexities of identity theory," by suggesting it's less about the craggy regions of post-Marxist identity theory, and more about shopping and trying on different outfits.

It occurs to me that a parallel exists between the various enclaves in which Lee places herself, and the group of critics (my own voice included) chosen for this review. The gatekeeper, the interlocutor, the apologist: what are their specific roles within the broader critical discourse? How does artist navigate the particular enclave they comprise? Lee provides one answer. Her persona, and the ideas connected to it, emerge through a series of documentary style photographs and film. In similar fashion 'Nikki S. Lee' emerges textually through critical inquiry. For me, what I 'got pretty quickly' upon first seeing her work receded, and what emerged was a changed understanding of 'self,' that mutable performer, who vies to assimilate even as it competes to stand out.

References:
Davis, B. (2006, October, 24). *Artnet* Magazine.
Saltz, J. (1999, September, 21). *Village Voice*

Vacario, G. (2008, April). "Seeing & Writing 3. ARTIST INTERVIEW: Nikki S. Lee"

WRITING ARTISTS' STATEMENTS

Anyone who exhibits photographs will sooner or later be asked to accompany her or his visual work with what is commonly referred to in art schools and the art-world as an *artist's statement*. An artist's statement is a brief, often one page or less, essay about the work being shown written by the one who made the work. Such requests can be daunting to artists. Some image makers resist explaining their work, believing that the work should stand on its own or that it speaks for itself. Some do not know what to say about their own work. Others know what they think their work means but do not want to give that meaning away, or constrain and limit viewers' readings of the work. In response to requests for artists' statements, some photographers resort to cynicism and write something intentionally obtuse and opaque, merely to fulfill the request. Others write so generally that their statements could apply to almost any group of images. Some fall prey to an assumed pressure to be "brilliant" or "theoretically grounded" and resort to arcane academic language that they think will impress.

A request for an artist's statement, however, presents positive challenges for the artist who has to write one. It presents occasions for artists to think about their visual expressions in a verbal medium. Thus, in exploring ideas in a different medium, they may gain insight into their own work through this process, and perhaps motivate further works of art.

An effective artist's statement can be helpful to viewers, especially if it meets some basic criteria: It is clear enough to be understood; it is specific enough to direct a viewer's attending to the work; and it is open enough to allow viewers room to build their own meanings about the work.

If in doubt about what to write about your own work, these questions might provide starting points:

- What would be helpful for viewers to know about this work so they can understand and enjoy what I have done?
- What motivated me as the artist who made this work? What were my starting points?
- What would I hope viewers would think about when viewing this work?
- Are there impressions that I clearly do not want to imply?

Following is an example of an effective artist's statement written by a candidate for a master of fine arts degree. It opens doors through which the viewer can enter into the work and find some of the meanings intended by the artist, and also encourages viewers to make meanings of their own (Plate 47).

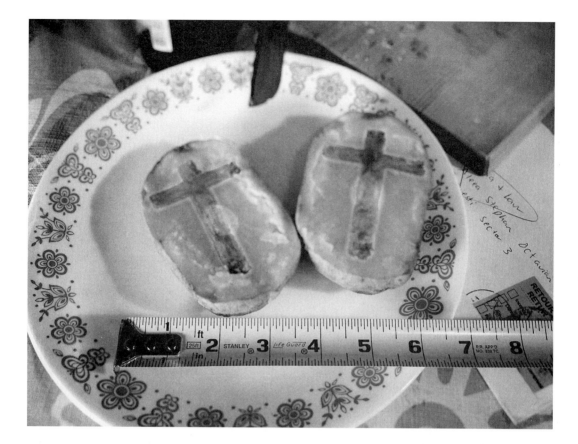

PLATE 47. Nate Larson, *Potato Manifestation,* 2001. Pigment print, 12 × 16 inches.
© Nate Larson. Courtesy of the artist.

Conjecture   NATE LARSON

When driving late at night, I listen to AM radio talk shows. In one of these shows, a caller had been preparing dinner, and when he took his potato out of the oven he sliced it to discover that there were glowing crosses in either half of the potato. This discovery placed the caller in a situation where he was unsure of the significance of the event as well as any ramifications it might have. The host of the broadcast offered some opinions, but what I found more fascinating were the responses of the other callers. These suggestions included everything from placing the potato halves on the eyes of the blind to cure blindness to slicing the potato into smaller slices to be sold on popular Internet auction sites. I would later document this found narrative as a photograph, titled Potato Manifestation.

    This body of work is a way of telling stories about an aspect of the culture in which I live. In our culture, people construct systems of beliefs, and these beliefs dictate the way that they live their lives and how they respond to others around them. These systems of belief include both religious traditions and secular myths, which are often interwoven to create new combinations of thought.

Religious systems of belief are constructed around abstract spirituality, based on centuries of ever-evolving manuscripts, and then completed by the personal faith of the individual. To validate this faith, many look for an external sign to corroborate their beliefs, and these signs can take the form of miracles, apparitions, and relics. Miracles and apparitions are usually supernatural visions or paranormal events perceived by the individual, while a relic is a physical remain of a saint or holy person with spiritual significance attached to it. Relics can also be used to invoke blessings or be called upon to perform miraculous events. Many would discredit these occurrences, yet many also seek them out as a part of their devotion. My role as an artist is to collect these events and objects that could be used to validate certain Christian belief systems, such as the potato manifestation, and then to examine and catalog these phenomena as photographic documents. All of these photographs have their genesis in either oral or textual narrative and are presented through photographs to examine the nature of the photographic document as well as the relationship of photography to both objective and subjective truth.

This visual project is neither an affirmation nor a denial of my personal beliefs, rather an examination of the influences that have touched my life during the various stages of my development, continuing through the present day. This reconstruction of found narratives creates a space in which to examine my perceptions of them as well as the underlying connection to western culture.

Taxidermy and My Southern Gothic   ELIZABETH DANIELLE WILSON

Growing up in small-town Alabama with parents who both worked full-time, I spent a great deal of time with my grandmothers in their kitchens, beauty parlors, churches, and cemeteries. On Sundays, I was ushered into a small country church lined with wooden pews and elderly women singing off-key from Missionary Baptist hymnals. On weekdays, I stacked curlers like Legos and absorbed old lady gossip on the floor of Grandmother's in-house beauty salon. In the Spring, I picked up plastic flowers fallen from headstone arrangements while Granny sold plots and raised cemetery funds from under a green awning in the Boldo Cemetery. Sometimes in the evenings, I tagged along to funeral home wakes, getting lost in the forest of black skirts and the thick scent of cut flowers. Before turning eighteen, I had probably only been to two weddings, but I cannot count the funerals and wakes I was taken to. Sermons on the afterlife and lifeless bodies were part of the regular fabric of life; lifeless forms dually repulsed and fascinated me.

I rarely ever really knew any of the bodies lying in the caskets. They did not differ much from the mannequins I saw in malls with my mother. I remember sticking my tongue out at the mannequins and touching their plastic skin, later becoming terrified that they would burst to life and vengefully attack me. Likewise, when Granny died during my seventh grade year, I remember leaning into her casket to touch her hand, knowing that I had to say goodbye, but terrified of actually feeling her rice paper skin. Later, I spent whole afternoons sitting all alone by her grave site and talking to her, while being simultaneously terrified that she would lurch her hand through the topsoil and pull me down to prematurely rot alive beside her.

Although I grew up in the South, I rarely encountered taxidermy except when we visited a distant cousin-by-marriage's house a few times. Taxidermy blanketed his living room—on the television set, next to the couch, hanging up and down every wall—a space so thick with mounted turkeys and squirrels that you could barely move without touching them—and touching them was too horrible a thing to imagine. These frozen animals captivated me just like the department store mannequins and dead bodies. (See Plate 48.)

Recently, I have found myself photographing bobcats mounted over beds, whole mountain lions lounging over fireplaces, snow sheep dawdling beside bookshelves, giraffe heads overlooking barware, foxes standing alert in the midst of toy car pileups, and deer heads guarding silver tea sets. "Leopard Sunning by Air Vent" was photographed in the corner of a master bedroom.

Initially encountering my taxidermy photographs, people are usually fairly shocked and dumbfounded. They often want to know whose side I am on—whether I hate hunting and condemn all hunters or if I spend my weekends in tree stands. I have never hunted, nor do I have any desire to judge anyone who does. I only want to document, collect, and present things as I find them. People regularly assume that I have set up props or digitally inserted the animals. I can rarely bring myself to touch the taxidermic objects, much less lug them across rooms. I am interested in capturing these creatures as their owners have arranged them. I find the wild (and often exotic) animals' re-contextualizations absolutely fascinating. I am also wildly fascinated by how the tension or power struggles between male and female partners is acted out through the acts of placement and repositioning of taxidermy as decoration in the home.

PROCESSES OF WRITING

Before you begin to write, determine whom you are writing to, how much background information your reader will have, and what information you will have to supply. Organize how you are going to proceed with your essay. Think about an opening that will draw your reader in—that will make someone want to read the rest of what you have written. Although we have studied criticism in the logical order of description, interpretation, evaluation, and theory, remember that critics rarely write in such a sequence. They write to be read with some enjoyment, in a

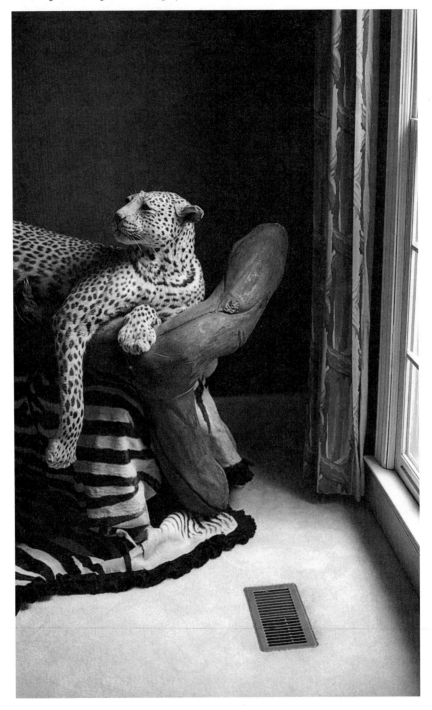

PLATE 48.   Elizabeth Danielle Wilson, *Leopard Sunning by Air Vent,* 2008. 6.09" × 10" at 300 dpi.

© Elizabeth Danielle Wilson. Courtesy of the artist.

way that will involve the reader in what they have to say. What do you want to tell your reader, and how do you want to tell it? What will be your main point, and what evidence do you need to establish it?

Next, sort and resort your notes, arranging them in a logical and interesting way. It may help to make a one-page outline or some other organizational pattern so that you can see all that you want to include and in what effective order. Then start writing! If you have difficulty getting started, begin with whatever section is the easiest for you to write, and then add the other sections. If you have a good organization for your essay, it does not matter where you begin, as long as you eventually put all the pieces into a logical and effective order.

Keep your reader in mind as you write and as you read what you have written. Read it through the eyes of your imaginary reader. First imagine a friendly reader who will be sympathetic to what you think. Then, for a second reading, imagine a reader who would be difficult to convince, so that you will build a strong case for what you believe. Don't assume too much of your reader: Describe the work sufficiently so that the reader can form a good mental picture of what you are writing about.

Convey your enthusiasm for the photograph with your choice of words. Once you've described it in sufficient detail, don't assume that the photograph's meaning is now evident. Provide your reader with your interpretation, and give reasons why you think it is a valid interpretation. Be sure that your judgment of the work is clear—that your reader knows that you strongly approve of it and why, or that you have reservations and what they are. If you are using specific criteria for evaluating the work, you may want to make them explicit. Be persuasive by your choice of language, and be convincing by the evidence you cite to support your claims.

Choose to write in first ("I"), second ("you"), or third person ("the viewer"), and then be consistent throughout your paper unless you have a good reason to change person. In critical writing, first person is probably most appropriate. You can own your own opinions directly: "I believe . . . I found . . . I object to . . . I favor . . ." If you use second person, you are likely to sound presumptuous about your readers: "You find . . . you notice . . . you see . . ." Similarly, it is safer to claim your own positions rather than attributing them to someone else: "The viewer notices . . . the viewer objects to . . ."

Use active voice and avoid passive voice in your writing. An example of passive voice: "It was believed that . . ." It can be rewritten into active voice: "Photographers adhering to a formalist aesthetic believed that . . ." Active voice is a more forceful way to write and will result in livelier, more engaging writing to read. You can revise this passive phrase, "The passive voice is to be avoided," to active voice: "Avoid the passive voice." Active voice is clearer and helps avoid ambiguity or misunderstanding (instead of "The images will be placed . . ." use the phrase "I will place the images"). Writing in active voice is also a more responsible way to write than using passive voice. Consider the irresponsible use of passive voice in the following brief calendar item published in the *New Yorker* magazine about an exhibition of photographs by Doug and Mike Starn: "New works by the Starn twins, who are known for melodramatic effects in vast, grainy photographs, explore the moth's pretty and sinister aspects in various formats, including sleek C-prints mounted on aluminum. Through March 20. (Lehmann Maupin, 540 W. 26th St. 212-255-2923.)"[3]

In the sentence, the use of passive voice occurs here: "the Starn twins, *who are known for.*" First, the comment is by an anonymous author. Peter Schjeldahl is the art critic for the magazine, but neither the arts calendar nor particular entries are identified with an author, so we do not know who wrote it. The one-sentence statement is a negative judgment, although somewhat subtly negative: *Dramatic* in art discourse may be complimentary, but *melodramatic* is not, unless something is ironically melodramatic. Similarly, *beautiful* is usually a compliment in art discourse, but *pretty,* when used by a critic to identify artworks, is rarely, if ever, a compliment. Similarly, in this context, *sleek* implies *too* sleek; *glossy* or *shiny* would be more neutral descriptors. Very importantly, *who* says the Starns are known for . . . whatever? "Known for" by whom: the unnamed critic? His or her circle of friends? The whole world? Had the critic written in active voice and said something to the effect that "*I find the Starns' work to be melodramatic and pretty,*" the statement would be much more honest, responsible, and courageous. Take responsibility for your thoughts and use active voice.

Each paragraph should focus on one major point with evidence to support the point. Your ideas should progress logically from paragraph to paragraph: If your paragraphs can be rearranged without loss of effectiveness, your essay is probably not as logically constructed as it ought to be. Provide your reader with transitions from one paragraph to another. Sometimes the whole first sentence of a new paragraph will provide the transition from one idea to another; other times a simple bridge such as *however* or *moreover* will suffice.

Write succinctly. Notice how much information the following calendar entries from the *New Yorker* contain in brief, economical, and lively writing.

Laurie Simmons

Home decoration goes haywire in these photographs of collages inspired by Frances Joslin Gold's 1976 do-it-yourself interior-design workbook, "The Instant Decorator." Perspective and proportions are skewed; tacky *objets d'art* teeter precariously on their perches; ladies clipped from postwar bra ads have invaded a bedroom, while a motley crew of bachelors lurks in the den. Fantasy decoration schemes collide with real life in "Black and White Living Room," which includes a painting by Simmons's husband, Carroll Dunham.[4]

Eugene Richards

Richards is arguably the most empathetic photographer working when it comes to showing the hard parts of people's lives. His record of his wife's fight with and death from breast cancer and his chronicles of inner-city drug users (collected in the books *Exploding into Life* and *Cocaine Blue, Cocaine True*) are harrowing and extraordinarily frank. Immediately after the attacks of September 11th, Richards hit the streets, visited people's homes, and attended funerals in search of images that might document the violence and loss that affected so many people that day. Once again, Richards has wrought a personal elegy for those who are just learning to cope with what has happened to them.[5]

Lee Friedlander

When Friedlander began to shoot landscapes, he traded his streetwise Leica for a square-format Hasselblad. But he doesn't follow the example of Ansel Adams and Edward Weston—he refuses to treat the American wilderness as an icon. Typical of his studies in composition is "Canyon de Chelly, 1998," which puts standard Adams fare (a lichen-stained monolith) in the foreground, then packs the rest of the frame with a graphic abundance of striated cliffside, headlong rushes of trees, rock-slide, and cloud. "Oregon, 1997" presents another outdoor piety (the sheer wall of rock), but stone has never been possessed by such a spirit of nervous energy.[6]

Make your conclusion brief, clear, and forceful. In a short essay it is not necessary to review your argument. Avoid the error of making the conclusion into a beginning of another essay by introducing a new idea or further evidence. Also avoid double endings. Consider your completed paper to be your first draft, and read it over critically. The following questions may help you to consider what you have written and perhaps to improve it.

- What is your main point? Do you state it soon enough and reinforce it throughout your essay?
- Does each paragraph have a topic?
- Do you proceed logically with your argument, with one point leading to the next?
- Do you move smoothly and effectively from one paragraph to another?
- Do you provide enough internal and external descriptive information for your reader to visualize the work you are discussing?
- Do you provide evidence for your interpretations?
- Do you provide reasons for your judgments?
- Have you been clear without being redundant?
- Do you get your reader's attention right at the beginning of your essay?

- Have you created the tone you want? Have you refrained from being sarcastic or insulting?
- Have you been fair in your judgments?
- Is the final paragraph a clear and forceful conclusion?
- Have you refrained from being and sounding dogmatic about your views?

Proofread your writing for proper grammar and correct spelling. Reading your paper aloud to yourself will help you discover errors, clumsy language, and poor transitions. Once you have done what you can to strengthen your essay, ask others to read what you have written and to tell you what they think about what you have done. Then reconsider your paper. Every writer can benefit from an editor. Polishing your writing at this point is similar to matting and framing a favorite photograph, presenting it in the best way possible.

If you enjoy writing and are good at it, consider writing for a publication. An increasing number of campus, local, and regional publications on art and photography need writers. Browse the periodical sections of libraries and bookstores. When you find a periodical you would like to write for, locate the name and address of the editor in the first several pages. Write to the editor and ask for writers' guidelines, or make an appointment to visit the editor of a local publication to discuss your possible contributions.

TALKING ABOUT PHOTOGRAPHS

Although talking about photographs is different from writing about them, the critical questions to consider are similar for both activities. When talking about a photograph or an exhibition of them, think about the questions asked in this book by the author and the critics quoted. Even in the presence of a photograph, we still need to describe it to one another because description is a way of noticing in words and a way of getting others to notice. Each of us may notice different things in different ways. We still need to interpret and to find evidence for our interpretations.

In casual conversations about photographs, we seem to have no trouble judging them. We tend to make readily apparent what we like and don't like. Too often, however, we do not offer sufficient reasons for our judgments, and rarely do we state criteria. Conversations about photographs would likely be more informative and more interesting if we did more than throw out casual judgments. We would have better conversations if we offered careful descriptions, full interpretations, and reasons and criteria with our judgments.

We all wander through exhibitions of photographs with assumptions about photography, art, and life. If we were to articulate these assumptions, we would be engaging in discussions of aesthetic theory and knowledge and social reality.

Theoretical discussions built on particular images or exhibitions, even in casual conversations, could be interesting, enjoyable, and valuable to each of us and those with whom we talk.

A significant difference between talking and writing is that writing is usually a solitary activity with an imagined reader in mind, and talking usually involves listeners. When writing, the audience is distant; in conversation the audience is present. Reactions to what we have written, when there are any (and often there are none or few), come long after our thoughts have been articulated on paper. It may be a year or more before the author of a book gets a response from a reader, and months before the author of an article gets a response. Responses from listeners to our articulated thoughts in conversation are often immediate. There can be quick give-and-take between speaker and listener. The writer of published material is sometimes allowed to revise after hearing others' reactions, but this is a long process of communication drawn out over months and years. In reaction to a listener, a speaker can revise immediately. To benefit from the advantage of having quick responses in conversations, we need to welcome responses and sometimes ask for responses when none are volunteered; and we need to listen to them, consider them, and acknowledge them. Monologues are not conversations, nor does talk without a response constitute a conversation.

The presence of the artist who made the work that is being discussed changes the discussion. Without the artist being present, when interpreting and judging the work, we appeal to evidence in the work, to what we know about the world, and perhaps to what others have said, including what that artist said if we have access to that information. When the artist is present, we may censor what we think for many reasons—we might be awed and thus silent, we might be self-conscious because we think we do not have anything of interest to say, we may disapprove of the work but do not want to offend the artist by saying so. Perhaps we mostly want to hear what the artist says about the work rather than tell the artist what we think about it.

From artists we can learn things about their work we can't learn from other sources. We can sometimes learn of the artist's motivations, state of mind when making the piece, intended meanings, methods of working, sources of inspiration, beliefs about art and the world, attitudes about other artists and movements; we can learn about the artist's personality and the way he or she relates to viewers of the piece. Does the artist's understanding of the work differ from that of the viewer or from that of critics who have written about the work? Which artwork does the artist think is his or her best? We can ask the artist about these matters. Information about some or all of these matters may help us to better understand and appreciate work we are considering. Ultimately, however, we don't want to depend solely on the artists' views of their own work.

The position offered in this book concerning artists' thoughts about their own work is that although they are sometimes enlightening and can provide us with insights, other times they seem irrelevant to what we see in the work. We get to decide. Artists make the work, and viewers interpret and judge it. The artist may greatly aid us in interpreting and judging it, but the artist doesn't own both the work and meaning. Artists may and do try to direct and set parameters around what they think their work is about and how it should be understood. A few of the artists whose work is reproduced in this book requested a copy of the text that would accompany their work before they would grant permission to reproduce it. Sometimes artists refuse an author permission to reproduce their work when they do not agree with the author's view of it.

An artist's interpretation of his or her work should meet the same criteria as anyone else's interpretation of that same work: Does it make sense? Does it offer insight? Is it interesting? Does it engage other interpretations? Is it reasonable and backed by relevant evidence? Does it overlook related and important issues? Is there sufficient reason, in addition to the fact that it comes from the artist, to accept it as a good interpretation and a worthy judgment?

STUDIO CRITIQUES

Critiques are a valuable part of studio courses, undergraduate through graduate school. When asked to define a *studio critique,* different art instructors[7] offered these seven spontaneous definitions:

An occasion for students to develop a critical awareness of their own work, or one might say the ability to step outside their own subjectivity regarding the work, and some idea of how the work relates to contemporary art.

The best opportunity for students to receive public reactions to their work. They can find out how their art is perceived by other students, and the faculty member can gain insight to the thought processes behind the student's creation.

An event during which the artist finds out viewers' responses so that the artist can evaluate how the image is interpreted and judged by others.

A means for a group to get at big issues, and to form a bond of purpose for a class.

An exchange of ideas about technique, form, concepts, production, theory, iconography . . . usually a collective group exchange between students and instructors.

An opportunity for artists to solicit informed opinions regarding their work.

An opportunity for students to receive feedback from their teacher and peers regarding the aesthetic, stylistic, creative, and innovative aspects of their studio work.

These definitions speak to group critiques, in which the whole class is present and participating. Critiques, however, are also conducted individually, between an instructor and a student, or student to student. Critiques can be informal and spontaneous in response to a statement or a question from a student or an instructor, perhaps in the middle of a working session. *In-process critiques* address a piece or a set of works while it is still being made. Often critiques are held at the culmination of a project or school term.

The preceding definitions are implicitly positive about critiques, seeing them as opportunities for growth. Many professional artists also look at critiques in a positive way. Carrie Mae Weems, for example, says, "I'm excited when my work is talked about in a serious manner—not because it's the work of Carrie Mae Weems, but because I think there's something that's important that's going on in the work that needs to be talked about, finally, legitimately, thoroughly."[8] Regarding the value of one-on-one critiques, Chuck Close says, "Having an old friend, a trusted eye, look at your work is so important—someone who's been there all along."[9]

Art instructors who conduct critiques hope that students have positive attitudes about them. The following spontaneous comments express the desires of instructors for what students should get out of critiques.

That the students learn how to maximize the benefits of the criticism given, and more importantly, to know how to decide what is useful and not useful in any feedback they get.

That the students try to disregard what they already think they know about their work.

I want my students not to be afraid to talk. What they have to say is important and is never stupid.

That they be courageous and really look at the image and the possible interpretations of it.

That they can gain insights into their own and others' work. That it is not a time to be defensive. They can take or leave what people say.

That the students' opinions are valid regardless of their backgrounds.

Productive critiques should be honest and open discussions.

I want students to look before they speak. Speak first about what is there, rather than about what is not there. Be honest. To realize that they know more than they think they know.

That we, as artists can learn a lot *after* the making of a thing by looking at that thing.

That critiques are another way for one to learn from one another.

I want my students to be honest about their observations. Not cruel, but honest.

I want the students to be aware of their cultural biases.

I want the students to talk about what we are *looking at*; tell us what the object is; go beyond "I like it; I don't like it."

That a critique is an opportunity to see what others are doing; to satisfy
their curiosity and to get new ideas and perspectives.

That a critique is a chance to learn about their own work.

That they learn to talk of the work itself rather than about the person or the
person's ability.

That the students provide a majority of the critical feedback about the work
of their peers.

That the students are the ones inquiring about their work and seeking criticism of it.

That the students are reflective, seek improvements, and discuss the work in
some context beyond only the formal aspects of the art.

That there is a triadic dialogue among the artist, the other students, and the
instructor.

That they can learn how to think and talk about work—others' work—not
just their own. Art class is not just about creating a piece. It is about how
the piece functions after one has presented it.

That the students get new ideas, new energy, enthusiasm, self-confidence,
and a sense of their own progress and accomplishments.

That critiques be learning events, not exercises in either humiliation or
negativity.

That each student walks away from the experience positively with ideas he
or she can apply to his or her own work.

Students have expressed some of the same sentiments about critiques as the
instructors. Students who have been part of many critiques during undergraduate
and graduate years made the following comments. The statements express what
students want and do not want from critiques. Note how often the students' wishes
and the instructors' wishes overlap.

I need to know how people respond to my work. Do they get anything out
of it? Then I want to know why—why do you respond to this and not
that? Most importantly, after I finish several pieces, I need direction to
start another bunch. I want to know where I could take this idea. How
could I push it, should I expand it or refine it?

I want harsh truth. My work will never progress to its potential unless I am
told what appear to be my strengths and weaknesses, what I'm doing
both well and not so well.

I want to know if my photographs work visually and what effect they have
emotionally and intellectually.

I don't want to feel uncomfortable or embarrassed. I do not want to defend
my artwork in front of a group of my peers.

I want to leave with the feeling that I can create art.

I want help in considering some of the big questions, for example, what is art, what is good art, how does art affect culture and vice versa?

I want to feel confident and motivated to continue making art.

I want to know if I met the criteria of the assignment. I also want to know how people related to or interpreted my work. A critique should be a supportive, positive experience.

I want to learn what works and what doesn't and why. If something really *shines,* I'd also like to know that and why.

I want my work to be viewed with respect.

I don't want someone to say, "Oh, I like it," just to be nice and then move on.

I want to hear many voices to gain insight on how people view my work and the work of other artists.

Tell me what you get from my work and what thoughts it arouses within your mind. Then let me decide whether your feedback is valid to me.

I want to see things from different points of view and to hear different interpretations.

Sometimes I get too close to the work and I need new insights into the work from others.

I want honesty. No sugar coating. No bogging down. Move along.

I want probing questions that help me expand my thinking; clarifying questions that require factual responses.

I want positive criticism—what can I work on rather than what I'm doing wrong.

I'd like to hear links between my work and other contemporary artists that may have done similar work to mine.

I want the viewer's first emotional and spontaneous impression.

I want a thorough interpretation of my artwork.

I don't want people to attack the artist and make negative remarks that only serve to belittle and humiliate rather than educate.

I do not want silence.

Most of the time my work gets misinterpreted solely on the fact that I have skin color. If I were to submit the work anonymously to an exhibition, color wouldn't be an issue purely because I am a minority. It's extremely frustrating when all people see of my work is a color and nothing else for no other reason than my skin tone. It's like a different version of racism where your work is scaled down and denied its true meaning and labeled a color.

I don't like to hear what I could have done or should have done if it totally changes my piece.

I do not want the person critiquing my work to try and change it to look like theirs.

I love it when I leave the critique with a burst of energy and ideas! I go
    straight to the studio and get busy.

Studio critiques should not be confused with art criticism. Studio critiques are
a special form of academic criticism, most often taking place in art courses, and
usually for the benefit of art students. *Criticizing Photographs,* however, is a study
of how professional critics criticize photographs made by professional photographers. While a common purpose of studio critiques is to improve students' abilities
to make art, published criticism is not written to improve how artists make art.
Professional critics do not try to change artists or their work; for better or worse,
participants in studio critiques, however, frequently focus on changing the art that
they see, trying to help the artist make it "better." Published criticism is generally
to engage interested readers (not single artists) in thought about new art or the
relevance of historical art. Improving art is a limited notion of art criticism, and
unfortunately, practices of studio critiques are often mistakenly conflated with art
criticism.

Professional criticism and studio critiques do share one important commonal-
ity: Both are attempts at deepening insights into art and furthering discussion of
it. A presupposition of *Criticizing Photographs* is that studio critiques would be
more effective if they relied more on the practices and activities of professional critics. For example, some descriptive, interpretive, and evaluative words and phrases
quoted from one randomly selected issue of *Aperture,* a journal of photography, are
presented here.[10] The excerpts are from an editorial, a letter to the editor, a book
review, and two short essays written by authors to accompany portfolios produced
by contemporary photographers.

The words and thoughts are given here for these reasons: Especially in critiques,
students often think there is nothing to say about a photograph. All these words
and thoughts show that there is indeed much to think about and talk about when
looking at images. Admittedly, the images to which the authors refer are made by
professional image makers, and granted, those using the words are, for the most
part, professional writers. Nevertheless, the quotations show that much can be said,
and the quotations might motivate or inspire deeper thinking about images made
by students. Some of the excerpts may provoke disagreement and might serve to
further counterarguments about topics and issues relevant to students and their
work.

As you read the phrases, consider whether any of the words, phrases, or ideas
might apply to work you and your classmates have made. You might also try
using some of these words and phrases to add content to your own talk about
photographs.

The quotations here are out of context. References to the sources of the excerpts
are provided so that you can see the thoughts in their proper context if you wish.

Also, should you use any of these excerpts, cite the source to honor their authors and to avoid plagiarism. The first set is selected from an editorial overview of the magazine written by Melissa Harris.

certain images strike a chord, something deeply visceral in the viewer

the sense is as ineffable as the concepts of home or loss or tenderness; profoundly subjective experiences

dream or fantasy or memory

the photographer works them lovingly and meticulously, despite their seeming randomness

a world engaged directly with the unconscious mind

a different otherworld

spellbinding, Lilliputian scenes

trying to recall some oddly affecting dreamland you once knew

they position us, discombobulatingly, outside-looking-in

it is after all a language that pictures speak

pictures that never have a chance to utter a word

the impact of photographs can be so provocative that . . .

depicted in postcard clichés

a surprising and stunning visual history

dispelling clichés outright

a body of work that demonstrates the great potential when two creative minds join forces

an electrifying, protean presence is explored and elaborated upon, but the partners manage to retain their individual sensibilities

playing a role, transforming, and acting

identity, like experience, exists as a mutable truth

a medium that is singularly suited to rendering that truth, in all its variations[11]

The following phrases are from a letter to the editor written by Zeev Deckel in response to photographs of the Middle East made by Larry Towell in a previous issue of the magazine.[12]

the camera and mind behind it are very subjective conceptually in judgment, interpretation, presentation, and message

one of the most powerful traits of this tool is its ability to extract subject matter and present it out of context, thus drawing the attention of the viewer to that particular detail; fleeting news programs, showing detailed close-ups without relevant context, causes the casual onlooker to believe in what he or she sees, and the current subjective interpretation becomes reality

lack of context is our most serious enemy

the photographer's abstract black-and-white pictures provoke mixed reactions of acceptance or rejection, even resentment, by their lack of a clue and message

they supply the pictures with the wrong context and a very narrow-minded interpretation

editorial duty should have added a balancing text

a very responsible editorial staff tries to understand the wider context in order to evaluate the entire presentation in terms of objectivity and put it in the right frame of reference

a permanent breeding ground for deadly, vicious, brutal, inhuman terror

I fail to see his human understanding, or how he is achieving the level of insight that only time and compassion can allow; status is conferred

meaningless self-sacrifice and carnage of innocent people

he chooses to ignore them for his personal reasons

there is a need to watch, observe, or report

if I had been given permission to take pictures and show Al Qaida villages and strongholds in Afghanistan devastated by American actions, would the resulting abstract pictures be published as art?[13]

This next set of quotations is from a book review by Michael Famighetti of *Underexposed: Pictures Can Lie and Liars Use Pictures,* a collection of historical and recent censored or deceivingly altered photographs edited by Colin Jacobson.

will photographs still serve as objective signposts of fact?

demonstrating that the assumption of photographic "truth" has been precarious and problematic since the start of the medium

visual information has been consistently mediated by tactical hands

the power of visual documentation was never lost on those occupying positions of influence and power

a cogent collection of images, a visual catalog of a century rife with social conflict, political oppression, labor struggle, famine, disease

censored by timid editors fearful of committing commercial or political offense

certain photographs have been surreptitiously doctored before publication; each image here was shrouded in a careful deception

dividing its numerous points of investigation into seven categories

probes the question

when news is not reported, does it fail to exist?

this image never ran in the South African media because of fear

the lack of photographic representation can not only erase the existence of an event, it can also negate the human form of an enemy

allowed the United States to invent and disseminate their own characteriza-
 tion of the enemy, one that lacked the basic feature of a human visage
shaped by ideology
the media have a responsibility to avoid sensationalism
paternalistic logic that violence and obscenity, even when difficult to stomach, still maintains a social or historical significance, and cannot simply
 be dismissed
countering the notion that advanced military technologies have transformed
 war into an antiseptic operation
resembles images found on the screens of an arcade
an exhaustive and intelligent account
clumsy, traditional propaganda
photographs can subtly misconstrue by design, to serve an agenda
histories are not simply written but constructed
selected for or rejected from inclusion
what is absent from the accepted genealogy constitutes a narrative of its
 own, often one belonging to those people who are denied access to
 power, those who are marginalized and disenfranchised
removed from its context
reminds us to digest information and images with a degree of skepticism
 that is essential to a healthy democratic society
selective information is misinformation[14]

This next set of quotations is from an essay by Carlo McCormick about a portfolio of fictional photographs made by Walter Martin and Paloma Muñoz.

home occupies a psychological space in our imaginations
an emotional construction
dysfunctional family dynamics
an idealized site of tranquility, safety, comfort, familiarity and all the other
 cherished attributes of the domestic
defined in contrasting opposition
wherever you are is also a place in and of itself
to occupy an ontological other space
this other realm is conjured
an exterior manifestation of internal topographies
adventure, alienation, dread, discovery, and destiny
beyond the window of the home front
sly inversions of dimensionality
a skewed perception
the typical aesthetic voyeurism of outside-looking-in
we are outside-looking-in-at-being-outside

the lure of these is their pure fantasy

invoking a frenzy

illusion and escapism

a picaresque adventure

plainly drawn from an internal reverie

a way of imagining

isolated, barren winterscapes

what the artists' gazes might fall upon from their rural vantage in the foot-
     hills of the Appalachian Mountains

the icy palette, the gray, leafless trees like jutting pikes, the land obfuscated
     by the blanket of snow

the work is perhaps more subtly informed by the alienation, paranoia, and
     dread of the artists' former urban environs

it offers a visual metaphor for the journey of two artists uprooted from a
     stable home life and set upon the road of itinerant exploration

an arc of perpetuated distance

so carefully delineated in these photographs

insubstantial yet absolute

perversely nasty black humor

enigmatic and cinematic scenes

open-ended narratives

suggest a more epic story of futile struggle, loss, and consequence

a kind of *film noir* rendered in white, the specifics bleached out

fragments that provoke us to fill in our own plot

an intonation of silent suffering

a meditation on temporal frailty, on mortality

the artists resist the easy amusements of camp

the artists are not celebrating the saccharine and sentimental

bitter and serious content

the articulation of the mundane within a poetics of the sublime

panoramic tableaux of misadventure

a parable of mock-moralistic consequences[15]

This last set of quotes is from an essay written by Charles Bowden about a portfolio of photographs made by Roger Ballen.

His images make me remember things, even if I lack any memory of this
     memory.
It tells me of where I have lived. And where I have been afraid to live.
The images seem to come from a place free of biography, of location.
The gallery walls are white, the images all silver-framed, placed like
     headstones.

The people in the photographs deserve better.

This is the safe country, which slowly kills us all.

No one in this country is on their way to the next appointment.

He invents a loose script—theater is part of his past—and then he and the people in the photographs improvise from that loose script.

Everyone I show the images to worries about whether he is exploiting the people within them. I don't think so or care.

There are few things better than being wrong. It is one of the rare moments when we actually learn and the blinders briefly lift from our studied eyes.

moments frozen by the machine he manipulates, of exact objects

imagine photography as a memory of something not remembered

. . . the texture feels warm, as if fresh from some loom

the walls not only could be touched, they also spoke

the peeling paint on the wall with its biography, its history

squares and rectangles of images all pinned like strange butterflies

a place that has nothing to do with the time and location of the print he is showing

a geography not of a place

my private life smears against his photographs

all of his work is autobiographical

he searches the faces of others for the parts of himself he cannot say or find on his own

visiting the rooms of his mind, doors suddenly flying open

his eyes are always darting and flickering over things. He explains that back where he comes from, a person has to be constantly alert[16]

Now that you have read through these excerpts, note how very few of the phrases, sentences, and thoughts are *negative*. Note that only one of the writers, in a letter to the editor, gives advice to editors and photographers on how to improve photographs and presentation by what *could have* or *should have* been done. Rather, most of the authors accept the work *as it is* and then make their observations and draw their implications. Note also that very few of the phrases refer directly to composition or printing technique but rather to the *meaning* and emotional and social *implications* of images. Unfortunately, however, critiques in photography classes are too often negative, focus exclusively on formal issues rather than *form in relation to meaning and values,* and frequently give advice to the photographers, whether or not the photographers have asked for it. (Unsolicited advice in normal living is rarely appreciated.)

In addition to furthering thinking abut existing images, the preceding lists of phrases can also be used as a basis for making new images. For example, can you make photographs of "profoundly subjective experiences" that you have had? Can you photographically construct "a world engaged directly with the unconscious mind"? Can you make images "dispelling clichés outright"? Which clichés would you choose to dispel? How would you visibly dispel them? How might you create "an ontological other space"? How might you make photographs of "an idealized site of tranquility, safety, comfort, familiarity, and all the other cherished attributes of the domestic"? Would you find these spaces and photograph them, or make the spaces to photograph them? What images does the phrase "perversely nasty black humor" conjure in your imagination? How might you, with one or a few photographs "suggest a more epic story of futile struggle, loss, and consequence"? What "fragments" might you give us that "provoke us to fill in our own plot"?

Kinds of Critiques

Different kinds of critiques can be run to meet different purposes and to achieve different learning. There can be more than the single purpose in critiques of judging a photograph and telling the photographer how to make it better. Critiques can be varied if we consider different purposes for having critiques.

One purpose of a critique is to aid photographers in improving their ability to articulate their thinking about the images they have made. In such a critique, attention would be given as much to the photographer's talk as to the photographer's work, and if and how the work and the talk relate. A related but different purpose may be to have all the photographers in the class be more verbally articulate about what they see in their classmates' photographs. If this is the case, then it is best that the photographer who made the image under discussion be silent so that the rest of the students can think on their own and bring their new ideas to a new image.

A critique might be held so that the instructor can see whether, based on the images, what has been taught has been learned, and if not, why not. Such a critique might be instructor driven and more like a lecture than a group discussion.

The purpose of a critique might simply be to have an interesting and engaging discussion about the photographs, and thus, merely judging them would be unnecessarily limited.

A critique might be used to bring joyful closure to a course or an assignment. In such a case, a celebratory critique would be appropriate, and negative judgmental remarks would be inappropriate.

INTENTIONALIST CRITIQUES   Many critiques are *explicitly* based on the artist's intent: "Tell us what you are trying to do with this image." Most critiques are *implicitly* intentionalist; that is, people assume that a critique should address the stated or implied intent of the artist who made the work. Thus, many photography critiques begin with a statement by the photographer whose work is being critiqued about what she or he meant by making the image. Then the critique proceeds to determine whether and how well the photographer met the stated intent for the photograph. The statement might include what the photographer wished he or she could or should have done, and so forth. The critique then follows with "if-then" statements directed to the photographer: "If this is what you wanted to show in this photograph, then you should have. . . ."

In some intentionalist critiques, the group must discover the photographer's intent by observing the image, not by hearing from the photographer. Sometimes critiques are based on the intent of the instructor who gave a specific assignment to be realized in photographs. In all cases, the critique will be more focused if ground rules are established and followed:

> Are we going to *hear* the intent from the photographer, or *infer* the intent from what we see in the photograph?
> Are we talking about the photograph *as it is,* or as the photographer *wished it were?* (Are we going to allow "could've-should've-wished I had" kinds of statements?)
> Are we talking about the photograph *as it is,* or as we the viewers *would like it to be?* (Are we going to disallow advice to the photographer?)

Intentionalist critiques can take either interpretive or evaluative directions or both. For example, the photograph can be *interpreted* according to the photographer's stated intent. Or the work might be *judged* as to whether it has met the artist's intent (or the instructor's assigned intent for the photograph). For example, it is a good photograph because it accomplishes what the photographer wants it to accomplish; or conversely, the work fails because it does not provide an adequate match between intent and final image.

Further, and importantly, the work might adequately meet the maker's intent, but the intent itself may not be a very good idea; thus, the photograph is probably not a good photograph. Also, a photograph may be *better than* or different from the photographer's stated intent, or it may successfully transcend the instructor's assignment: In such cases it would likely be judged a good photograph.

Intentionalist methods of critiquing work have advantages and disadvantages. A major theoretical objection to using intent as a basis for criticism is known as the *intentionalist fallacy.* Briefly, objections are that we cannot know the intent: The photographer may not consciously know the intent for the work; photographers are often not present to tell their intents; photographers may be unwilling or unable to reveal their intents; a photograph may well mean something different from what the photographer intended.

Intentionalist critiques also have educational advantages and disadvantages. A significant disadvantage to intentionalist critiques is that they put viewers in a relatively passive position, relying on the maker to get them started and to see if they interpret the image "correctly." Intentionalist critiques tend to reinforce the false belief that the photograph means what the photographer says it means. Relying on stated intents can lead to passive interpreters and overreliance on what the photographer says rather than what the photograph itself expresses.

An educational advantage of intentionalist critiques is that they can aid the photographer in getting clear on what and why he or she is making an image. Intentionalist critiques may give photographers opportunities to become more articulate about their own work. Being able to articulate one's purpose is important in school, and it is often a necessary part of obtaining scholarships, grants, awards, and obtaining shows.

There is a solution to the weaknesses of using intentionalism as the basis for or a significant part of group critiques. Discussions about intent can be conducted one-on-one, instructor to student, or individual student to student rather than as the basis of a large group discussion.

DESCRIPTIVE CRITIQUES   Many instructors believe that a primary purpose of engaging students in critiques is to increase the students' abilities *to see*. We can learn to see by describing what we are looking at, and we can learn to be linguistically descriptive by observing and by learning and choosing words to name what we see.

By hearing others talk about a work of art, we can see it through the others' eyes and hear it in words different from our own. Such an experience can greatly expand our awareness of what is being described. Niketas, one of Umberto Eco's fictional characters, reinforces this point: "Niketas was curious by nature. He loved to listen to the stories of others, and not only concerning things unknown to him. Even things he had seen with his own eyes, when someone recounted them to him, seemed to unfold from another point of view."[17]

Instructors sometimes have difficulty getting students to describe what is in front of them because many students wrongly assume that what they see, everyone sees, and to tell what one sees is to say what is too obvious. On the contrary, we all notice different things because of personal and cultural differences; we use different words to express what we see, and our words will inflect the meanings of what we describe. For a photographer to hear what others do and do not notice about a photograph can be revealing and helpful in future image making.

Description is not a prelude to criticism. In itself, description is criticism. Sandy Skoglund, photographer and installation artist, frequently begins the critiques she engages in with the phrase "I see. . . ."[18] Description can be a valuable means to survey what is being critically considered. In this sense, description is a data-gathering process. When in doubt about what to say about a piece, begin by describing what you see: its medium, how it was made, its subject matter if it has subject matter, its form, and in what context it is presented. Description can also serve as a way to present visual data in language so that others can see what the describer has seen and hear about it in the describer's individual language, expanding everyone's awareness of what is before them.

INTERPRETIVE CRITIQUES   Too often, student critics rush to judgment (Is this a good photograph?) much more quickly than professional critics who, when writing about photographs, spend considerable column space describing and interpreting what they see before (and if) they offer a judgment of it.

Interpretive critiques can be ordered around these questions: What do I see? What's it about? How do I know? The third question, How do I know? asks for evidence and reasons for interpretive claims. A photograph is not about anything we wish it to be about. Photographs offer us constraints for interpretation by how they use media, form, subject matter, and by the time and place in which they were made, and by whom.

For an exhibition by Fred Wilson, who is best known for rearranging objects in the permanent collections of museums, giving them new contexts and forcing new associations and interpretations, museum educators devised four questions to accompany visitors. These questions posed by museum educators can also be asked of student work during a critique:

> For whom was it created?
> For whom does it exist?
> Who is represented?
> Who is doing the telling? The hearing?[19]

This list of questions can be used to further interpretive thought. A critique could be built around one of them or a few combined:

> What do you think the photograph is for or against?
> What political, religious, or racial views does the photograph seem to
>   uphold?
> What would the photograph have you believe about the world?
> Does the photograph represent a gendered point of view?
> What does the photograph assume about the viewer?
> Is the photograph directed at a certain age group, a certain class of people?
> Who might most appreciate the photograph?
> Might some be offended by the photograph?[20]

JUDGMENTAL CRITIQUES   Many people (falsely) assume that critiques are judgmental and worse, that they are *negatively* judgmental, forgetting that judgments can be positive or negative. Critiques can be descriptive and interpretive without entering into explicit judgments—it is a good work of art; it is not a good work of art. Once a photograph is carefully described and reasonable interpretations of it are offered, judgments usually are implied: "This photograph has many aspects to it; it generates meaning and offers insight into experience and the world (and by implication, it is therefore a good photograph)." Conversely, if we carefully describe and interpret a photograph and there is not much substance to be found in it, implicitly it is likely not a successful piece.

Judgments of value, when they are given, must contain a clear appraisal and be accompanied by reasons. It is a good (successful, stimulating, interesting, unique, or some other adjective) photograph *because* it. . . . A complete judgment entails an appraisal (rating) and reasons for the appraisal that are based in *criteria*. Realism, expressionism, formalism, and activism are four major sets of criteria. Thus, for example, "X is a good photograph (appraisal) because it . . . (reasons), and photographs in general ought to (criterion). . . ."

Preferences are not judgments. Preferences are mere psychological reports on what an individual likes or dislikes. Whether one "likes" or "dislikes" a photograph is critically irrelevant in critical discourse. We all get to like what we like. When we make a judgment, however, we are making statements about the image, not ourselves, and these judgments ought to be backed with reasons that other people can understand. The judgmental question in criticism is not whether one *likes* a work but whether one thinks the work is good or not and for what reasons. During your next critique, try to ban the word *like* from your vocabulary for the whole critique. You may find it to be a surprisingly difficult limitation, but the exercise can further your critical prowess and intellectual development. Every time you wish to say, "I like . . . ," edit the phrase to "I think this is good because. . . ."

Judgments can be, but need not be, comparative. For example, "Jose's photograph uses contrast more effectively than Li-Yan's photograph." To compare and contrast works of art is a standard and effective procedure of analysis used in art history classes, but the artists who made the works that are being compared are not present. One could rephrase the thought and simply say, "This photograph uses contrast very effectively" and then go on to explain how it does that.

A criterion or many criteria can be imposed on a photograph, or the critic can allow the work to suggest the criteria by which it should be judged. For example, some socially minded critics insist that all photographs be considered for their social impact, not merely their aesthetic value. In some critiques, objects made in response to an assignment by the instructor may already have a criterion stated in the assignment. In such cases, it would seem fairest to follow that criterion when judging the work.

When the instructor does not set a criterion for the assignment, choices emerge. Should the work be judged by one of many criteria? Should the photograph be judged by the critic's criterion? Should the photograph establish the criterion by which it should be judged? To take an obvious example, many viewers think art ought to be representational, realistic, and conventionally beautiful. When such viewers face an Edward Weston photograph of a nude, they will likely conclude that it is a good work of art; and when those same viewers face a photograph of an obviously distorted nude by Bill Brandt, they are likely to believe that it is an unsuccessful photograph. If viewers go through life only able to appreciate realistic and conventionally beautiful works, they will have a very limited repertoire. A more generous approach would be to allow the work to determine by what criterion it will be judged. It seems unreasonable to insist, for example, that a nonrepresentational photograph is unsuccessful because it does not realistically represent reality.

Evaluative critiques need not be negative. Nor do evaluative critiques need to take the form of giving advice to the artist, such as "You should have done this," or "It would be a better piece if. . . ." One can ask questions such as the following and let photographers decide how they might improve the work if they think it needs to be improved.

What is good about this photograph?
What are the most successful aspects of this work?
Which (professional) photographers might be drawn to this work and why?

THEORETICAL CRITIQUES   Critiques often prompt spontaneous theoretical discussions, for example: "What makes *that* art?" "Who decides what's a good photograph?" "That's pornography, not art!" When a big issue arises, the instructor and the group can decide whether to pursue a theoretical discussion during a critique or to table it for another time.

Critiques can also be used expressly as occasions for a serious theoretical pursuit of ideas based on the images that students have made. Such open-ended discussions can further thinking about the medium, purposes of image making, and consequences of images, and sharpen students' intellectual abilities and skills of philosophical thinking. Such discussion might also prompt the making of new work and seeing old work in new light. Here are some topics for discussion:

What is factual and what is fictional about these documentary photographs? What is factual and fictional about *any* given photograph? Is there truth in fiction?
What does digital technology add to or take from chemistry-based photography?
Do digital photographic images change the ontological (what they are) or epistemological (how they mean) status of photographs?
Do photographs get us closer to "truth" than paintings or writing? What is the truth-value of a photograph, a painting, a written report, a novel?
What are the consequences of labeling photographs "art" rather than objects of "visual culture"?
How are these images "gendered"?

Engaging in theoretical discussions can leave students frustrated by beliefs that "anything goes," that such discussions are merely a matter of opinion, or that "it's all subjective anyway." Providing or asking for reasons and evidence in support of theoretical claims will help to counter such negatively and unproductive relativist positions. Theoretical positions, like interpretations and judgments, should be solidly built arguments, and some arguments should be shown to be more thoughtful and enlightening than other arguments. Theory is not just a matter of opinion but also of positions informed by logic and empirical evidence.

Before ending theoretical discussions, it is helpful if positions are summarized and if some conclusions, however tentative, can be agreed upon. Where there is disagreement, it is helpful if counterpositions are clearly identified regarding points of agreement and disagreement so that everything is not left "up for grabs."

CRITIQUES WITHOUT ADVICE   *Critiques need not include advice* to the photographer. Unsolicited advice is rarely appreciated in daily living, yet we generally believe that critiques give us license to identify problems in other people's work and then to offer them our solutions to those problems, usually in a series of "shoulds." Relatedly, some critiques also nurture an unhealthy psychological environment in which active, independent artists become passive and dependent upon others' statements of approval. If they are not careful, image makers can also allow critiques to be disempowering, in effect, leading makers to the impotent position of "solve my problems for me," "I can't make a good image without you," "I won't know if I have made a good image unless you tell me so."

Even judgmental critiques can offer statements and reasons why a particular image is not successful without adding a solution for a fix to what the critic sees as a problem—"I think it would be better if you. . . ." Why not offer a statement and reasons and let the maker decide *if* and *how* he or she wants to change the image?

Why not fully interpret an image without giving any advice and then let the photographer decide whether he or she wants to leave the image as it is or alter it based on what he or she heard you say? Why not carefully describe the image, and let the maker decide, based on your descriptive insights, whether to leave the image as is or to change it?

Conducting Successful Critiques

Critiques can take the form of lectures by instructors. Sometimes this is a wise choice by the instructor because he or she wants to reinforce something being taught, to efficiently correct simple technical flaws, or to explain something directly. Holding a group discussion on such matters as increasing depth of field, using a tool in Photoshop, or cleanly matting a picture is probably not a good use of time: A simple lecture and demonstration better serves such purposes.

Other times, however, during group discussions, instructors resort to lecturing by default because too few students are talking, and the instructor fills the void of an uncomfortable silence. The following suggestions are offered to enliven any discussion about photographs with and without the photographer who made the image present.

- *Allow segments of silence.* When a good question is asked, respondents need quiet time to think or to build confidence to speak. Allow the discomfort of silence: Good thoughts can come from silence, even when it seems uncomfortable.
- *Describe what you see.* To describe a photograph to a group when everyone can see the image may seem silly; we tend to believe that everyone can see what we see, so we feel awkward in describing what we perceive to be obvious. But what is apparent to one person might be overlooked by someone else. If a group of twenty people describe a photograph, each will attend to different aspects of it with different points of emphasis, varying degrees of enthusiasm, and different vocabularies.
- *Consider subject matter.* Photographers tend to discuss photographic form and shy away from considering subject matter, thinking it too obvious to discuss. But considerations of subject matter in professional critics' writing about Avedon or Mapplethorpe, for example, are essential to their criticisms. The act of description also extends the time a group will actively attend to a photograph. Descriptive discussions can be enlightening to the group and to the photographer. What others notice and what they miss or choose to ignore can be surprising.
- *Consider how form relates to subject matter.* When discussing the formal properties of a photograph, seek to relate choices the photographer made about density, contrast, focus, and other compositional elements in terms of how those choices affect the subject matter of the photograph and ultimately the meaning of the photograph. The interpretive equation **subject matter + form = content** can yield rich meanings.
- *Let interpretation be a communal endeavor.* When talking about photographs casually or in organized critiques, people often neglect interpretation altogether or treat it superficially. This is especially true when the photographer is present. Often the photographer will supply the meaning of what the work is about. What the photographer thinks the image is about should be only one among several competing interpretations, and it is not necessarily the best interpretation, even though he or she may pronounce the meaning with great confidence and authority.

If you are in a group that is interpreting a photograph or body of work, you are part of an interpretive community. Individuals in the group of interpreters should build on one another's thoughts about the work in question. You can work communally to arrive at a consensus interpretation or agree to accept diverse interpretations. To be part of a group but not to listen to and build on one another's interpretations defeats the advantages of being in a group.

- *Suggest that the photographer be silent.* When conducting critiques with those who make images, the discussions might be more productive if the photographer whose work is being considered does not contribute to the discussion of his or her pictures. This way, the photographer is much less likely to tell nervous jokes or irrelevant anecdotes, make defensive statements, or verbally justify the images. Without the responsibility to defend, the photographer is better able to absorb what is being said about the photographs. The silence of the photographer also puts the responsibility for criticism on the viewers, where it should be.

- *Interpret the photograph by questions it raises.* Let the interpretation be by questions the photograph seems to pose. Conversely, ask questions about the photograph that the photograph seems to ignore. What is excluded from the photograph? What does the photographer take for granted? Questions do not need to be directed to the photographer—ask about the photograph itself, and let the interpreter provide the answer.

- *Avoid hasty judgments.* When judging photographs, avoid impulsive judgments and premature evaluative closures. If an evaluative conversation begins with a judgment, it should be backed up with reasons and an appeal to criteria on which the judgment is based. Listen sympathetically to views that challenge your own.

- *Consider presentational environments.* Where is the work being shown or meant to be shown? Who is sponsoring its showing? Why are you seeing it here and now in this environment? Answers to questions such as these can situate the work in a social context. Now the interpretive equation can be expanded to **subject matter + form + context = content.**

- *Ask how the photograph would want to be judged.* Does the photograph suggest that it be judged by certain criteria? Does it resist certain criteria? To be generous in spirit when judging a photograph or an exhibition, you may judge the work by criteria it suggests. *Under what criteria does the work best succeed?* Then consider the photograph with criteria that would not be sympathetic to it. Ultimately, you have to decide whether you are going to let the photograph choose the criteria by which you judge it or whether you will impose your criteria on it.

- *Consider implications.* Is a digital photograph less "real" than a traditional photograph? Who in a photograph is being shown and who is not? Who might be offended by a particular image and why? What does an image demand of a viewer in order that the image be understood? What are the social implications of an image?

- *Consider assumptions.* Theories, either consciously or unconsciously held, about life, art, and photography affect the making of photographs and talk about photographs. Consider your assumptions about art and photography and their relation to life. Consider what assumptions buoy the photograph. What do you assume a photograph to be? What are you being taught about a photograph?

- *Be honest and open.* Attitudes of honesty and openness improve critiques and other discussions about photographs. If participants resolve to try to express rather than to impress, the discussions will be much livelier and will include more participants. Avoiding dogmatic responses will also further discussions. Dogmatic pronouncements irritate people, cause nonproductive arguments, and end conversations rather than extend thinking and talking.

Valuable qualities to bring to any discussion are to actively listen, acknowledge to the speaker that you have heard what he or she has said, respond to it, and build on it, even though you may disagree with it. Speaking aloud is a risky act, especially in a group, and the more comfortable we can make such situations for ourselves and others, the more enjoyable and productive the discussions will be. Criticism can be kind and critical.

Principles for Effective Critiques

The following principles serve as both a summary of material in this chapter that applies to studio critiques with groups of people and a guide to direct critiques.

- Critiques are opportunities for learning about images to be articulated.
- Critiques present opportunities to increase observational, interpretive, and judgmental abilities.
- Critiques can offer artists alternate ways to think about their images.
- Critiques require participation: Speak thoughtfully and listen actively.
- Describing what you see is a vital part of the critical process.
- Description is both a data-gathering process and a reporting process.
- Everything counts in a photograph.
- Effectively communicating your insights is preferable to impressing with your intelligence.
- When interpreting an image, you need not be overly constrained by the artist's stated intent for the image.
- Images can carry multiple meanings and support multiple interpretations.
- Judgments of the value of an image ought to be dependent on an interpretive interpretation of that image.
- Judgments without reasons are irresponsive and irresponsible.
- Preferences are personal and indisputable; judgments need to be defended.
- Critiques need not be judgmental.
- Being critical and being kind are not mutually exclusive activities.

Notes

Chapter 1 • About Art Criticism

1. bell hooks, "Critical Reflections," *Artforum*, November 1994, p. 64.

2. Peter Schjeldahl, "Critical Reflections," *Artforum*, Summer 1994, p. 69.

3. Christopher Knight, quoted by Hunter Drohojowska, "Christopher Knight," *Artnews*, September 1992, p. 88.

4. Rene Ricard, "Not About Julian Schnabel," *Artforum*, Summer 1981, pp. 74–80.

5. Michael Feingold, "The Truth About Criticism, Part I," *Village Voice*, June 16, 1992, p. 93.

6. Lucy Lippard, "Headlines, Heartlines, Hardlines: Advocacy Criticism as Activism," in *Cultures in Contention*, ed. Douglas Kahn and Diane Neumaier (Seattle: Real Comet Press, 1985), pp. 242–47.

7. Morris Weitz, *Hamlet and the Philosophy of Literary Criticism* (Chicago: University of Chicago Press, 1964), p. vii.

8. Schjeldahl, p. 69.

9. Michael Feingold, "The Truth About Criticism, Part II," *Village Voice*, June 23, 1992, p. 101.

10. Abigail Solomon-Godeau, interviewed by Vince Leo, "What's Wrong with This Picture?" *Artpaper*, December 1987, pp. 12–14.

11. Edmund B. Feldman, "The Teacher as Model Critic," *Journal of Aesthetic Education* 7, no. 1 (1973): pp. 50–57.

12. A. D. Coleman, "Because It Feels So Good When I Stop: Concerning a Continuing Personal Encounter with Photography Criticism," in *Light Readings: A Photography Critic's Writings 1968–1978*, by A. D. Coleman (New York: Oxford University Press, 1979). Originally published in *Camera 35*, October 1975.

13. Weitz, p. vii.

14. Harry S. Broudy, *Enlightened Cherishing* (Champaign-Urbana: University of Illinois Press, 1972).

15. *New Art Examiner*, "Reviewer's Guidelines," editorial office, Chicago, 1988.

16. *Dialogue: An Art Journal*, "Writer's Guidelines," editorial office, Columbus, Ohio, 1987.

17. Kay Larson, quoted by Amy Newman, "Who Needs Art Critics?" *Artnews*, September 1982, p. 60.

18. Ingrid Sischy, Afterword, in *Nudes*, by Lee Friedlander (New York: Pantheon, 1991).

19. Ingrid Sischy, "Good Intentions," *New Yorker*, September 9, 1991, pp. 89–95.

20. Andy Grundberg, "Toward a Critical Pluralism," in *Reading into Photography: Selected Essays, 1959–1982*, ed. Thomas

Barrow, et al. (Albuquerque: University of New Mexico Press, 1982), pp. 247–53. Originally published in *Afterimage,* October 1980.

21. See for example, Edward Leffingwell, "Andreas Gursky: Making Things Clear," *Art in America,* June 2001, p. 76; "Thomas Ruff at David Zwirner," *Art in America* (November 2003): 166; "Jeremy Blake at Feigen Contemporary," *Art in America,* February 2004, p. 119.

22. Louis Kaplan, "Photography and the Exposure of Community: Sharing Nan Goldin and Jean-Luc Nancy," *Angelaki* 6, no. 3, December 2001, p. 7.

23. A. D. Coleman, "An Apologia/A Jeremiad," panel discussion, Mendel Art Gallery, Saskatoon, Saskatchewan, October 19, 1984.

24. Solomon-Godeau, interviewed by Leo, "What's Wrong with This Picture?" p. 12.

25. Abigail Solomon-Godeau, *Photography at the Dock: Essays on Photographic History, Institutions, and Practices* (Minneapolis: University of Minnesota, 1991).

26. Grace Glueck and Mark Stevens, quoted by Newman, "Who Needs Art Critics?"

27. Solomon-Godeau, interviewed by Leo, p. 12.

28. Kay Larson, quoted by Margot Mifflin, "Kay Larson," *Artnews,* September 1992, pp. 87–88.

29. Grace Glueck, quoted by Newman, p. 56.

30. Coleman, "Because It Feels So Good," p. 207.

31. Ibid., p. 208.

32. Mark Stevens, quoted by Newman, p. 58.

33. Lippard, "Headlines, Heartlines, Hardlines," p. 243.

34. Schjeldahl, "Critical Reflections," p. 69.

35. Kay Larson, quoted by Newman, p. 59.

36. Stevens, quoted by Newman, p. 59.

37. Jerry Saltz in *M/E/A/N/I/N/G: An Anthology of Artists' Writings, Theory, and Criticism,* eds. Susan Bee and Mira Schor (Durham, N.C.: Duke University, 2000), pp. 334–35.

38. Christopher Knight, quoted by Drohojowska, "Christopher Knight," p. 88.

39. Michael Feingold, "The Truth About Criticism, Part II," p. 101.

40. Terry Barrett, "A Comparison of the Goals of Studio Professors Conducting Critiques and Art Education Goals for Art Criticism," *Studies in Art Education,* Fall 1988, pp. 22–27.

41. Hilton Kramer, in *The New Criterion,* 1982, quoted by Lippard in "Headlines, Heartlines, Hardlines," p. 242.

42. Terence Pitts, book review of *Mining Photographs and Other Pictures 1948–1968,* eds. Robert Wilke and Benjamin Buchloh (Cape Breton: Nova Scotia College of Art and Design, 1983), *Exposure* 22, no. 3 (1984): 48–53.

43. Saltz in *M/E/A/N/I/N/G,* pp. 333–34.

44. Stevens, quoted by Newman, "Who Needs Art Critics?" p. 57.

45. Nicholas Jenkins, "Robert Hughes," *Artnews,* September 1992, pp. 84–86.

46. Saltz, pp. 333–34.

47. Schjeldahl, p. 69.

48. Marcia Siegel, quoted by Irene Ruth Meltzer, *The Critical Eye: An Analysis of the Process of Dance Criticism as Practiced by Clive Barnes, Arlene Croce, Deborah Jowitt, Elizabeth Kendall, Marcia Siegel, and David Vaughan* (Master's thesis, The Ohio State University, 1979), p. 55.

49. Coleman, "Because It Feels So Good," p. 254.

Chapter 2 • Describing Photographs: What Do I See?

1. Mary Ellen Mark, Foreword, in *The Bathers* by Jennette Williams (Durham, N.C.: Duke University Press, 2009).

2. Richard Avedon, *In the American West* (New York: Abrams, 1985).

3. Douglas Davis, "A View of the West," *Newsweek,* September 23, 1985, p. 82.

4. William Wilson, Review, *Artforum,* September 1985, p. 7.

5. Susan Weiley, "Avedon Goes West," *Artnews,* March 1986, pp. 86–91.

6. Wilson, p. 7.

7. Weiley, p. 91.

8. *Art in America,* March 2003, p. 35.

9. Davis, p. 83.

10. Wilson, p. 7.

11. Weiley, p. 86.

12. Richard Bolton, "In the American East: Avedon Incorporated," *Afterimage* 15, no. 2 (1987): 14.

13. Susan Kismaric, Introduction, *Jan Groover* (New York: Museum of Modern Art, 1987).

14. Michael Brenson, "Art: Whitney Shows Cindy Sherman Photos," *New York Times,* July 24, 1987.

15. Eleanor Heartney, "Cindy Sherman," *Afterimage,* October 1987, p. 18.

16. Arthur Danto, "Photography and Performance: Cindy Sherman's Stills," in *Cindy Sherman, Untitled Film Stills* (New York: Rizzoli, 1990), p. 13.

17. In Terry Barrett, *Why Is That Art?* (New York: Oxford, 2008), p. 152.

18. Ibid., pp. 176–177.

19. Gagosian Gallaery, http://www.gagosian.com/exhibitions/2009-06-07_cindy-sherman/, March 1, 2010.

20. Cynthia Chris, "Witkin's Others," *Exposure* 26, no. 1 (1988): p. 17.

21. Hal Fischer, "Looking into Darkness," *Artweek,* August 13, 1983.

22. Chris, p. 17.

23. Van Deren Coke, Introduction, *Joel-Peter Witkin* (San Francisco: Museum of Modern Art, 1985), pp. 6–18.

24. Edward Weston, "Seeing Photographically," in *A Modern Book of Esthetics,* 4th ed., ed. Melvin Rader (New York: Holt, Rinehart & Winston, 1973), p. 207.

25. John Szarkowski, *Looking at Photographs: 100 Pictures from the Collection of the Museum of Modern Art* (New York: Museum of Modern Art, 1973), p. 134.

26. Kismaric, Introduction, *Jan Groover.*

27. "Musings: Contemporizing Tradition," Gallery 312, Chicago, http://members.core.com/~gall312/musings.html, February 21, 2004.

28. Weiley, "Avedon Goes West," p. 87.

29. Kismaric.

30. Gary Indiana, "Joel-Peter Witkin at Hardison Fine Arts," *Art in America,* September 1983, p. 175.

31. Fischer, "Looking into Darkness."

32. Jim Jordan, "Chaplin in Hell," *Artweek,* November 10, 1984.

33. Andrew Perchuk, "Uta Barth, Bonakdar Jancou Gallery," *Artforum,* September 1998, p. 152.

34. Annette Grant, "Lights, Camera, Stand Really Still: On Set with Gregory Crewdson," *New York Times,* Sunday, May 30, 2004, pp. 1, 20–21.

35. A. D. Coleman, "The Directorial Mode: Notes Toward a Definition," in *Light Readings,* pp. 246–57.

36. Jonathan Green, ed., *The Snapshot* (Millerton, N.Y.: Aperture, 1974).

37. Weiley, "Avedon Goes West," p. 87.

38. Davis, "A View of the West," p. 83.

39. Weiley, p. 89.

40. Coke, Introduction, *Joel-Peter Witkin.*

41. Chris, "Witkin's Others," p. 17.

42. Michael Fried, "Living in America," *Artforum,* January 2010, p. 43.

43. Chris, "Witkin's Others," p. 18.

44. Fischer, "Looking into Darkness."

45. Gene Thornton, "A Gothic Vision of Man Seen with the Camera's Eye," *New York Times,* August 24, 1986, p. 27.

46. Indiana, "Joel-Peter Witkin at Hardison Fine Arts," p. 175.

47. Bill Berkson, *Artforum,* February 1984, p. 117.

48. Jim Jordan, "Chaplin in Hell."

Chapter 3 • Interpreting Photographs: What Does It Mean?

1. Susan Sontag, "Looking at War: Photography's View of Devastation and Death," *New Yorker,* December 9, 2002, p. 98.

2. Graham Nash, "On Diane Arbus's *Child with a Toy Hand Grenade in Central Park, N.Y.C.,*" *Aperture,* Winter 2009.

3. Paul Thom, *Making Sense: A Theory of Interpretation* (New York: Roman & Littlefield, 2000), p. 64.

4. Andy Grundberg, "A Quintessentially American View of the World," *New York Times*, September 18, 1988, p. 35.

5. Ernst Gombrich, *Art and Illusion* (New York: Pantheon Books, 1960), pp. 297–98.

6. Nelson Goodman, *Languages of Art* (Indianapolis: Hackett, 1976), p. 7.

7. Hans-Georg Gadamer, quoted by Klaus Davi in *Art and Philosophy,* ed. Giancarlo Politi (Milan: Flash Art Books, 1991), p. 20.

8. Goodman, p. 6.

9. Roland Barthes, "Rhetoric of the Image," 1964, in *Image-Music-Text,* ed. Roland Barthes (New York: Hill & Wang, 1971), pp. 32–51.

10. Ibid.

11. John Szarkowski, *Looking at Photographs: 100 Pictures from the Collection of the Museum of Modern Art* (New York: Museum of Modern Art, 1973), p. 202.

12. Sally Eauclaire, *American Independents: Eighteen Color Photographers* (New York: Abbeville Press, 1984), p. 219.

13. Shelley Rice, "Mary Ellen Mark," in *4 × 4: Four Photographers by Four Writers* (Boulder: University of Colorado, 1987).

14. Jonathan Green, *American Photography: A Critical History* (New York: Abrams, 1984), p. 163.

15. Edward Bryant, Introduction, *Picture Windows: Photographs by John Pfahl,* ed. John Pfahl (New York: New York Graphic Society, 1987), p. 1.

16. Ronald Dworkin, "Law as Interpretation," in *The Politics of Interpretation,* ed. W. J. T. Mitchell (Chicago: University of Chicago Press, 1983), pp. 249–70.

17. Eleanor Heartney, "Cindy Sherman," *Afterimage,* October 1987, p. 18.

18. Szarkowski, p. 166.

19. Green, pp. 66, 67.

20. Diane Neumaier, "Alfred, Harry, Emmet, Georgia, Eleanor, Edith, and Me," *Exposure* 22, no. 2 (1984): 6, 7.

21. Anne H. Hoy, *Fabrications: Staged, Altered, and Appropriated Photographs* (New York: Abbeville Press, 1987), p. 47.

22. Donald Kuspit, "Sally Mann, Gagosian Gallery," *Artforum,* January 2010, pp. 198–199.

23. Kathleen McCarthy Gauss, *New American Photography* (Los Angeles: Los Angeles County Museum of Art, 1985), p. 30.

24. Bill Nichols, *Ideology and the Image: Social Representation in the Cinema and Other Media* (Bloomington: Indiana University Press, 1981), pp. 60–61.

25. Linda Andre, "Dialectical Criticism and Photography," *Exposure* 22, no. 4 (1984): 8.

26. Hoy, p. 16.

27. Van Deren Coke, Introduction, *Joel-Peter Witkin: Forty Photographs* (San Francisco: Museum of Modern Art, 1985), pp. 6–18.

28. Lauren Greenfield, *Girl Culture* (San Francisco: Chronicle Books, 2002), p. 150.

29. Monroe C. Beardsley, "The Testability of an Interpretation," in *Philosophy Looks at the Arts,* 3rd ed., ed. Joseph Margolis (Philadelphia: Temple University Press, 1987), pp. 466–83.

30. Joseph Margolis, ed., *Philosophy Looks at the Arts,* p. 366.

31. E. D. Hirsch, Jr., *Validity in Interpretation* (New Haven, Conn.: Yale University Press, 1967), p. 54.

32. Dworkin, "Law as Interpretation," p. 253.

33. Minor White, "Criticism," *Aperture* 2, no. 2 (1957): 29–30.

34. Monroe C. Beardsley and William Wimsatt, Jr., "The Intentional Fallacy," in *Philosophy Looks at the Arts,* pp. 367–80.

35. Cindy Sherman, quoted by Jeanne Siegel in *Artwords 2: Discourse on the Early 80s* (Ann Arbor: UMI Press, 1988), p. 275.

36. Jerry Uelsmann, *Uelsmann: Process and Perception* (Gainesville: University Press of Florida, 1985), p. 23.

37. Sandy Skoglund, quoted by Jude Schwendenwien, "Sandy Skoglund," *Journal of Contemporary Art* 6, no. 1 (1993): pp. 87–88.

38. Nathan Lyons, ed., *Photographers on Photography* (Englewood Cliffs, N.J.: Prentice Hall, 1966); Alan Trachtenberg, ed., *Classic Essays on Photography* (New Haven, Conn.: Leete's Island Books, 1980).

39. Tom Anderson, "A Structure for Pedagogical Art Criticism," *Studies in Art Education* 30, no. 1 (1988): p. 28.

40. Hirsch, *Validity in Interpretation,* p. 62.

41. Ibid., p. 63.

42. Anderson, pp. 34–35.

43. Julia Kristeva, quoted by Catherine Franchlin, in *Art and Philosophy,* ed. Giancarlo Politi (Milan: Flash Art Books, 1991), p. 63.

44. Michael Parsons, *How We Understand Art: A Cognitive Developmental Account of Aesthetic Experience* (Cambridge, England: Oxford University Press, 1987), pp. 84–85.

Chapter 4 • Types of Photographs

1. Dominique François Arago, "Report," 1839, in *Classic Essays in Photography,* ed. Alan Trachtenberg (New Haven, Conn.: Leete's Island Books, 1980).

2. C. Jabez Hughes, "On Art Photography," 1891, *The American Journal of Photography,* quoted by Beaumont Newhall, *The History of Photography:1839 to the Present Day,* 4th ed. (New York: Museum of Modern Art, 1982), p. 73.

3. Sadakichi Hartmann, "A Plea for Straight Photography," *American Amateur Photography,* 1904, quoted by Newhall, *History of Photography,* p. 167.

4. Edward Weston, quoted by Newhall, p. 188.

5. Newhall, pp. 196–97.

6. John Szarkowski, *The Photographer's Eye* (New York: Museum of Modern Art, 1966).

7. John Szarkowski, *Mirrors and Windows: American Photography Since 1960* (New York: Museum of Modern Art, 1978), pp. 18–19.

8. Andy Grundberg, "Photography," *New York Times,* Book Review section, December 4, 1988, p. 20.

9. Jonathan Green, *American Photography: A Critical History 1945 to the Present* (New York: Abrams, 1984).

10. Manabu Yamanaka, http://www.ask.ne.jp/~yamanaka/, August 18, 2004.

11. Michael Amy, "Manabu Yamanaka at Stefan Stux," *Art in America,* May 2000.

12. Lawrence Weschler, "Afterword: Why Is the Human on Earth?" in Michael Benson, *Beyond: Visions of the Interplanetary Probes* (New York: Abrams: 2003, p. 317.

13. Edward Curtis, *Native Nations, First Americans as Seen by Edward Curtis* (Boston: Bullfinch, 1993).

14. James Van Der Zee, *Van Der Zee Photographer: 1886–1983* (New York: Abrams, 1993).

15. Lauren Greenfeld Photography, http://www.laurengreenfield.com/index.php?p=4O2GUTFT, accessed March 1, 2010.

16. KayLynn Deveney, *The Day-to-Day Life of Albert Hastings,* Princeton Architectural Press, 2007.

17. Szarkowski, *Mirrors and Windows,* p. 23.

18. For a good selection of press photographs, see Sheryle and John Leekley, *Moments: The Pulitzer Prize Photographs* (New York: Crown, 1978).

19. Elizabeth Hess, "Family of Nan," *Village Voice,* May 18, 1993, p. 101.

20. Fazal Sheikh in *In Response to Place: Photographs from the Nature Conservancy's Last Great Places,* Nature Conservancy (New York: Bulfinch Press, 2001), p. 136.

21. Fraenkel Gallery, http://www.fraenkelgallery.com/index.php#s=0&p=0&a=11&mi=4&pt=1&pi=10000&at=1, February 25, 2010.

22. Phillip Lopate, "Sally Gall Crawl," *Aperture* 196, Fall 2009.

23. A. D. Coleman, "The Directorial Mode: Notes Toward a Definition," *Artforum,* September 1976, in *Light Readings: A Photography Critic's Writings 1968–1978,* Coleman (New York: Oxford University Press, 1979), p. 250.

24. Janine Antoni and Douglas Dreishpoon, "Escape Hatch," *Art in America,* October 2009, p. 127.

25. Nancy Princethal, "Party of Two," *Art in America,* November 2009, p. 114.

26. Ibid.

27. Jerry Uelsmann, *Twentieth Century Encyclopedia of Photography* (New York: Routledge, 2006), p. 1570.

28. Ibid., p. 1043.

29. "Neil Folberg's Serpent's Chronicle to Open at Flomenhaft Gallery 3/11," Broadway World, February 25, 2010, http://www.broadwayworld.com/article/Neil_Folbergs_SERPENTS_CHRONICLE_To_Open_at_Flomenhaft_Gallery_311_20100225, accessed March 5, 2010.

30. Carlo McCormick, Elegy in White," *Aperture* 173, Winter 2003, p. 18.

31. Peter Galassi, "Philip-Lorca diCorcia," *Artforum,* Summer 2001, p. 189.

32. Vicki Goldberg, "Everyman Tries to Save the Earth, One Image at a Time," *New York Times,* February 4, 2000.

33. Jean Lawlwer Cohen, "Rimma Gerlovina and Valeriy Gerlovin," *Artnews,* April 1994, p. 175.

34. Alfredo Jaar and David Levi Strauss, "A New Lament," *Aperture,* 197, Winter 2009, p. 22.

35. Wendy Ewald, Catherine Chermayeff, and Nan Richardson, *I Dreamed I Had a Girl in My Pocket: The Story of an Indian Village* (New York: Norton, 1996).

36. Vince Aletti, "Dark Passage," *Village Voice,* December 22, 1992, p. 103.

37. Deborah Willis, *Lorna Simpson* (San Francisco: Friends of Photography, 1992).

38. Chad Elias, "Allan Sekula, The Renaissance Society," *Artforum,* January 2010, p. 207.

39. Allan Sekula, quoted by Benjamin H. D. Buchloh in *Fish Story,* by Sekula (Art Publishers, 1995), p. 190.

40. Ibid., quoting Sekula.

41. Nicholas Jenkins, *Artnews,* January 1992, p. 119.

42. Gerald Slota and Neil LaBute, "Because the Darkness Feeds My Soul," *Aperture,* Winter 2009.

43. Edward Burtynsky, Three Georges Dam, http://www.edwardburtynsky.com/WORKS/China/Chapters/TGD.html, accessed January 3, 2011.

44. Nina Berman, *Aperture,* Summer 2008, p. 81.

45. Szarkowski, *Mirrors and Windows,* p. 17.

46. The Cleveland Museum of Art, "Aftermath: Laura Letinsky Still-Life Photographs," January 24–April 7, 2004, http://www.clevelandart.org/.

47. Ibid.

48. Heather Snider, "Mona Kuhn: Native," *Eyemazing,* November 2009.

49. Mark Johnstone, *New American Photography* (NY: Farrar Straus & Giroux, 1989).

50. Magnum Photos, http://events.magnumphotos.com/exhibition/martin-parr, accessed March 1, 2010.

51. Randy Kennedy, "Larry Sultan, California Photographer, Dies at 63," *New York Times,* December 14, 2009, p. 1.

52. Cindy Sherman's photographs can be seen in Hoy, *Fabrications,* pp. 90–93.

53. Sherrie Levine's photographs can be seen in Hoy, pp. 122–23.

54. Richard Prince's photographs can be seen in Hoy, pp. 124–27.

55. Kate Linker, "Artifacts of Artifice," *Art in America,* July 1998, p. 78.

56. Dave Hickey, "Sarah Charlesworth: The Pleasures of Knowing," in *Sarah Charlesworth: A Retrospective* (Santa Fe, N.M.: Site Santa Fe, 1998), p. 109.

57. Andy Grundberg, quoted in Zeke Berman, *Optiks* (San Francisco: Friends of Photography, 1991).

58. Zeke Berman, "Introduction," http://zekeb.com/bio/intro.shtml.

59. David Zwirner, Thomas Ruff, February 11–March 13, 2010, press release, http://www.davidzwirner.com/resources/50252/2010%20DZG%20TR%20Press%20Release.pdf, accessed February 22, 2010.

60. Rod Slemmons, "Persistence of Vision," catalogue essay, Paul Berger: 1973–2003, Museum of Contemporary Photography, Columbia College, Chicago, 2003.

61. Thomas Demand, Matthew Marks Gallery, http://www.matthewmarks.com/artists/thomas-demand/, accessed on March 7, 2010.

62. Liz Kotz, "The Medium and the Messages," *Artforum,* October 2009, p. 68.

63. Carmela Ciuraru, Elle Décor, Art Show: Carter Mull, http://www.pointclickhome.com/style_guide/articles/art_show_carter_mull, accessed March 6, 2010.

Chapter 5 • Photographs and Contexts

1. Sheryle Leekley and John Leekley, *Moments: The Pulitzer Prize Photographs* (New York: Crown, 1978), p. 46.

2. Edward Weston, *The Daybooks of Edward Weston, Volume II: California* (Millerton, N.Y.: Aperture, 1973).

3. A Sherrie Levine "After Walker Evans" photograph may be seen in Anne Hoy, *Fabrications: Staged, Altered, and Appropriated Photographs* (New York: Abbeville Press, 1987), p. 123.

4. In Leekley and Leekley, *Moments,* p. 89.

5. Gisèle Freund, *Photography and Society* (Boston: David R. Godine, 1980), pp. 178–79.

6. John Szarkowski, *Looking at Photographs: 100 Pictures from the Collection of the Museum of Modern Art* (New York: Museum of Modern Art, 1973), p. 172.

7. Roland Barthes, "The Photographic Message," in *Image-Music-Text,* ed. Barthes (New York: Hill & Wang, 1977), p. 17.

8. Martha Rosler, "Lookers, Buyers, Dealers, and Makers: Thoughts on Audience," *Exposure* 17, no. 1 (1979): p. 21.

9. Walter Benjamin, a 1934 address delivered in Paris at the Institute on the Study of Fascism, quoted by Susan Sontag, *On Photography* (New York: Farrar, Straus & Giroux, 1978), p. 105.

10. Ibid.

11. John Szarkowski, *Mirrors and Windows: American Photography Since 1960* (New York: Museum of Modern Art, 1972), p. 30.

12. Carol Squiers, "Diversionary (Syn)tactics," *Artnews,* February 1987, p. 81.

13. Ibid., p. 82.

14. Craig Owens, "The Medusa Effect or, The Specular Ruse," *Art in America,* January 1984, p. 98.

15. Squiers, pp. 84–85.

16. Barbara Kruger, in Squiers, p. 85.

17. Ibid.

18. Ibid., p. 80.

19. Kruger, quoted in Anne Hoy, *Fabrications,* p. 134.

20. Kruger, quoted in Le Anne Schreiber, "Talking to Barbara Kruger," *Vogue,* October 1987, p. 268.

21. Ibid.

22. Lynn Zelevansky, "Barbara Kruger," *Artnews,* May 1983, p. 154.

23. Squiers, "Diversionary (Syn)tactics," p. 85.

24. Owens, "The Medusa Effect or, the Specular Ruse," p. 98.

25. Hal Foster, "Subversive Signs," *Art in America,* November 1982, pp. 88–90.

26. Schreiber, p. 268.

27. Zelevansky, p. 154.

28. Jean Fisher, review of Barbara Kruger at Annina Nosei Gallery, *Artforum,* January 1984, pp. 115–16.

29. John Sturman, "Barbara Kruger, Annina Nosei," *Artnews,* May 1986, p. 129.

30. Fisher, pp. 115–16.

31. Hoy, *Fabrications,* p. 131.

32. Shaun Caley, "Barbara Kruger," *Flash Art,* May/June 1986, p. 55.

33. Squiers, p. 85.

34. S. H. M., "Documenta: Making the Pointed Pointless," *Artnews,* September 1987, pp. 160–61.

35. See, for example, Susan Sontag, *On Photography,* and Allan Sekula, "The Instrumental Image: Steichen at War," in *Photography Against the Grain* (Halifax: The Press of the Nova Scotia College of Art and Design, 1984), pp. 32–51.

Chapter 6 • Judging Photographs: Is It Good?

1. *New Yorker,* February 23, 2010, p. 3.

2. Richard Lacayo, "Drunk on a World Served Straight," *Time,* October 12, 1987, p. 88.

3. Lisa Phillips, "Cindy Sherman's Cindy Sherman," catalogue essay in *Cindy Sherman* (New York: Whitney Museum of American Art, 1987), p. 16.

4. Rod Slemmons, "Conversations: Text and Image," catalogue brochure, Museum of Contemporary Photography, Columbia College, Chicago, February 26–April 17, 2004.

5. Kate Linker, "Artifacts or Artifice," *Art in America,* July 1988, pp. 74–79.

6. Janet Kopolos, "Humorist of the Everyday," *Art in America,* March 2004, p. 115.

7. Susan Weiley, "Avedon Goes West," *Artnews,* March 1986, p. 91.

8. Jonathan Green, *American Photography: A Critical History 1945 to the Present* (New York: Abrams, 1983), p. 157.

9. Arthur Danto, "Playing with the Edge," in *Mapplethorpe,* by Robert Mapplethorpe (New York: Random House, 1992), p. 312.

10. *New Yorker,* September 23, 2002, p. 22.

11. Ibid.

12. Allan Sekula, "The Traffic in Photographs," in *Photography Against the Grain* (Halifax: Nova Scotia Schools of Art and Design, 1987), p. 89.

13. Hilton Kramer, "From Fashion to Freaks," *New York Times Magazine,* November 5, 1972, p. 38.

14. Susan Sontag, *On Photography* (New York: Farrar, Straus & Giroux, 1978), pp. 33, 34.

15. Owen Edwards, "Small World in a Room," *Saturday Review,* October 1, 1997.

16. Mark Stevens, "The Bad and the Beautiful," *Newsweek,* September 26, 1977.

17. Amy Goldin, "Diane Arbus: Playing with Conventions," *Art in America,* March/April 1973, p. 73.

18. Phillips, "Cindy Sherman's Cindy Sherman."

19. Deborah Drier, "Cindy Sherman at Metro Pictures," *Art in America,* January 1986, p. 138.

20. Green, *American Photography.*

21. Kramer, "From Fashion to Freaks."

22. Douglas Davis, "A Way of Seeing," *Newsweek,* December 3, 1979, pp. 108–12.

23. Gene Thornton, "A Show That Reveals an Artist at the Height of His Powers," *New York Times,* Arts and Leisure section, January 20, 1985, p. 29.

24. John Szarkowski, *Mirrors and Windows: American Photography Since 1960* (New York: Museum of Modern Art, 1978), p. 9.

25. Paul Strand, "Photography," 1917, in *Photographers on Photography,* ed. Nathan Lyons (Englewood Cliffs, N.J.: Prentice Hall, 1966), p. 136.

26. Edward Weston, quoted by Beaumont Newhall, *The History of Photography* (New York: Museum of Modern Art, 1982), p. 184.

27. John Szarkowski, *The Photographer's Eye* (New York: Museum of Modern Art, 1966), p. 8.

28. Charles Hagen, "Seeing *Olympia* Afresh," *New York Times,* August 4, 1991, pp. 25–26.

29. Kramer, "From Fashion to Freaks," p. 38.

30. Sadakichi Hartmann, "A Plea for Straight Photography," 1904, in *American Amateur Photographer*, 1964, quoted by Newhall, *History of Photography*, p. 171.

31. Strand, in *Photographers on Photography*, ed. Lyons, p. 136.

32. Edward Weston, "Seeing Photographically," 1943, in *A Modern Book of Esthetics*, 4th ed., ed. Melvin Rader (New York: Holt, Rinehart & Winston, 1973), p. 207.

33. Minor White, "Found Photographs," 1957, in *Photography: Essays and Images*, ed. Beaumont Newhall (New York: Museum of Modern Art, 1980), p. 77.

34. Lange, in *Photographers on Photography*, ed. Lyons, p. 67.

35. C. Jabez Hughes, quoted by John L. Ward, *The Criticism of Photography as Art: The Photographs of Jerry N. Uelsmann* (Gainesville: University of Florida Press, 1970), p. 4.

36. Robert Rosenblum, "Introduction," in *Mike and Doug Starn: 1985–1990* by Mike Starn and Doug Starn (New York: Abrams, 1990), p. 14.

37. Roger Fry, "Pure and Impure Art," 1924, in *A Modern Book of Esthetics*, 3rd ed., ed. Melvin Rader (New York: Holt, Rinehart & Winston, 1965); Clive Bell, *Art* (New York: Putnam, 1985).

38. Jan Zita Grover and Lynette Molnar, in *AIDS: The Artists' Response*, exhibition catalogue (Columbus: The Ohio State University Gallery of Fine Arts, 1989), p. 56.

39. Michael Kimmelman, "Bitter Harvest: AIDS and the Arts," *New York Times*, Arts and Leisure section, March 19, 1989, pp. 1, 6.

40. Nicholas Nixon, in *AIDS: The Artists' Response*, p. 45.

41. Greg Bordowitz, in "Art and Activism," by Douglas Crimp, in *AIDS: The Artists' Response*, p. 10.

42. Robert Atkins, "Photographing AIDS," in *AIDS: The Artists' Response*, pp. 26–27.

43. Hans-Georg Gadamer, quoted by Klaus Davi, in *Art and Philosophy*, ed. Giancarlo Politi (Milan: Flash Art Books, 1991), p. 28.

44. Szarkowski, *Mirrors and Windows*, pp. 16–17; Sekula, *Photography Against the Grain*, pp. 76–101; Green, *American Photography*, pp. 46–51.

45. John Corry, "Hollywood Virtue, Hollywood Vice," *New York Times*, Arts and Leisure section, February 17, 1985, p. 1.

46. Philip Gefter, "Two Robert Mapplethorpe Symposia," *Aperture*, 197, (Winter 2009), pp. 82–85.

47. Vince Aletti, "Critic's Notebook Shoot to Thrill," *New Yorker*, May 26, 2008.

48. Raf Casert, "A Different World," Reading, Pennsylvania *Eagle*, August 1, 1993.

49. Serrano's photograph may be seen in *Art in America*, September 1989, p. 43.

50. Schuyler Chapin, "An Advocate for the Arts," *New York Times*, July 24, 1989, p. 19.

51. Hilton Kramer, "Is Art Above the Laws of Decency?" *New York Times*, Arts and Leisure, July 2, 1989, pp. 1, 7.

52. Grace Glueck, "Art on the Firing Line," *New York Times*, Arts and Leisure section, July 9, 1989, pp. 1, 9.

53. Veronica Vera, "Letters," *New York Times*, Arts and Leisure section, July 30, 1989, p. 3.

54. Ibid.

55. Kay Larson, "Getting Graphic," *New York Magazine*, August 15, 1988, pp. 66–67.

56. Stephen Koch, "Guilt, Grace, and Robert Mapplethorpe," *Art in America*, November 1986, pp. 146, 150.

57. Stuart Morgan, "Something Magic," *Artforum*, May 1987, pp. 119–23.

58. Andy Grundberg, "The Allure of Mapplethorpe's Photographs," *New York Times*, Arts and Leisure section, July 31, 1988, pp. 29–30.

59. Andy Grundberg, "Blaming the Medium for the Message," *New York Times*,

Arts and Leisure section, August 6, 1989, p. 33.

60. Ingrid Sischy, "Photography: White and Black," *New Yorker,* November 13, 1989, p. 124; Danto, in *Mapplethorpe,* p. 314.

61. Doug Ischar, "Endangered Alibis," *Afterimage,* 17, no. 10 (1990): pp. 8–11.

Chapter 7 • Photography Theory: Is It Art? Is It True? Is It Moral?

1. Owen Edwards, "Small World in a Room," *Saturday Review,* October 1, 1977.

2. Andy Grundberg, "Hands Pose for Their Portraits," *New York Times,* Arts and Leisure section, January 29, 1989, p. 35.

3. A. D. Coleman, *Light Readings: A Photography Critic's Writings 1968–1978* (New York: Oxford University Press, 1979).

4. Allan Sekula, "Dismantling Modernism, Reinventing Documentary (Notes on the Politics of Representation)," in *Photography Against the Grain: Essays and Photo Works 1973–1983* (Halifax: The Press of the Nova Scotia College of Art and Design, 1984), p. ix.

5. Lauri Firstenberg, "Autonomy and the Archive in America: Reexamining the Intersection of Photography and Stereotype," in *Only Skin Deep: Changing Visions of the American Self,* eds. Coco Fusco and Brian Wallis (New York: Abrams, 2003), p. 316.

6. Ibid., p. 317.

7. Roland Barthes, *Camera Lucida: Reflections on Photography* (New York: Hill & Wang, 1981).

8. Joel Snyder, "Picturing Vision," in *The Language of Pictures,* ed., W. J. T. Mitchell (Chicago: University of Chicago Press, 1980).

9. Fred Ritchin, "Photojournalism in the Age of Computers," in *The Critical Image: Essays on Contemporary Photography,* ed. Carol Squiers (Seattle: Bay Press, 1990), p. 28.

10. Lauren Collins, "Pixel Perfect," *New Yorker,* May 12, 2008, p. 94.

11. Martin Lister, "Photography in the Age of Electronic Imaging," in *Photography: A Critical Introduction,* 2nd ed., ed. Liz Wells (London: Routledge, 2000), p. 311.

12. Ibid., p. 334.

13. Boder and Wombell in Lister, p. 306.

14. Fred Ritchin in Sarah Kember, "The Shadow of the Object: Photography and Realism" in *The Photography Reader,* ed. Liz Wells (London: Routledge, 2003), p. 202.

15. W. J. T. Mitchell in Lister, p. 312.

16. Jonathan Crary, ibid.

17. Dominique François Arago, "Report," in *Classic Essays on Photography,* ed. Alan Trachtenberg (New Haven, Conn.: Leete's Island Books, 1980), pp. 11–13.

18. Louis-Jacques-Mandé Daguerre, "Daguerreotype," in *Classic Essays,* p. 12.

19. Edgar Allan Poe, cited by Trachtenberg, p. 71.

20. Berger quoted by Lister, p. 314.

21. Allan Sekula, "Reading an Archive: Photography Between Labour and Capital," *The Photography Reader,* p. 447.

22. Coleman, "The Directorial Mode: Notes Toward a Definition," in *Light Readings,* p. 248.

23. Andy Grundberg, "Blaming a Medium for Its Message," *New York Times,* Arts and Leisure section, August 6, 1989, p. 1.

24. Lewis Hine, "Social Photography, How the Camera May Help in the Social Uplift," in *Classic Essays,* p. 111.

25. Paul Strand, "Photography," in *Photographers on Photography,* ed. Nathan Lyons (Englewood Cliffs, N.J.: Prentice Hall, 1966), pp. 136–37.

26. Gisele Freund, *Photography and Society* (Boston: David R. Godine, 1980), p. 149.

27. David Ogilvy, *Confessions of an Advertising Man* (New York: Scribner, 1980).

28. Susan Sontag, *On Photography* (New York: Farrar, Straus & Giroux, 1978), p. 178.

29. Barthes, *Camera Lucida.*

30. Kendall Walton, "Transparent Pictures," an address delivered at The Ohio State University, Columbus, June 2, 1982.

31. Abigail Solomon-Godeau, "Remote Control," *Artforum,* Summer 2004, p. 64.

32. Susan Sontag, "Regarding the Torture of Others: Notes on What Has Been Done—and Why—to Prisoners, by Americans," *New York Times Magazine,* May 23, 2004, p. 42.

33. Joel Snyder and Neil Allen Walsh, "Photography, Vision, and Representation," *Critical Inquiry 2,* no. 1 (1975): p. 152.

34. Joel Snyder, "Picturing Vision."

35. Snyder and Walsh, p. 156.

36. Geoffrey Batchen, *Burning with Desire: The Conception of Photography* (Cambridge, Mass.: MIT Press, 1997), p. 56.

37. In Batchen, pp. 73–75.

38. Diana C. Stoll, "Interview of Adrian Piper," *Afterimage,* No. 166, Spring 2002, p. 46.

39. Lister, "Photography in the Age of Electronic Imaging," p. 315.

40. http://www.eso.org/lasilla/ Telescope/2p2T/ E2p2M/WFI/ VVFI.html.

41. Arcturus Observatory, "The Messier Objects," http://cometman.com/ Messier.html, accessed March 24,1999.

42. Editorial, "Seeing Isn't Believing," *Columbus Dispatch,* February 26, 2004, p. A10.

43. Colin Jacobson, ed., *Underexposed: Censored Pictures and Hidden History* (London: Vision On Publishing, 2002).

44. Kenneth Brower, "Photography in the Age of Falsification," *Atlantic Monthly,* May 1998, http://www.theatlantic.com/ issues/98/photo.htm, accessed January 16, 2004.

45. *International Center of Photography Encyclopedia of Photography* (New York: Crown Press, 1984), pp. 395–96.

46. Coco Fusco, "Racial Time, Racial Marks, Racial Metaphors," in *Only Skin Deep: Changing Visions of the American Self,* eds. Coco Fusco and Brian Wallis (New York: Abrams, 2003), p. 41.

47. Brower, "Photography in the Age of Falsification."

48. Ibid.

49. Jacobson, ed., *Underexposed.*

50. Ibid., p. 32.

51. Ibid.

52. Harold Evans, "Banned," in Jacobson, p. 7.

53. Jacobson, p. 180.

54. Andy Grundberg, "A Medium No More (Or Less): Photography and the Transformation of Contemporary Art," in *Visions from America: Photographs from the Whitney Museum of American Art, 1940–2001,* by Sylvia Wolf (New York: Prestel, 2002), p. 29.

55. Ibid., p. 38.

56. Ibid., pp. 42–43.

57. George Dickey, *Art and the Aesthetic: An Institutional Analysis* (Ithaca, N.Y.: Cornell University Press, 1974), p. 464.

58. Richard B. Woodward, "It's Art, but Is It Photography?" *New York Times Magazine,* October 9, 1988, p. 42.

59. Eleanor Heartney, "Cindy Sherman," *Afterimage,* October 1987, p. 18.

60. Edward Weston, "Seeing Photographically," 1943, in *A Modern Book of Esthetics,* 4th ed., ed. Melvin Rader (New York: Holt, Rinehart & Winston, 1973), p. 207.

61. Max Kozloff, "The Etherealized Figure and the Dream of Wisdom," in *Vanishing Presence,* exhibition catalogue (Minneapolis, Minn.: Walker Art Center, 1989), p. 33.

62. Sekula, "Dismantling Modernism."

63. Abigail Solomon-Godeau, "Winning the Game When the Rules Have Been Changed, Art Photography and Postmodernism," *Exposure* 23, no. 1 (1985): p. 15.

64. Douglas Crimp, "The Museum's Old! The Library's New Subject," *Parachute*, no. 22 (Printemps 1981): pp. 32–37.

65. Woodward, p. 42.

66. Desmarais, quoted in Woodward, p. 46.

67. Richard Woodward, "Serendipity All Over Again: Joel Sternfeld Versus His Successors," *New York Times*, January 18, 2004, p. 30.

68. Jean-François Lyotard, interviewed by Bernard Blistene, in *Art and Philosophy*, ed. Giancarlo Politi (Milan: Flash Art Books, 1991), p. 72.

69. Jacques Derrida, quoted by Mitchell Stephens, "Jacques Derrida," *New York Times Magazine*, January 23, 1994, p. 22.

70. Robert Scholes, *Textual Power: Literary Theory and the Teaching of English* (New Haven, Conn.: Yale University Press, 1985), pp. 1–2.

71. Todd Gitlin, "Hip-Deep in Postmodernism," *New York Times Review of Books*, November 6, 1988, p. 35.

72. Scholes.

73. James Hugunin, "The Map Is Not the Territory." *Exposure* 22, no. 1 (1984): p. 11.

74. For a sarcastically critical treatment of modernist painting, see Tom Wolfe, *The Painted Word* (New York: Farrar, Straus & Giroux, 1975).

75. John Szarkowski, *The Photographer's Eye* (New York: The Museum of Modern Art, 1966).

76. Richard B. Woodward, "Picture Perfect," *Artnews*, March 1988.

77. Michael Köhler, "Arranged, Constructed and Staged—From Taking to Making Pictures," in *Constructed Realities: The Art of Staged Photography*, ed. Michael Köhler (Zurich: Edition Stemmle, 1989), pp. 18–19.

78. Weston Naef quoted by Holly Myers, "Flashes of Genius: The Getty Pursue the Great Man (and Woman) Theory of Photography," *New York Times*, Sunday, May 9, 2004, Arts, p. 19.

79. Abigail Solomon-Godeau, "Photography After Photography," in *Art After Modernism: Rethinking Representation*, ed. Brian Wallis (New York: New Museum of Contemporary Art, 1984), p. 80.

80. Köhler.

81. Jan Zita Grover, "Introduction to AIDS: The Artists' Response," in AIDS: The Artists' Response, exhibition catalogue (Columbus: The Ohio State University Gallery of Fine Arts, 1989), p. 2.

82. Walter Benjamin, "A Short History of Photography," 1931, in *Classic Essays in Photography*, ed. Alan Trachtenberg (New Haven, Conn.: Leete's Island Books, 1980); "The Work of Art in the Age of Mechanical Reproduction," 1935, in *Film Theory and Criticism*, eds. Gerald Mast and Marshall Cohen (London: Oxford University Press, 1979).

83. Woodward, "It's Art but Is It Photography?" p. 30.

84. Solomon-Godeau, "Winning the Game," p. 80.

85. Stephens, "Jacques Derrida," p. 22.

86. Susan Sontag, "Looking at War: Photography's View of Devastation and Death," *New Yorker*, December 9, 2002, p. 97.

87. Robert Hirsch, *Exploring Color Photography*. 3rd ed. (New York: McGraw-Hill, 1997), p. 137.

88. Edward Leffingwell, "Jeremy Blake at Feigen Contemporary," *Art in America*, February 2004, p. 119.

89. Edward Leffingwell, "Andreas Gursky: Making Things Clear," *Art in America*, June 2001, p. 76.

90. David Zwirner and Thomas Ruff, Press Release, February 11–March 13, 2010, http://www.davidwirner.com/resources/50252/2010%20DZG%20TR%20Press%20Release.pdf, accessed February 22, 2010.

91. Michael Kaplan, "Extreme Paparazzi," *American Photo Magazine*, September–October, 2003, p. 14.

92. Bruno Ceschel, "Photos Not Taken," *Utne*, September–October 2004, p. 114.
93. Ibid.
94. Sekula, "Dismantling Modernism," p. 74.
95. Ibid., p. 60.
96. Ibid., p. 62.
97. Hugunin, "The Map Is Not the Territory," p. 12.
98. Victor Burgin, ed., *Thinking Photography* (London: Macmillan, 1982), p. 2.
99. Suzi Gablik, "We Spell It Like the Freedom Fighters': A Conversation with the Guerrilla Girls," *Art in America,* January 1994, pp. 43–47.
100. Sally Hagaman McRorie, "Education in Philosophy and Art in the United States: A Feminist Account," in *Das Philosophische Denken von Kindern* (Sankt Augustin, Germany: Academia Verlag), pp. 213–19.
101. Solomon-Godeau, "Winning the Game," p. 13.
102. Barbara DeGenevieve, "Guest Editorial: On Teaching Theory," Exposure 26, no. 213 (1988): p. 10.
103. Deborah Cherry and Griselda Pollock, quoted by Pollock, "Art, Art School, Culture: Individualism After the Death of the Artist," Exposure 24, no. 3 (1986): p. 22.
104. Solomon-Godeau, p. 13.
105. Ibid., p. 15.
106. Laura Cottingham, "Re-Framing the Subject: Feminism and Photography," in *Veronica's Revenge: Contemporary Perspectives on Photography,* ed. Elizabeth Janus (New York: Scalo, 1988), p. 61.
107. Patricia Stuhr, "Multicultural Art Education and Social Reconstruction," *Studies in Art Education,* 35(3), 1994, pp. 178–87.
108. Richard Dyer, "On the Matter of Whiteness," in *Only Skin Deep,* eds. Fusco and Wallis, p. 304.
109. Ibid., pp. 304–5.
110. Ibid., 303.
111. Coco Fusco, "Racial Time, Racial Marks, Racial Metaphors" in Fusco and Wallis, p. 29.
112. Ibid., p. 37.
113. Nicholas Mirzoeff, *An Introduction to Visual Culture* (New York: Routledge, 1999), p. 195.
114. Nicholas Mirzoeff, "The Shadow and the Substance: Race, Photography, and the Index" in Fusco and Wallis, pp. 120–22.
115. Linda Weintraub, *In the Making: Creative Options for Contemporary Art,* New York: DAP, 2003, p. 262.
116. Ibid.
117. Kobena Mercer, "Skin Head Sex Thing: Racial Difference and the Homoerotic Imaginary," in Fusco and Wallis, p. 237.
118. Ibid., p. 250.
119. Holland Cotter, "A Retrospective of Many Artists, All of Them One Woman," Art & Design, *New York Times,* September 25, 2008.
120. Thanks to James Sanders, who informed me of the origin of this term. He found reference to it in J. C. Hawley, ed., *Postcolonial, Queer: Theoretical Intersections* (Albany, N.Y.: State University of New York Press, 2001), p. 5. Sanders also directed me to Jeffrey Weeks, Teresa de Laurentis, and David Halperin.
121. Michel Foucault, *The History of Sexuality Volume 1: An Introduction.* Robert Hurley, trans. (New York: Pantheon 1978).
122. Andrew Wikholm, "Words: Queer Theory," http://www.gayhistory.com/rev2/words/queertheory.htm, July 8, 2004.
123. Ibid.
124. Rictor Norton, *The Myth of the Modern Homosexual: Queer History and the Search for Cultural Unity* (Washington, D.C.: Cassel, 1997).
125. Jeffery Weeks, "The Challenge of Lesbian and Gay Studies," in *Lesbian and Gay Studies: An Introductory,*

Interdisciplinary Approach (London: Sage, 2000), preface.

126. Teresa de Laurentis, "Queer Theory: Lesbian and Gay Sexualities," *Differences* 3, no. 2, p. iii.

127. David Halperin, *Saint Foucault: Toward a Gay Hagiography* (New York: Columbia University Press, 1995).

128. Gran Fury, in *Contemporary Art and Multicultural Education,* eds. Susan Cahan and Zoya Kocur (New York: Routledge, 1996), p. 123.

129. Amy Scholder, ed., *In the Shadow of the American Dream: The Diaries of David Wojnarowicz* (New York: Grove, 2000).

130. "David Wojnarowicz interviewed by Barry Blinder man," October 1989, http://www.arts.ilstu.edu/cfa/galleries/old_site/wojnint1.html, January 14, 2004.

131. "The Imperial Archive, Key Concepts in Postcolonial Studies." School of English, the Queen's University of Belfast, Northern Ireland, http://www.qub.ac.uk/en/imperial/key-concepts/African-American-PC-Studies.htm, July 10, 2004.

132. Christine Roth and Cary Henson, "Postcolonialism," University of Wisconsin at Oshkosh, http://www.english.uwosh.edu/core/postcol.html, July 9, 2004.

133. Tim Spurgin, "Contemporary Critical Theory," Lawrence University in Appleton, Wisconsin, http://www.lawrence.edu/dept/english/courses/60A/handouts/poco.html, July 9, 2004.

134. Edward Said, *Orientalism* (New York: Vintage Books, 1979).

135. Postcolonial Studies at Emory, English Department, http://www.emory.edu/ENGLISH/Bahri/Orientalism.html, July 9, 2004.

136. Anandi Ramamurthy, "Constructions of Illusion: Photography and Commodity Culture," in *Photography: A Critical Introduction,* ed. Liz Wells, pp. 165–216.

137. Ibid, pp. 202–3.

138. Krista Thompson, "Exhibiting 'Others' in the West," 1998, Postcolonial Studies at Emory, http://www.english.emory.edu/ Bahri/Exhibition.html, November 3, 2004.

Chapter 8 • Writing and Talking About Photographs

1. *Cindy Sherman,* boxed set proof reproductions (New York: Fotofolio).

2. V. Patterson and F. Rudolf, *Carrie Mae Weems: The Hampton Project* (New York: Aperture, 2000).

3. *New Yorker,* "Goings on About Town," March 8, 2004, p. 17.

4. Ibid.

5. Ibid., September 23, 2002, p. 21.

6. Ibid.

7. The author obtained completed questionnaires about critiques from art instructors (professors and graduate teaching associates) at many schools, including the American Photography Institute, Austin Peay State University, Ball State University, Boise State University, Colorado State University, Moore College of Art and Design, Mount Mary College, Northern Illinois University, Nova Scotia School of Art and Design, The Ohio State University, Old Dominion University, Portland Community College, Pratt School of Art and Design, Rhode Island School of Art and Design, Redeemer University College (Waterloo, Canada), Southern Connecticut State University, Southern Illinois University at Carbondale, Texas Christian University, The University of Arizona, The University of Central Arkansas, University of Florida, University of Memphis, The University of New South Wales (Australia), The University of Northern Iowa, University of Toledo, Webster University.

8. Carrie Mae Weems, in *Artists, Critics, Context: Readings in and Around American Art Since 1945,* ed. Paul F. Fabozzi

(Upper Saddle River, N.J.: Prentice Hall, 2002), p. 430.

9. Chuck Close, *The Portraits Speak: Chuck Close in Conversation with 27 of His Subjects* (New York: A.R.T. Press, 1997), p. 222.

10. *Aperture,* 173, Winter, 2003.

11. Words and phrases by Melissa Harris, "Editor's Note," *Aperture,* 173, Winter, 2003, p. 5.

12. Larry Towell, "Images from No Man's Land," *Aperture,* 171, Summer 2003.

13. Zeev Deckel, "Letters," Ibid., pp. 8–9.

14. Michael Famighetti, review of *Underexposed,* Ibid., pp. 13–14.

15. Carlo McCormick, "Elegy in White: Walter Martin and Paloma Munoz," Ibid., pp. 19, 27.

16. Charles Bowden, "Roger Ballen's World," *Aperture,* 173, Winter 2003, pp. 55–57.

17. Umberto Eco, *Baudolino* (New York: Harcourt, 2000), p. 13.

18. Based on observed critiques run by Sandy Skoglund at The Ohio State University, 2000.

19. Museum for Contemporary Arts, Baltimore, 1992.

20. Terry Barrett, *Talking About Student Art* (Worcester, Mass.: Davis, 1997), p. 56.

Bibliography

Adams, Ansel. *Ansel Adams*. Hastings-on-Hudson, N.Y.: Morgan and Morgan, 1972.

Aletti, Vince. "Dark Passage." *Village Voice,* December 22, 1992, pp. 102–3.

Alpern, Mary. *Dirty Windows*. New York: Scalo, 1995.

Anderson, Tom. "A Structure for Pedagogical Art Criticism." *Studies in Art Education* 30, no. 1 (1988): 28–38.

Andre, Linda. "Dialectical Criticism and Photography." *Exposure* 22, no. 4 (1984): 5–18.

Arago, Dominique François. "Report," 1939. In *Classic Essays in Photography,* edited by Alan Trachtenberg. New Haven, Conn.: Leete's Island Books, 1980, pp. 15–25.

Aristotle *Poetics*. London: Macmillan, 1911.

Arnheim, Rudolph. "On the Nature of Photography." *Critical Inquiry* 1, no. 1 (1974): 149–61.

Aschner, Mary Jane. "Teaching the Anatomy of Criticism." *The School Review* 64, no. 7 (1956): 317–22.

Atkins, Robert. "Photographing AIDS." In *AIDS: The Artists' Response,* exhibition catalogue. Columbus: The Ohio State University Gallery of Fine Arts, 1989, pp. 26–28.

Avedon, Richard. *In the American West.* New York: Abrams, 1985.

Barney, Tina. *Theaters of Manners*. New York: Scalo, 1998.

Barrett, Terry. "A Comparison of the Goals of Studio Professors Conducting Critiques and Art Education Goals for Art Criticism." *Studies in Art Education* 30, no. 1 (1988): 22–27.

———. *Criticizing Art: Understanding the Contemporary*. Mountain View, Calif.: Mayfield, 1994.

———. *Talking About Student Art*. Worcester, Mass.: Davis, 1997.

Barthes, Roland. *Camera Lucida: Reflections on Photography*. New York: Hill & Wang, 1981.

———. "The Photographic Message," 1961. In *Image-Music-Text,* pp. 15–31. New York: Hill & Wang, 1971.

———. "Rhetoric of the Image," 1964. In *Image-Music-Text,* pp. 30–51. New York: Hill & Wang, 1971.

Batchen, Geoffrey. *Burning with Desire: The Conception of Photography*. Cambridge, Mass.: MIT Press, 1997.

Beardsley, Monroe C. "The Testability of an Interpretation." In *Philosophy Looks at the Arts,* 3rd ed., edited by Joseph Margolis, pp. 466–83. Philadelphia: Temple University Press, 1987.

Becher, Bernd, and Hilla Becher. *Water Towers*. Cambridge, Mass.: MIT Press, 1988.

Becker, Howard. *Exploring Society Photographically.* Chicago: Northwestern University Press, 1981.

Bee, Susan, and Mira Schor, eds. *M/E/A/N/I/N/G: An Anthology of Artists' Writings, Theory, and Criticism.* Durham, N.C.: Duke University, 2000.

Bell, Clive. *Art.* New York: Putnam, 1985.

Benjamin, Walter. "A Short History of Photography," 1931. *Classic Essays in Photography,* edited by Alan Trachtenberg, pp. 199–216. New Haven, Conn.: Leete's Island Books, 1980.

———. "The Work of Art in the Age of Mechanical Reproduction," 1935. In *Film Theory and Criticism,* edited by Gerald Mast and Marshall Cohen. London: Oxford University Press, 1979.

Berkson, Bill. Review *Artforum,* February 1984, p. 117.

Berman, Zeke. *Optiks.* San Francisco: The Friends of Photography, 1991.

Bernhard, Ruth. *Ruth Bernhard: The Collection of Ginny Williams.* Tallgrass Press, 1993.

Bolton, Richard. *The Contest of Meaning: Critical Histories of Photography.* Cambridge, Mass.: MIT Press, 1989.

———. "In the American East: Avedon Incorporated." *Afterimage* 15, no. 2 (1987): 12–17.

Bowden, Charles. "Roger Ballen's World." *Aperture* 173, Winter 2003, pp. 55–57.

Brandt, Bill. *Nudes.* London: G. Fraser, 1980.

Brenson, Michael. "Art: Whitney Shows Cindy Sherman Photos." *New York Times,* July 24, 1987.

Bresson, Henri-Cartier. *The World of Henri-Cartier Bresson.* New York: Viking, 1968.

Broudy, Harry S. *Enlightened Cherishing.* Champaign-Urbana: University of Illinois Press, 1972.

Brower, Kenneth. "Photography in the Age of Falsification." *Atlantic Monthly,* May 1998, http://www.theatlantic.com/isues/98/photo.htm, accessed January 16, 2004.

Bryant, Edward. Introduction. *Picture Windows: Photographs by John Pfahl,* edited by John Pfahl. New York: New York Graphic Society, 1987.

Bullock, Wynn. *The Enchanted Landscape: The Photographs of Wynn Bullock, The Years 1940–1975.* New York: Aperture, 1993.

———. *Wynn Bullock.* San Francisco: Scrimshaw Press, 1971.

Burgin, Victor, ed. *Thinking Photography.* London: Macmillan, 1982.

Caley, Shaun. "Barbara Kruger." *Flash Art,* May/June 1986, p. 55.

Callahan, Harry. *Callahan.* Millerton, N.Y.: Aperture, 1976.

———. *Harry Callahan: Color.* Providence, R.I.: Matrix, 1980.

———. *Harry Callahan: New Color, 1978–1987.* Kansas City, Mo.: Hallmark Cards, 1988.

Cameron, Julia Margaret. "Annals of My Glass House," 1874. In *Photography in Print, Writings from 1816 to the Present,* edited by Vicki Goldberg, pp. 180–87. New York: Touchstone, 1981.

Caponigro, Paul. *Megaliths.* New York: New York Graphic Society, 1986.

———. *Paul Caponigro.* Millerton, N.Y.: Aperture, 1972.

Casert, Raf. "A Different World." Reading, Pennsylvania, *Eagle,* August 1, 1993.

Ceschel, Bruno. "Photos Not Taken." *Utne,* September–October 2004.

Chapin, Schuyler. "An Advocate for the Arts." *New York Times,* July 24, 1989.

Chris, Cindy. "Witkin's Others." *Exposure* 26, no. 1 (1988): p. 17.

Cindy Sherman. New York: Whitney Museum of American Art, 1987.

Clark, Larry. *Tulsa.* New York: Lustrum Press, 1971.

Close, Chuck. *The Portraits Speak: Chuck Close in Conversation with 27 of His Subjects.* New York: A.R.T. Press, 1997.

Cohen, Jean Lawler. "Rimma Gerlovina and Valeriy Gerlovin." *Artnews,* April 1994.

Coke, Van Deren. *Joel-Peter Witkin*. San Francisco: Museum of Modern Art, 1985.

Coleman, A. D. "An Apologia/A Jeremiad," panel discussion. Saskatoon, Saskatchewan: Mendel Art Gallery, October 19, 1984.

———. *Critical Focus*. Tucson, Ariz.: Nazareli Press, 1994.

———. *Light Readings: A Photography Critic's Writings 1968–1978*. New York: Oxford University Press, 1979.

Contemporary American Photograph, Part I. Tokyo: Gallery Min, 1986.

Coplans, John. *John Coplans: A Self-Protrait, 1984–1987*. New York: P. S. 1 Contemporary Art Center, 1997.

Corry, John. "Hollywood Virtue, Hollywood Vice." *New York Times,* Arts and Leisure section, February 17, 1985, p. 1.

Cosindas, Marie. *Marie Cosindas: Color Photographs*. Boston: New York Graphic Society, 1978.

Cottingham, Laura. "Re-Framing the Subject: Feminism and Photography." In *Veronica's Revenge: Contemporary Perspectives on Photography,* edited by Elizabeth Janus. New York: Scalo, 1998.

Crane, Barbara. *Barbara Crane: Photographs 1948–80*. Tucson, Ariz.: Center for Creative Photography, 1981.

Crimp, Donald. "Art and Activism." In *AIDS: The Artists' Response,* exhibition catalogue. Columbus: The Ohio State University Gallery of Fine Arts, 1989, pp. 8–11.

———. "The Museum's Old/ The Library's New Subject." *Parachute,* no. 22 (Printemps 1981): 32–37.

———. "Pictures." In *Art After Modernism: Rethinking Representation,* edited by Brian Wallis, pp. 175–87. New York: New Museum of Contemporary Art, 1984.

Cross References: Sculpture into Photography, exhibition catalogue. Minneapolis: Walker Art Center, 1987.

Cunningham, Imogen. *Imogen Cunningham: Photographs*. Seattle: University of Washington Press, 1971.

Curtis, Edward. *Native Nations, First Americans as Seen by Edward Curtis*. Boston: Bullfinch Press, 1993.

Daguerre, Louis-Jacques-Mandé. "Daguerreotype." In *Classic Essays in Photography,* edited by Alan Trachtenberg, pp. 11–13. New Haven, Conn.: Leete's Island Books, 1980.

Danto, Arthur. "Photography and Performance: Cindy Sherman's Stills." In *Cindy Sherman, Untitled Film Stills* by Cindy Sherman. New York: Rizzoli, 1990.

———. *The Transfiguration of the Commonplace: A Philosophy of Art*. Cambridge, Mass.: Harvard University Press, 1981.

Dater, Judy. *Judy Dater: Twenty Years*. Tucson: University of Arizona Press, 1986.

Dater, Judy, and Jack Welpott. *Women and Other Visions*. Dobbs Ferry, N.Y.: Morgan and Morgan, 1975.

Davidson, Bruce. *East 100th Street*. Cambridge, Mass.: Harvard University Press, 1970.

Davis, Douglas. "A View of the West." *Newsweek,* September 23, 1985, pp. 82–83.

———. "A Way of Seeing." *Newsweek,* December 3, 1979, pp. 108–12.

Deckel, Zeev. "Letters." *Aperture* 173, Winter 2003, pp. 8–9.

DeGenevieve, Barbara. "Guest Editorial: On Teaching Theory." *Exposure* 26, no. 2/3 (1988): 10–13.

Dickey, George. *Art and the Aesthetic: An Institutional Analysis*. Ithaca: N.Y.: Cornell University Press, 1974.

Drier, Deborah. "Cindy Sherman at Metro Pictures." *Art in America,* January 1986, pp. 136–38.

Drohojowska, Hunter. "Christoper Knight." *Artnews,* September 1992, pp. 88–89.

Dubin, Steven. *Arresting Images: Impolitic Art and Uncivil Actions*. New York: Routledge, 1992.

Dworkin, Ronald. "Law as Interpretation." In *The Politics of Interpretation,* edited by W. J. T. Mitchell, pp. 249–70. Chicago: University of Chicago Press, 1983.

Dyer, Richard. "On the Matter of Whiteness." In *Only Skin Deep: Changing Visions of the American Self,* edited by Coco Fusco and Brian Wallis. New York: Abrams, 2003.

Easter, Eric, D. Michael Cheers, and Dudley Brooks. *Songs of My People: African Americans: A Self-Portrait.* Boston: Little Brown, 1992.

Eauclaire, Sally. *American Independents: Eighteen Color Photographers.* New York: Abbeville Press, 1984.

———. *The New Color Photography.* New York: Abbeville Press, 1981.

Eco, Umberto. *Baudolino.* New York: Harcourt, 2000.

Edgerton, Harold. *Moments of Vision: The Stroboscopic Revolution in Photography.* Cambridge, Mass.: MIT Press, 1979.

———. *Stopping Time: The Photographs of Harold Edgerton.* New York: Abrams, 1987.

Edwards, Owens. "Small World in a Room." *Saturday Review,* October 1, 1977.

Evans, Harold. "Banned." In *Underexposed: Censored Pictures and Hidden History,* edited by Colin Jacobson. New York: Vision On, 2002.

Ewald, Wendy, Catherine Chermayeff, and Nan Richardson. *I Dreamed I Had a Girl in My Pocket: The Story of an Indian Village.* New York: Norton, 1996.

Fabozzi, Paul F., ed. *Artists, Critics, Context: Readings in and Around American Art Since 1945.* Upper Saddle River, N.J.: Prentice Hall, 2002.

Famighetti, Michael. Book review of *Underexposed. Aperture* 173, Winter 2003, pp. 14–16.

The Family of Man. New York: Museum of Modern Art, 1955.

Fastman, Raisa. *A Portrait of American Mothers and Daughters.* Pasadena, Calif.: New Sage Press, 1987.

Feingold, Michael. "The Truth About Criticism, Part I." *Village Voice,* June 16, 1992.

———. "The Truth About Criticism, Part II." *Village Voice,* June 23, 1992.

Feldman, Edmund B. "The Teacher as Model Critic." *Journal of Aesthetic Education* 7, no. 1 (1973): 50–57.

———. *Thinking About Art.* Englewood Cliffs, N.J.: Prentice Hall, 1984.

———. *Varieties of Visual Experience: Art as Image and Idea,* 3rd ed. Englewood Cliffs, N.J.: Prentice Hall and Abrams, 1987.

Firstenberg, Lauri. "Autonomy and the Archive in America: Reexamining the Intersection of Photography and Stereotype." In *Only Skin Deep: Changing Visions of the American Self,* edited by Coco Fusco and Brian Wallis. New York: Abrams, 2003.

Fischer, Hal. "Looking into Darkness." *Artweek,* August 13, 1983.

Fisher, Jean. "Barbara Kruger, Annina Nosei Gallery." *Artforum,* January 1984, pp. 115–16.

Foster, Hal. "Subversive Signs." *Art in America,* November 1982.

4 × 4: Four Photographers by Four Writers, exhibition catalogue. Boulder: University of Colorado at Boulder, 1987.

Frank, Robert. *The Americans.* New York: Grove Press, 1959.

Freund, Gisèle. *Photography and Society.* Boston: David R. Godine, 1980.

Friedlander, Lee. *Lee Friedlander Photographs.* New City, N.Y.: Haywire Press, 1978.

Fry, Roger. "Pure and Impure Art," 1924. In *A Modern Book of Esthetics,* 3rd ed., edited by Melvin Rader. New York: Holt, Rinehart & Winston, 1965.

Fusco, Coco. "Racial Time, Racial Marks, Racial Metaphors." In *Only Skin Deep: Changing Visions of the American Self,* edited by Coco Fusco and Brian Wallis. New York: Abrams, 2003.

Fusco, Coco, and Brian Wallis, eds. *Only Skin Deep: Changing Visions of the American Self.* New York: Abrams, 2003.

Gablik, Suzi. "'We Spell It Like the Freedom Fighters': A Conversation with the Guerrilla Girls." *Art in America,* January 1994, pp. 43–47.

Galassi, Peter. "Philip-Lorca diCorcia." *Artforum,* Summer 2001, p. 189.

Gauss, Kathleen McCarthy. *New American Photography.* Los Angeles: Los Angeles County Museum of Art, 1985.

Gerlovina, Rimma, and Valeriy Gerlovin. *Photoglyphs.* New Orleans: New Orleans Museum of Art, 1993.

Gibson, Ralph. *Days at Sea.* New York: Lustrum Press, 1974.

———. *Déjà-Vu.* New York: Lustrum Press, 1973.

———. *The Somnambulist.* New York: Lustrum Press, 1973.

Gitlin, Todd. "Hip-Deep in Post-modernism." *New York Times Review of Books,* November 6, 1988.

Glueck, Grace. "Art on the Firing Line." *New York Times,* Arts and Leisure section, July 9, 1989, pp. 1, 9.

Goldberg, Jim. *Raised by Wolves.* New York: Scalo, 1995.

Goldin, Amy. "Diane Arbus: Playing with Conventions." *Art in America,* March/April 1973, p. 73.

Goldin, Nan. *The Devil's Playground.* London: Phaidon, 2004.

———. *The Other Side.* New York: Scalo, 1993.

Gombrich, E. H. *Art and Illusion: A Study of the Psychology of Pictorial Representation.* Princeton, N.J.: Princeton University Press, 1960.

———. "Standards of Truth: The Arrested Image and the Moving Eye." In *The Language of Images,* edited by W. J. T. Mitchell. Chicago: University of Chicago Press, 1980.

Goodman, Nelson. *Languages of Art.* Indianapolis, Ind.: Hackett, 1976.

Gowin, Emmet. *Photographs.* New York: Knopf, 1976.

Grant, Annette. "Lights, Camera, Stand Really Still: On Set with Gregory Crewdson." *New York Times,* Sunday, May 30, 2004, pp. 1, 20–21.

Green, Jonathan. *American Photography: A Critical History 1945 to the Present.* New York: Abrams, 1983.

———. *The Snapshot.* Millerton, N.Y.: Aperture, 1974.

Greenfield, Lauren. *Fastforward.* New York: Knopf, 1997.

———. *Girl Culture.* San Francisco: Chronicle Books, 2002.

Greenough, Sarah, and Juan Hamilton, eds. *Alfred Stieglitz: Photographs and Writings.* New York: Calloway Editions, 1982.

Groover, Jan. *Jan Groover.* New York: Museum of Modern Art, 1987.

Grover, Jan Zita. Introduction. *AIDS: The Artists' Response,* exhibition catalogue. Columbus: The Ohio State University Gallery of Fine Arts, 1989, pp. 2–7.

Grundberg, Andy. "The Allure of Mapplethorpe's Photographs," *New York Times,* Arts and Leisure section, July 31, 1988, pp. 29–30.

———. "Blaming a Medium for Its Message." *New York Times,* Arts and Leisure section, August 6, 1989.

———. "Hands Pose for Their Portraits." *New York Times,* Arts and Leisure section, January 29, 1989, p. 35.

———. "Homelessness at a Remove: An Urge to Stare." *New York Times,* Arts and Leisure section, September 25, 1988, pp. 33, 40.

———. "Images from Winogrand's Mosaic of Life." *New York Times,* May 15, 1988, p. 45.

———. "A Medium No More (Or Less): Photography and the Transformation of Contemporary Art." In *Visions from America: Photographs from the Whitney Museum of American Art, 1940–2001,* by Sylvia Wolf. New York: Prestel, 2002.

———. "Photography." *New York Times,* Book Review section, December 4, 1988, p. 20.

———. "A Quintessentially American View of the World." *New York Times,* September 18, 1988, p. 35.

———. "Review of *Water Towers.*" *New York Times Review of Books,* December 4, 1988, p. 20.

———. "Toward a Critical Pluralism." In *Reading into Photography: Selected Essays, 1959–1982,* edited by Thomas Barrow et al., pp. 247–53. Albuquerque: University of New Mexico Press, 1982. (Originally published in *Afterimage,* October 1980.)

Hagaman, Sally. "Education in Philosophy and Art in the United States: A Feminist Account." In *Das Philosophische Denken von Kindern.* Sankt Augustin, Germany: Academia Verlag, pp. 213–19.

Hagan, Charles. "Seeing *Olympia* Afresh." *New York Times,* August 4, 1991, pp. 25–26.

Harris, Melissa. "Editor's Note." *Aperture* 173, Winter, 2003, p. 5.

Heartney, Eleanor. "Cindy Sherman." *Afterimage,* October 1987, p. 18.

Heinecken, Robert. *Heinecken: Selected Works, 1966–86.* Tokyo: Gallery Min, 1986.

Hess, Elizabeth. "Family of Nan." *Village Voice,* May 18, 1993, p. 101.

Hickey, Dave. "Sarah Charlesworth: The Pleasure of Knowing." In *Sarah Charlesworth: A Retropsective.* Santa Fe, N.M.: Site Santa Fe, 1998.

Hine, Lewis. "Social Photography, How the Camera May Help in the Social Uplift." In *Classic Essays in Photography,* edited by Alan Trachtenberg. New Haven, Conn.: Leete's Island Books, 1980.

Hirsch, E. D. *Validity in Interpretation.* New Haven: Yale University Press, 1967.

Hirsch, Robert. *Exploring Color Photography,* 3rd ed. New York: McGraw-Hill, 1997.

Hockney, David. *Photoworks.* New York: Alfred A. Knopf, 1984.

Hollander, Paul den. *Les Pyradmides du Nord.* Breda, the Netherlands: Den Hollander, 1992.

hooks, bell. "Critical Reflections." *Artforum,* November 1994.

Hoy, Anne H. *Fabrications: Staged, Altered, and Appropriated Photographs.* New York: Abbeville Press, 1987.

Hughes, Robert. "To Hades with Lens." *Time,* November 13, 1972, p. 84.

Hugunin, James. "The Map Is Not the Territory." *Exposure* 22, no. 1 (1984): 5–15.

In Response to Place: Photographs from the Nature Conservancy's Last Great Places. New York: Bulfinch Press, 2001.

Ina, Eiji. *Waste.* Tucson, Ariz.: Nazareli Press, 1989.

Indiana, Gary. "Joel-Peter Witkin at Hardison Fine Arts." *Art in America,* September 1983, p. 175.

The International Center of Photography Encyclopedia of Photography. New York: Crown, 1984.

Irvine, Karen. "The Furtive Gaze: Merry Alpern, Sophie Calle, Melanie Manchot, Chris Verene, Shizuka Yokomizo," exhibition catalogue. Chicago: Museum of Contemporary Photograph, Columbia College of Art, 2003.

Ischar, Doug. "Endangered Alibis." *Afterimage* 17, no. 10 (1990): pp. 8–11.

Isenberg, Arnold. "Critical Communication." *Philosophical Review* 58 (1959).

Jacobson, Colin, ed. *Underexposed: Censored Pictures and Hidden History.* New York: Vision On, 2002.

Janus, Elizabeth, ed. *Veronica's Revenge: Contemporary Perspectives on Photography.* New York: Scalo, 1998.

Jenkins, Nicholas. *Artnews,* January 1992, p. 119.

Jones, Carolyn. *Living Proof: Courage in the Face of AIDS.* New York: Abbeville Press, 1994.

Jones, Jr., Malcolm. "The World in Focus." *Newsweek,* June 6, 1994, pp. 74–76.

Jordan, Jim. "Chaplin in Hell." *Artweek,* November 10, 1984.

Jussim, Estelle, and Elizabeth Lindquist-Cock. *Landscape as Photograph.* New Haven, Conn.: Yale University Press, 1985.

Kahn, Douglas. *John Heartfield: Art and Mass Media.* New York: Tanam Press, 1985.

Kaplan, Louis. "Photography and the Exposure of Community: Sharing Nan Goldin and Jean-Luc Nancy." *Angelaki 6,* no. 3 (December 2001): 7–30.

Kaplan, Michael. "Extreme Paparazzi." *American Photo Magazine,* September–October, 2003, p. 14.

Kelly, Mary. "Re-viewing Modernist Criticism." In *Art After Modernism: Rethinking Representation,* edited by Brian Wallis, pp. 87–103. New York: New Museum of Contemporary Art, 1984. (Originally published in *Screen* 22, no. 3, 1981.)

Kember, Sarah. "The Shadow of the Object: Photography and Realism." In *Photography: A Critical Introduction,* 2nd ed., edited by Liz Wells. London: Routledge, 2000.

Kimmelman, Michael. "Bitter Harvest: AIDS and the Arts." *New York Times,* Arts and Leisure section, March 19, 1989, pp. 1, 6.

Kismaric, Susan. *Jan Groover.* New York: Museum of Modern Art, 1987.

Koch, Stephen. "Guilt, Grace, and Robert Mapplethorpe." *Art in America,* November 1986, pp. 144–46.

Kon, Michiko. *Still Lifes.* New York: Aperture, 1997.

Kopolos, Janet. "Humorist of the Everyday." *Art in America,* March 2004, pp. 112–15.

Kozloff, Max. "The Etherealized Figure and the Dream of Wisdom." In *Vanishing Presence,* exhibition catalogue. Minneapolis: Walker Art Center, 1989, pp. 30–61.

Kramer, Hilton. "From Fashion to Freaks." *New York Times Magazine,* November 5, 1972, p. 38.

———. "Is Art Above the Laws of Decency?" *New York Times,* Arts and Leisure section, July 2, 1989, pp. 1, 7.

Krims, Les. *The Deerslayers.* Buffalo, N.Y.: Les Krims, 1972.

———. *Fictcryptokrimsographs: A Bookwork.* Buffalo, N.Y.: Humpy Press, 1975.

———. "Idiosyncratic Pictures," postcard portfolio. New York: Mythology Unlimited, 1980.

———. *Making Chicken Soup.* Buffalo, N.Y.: Humpy Press, 1972.

Kruger, Barbara. *Remote Control: Power, Cultures, and the World of Appearances.* Cambridge, Mass.: MIT Press, 1993.

Kuspit, Donald, series ed. *Contemporary American Art Critics.* Ann Arbor, Mich.: UMI Research Press, 1986.

Lacayo, Richard. "Drunk on a World Served Straight." *Time,* October 12, 1987, p. 88.

Lange, Dorothea. *Dorothea Lange: Photographs of a Lifetime.* Millerton, N.Y.: Aperture, 1982.

Lanker, Brian. *I Dream a World: Portraits of Black Women Who Changed America.* New York: Stewart, Tabori & Chang, 1989.

Larson, Kay. "Getting Graphic." *New York Magazine,* August 15, 1988, pp. 66–67.

Leekley, Sheryle, and John Leekley. *Moments: The Pulitzer Prize Photographs.* New York: Crown, 1978.

Leffingwell, Edward. "Andreas Gursky: Making Things Clear." *Art in America,* June 2001, p. 76.

———. "Jeremy Blake at Feigen Contemporary." *Art in America,* February 2004, p. 119.

———. "Thomas Ruff at David Zwirner." *Art in America,* November 2003, p. 166.

Leibovitz, Annie. *Annie Leibovitz: Photographs 1970–1990.* New York: HarperCollins, 1991.

Leo, Vince. "What's Wrong with This Picture?" Interview with Abigail Solomon-Godeau. *Artpaper,* Minneapolis, December 1987, pp. 12–14.

Linker, Kate. "Artifacts of Artifice." *Art in America,* July 1998, p. 78.

Lippard, Lucy. "Headlines, Heartlines, Hardlines: Advocacy Criticism as Activism." In *Cultures in Contention,* edited by Douglas Kahn and Diane Neumaier, pp. 242–47. Seattle: Real Comet Press, 1985.

Lister, Martin. "Photography in the Age of Electronic Imaging." In *Photography: A Critical Introduction,* 2nd ed., edited by Liz Wells. London: Routledge, 2000.

Lyon, Danny. *Conversations with the Dead.* New York: Macmillan, 1971.

Lyons, Nathan. *Photographers on Photography.* Englewood Cliffs, N.J.: Prentice Hall, 1966.

M., S. H. "Documenta: Making the Pointed Pointless." *Artnews,* September 1987, pp. 160–61.

Madoff, Steven Henry. "Michael Kimmelman." *Artnews,* September 1992, pp. 86–87.

Mandel, Mike. *Making Good Time.* Santa Cruz, Calif: Mike Mandel, 1989.

Mann, Sally. *Immediate Family.* New York: Aperture, 1992.

Mapplethorpe, Robert. *Black Book.* New York: St. Martin's Press, 1986.

———. *Mapplethorpe.* New York: Random House, 1992.

———. *Robert Mapplethorpe: The Perfect Moment.* Philadelphia: Institute of Contemporary Art, University of Pennsylvania, 1988.

Marey, Etienne Jules. *Movement.* Appleton, N.Y.: 1895.

Margolis, Joseph, ed. *Philosophy Looks at the Arts,* 3rd ed. Philadelphia: Temple University Press, 1987.

Margolis, Richard. "The Battle at the SPE Conference." *Images/Ink* 4, no. 2 (1989): 40.

Mark, Mary Ellen. *Falkland Road.* New York: Knopf, 1981.

———. *Passport.* New York: Lustrum, 1974.

———. *Ward 81.* New York: Fireside Books, 1979.

McCormick, Carlo. "Elegy in White: Walter Martin and Paloma Munoz." *Aperture* 173, Winter 2003, pp. 19, 27.

Meatyard, Ralph Eugene. *The Family Album of Lucybelle Crater.* Louisville, Ky.: Jargon Society, 1974.

Meltzer, Irene Ruth. *The Critical Eye: An Analysis of the Process of Dance Criticism as Practiced by Clive Barnes, Arlene Croce, Deborah Jowitt, Elizabeth Kendall, Marcia Siegel, and David Vaughan.* Master's thesis, The Ohio State University, 1979.

Mendoza, Tony. *Ernie: A Photographer's Memoir.* Santa Barbara, Calif.: Capra Press, 1985.

———. *Stories.* New York: Atlantic Monthly Press, 1987.

Meyerowitz, Joel. *Bay/Sky.* Boston: Bullfinch Press, 1993.

———. *Cape Light.* Boston: New York Graphic Society, 1978.

———. *St. Louis and the Arch.* Millerton, N.Y.: Aperture, 1980.

Michals, Duane. *Real Dreams.* Danbury, N.H.: Addison House, 1976.

Mifflin, Margot. "Kay Larson." *Artnews,* September 1992, pp. 87–88.

Mirzoeff, Nicholas. *An Introduction to Visual Culture.* New York: Routledge, 1999.

———. "The Shadow and the Substance: Race, Photography, and the Index." In *Only Skin Deep: Changing Visions of the American Self,* edited by Coco Fusco and Brian Wallis. New York: Abrams, 2003.

Misrach, Richard. *Violent Legacies: Three Cantos.* New York: Aperture, 1992.

Morgan, Stuart. "Something Magic." *Artforum,* May 1987, pp. 119–23.

Morton, Margaret. *The Tunnel: The Underground Homeless of New York City.* New Haven, Conn.: Yale University Press, 1995.

Muybridge, Eadweard. *Animal Locomotion: An Electro-photographic Investigation of Consecutive Phases of Animal Movement,* 11 volumes. Philadelphia: University of Pennsylvania, 1887.

Myers, Holly. "Flashes of Genius: The Getty Pursue the Great Man (and Woman) Theory of Photography." *New York Times,* Sunday, May 9, 2004, Arts, p. 19.

NASA. *A Meeting with the Universe: Science Discoveries from the Space Program.* Washington, D.C.: NASA, 1981.

Nettles, Bea. *The Elsewhere Bird.* Inky Press, 1974.

———. *Events in the Sky.* Inky Press, 1973.

———. *Mountain Dream Tarot.* Inky Press, 1975.

Neumaier, Diane. "Alfred, Harry, Emmet, Georgia, Eleanor, Edith, and Me." *Exposure* 22, no. 2 (Summer 1984): 5–8.

Newhall, Beaumont. *The History of Photography: 1839 to the Present Day,* 4th ed. New York: Museum of Modern Art, 1964.

———. *The History of Photography: 1839 to the Present Day,* 5th ed. New York: Museum of Modern Art, 1982.

Newman, Amy. "Who Needs Art Critics?" *Art News,* September 1982, pp. 55–60.

Nichols, Bill. *Ideology and the Image: Social Representation in the Cinema and Other Media.* Bloomington: Indiana University Press, 1981.

Owens, Bill. *Our Kind of People: American Groups and Rituals.* San Francisco: Straight Arrow Press, 1975.

———. *Suburbia.* San Francisco: Straight Arrow Press, 1973.

Owens, Craig. "The Medusa Effect, or The Spectacular Ruse." *Art in America,* January 1984, pp. 97–105.

Parsons, Michael. *How We Understand Art: A Cognitive Developmental Account of Aesthetic Experience.* New York: Oxford University Press, 1987.

Perchuk, Andrew. "Uta Barth, Bonakdar Jancou Gallery." *Artforum,* September 1998, p. 152.

Pitts, Terence. Book review of *Mining Photographs and Other Pictures 1948–1968,* edited by Robert Wilke and Benjamin Buchloh. Cape Breton, Nova Scotia: Nova Scotia College of Art and Design, 1983. In *Exposure* 22, no. 3 (1984): 48–53.

Plagens, Peter. "Keeping a Stiff Upper Lip." *Newsweek,* February 15, 1993, p. 56.

Politi, Giancarlo, ed. *Art and Philosophy.* Milan: Flash Art Books, 1991.

Pollock, Griselda. "Art, Art School, Culture: Individualism After the Death of the Artist." *Exposure* 24, no. 3 (1986): 20–33.

Prince, Richard. *Women.* Germany: Hatje Cantz Publishers, 2004.

Ricard, Rene. "Not About Julian Schnabel." *Artforum* 19, no. 10 (1981): 74–80.

Rice, Shelley. "Mary Ellen Mark." In *4 × 4: Four Photographers by Four Writers.* Boulder: University of Colorado, 1987.

Richards, Eugene. *Below the Line: Living Poor in America.* Mount Vernon, N.Y.: Consumers Union, 1987.

———. *Cocaine True, Cocaine Blue.* New York: Aperture, 1994.

Rickey, Carrie. Lecture at the *Dialogue* Criticism Conference. Upper Arlington, Ohio, November, 1982.

Riis, Jacob. *How the Other Half Lives, 1901.* New York: Dover, 1971.

Ritchin, Fred. "Photojournalism in the Age of Computers." In *The Critical Image: Essays on Contemporary Photography,* edited by Carol Squiers, pp. 28–37. Seattle: Bay Press, 1990.

Robbins, Mark. "Participant/Observer." In *Evidence: Photographs and Site,* exhibition and catalogue. Columbus, Ohio: Wexner Center for the Arts, 1997.

Rosenblum, Naomi. *A History of Women Photographers.* New York: Abbeville, 1994.

Rosler, Martha. "Lookers, Buyers, Dealers, Makers, Thoughts on Audience." *Exposure* 17, no. 1 (1980).

———. *3 Works.* Halifax, Nova Scotia: Nova Scotia College of Art and Design, 1981.

Salgado, Sebastião. *Workers: An Archeology of the Industrial Age.* New York: Aperture, 1993.

Samaras, Lucas. *Phantasmata: Photo-transformations.* New York: Pace Gallery, 1976.

Sander, August. "Lecture 5: Photography as a Universal Language," 1931. In *Massachusetts Review,* Winter 1978, pp. 674–79.

Scharf, Aaron. *Art and Photography.* Middlesex, England: Pelican Books, 1974.

Schjeldahl, Peter. "Critical Reflections." *Artforum,* Summer 1994.

Schreiber, Le Anne. "Talking to Barbara Kruger." *Vogue,* October 1987.

Schwendenwien, Jude. "Sandy Skoglund." *Journal of Contemporary Art* 6, no. 1 (1993): 87–98.

Scruton, Roger. "Photography and Representation." *Critical Inquiry* 7 (1981): 577–603.

"Seeing Isn't Believing," editorial. *Columbus Dispatch,* February 26, 2004, p. A10.

Sekula, Allan. *Fish Story.* Düsseldorf: Richter Verlag, Art Publishers, 1995.

———. *Geography Lesson: Canadian Notes.* Cambridge, Mass.: MIT Press, 1997.

———. *Photography Against the Grain: Essays and Photo Works 1973–1983.* Halifax: Nova Scotia College of Art and Design, 1983.

Sherman, Cindy. *Cindy Sherman 1975–1993.* New York: Rizzoli, 1990.

———. *Cindy Sherman, Untitled Film Stills.* New York: Rizzoli, 1990.

———. *Film Stills.* New York: Rizzoli, 1993.

Siegel, Jeanne, ed. *Artwords 2,* Ann Arbor, Mich.: UMI Research Press, 1988.

Simpson, Lorna. *For the Sake of the Viewer.* New York: Universe, 1992.

Sischy, Ingrid. Afterword. In *Nudes,* by Lee Friedlander. New York: Pantheon, 1991.

———. "Good Intentions." *New Yorker,* September 9, 1991, pp. 89–95.

———. "Photography: White and Black." *New Yorker,* November 13, 1989, p. 124.

Siskind, Aaron. *Aaron Siskind: Photographs, 1966–1975.* New York: Farrar, Straus & Giroux, 1976.

Skoglund, Sandy. *Reality Under Siege: A Retrospective.* New York: Abrams, 1998.

Slemmons, Rod. "Conversations: Text and Image," catalogue brochure. Chicago: Museum of Contemporary Photography, Columbia College, February 26–April 17, 2004.

———. "Persistence of Vision," catalogue essay, Paul Berger: 1973–2003. Chicago: Museum of Contemporary Photography, Columbia College, 2003.

Smith, Loren. *The Visionary Pinhole.* Salt Lake City: Peregrine Books, 1985.

Smith, Ralph A. "Teaching Aesthetic Criticism in the Schools." *Journal of Aesthetic Education* 7, no. 1 (1973): 38–49.

Smith, W. Eugene, and Aileen M. Smith. *Minamata.* New York: Alskog, 1975.

Snyder, Joel. "Picturing Vision." In *The Language of Images,* edited by W. J. T. Mitchell. Chicago: University of Chicago Press, 1980.

Snyder, Joel, and Neil Allen Walsh. "Photography, Vision, and Representation." *Critical Inquiry* 2, no. 2 (1975): 148–69.

Solomon-Godeau, Abigail. "Photography After Art Photography." In *Art After Modernism: Rethinking Representation,* edited by Brian Wallis, pp. 74–85. New York: New Museum of Contemporary Art, 1984.

———. *Photography at the Dock: Essays on Photographic History, Institutions, and Practices.* Minneapolis: University of Minnesota, 1991.

———. "Winning the Game When the Rules Have Been Changed, Art Photography and Postmodernism." *Exposure* 23, no. 1 (1985): 5–15.

Sommer, Frederick. *Words/Images.* Tucson, Ariz.: Center for Creative Photography, 1984.

Sonneman, Eve. *Real Time.* New York: Printed Matter, 1976.

Sontag, Susan. "Looking at War: Photography's View of Devastation and Death." *New Yorker,* December 9, 2002, pp. 82–98.

———. *On Photography.* New York: Farrar, Straus & Giroux, 1978.

———. *Regarding the Pain of Others.* New York: Picador, 2003.

———. "Regarding the Torture of Others: Notes on What Has Been Done—and Why—to Prisoners, by Americans." *New*

York Times Magazine, May 23, 2004, pp. 23–29.

Squiers, Carol. "Diversionary (Syn)tactics." *Artnews,* February 1987, pp. 77–85.

Starn, Mike, and Doug Starn. *Attracted to Light.* New York: Power House Books, 2004.

———. *Mike and Doug Starn: 1985–1990.* New York: Abrams, 1990.

Stephens, Mitchell. "Jacques Derrida." *New York Times Magazine,* January 23, 1994, pp. 22–25.

Stevens, Mark. "The Bad and the Beautiful." *Newsweek,* September 26, 1977.

Stoll, Diana C. "Interview of Adrian Piper." *Afterimage,* no. 166, Spring 2002.

Storr, Robert. *Tom Friedman.* New York: Phaidon, 2001.

Strand, Paul. "Photography." In *Photographers on Photography,* edited by Nathan Lyons. Englewood Cliffs, N.J.: Prentice Hall, 1966.

Stuhr, Patricia. "Multicultural Art Education and Social Reconstruction." *Studies in Art Education* 35, no. 3 (1994): 178–87.

Sturges, Jock. *Evolution of Grace.* Tokyo: GAKKEN, 1994.

———. *The Last Day of Summer.* New York: Aperture, 1991.

———. *Radiant Identities.* New York: Aperture, 1994.

Sturman, John. "Barbara Kruger, Annina Nosei Gallery." *Artnews,* May 1986.

Sugarman, Martin. *God Be with You: War in Croatia and Bosnia-Herzegovina.* Malibu, Calif.: Sugarman Productions, 1993.

Szarkowski, John. *Irving Penn.* New York: Museum of Modern Art, 1984.

———. *Looking at Photographs: 100 Pictures from the Collection of the Museum of Modern Art.* New York: Museum of Modern Art, 1973.

———. *Mirrors and Windows: American Photography Since 1960.* New York: Museum of Modern Art, 1978.

———. *The Photographer's Eye.* New York: Museum of Modern Art, 1966.

———. *Winogrand: Figments for the Real World.* New York: Museum of Modern Art, 1988.

Thom, Paul. *Making Sense: A Theory of Interpretation.* New York: Roman & Littlefield, 2000.

Thornton, Gene. "A Gothic Vision of Man Seen with the Camera's Eye." *New York Times,* August 24, 1986.

———. "A Show That Reveals an Artist at the Height of His Powers." *New York Times,* Arts and Leisure section, January 20, 1985, p. 29.

Time-Life Series on Photography. *The Great Themes.* New York: Time-Life Books, 1970.

———. *Photography as a Tool.* New York: Time-Life Books, 1970.

Towell, Larry. "Images from No Man's Land." *Aperture* 171, Summer 2003.

Trachtenberg, Alan. *Classic Essays on Photography.* New Haven, Conn.: Leete's Island Books, 1980.

Tress, Arthur. *The Teapot Opera.* New York: Abbeville Press, 1988.

———. *Theatre of the Mind.* Dobbs Ferry, N.Y.: Morgan and Morgan, 1976.

Uelsmann, Jerry. *Jerry N. Uelsmann.* New York: Aperture, 1973.

Van Der Zee, James. *Van Der Zee Photographer: 1886–1983.* New York: Abrams, 1993.

Vanishing Presence, exhibition catalogue. Minneapolis: Walker Art Center, 1989.

Walton, Kendall K. "Transparent Pictures." Address delivered at The Ohio State University, Columbus, Ohio, June 2, 1982.

———. "Transparent Pictures: On the Nature of Photographic Realism." *Critical Inquiry* 11 (December 1984).

Ward, John L. *The Criticism of Photography as Art: The Photographs of Jerry N. Uelsmann.* Gainesville: University of Florida Press, 1970, p. 4.

Wegman, William. *ABC.* New York: Hyperion, 1994.

———. *Cinderella.* New York: Hyperion, 1993.

———. *Little Red Riding Hood.* New York: Hyperion, 1994.

———. *Man's Best Friend.* New York: Abrams, 1982.

———. *William Wegman: Paintings, Drawings, Photographs, Videotapes.* New York: Abrams, 1990.

Weiley, Susan. "Avedon Goes West." *Artnews,* March 1986, pp. 86–91.

Weintraub, Linda. *In the Making: Creative Options for Contemporary Art.* New York: DAP, 2003.

Weitz, Morris. *Hamlet and the Philosophy of Literary Criticism.* Chicago: University of Chicago Press, 1964.

Weston, Edward. *The Daybooks of Edward Weston, Volume II California.* Millerton, N.Y.: Aperture, 1973.

———. *Edward Weston: Fifty Years.* Millerton, N.Y.: Aperture, 1973.

———. "Seeing Photographically." In *A Modern Book of Esthetics,* 4th ed., edited by Melvin Rader. New York: Holt, Rinehart & Winston, 1973.

———. "Techniques of Photographic Art." *Encyclopedia Britannica,* 1964 edition, pp. 942–43.

White, Minor. "Criticism." *Aperture* 2, no. 2, 1957.

———. "Found Photographs," 1957. In *Photography: Essays and Images,* edited by Beaumont Newhall, pp. 307–9. New York: Museum of Modern Art, 1980.

———. *Mirrors Messages Manifestations.* Millerton, N.Y.: Aperture, 1969.

Whyte, Murray. "Burtynsky's Account: Adding Up the Price That Nature Pays." *New York Times,* January 4, 2004, pp. 34, 37.

Willis, Deborah. *Lorna Simpson.* San Francisco: The Friends of Photography, 1992.

Wilson, William. Review of Avedon's "In the American West." *Artforum,* September 1985, p. 7.

Wimsatt, William, and Monroe Beardsley. "The Intentional Fallacy." In *The Verbal Icon,* edited by Wimsatt and Beardsley. Louisville: University of Kentucky Press, 1954.

Winogrand, Garry. *The Animals.* New York: Museum of Modern Art, 1969.

———. *Women Are Beautiful.* New York: Light Gallery, 1975.

Wise, Kelly. *The Photographers' Choice.* Danbury, N.H.: Addison House, 1975.

Witkin, Joel-Peter. *Joel-Peter Witkin.* San Francisco: Museum of Modern Art, 1985.

Wolfe, Tom. *The Painted Word.* New York: Farrar, Straus & Giroux, 1975.

Woodward, Richard B. "It's Art, But Is It Photography?" *New York Times Magazine,* October 9, 1988, p. 29ff.

———. "Picture Perfect." *Artnews,* March 1988.

———. "Serendipity All Over Again: Joel Sternfeld Versus His Successors." *New York Times,* Sunday, January 18, 2004.

Zelevansky, Lynn. "Barbara Kruger, Annina Nosei Gallery." *Artnews,* May 1983, p. 154.

Index

Page references in italics refer to photographs.